Consumer Policy from Below

Kai-Uwe Hellmann · Ansgar Klein ·
Bernward Baule
Editors

Consumer Policy from Below

Paradoxes, Perspectives, Problematizations

Second edition

Springer

Editors
Kai-Uwe Hellmann
Institut für Soziologie, TU Berlin
Berlin, Germany

Ansgar Klein
Berlin, Germany

Bernward Baule
Berlin, Germany

ISBN 978-3-658-44477-8 ISBN 978-3-658-44478-5 (eBook)
https://doi.org/10.1007/978-3-658-44478-5

The translation was done with the help of an artificial intelligence machine translation tool. A subsequent human revision was done primarily in terms of content.

This Springer imprint is published by the registered company Springer Fachmedien Wiesbaden GmbH, part of Springer Nature.
The registered company address is: Abraham-Lincoln-Str. 46, 65189 Wiesbaden, Germany

Paper in this product is recyclable.

Preface

This anthology is based on a conference of the same name, which took place on June 14, 2019 at the Institute for Sociology at the TU Berlin. It owes its existence to the suggestion of Bernward Baule, the then head of the department V B 4, Consumer Research, Consumer Education at the Federal Ministry of Justice and Consumer Protection (Bundesministerium der Justiz und für Verbraucherschutz (BMJV)).

The conference was financially supported by the BMJV. Thanks also go to Steffi Schinschke from the office of the Consumer Research Network at the BMJV and Sebastian Gülland, Silke Kirchhoff and Leonie Mader from the Institute for Sociology at the TU Berlin, who were very helpful in preparing and conducting the conference.

The metaphor 'from below' obviously reflects a 'from above'. To what extent these attributions are accurate is an empirical question. However, a special dialectic and interaction between the state and civil society regarding consumer policy issues have now become unmistakable, although the lethargy of state consumer policy due to a long-practiced power asymmetry is still very pronounced.

It is to be hoped that the existentially important field of consumer policy will not remain an appendage of unrelated policy fields and will not only find temporary attention due to opportunism or even scandal-driven, but that it will finally receive the institutional and not least budget-appropriate recognition it deserves, which has been denied to it for decades.

Berlin
Beginning of July 2020

Kai-Uwe Hellmann

Contents

Editors and Contributors

About the Editors

Kai-Uwe Hellmann, apl. Prof. Dr., born 1962, teaches consumer and economic sociology at the Institute for Sociology at the Technical University of Berlin and co-leads the AG Consumer Sociology with Prof. Dr. Dominik Schrage.

Ansgar Klein, Dr., born in 1959, is the managing director of the Federal Network for Civic Engagement (BBE). The habilitated political scientist and diploma sociologist has been a co-editor of the "Research Journal New Social Movements" since 1988. After working for several years as a scientific author, freelance publicist, editor, and lecturer in political education, he worked from 2000 to 2002 as a scientific coordinator of the SPD parliamentary group for the Enquete Commission "Future of Civic Engagement". The editor of several book series and private lecturer at the Humboldt University in Berlin has been the (founding) managing director of the Federal Network for Civic Engagement (BBE) since 2002.

Bernward Baule is a political scientist and has worked in various leadership positions in political institutions, most recently in the Federal Ministry of Justice and Consumer Protection responsible for consumer research and consumer education. His main areas of work, in addition to consumer research/consumer policy, are the cultural, technological, and political-philosophical foundations of consumers and consumption.

Contributors

Georg Abel VERBRAUCHER INITIATIVE e. V., Berlin, Germany

Daniel Affelt BUND Berlin e. V., Berlin, Germany

Thomas Cannaday Berlin, Germany

Karsten Fischer Geschwister-Scholl-Institut für Politikwissenschaft, Ludwig-Maximilians-Universität München, München, Germany

Jonas Grauel Ernährung und Umwelt, Verbraucherzentrale NRW, Düsseldorf, Germany

Marianne Heinze Akkon University of Applied Sciences, Berlin, Germany

Kai-Uwe Hellmann Institut für Soziologie, TU Berlin, Berlin, Germany

Ansgar Klein Bundesnetzwerk Bürgerschaftliches Engagement, Berlin, Germany

Daniel Kofahl Büro für Agrarpolitik und Ernährungskultur – APEK, Kassel, Germany

Jörn Lamla Universität Kassel, Fachbereich Gesellschaftswissenschaften, Kassel, Germany

Kathrin Loer Fakultät Wirtschafts- und Sozialwissenschaften, Hochschule Osnabrück, Osnabrück, Germany

Günther Rosenberger Institut für Verbraucherjournalismus ifv, Berlin, Germany

Kristina Schimpf Humboldt Universität zu Berlin, Berlin, Germany

Stefan Schridde MURKS? NEIN DANKE! e. V., Berlin, Germany

Reinhard Singer Humboldt Universität zu Berlin, Berlin, Germany

Heiko Steffens ALOENK, Berlin, Germany

Kathrin Steinbach Humboldt Universität zu Berlin, Berlin, Germany

Christoph Strünck Fakultät I, Seminar für Sozialwissenschaften, Universität Siegen, Siegen, Germany

Nina Birkner-Tröger Abteilung Konsumentenpolitik, Arbeiterkammer Wien, Wien, Austria

Wolfgang Ullrich München, Germany

Consumer Policy from Below: An Introduction

Kai-Uwe Hellmann and Ansgar Klein

Abstract

Consumer policy in Germany has long been a network of actions, organizations, and strategies that was particularly close to the state, i.e., oriented towards and around the state. Most of the time, orders were issued by the state or with the state's approval and support, funding models were set up, and laws were enacted, which could give the impression that there was essentially only a 'consumer policy from above' dictated by macro politics. However, in recent years, this asymmetry has shifted significantly in favor of civil society, keyword 'Political Consumption', and by now there are so many actions, initiatives, and organizations that one can probably speak of an increasingly stronger 'consumer policy from below'. This anthology traces these changes to some extent.

Keywords

Engagement policy · Consumer morality · Guiding principle · Maturity · Political consumption · Prosumism · Participation · Responsibility · Grassroots consumer policy

K.-U. Hellmann (✉)
Institut für Soziologie, TU Berlin, Berlin, Germany
e-mail: kai-uwe.hellmann@campus.tu-berlin.de

A. Klein
Bundesnetzwerk Bürgerschaftliches Engagement, Berlin, Germany
e-mail: ansgar.klein@snafu.de

K.-U. Hellmann et al. (eds.), *Consumer Policy from Below*,
https://doi.org/10.1007/978-3-658-44478-5_1

1 Long Time from Above—Now also from Below

German consumer policy[1] has been characterized since its first, tentative beginnings in the 1950s by the fact that it was not only related to the state, predominantly at least, but was also largely operated by the state. Not that there were not also isolated initiatives in and from the civil society sector that were motivated and active in consumer policy (Selter 1973; Scherhorn 1975; Biervert et al. 1984; Baule 2012, p. 568 ff.; Jaquemoth and Hufnagel 2018, p. 163 ff.). However, in terms of their effectiveness, including their self-understanding, and even more so in terms of their institutionalization and organizational forms, one primarily dealt with a 'consumer policy from above' that was predominantly state-oriented and oriented towards the state (Bock and Specht 1958; Kuhlmann 1990; Lübke 1991; Janning 2003, 2011). Not much came from the middle of the citizens (von Braunschweig 1965; Rick 2018)—certainly also a legacy of the political culture of the decades before.

In contrast to this decades-long dominance of a 'consumer policy from above', a civil society counterpower has only formed over the last good thirty years, which advocates a 'consumer policy from below' and increasingly self-initiatively and stubbornly, creatively and obstinately fights for it, yes, to actively and effectively co-design the agenda of German consumer policy from below, to set its own topics and to noticeably accelerate the pace of the intended transformations (Baringhorst et al 2007; Baringhorst and Witterhold 2015).[2]

The reasons for this are manifold. One could refer to the change in values as described by Ronald Inglehart (1977) in 'Silent Revolution', or speak of an 'uprising of the audience' as Jürgen Gerhards (2001) has done. This spirit of departure began in the course of the 1960s. However, it took another twenty years, if one considers the founding of the Verbraucher Initiative e. V. 1985 as a

[1] Where it should be questioned right away whether this ensemble of issues and initiatives actually already constitutes an independent policy field that puts consumers (of both sexes) at the center of its attention, or whether it is still rather attempts, approaches, efforts in this direction, without real systematics and determination, so that it would be better to speak of highly scandal-driven, poorly coordinated consumer protection measures, without real field or 'policy' quality. Cf. Müller (2001); Lamla and Klein (2005).

[2] Cf. issue 4 (2005) 'Unterschätzte Verbrauchermacht' and issue 2 (2015) 'Das Private ist Politisch. Konsum und Lebensstile', both published by the *Forschungsjournal Neue Soziale Bewegungen*.

kind of turning point (because for the first time the self-organization[3] of consumers was really in the foreground), until this consumer policy counterpower had mobilized and organized itself to such an extent that it had also grown into a relevant size and strength of influence (Nessel 2016).

A situation has now arisen that fully justifies the assumption of a fully developed 'consumer policy from below'. Its effectiveness may still prove to be limited. However, its volume, its diversity, its sense of mission, and its will to shape are undeniable. In this respect, what was discussed about almost 30 years ago as 'Demokratie von unten' (Roth 1994) respectively 'Democracy from below' (Koopmans 1995) now also applies to the field of consumer policy: the increased inclusion and participation of citizens in the initiation and implementation of consumer policy and specific consumer protection reforms.

2 With a Big P and a small p

In science, the internationally highly agile research field 'Political Consumerism' primarily deals with what is generally meant here by 'consumer politics from below'. Although there were already initial approaches to this long before, academically a kind of 'tipping point' can probably be identified with the publication of the anthology 'Politics, Products, and Markets. Exploring Political Consumerism Past and Present' by Michele Micheletti, Andreas Føllesdal, and Dietlind Stolle in 2004. This was followed in 2013 by the systematically designed overall presentation 'Political Consumerism. Global Responsibility in Action' by Stolle and Micheletti (2013). Since then, this field of topics has experienced an impressive boom (Böstrum et al. 2019).

However, it remains peculiarly vague what the political aspect of political consumption actually is. Intentions and motives, forms of action and organization, and not least successes and effects are of course discussed (Micheletti et al. 2004; Boström et al. 2005; Baek 2010; Newman and Bartels 2011; Koos 2012).[4] Nevertheless, the answer is not entirely simple as to when exactly forms of expression

[3] Cf. Biervert et al. (1984); Nessel (2016).

[4] In general, it seems advisable, in addition to motive research, which promises little reliability in terms of practical consequences, keyword 'attitude-behavior-gap', to focus even more on the analysis of forms of action and not just to observe 'boycotts' and 'buycotts', as is predominantly done, but the entire spectrum, as it has already been systematically recorded, see Barnes and Kaase (1979).

and action of political consumption are to be taken seriously politically. How should this be dealt with?

To briefly refer back to movement research at this point: In 1985, Joachim Raschke (1985, p. 109 ff.) proposed a 'typology' for discussion that distinguished between power-oriented and culture-oriented movements. While power-oriented movements strategically aim at the center of the political system, more precisely the state in the form of the government, in order to bring about, prevent or reverse a more fundamental social change for all, culture-oriented movements are more interested in fundamental changes in the respective way of life of their followers, so they show a strong self-reference—but sometimes also tend to want to prescribe their philosophy of life to the general population, just not politically.

If this distinction is transferred to political consumption, it could be assumed: As long as political consumption primarily acts power-oriented, i.e. clearly appeals to the state in order to initiate a more fundamental change in our production and consumption routines, it is consumer politics with a big P, and the question of the political would be comparatively easy to answer. Otherwise, one would be dealing with a form of political consumption that is much more culture-oriented, engages at most at the periphery of the political system, and thus rather practices politics consumption with a small p—whereby this political consumption with a small p experiences enormous demand, as is known from the 1968 slogan 'The private is political'[5]. To what extent this implies more than mere lifestyle behavior would have to be examined in detail (Connolly and Prothero 2008; Holzer 2010; Baringhorst 2015; Wahlen and Laamanen 2015).

3 Responsibility and Participation

In any case, political consumption is currently receiving considerable attention and resonance. Greta Thunberg has become a representative icon. Often associated with this is the question of consumer responsibility. After all, almost everything that is produced worldwide is available on markets sooner or later and can be purchased by us consumers, in line with the famous formulation by Adam Smith from 1776: 'Consumption is the sole end and purpose of all production'. In the end, it depends on each individual how he or she behaves at the 'Point of

[5] See issue 2 'Das Private ist Politisch. Konsum und Lebensstile' by the *Forschungsjournal Neue Soziale Bewegungen* 2015.

Purchase' regarding the issue of political consumption, and accordingly, each of us has a certain responsibility—but how much and with what consequence? What does 'Politics in the Supermarket' (Stolle et al. 2005) achieve politically? And wouldn't 'Politik statt Einkaufswagen' (Hartmann 2013) be much more effective?

The debate about the relevance of consumer responsibility ('Consumer Social Responsibility') has found great interest in Germany in the last ten years (Schrader 2007; Heidbrink et al. 2011; Schmidt 2016). However, it repeatedly appears that the 'attitude-behavior-gap' often seems insurmountable. In certain circles, the vehement advocacy and promotion of consumer responsibility may have become enormously popular, almost fashionable. But it remains questionable to what extent this can be demanded of everyone else, and even more, whether one actually lives up to it—or whether a special version of double standards shapes one's own consumer behavior. At least the impression often arises that water is preached here, but wine is very gladly drunk, be it in questions of nutrition, leisure activities, mobility, use of technology, tourism, basically everything included.

A related question focuses on the conditions of the possibility of consumer participation. Fundamental to the issue of participation is likely the idea of expanding membership and participation rights in modern society by Thomas H. Marshall (Marshall 1950; Hellmann 2012). It started with the expansion of civil liberties, later political participation rights such as universal suffrage were added, to find their provisional conclusion in the participation of all in the blessings of the welfare state.

By now, we have reached a stage of development where the impression sometimes arises that participation in society is largely guaranteed by comprehensive participation in consumption, almost a new human right (Riesman and Roseborough 1964; Hellmann 2010). Otherwise, exclusion threatens if a certain consumption standard is not reached (Bosch 2010; Chen et al. 2017). This is still about participation in society as such (Kraemer 2002).

To be distinguished from this is political inclusion through consumer protest, which again leads back to the distinction of political consumption with a big P and a small p (Stolle and Hooghe 2011). Because it is quite conceivable that a power-oriented execution of political consumption, which is explicitly related to the state, also leads to a real inclusion in the political system, just like with all other concerns that are brought forward with the intention of becoming the subject of collectively binding decisions that are then to become effective for all without exception.

The situation is different when it comes to the culture-oriented execution of political consumption. This variant does not aspire to an active role in political events, but mainly remains outside the political system and deals with questions of one's own lifestyle, or as Raschke has put it, with a new "paradigm of lifestyle" (Raschke 1985, p. 421). However, this differentiation also remains admittedly vague, as the current state of research does not yet allow for a precise clarification (Lamla and Neckel 2006).

4 Consumer Morality—Both Bright and Dark

Closely linked to the debate on responsibility and participation is the discussion about the ethics of consumption (Carrigan and Attalla 2001; Koslowski and Priddat 2006; Devinney et al. 2010). Sometimes, there is also talk of moral consumption (Hedtke 2005; Brandl 2007; Ullrich 2008; Barnett et al. 2010, p. 1 ff.).[6] This perspective directly corresponds with the culture-oriented execution of political consumption when it comes to questions of the right, especially sustainable, way of life.

Of course, in the debate about morality, as Theodor Geiger had already stated early on, it is difficult for modern society to reach a comprehensive consensus. Instead, one should assume a fundamental 'moral schism' (Geiger 1964; Hellmann 2003). Thus, each class, each lifestyle, each subculture forms its own moral standards, which by no means find general approval.

This insight can easily be transferred to consumption, which considerably complicates the chances of success of political consumption. Because there we already find such a plurality and unstoppable pluralization of consumer behavior today that it is hard to imagine how this diversity could be brought back to a higher-level unity—a question that Émile Durkheim had already dealt with on a larger scale (Hellmann 2004).

Given the entire spectrum of consumer moralities as they are practiced globally today, political consumption, whether culture- or power-oriented, thus represents only one facet, which, considered in isolation, may believe it is propagating the only right thing; but this does not apply without objection to everyone else and sometimes even provokes massive reservations and defensive reflexes. In this respect, such a 'consumer politics from below' almost dialectically provokes counter-positions, as we know well from movement research (Zald and Useem 1987).

[6] See also the Spiegel eBook 'Moral Consumption—Why it is so difficult to improve the world as a customer' from 2015.

5 Maturity ('Mündigkeit') in the Defensive

As controversial as the debate about the correct consumer morality is, the question of the correct consumer model is also controversial in consumer policy. The main line of conflict is drawn at the distinction between mature (sovereign) or not mature (manipulable). If the model of the mature consumer is about fundamentally attributing to him the ability to freely decide for himself in matters of his own consumption, with all the consequences that may arise from the responsibility of the associated consequences, the criticism of this points to the difficulties, sometimes impossibility, of behaving sovereignly in markets at all, because the information asymmetry between producers and consumers structurally always works to the disadvantage of the latter.

Without being able to go into the changing history of a consumer model debate that has been going on for some time, it is currently recognizable that the model of the mature consumer, which is represented and decisively enforced by EU jurisprudence, has at least come on the defensive in Germany (Mickletz et al. 2010; Kenning and Wobker 2013; Oehler 2013; Schmidt-Kessel and Germelmann 2016). There are good reasons for this. To what extent the fundamental skepticism about the maturity of consumers, however, is compatible with the self-understanding and concerns of the supporters of political consumption, in other words, to what extent an engaged 'consumer policy from below' does not just testify to the maturity of consumers, would still need to be clarified separately.

In any case, consumer policy, both below and above, as well as consumer research, are at a kind of crossroads where a single model has come under strong criticism, other, older and newer ones, are being put up against it, but it is still completely open, based on which rationality, which political strategy a certain consumer model, whether monomaniac or highly differentiated, can provide that orientation in the future, which is so urgently needed for policy making, legislation and consumer research (Bala and Schuldzinski 2019).

6 Consumer Policy and Engagement Policy: Challenges Posed by Prosumption and Co-production

The connections between the roles as consumers and as engaged citizens are increasingly coming into focus. This is particularly true where it is becoming increasingly clear that responsible individual consumption patterns and practices alone do not contribute to the necessary change. The change on the supply and production side, as the realization from numerous discussions about climate change and sustainability, is absolutely necessary in order to achieve political goals such as stopping climate change. Regional goods, decentralized cycles, or sustainable production (such as renewable energy) are therefore among the priority goals that motivate the newly emerging role of the 'prosumer' and suggest to civil society an active participation in the change of the market's supply structures.

The relationship between civil society and the economy has known approaches of mutual penetration and influence since the nineteenth century,[7] keywords would be the social housing for workers already discussed by early socialist Robert Owen, cooperative and other communal forms of organization in the production of important economic goods, debates about public goods and common good economy, or also the concept of the 'activity society', which clearly shows the close interweaving of gainful employment, informal work, and engagement (Klein and Röbke 2018). Critical keywords to the tense relationship between gainful employment and engagement and to the gray zones of transitions would be a 'monetization' of engagement or its instrumental use as a 'resource' in times of scarce public funds (BBE 2008).

The co-production of public goods has been discussed since the 1980s in the social policy debate of a development from the welfare state to the welfare society (Welfare Mix) (Evers and Olk 1996). For civil society, this resulted in the insight into 'hybrid' organizational patterns of the so-called 'third sector', in which civil society goals and economic principles of action reconnect with each other. It quickly became clear that engagement-based co-productions can gain dense illustrative material, both for better and worse, especially with regard to the developments of initially engagement-based welfare care, which in the form of welfare associations now belong to the largest national and European employers (Klein 2019).

The foreseeable co-productions in the field of climate, especially of renewable energy production and sustainable economy, should therefore learn from the experiences of the welfare associations, also with a view to avoiding wrong paths in dealing with engagement as only cost-saving 'resource'. Co-production and prosumption, the importance of public goods, and the increasingly important role of municipal companies represent central themes for the future of consumer policy.

[7] On the relationship between civil society and the economy, see Adloff et al. (2016).

7 Activists, Actors, Initiatives, Organizations, Associations

In conclusion, as this volume is about 'consumer policy from below', it should be emphasized once again that the main drivers for dealing with this topic are the sheer number of actors and the diversity of topics with which this 'consumer policy from below' is pursued, and have now increased to such an extent that they would deserve a systematic survey and evaluation on their own. This cannot be achieved with such a collection alone. Nevertheless, it should be emphasized that, in comparison with time, looking back about twenty years, the current situation has fundamentally changed. Never before have there been so many initiatives, organizations, projects dealing with consumer policy issues, from very small to quite large, just think of the Federal Association of Consumer Centers and the affiliated consumer centers in the states. It is now a hardly manageable mix, a hustle and bustle of actions, measures, goals in this increasingly complex field of consumer policy, that the state of development of this field should now fully justify the term 'consumer *policy*'.[8]

In this volume, only a few actors, activists, initiatives, and organizations will be able to speak and introduce themselves. Therefore, there is no claim to completeness or representativeness. Rather, the aim is to provide an impetus to deal more systematically with what has emerged and happened in the field of 'consumer policy from below' over the last twenty years.

8 The Individual Contributions

In a first block, which deals with the question 'The mature consumer as an obsolete model?', Christoph Strünck, who has made important contributions to the ongoing consumer role debate in the past, once again intervenes in this debate and critically refers to its course, which has severely affected the model of the mature consumer in recent years; on the other hand, Strünck ruminates about the sense and purpose of consumer models in general. This is followed by Thomas Cannaday with a contribution that deals with the model of the mature consumer from a philosophical perspective and breaks a lance for this model, provided one considers a practice-theoretical revision.

[8] See footnote 1.

The second block deals with the relationship between political consumption and political participation. First, Karsten Fischer, from a political science perspective, addresses the central question of what is political about political consumption. The different variants of participation that can be identified in the context of political consumption play a significant role in this. Jörn Lamla then focuses on those forms of participation that are used on internet rating portals and asks what relevance these experiences and their justification patterns have for the expectation of participation associated with (political) consumption.[9]

The third block deals with the responsibility and responsibilities of consumers. Kathrin Loer approaches this topic from the political science side, repeatedly engages constructively with the idea of a 'consumer policy from below' and considers how the question of responsibility could be conceived from this perspective. Subsequently, Wolfgang Ullrich turns to the connection between consumption and responsibility with reference to Hans Jonas' 'Principle of Responsibility' and toys with the possibility of a duty ethics that could receive more attention in this context.

In the fourth block, the three contributions are interested in the cultural-moral dimension of (political) consumption. Marianne Heinze starts by examining the circumstances of origin and forms of expression of the alternative consumption discourse from the 1970s and asks about its significance for the present. Daniel Kofahl then turns to the figure of the moral entrepreneur and illustrates his appearance, among other things, in conflicts that can arise from a preference for different food cultures. Finally, Günther Rosenberger introduces the dark sides of consumption, i.e., consumption behavior that is considered morally dubious and questionable or should even be referred to as criminal consumption.

The fifth and final block brings together actors, activists, initiatives, organizations, and associations, most of which can be assigned to the field of 'consumer politics from below'. In the first contribution, Nina Birkner-Tröger first deals with the two distinctions of self- or external organization of consumer organizations as well as the mono- or poly-thematic treatment of policy fields and then provides an overview of the consumer political landscape of Austria, with a special focus on grassroots movements. In the second contribution, Heiko Steffens deals with the history of the Working Group of Consumer Centers (AgV, Arbeitsgemeinschaft der Verbraucherverbände), which represented the principle of external organization of consumer interests and was transformed into the Consumer

[9] See also Kornberger (2017).

Center Federal Association (vzbv) in 2000, as well as related consumer organizations. Georg Abel then explains the position of the Verbraucher Initiative e. V., which was founded in 1985 as a representation of consumers through self-organization.[10] Next, Daniel Affelt presents several initiatives of the Bund für Umwelt- und Naturschutz Deutschland (BUND) Berlin, in which consumers in Berlin are offered various opportunities to become active themselves in the context of political consumption, such as sewing cafes, repair cafes, etc. The same applies to a bouquet of initiatives initiated and organized by the Verbraucherzentrale Nordrhein-Westfalen and presented by Jonas Grauel. The sixth contribution comes from Stefan Schridde and discusses measures on how to counter planned obsolescence or how to avoid it as much as possible, for example within the framework of the association 'Murks? Nein Danke!'. Finally, Reinhard Singer, Kristina Schimpf, and Kathrin Steinbach explain the social innovation of 'Law Clinics' using the example of the 'Humboldt Consumer Law Clinic' of the Law Faculty of Humboldt University in Berlin, where consumers can receive free advice from law students for very specific consumer problems such as unjustified rent increases.

References

Adloff, Frank, Ansgar Klein, and Jürgen Kocka. 2016. Kapitalismus und Zivilgesellschaft. *Forschungsjournal Soziale Bewegungen* 29:14–21.

Baek, Young Min. 2010. To buy or not to buy: Who are political consumers? What do they think and how do they participate? *Political Studies* 58:1065–1086.

Bala, Christian, and Wolfgang Schuldzinski, eds. 2019. *Der vertrauende Verbraucher. Zwischen Regulation und Information*. Düsseldorf: Verbraucherzentrale NRW.

Baringhorst, Sigrid. 2015. Konsum und Lebensstile als politische Praxis – Systematisierende und historisch kontextualisierende Annäherungen. *Forschungsjournal Soziale Bewegungen* 28:17–27.

Baringhorst, Sigrid, Veronika Kneip, Annegret März, and Johanna Niesyto, eds. 2007. *Politik mit dem Einkaufswagen. Unternehmen und Konsumenten als Bürger in der globalen Mediengesellschaft*. Bielefeld: transcript.

Baringhorst, Sigrid, and Katharina Witterhold. 2015. Verbraucherinformation – Top down oder bottom up? Neue Formen netzbasierter Generierung einer kritischen Verbraucheröffentlichkeit. In *Abschied vom Otto Normalverbraucher*, ed. C. Bala, 145–165. Düsseldorf: Klartext und Landeszentrale für politische Bildung.

[10] See also Verbraucher Initiative (1996).

Barnes, Samuel H., and Max Kaase. 1979. *Political action: Mass participation in five western democracies*. Beverly Hill: Sage.

Barnett, Clive, Paul Cloke, Nick Clarke, and Alice Malpass. 2010. *Globalizing Responsibility. The Political Rationalities of Ethical Consumption*. Oxford: Wiley.

Baule, Bernward. 2012. §72 Kommerzkultur, Verbrauchermacht, moralischer Konsum – zur Verbraucherpolitik im Föderalismus. In *Handbuch Föderalismus. Föderalismus als demokratische Rechtsordnung und Rechtskultur in Deutschland, Europa und der Welt*, ed. I. Härtel, 515–613. Berlin: Springer.

Biervert, Bernd, Kurt Monse, and Reinhard Rock. 1984. *Organisierte Verbraucherpolitik. Zwischen Ökonomisierung und Bedürfnisorientierung*. Frankfurt/New York: Campus.

Bock, Josef, and Karl Gustav Specht. 1958. *Verbraucherpolitik*. Köln: Westdeutscher Verlag.

Bosch, Aida. 2010. *Konsum und Exklusion. Eine Kultursoziologie der Dinge*. Bielefeld: Transcript.

Boström, Magnus, Andreas Føllesdal, Mikael Klintman, Michele Micheletti, and Mads P. Søresen, eds. 2005. *Political Consumerism: Ist motivations, power, and conditions in the Nordic countries and elsewhere. Proceedings from the 2nd International Seminar on Political Consumerism, Oslo August* 26–29, 2004. Kopenhagen: TemaNord.

Boström, Magnus, Michele Micheletti, and Peter Oosterveer, eds. 2019. *Oxford Handbook of Political Consumerism*. New York: Oxford University Press.

Brandl, Werner. 2007. Konsum und Moral – Ein orthodoxes Paradox der Mode? *Haushalt in Bildung und Forschung* 7:90–111.

Braunschweig, Christa. 1965. *Der Konsument und seine Vertretung. Eine Studie über Verbraucherverbände*. Heidelberg: Quelle & Meyer.

Bundesnetzwerk Bürgerschaftliches Engagement (BBE). 2008. *Engagement und Erwerbsarbeit*. Berlin: BBE-Eigenverlag.

Carrigan, Marylyn, and Ahmad Attalla. 2001. The myth of the ethical consumer – Do ethics matter in purchase behaviour? *Journal of Consumer Marketing* 18:560–578.

Chen, Rocky Peng, Echo Wen Wan, and Eric Levy. 2017. The effect of social exclusion on consumer preference for anthropomorphized brands. *Journal of Consumer Psychology* 27:23–34.

Connolly, John, and Andrea Prothero. 2008. Green consumption. Life-politics, risk and contradictions. *Journal of Consumer Culture* 8:117–145.

Devinney, Timothy M., Pat Auger, and Giana M. Eckhardt. 2010. *The myth of the ethical consumer*. Cambridge: Cambridge University Press.

Evers, Adalbert, and Thomas Olk. 1996. *Wohlfahrtspluralismus. Vom Wohlfahrtsstaat zur Wohlfahrtsgesellschaft*. Opladen: Westdeutscher Verlag.

Geiger, Theodor. 1964. *Vorstudien zu einer Soziologie des Rechts. Mit einer Einleitung und internationalen Bibliographie von Paul Trappe*. Neuwied: Luchterhand.

Gerhards, Jürgen. 2001. Der Aufstand des Publikums. Eine systemtheoretische Interpretation des Kulturwandels in Deutschland zwischen 1960 und 1989. *Zeitschrift für Soziologie* 30:163–184.

Hartmann, Kathrin. 2013. Politik statt Einkaufswagen. *Haushalt in Bildung und Forschung* 2:14–17.

Hedtke, Reinhold. 2005. Die Moral des Konsums und der Konsum der Moral. Anmerkungen zu den Paradoxien des Marktes. In *Warenethik und Berufsmoral im Handel.*

Beiträge zur Innovation der kaufmännischen Bildung. Schriftenreihe der Deutschen Stiftung für Warenlehre, eds. H. Lungershausen and R. Retzmann, 47–53. Essen: Deutsche Stiftung für Warenlehre.

Heidbrink, Ludger, Imke Schmidt, and Björn Ahaus, eds. 2011. *Die Verantwortung des Konsumenten. Über das Verhältnis von Markt, Moral und Konsum*. Frankfurt: Campus.

Hellmann, Kai-Uwe. 2003. Sind wir eine Gesellschaft ohne Moral? Soziologische Anmerkungen zum Verbleib der Moral in der Moderne. In *Interesse und Moral als Orientierungen politischen Handelns*, ed. U. Willems, 101–133. Baden-Baden: Nomos.

Hellmann, Kai-Uwe. 2004. Solidarität, Sozialkapital und Systemvertrauen. Formen sozialer Integration. In *Zivilgesellschaft und Sozialkapital. Herausforderungen politischer und sozialer Integration*, eds. A. Klein, K. Kern, B. Geißel, and M. Berger, 131–149. Opladen: VS Verlag.

Hellmann, Kai-Uwe. 2010. Konsum zwischen Risiko und Gefahr. In *Unsichere Zeiten. Herausforderungen gesellschaftlicher Transformation. Verhandlungen des 34. Kongresses der Deutschen Gesellschaft für Soziologie in Jena 2008*, ed. H.G. Soeffner. Frankfurt: Campus, CD-ROM.

Hellmann, Kai-Uwe. 2012. Inklusion als Teilnahme und Teilhabe an Gesellschaft. Die soziologische Perspektive. In *Inklusion und Individualität. Aspekte einer systematischen Spannung*, ed. R. Mehring, 61–76. Heidelberg: Mattes.

Holzer, Boris. 2010. Political consumerism between individual choice and collective action social movements, role mobilization, and signalling. *International Journal of Consumer Studies* 30:405–415.

Inglehart, Ronald. 1977. *The silent revolution. Changing values and political styles among western publics*. Princeton: Princeton University Press.

Janning, Frank. 2003. Der Staat der Konsumenten. Plädoyer für eine politische Theorie des Verbraucherschutzes. *Politische Vierteljahresschrift*, Sonderheft (Politik und Markt): 151–185.

Janning, Frank. 2011. *Die Spätgeburt eines Politikfeldes. Die Institutionalisierung der Verbraucherschutzpolitik in Deutschland und im internationalen Vergleich*. Baden-Baden: Nomos.

Jaquemoth, Mirjam, and Rainer Hufnagel. 2018. *Verbraucherpolitik. Ein Lehrbuch mit Beispielen und Kontrollfragen*. Stuttgart: Schäffer-Poeschel.

Kenning, Peter, and Inga Wobker. 2013. Ist der ‚mündige Verbraucher' eine Fiktion? Ein kritischer Beitrag zum aktuellen Stand der Diskussion um das Verbraucherleitbild in den Wirtschaftswissenschaften und der Wirtschaftspolitik. *Zeitschrift für Wirtschafts- und Unternehmensethik* 14:282–300.

Klein, Ansgar. 2019. Wohlfahrtsverbände und die Dynamik des Engagements in der Gesellschaft. In *Demokratie und Wohlfahrtspflege. Sonderband 2019 der Zeitschriften Blätter der Wohlfahrtspflege und Sozialwirtschaft*. eds. K. Hummel and G. Timm, 213–226. Baden-Baden: Nomos.

Klein, Ansgar and Thomas Röbke. 2018. Monetarisierung und Engagement. Ausblicke auf die Tätigkeitsgesellschaft. In *Jahrbuch Engagementpolitik 2018*, 99–110. Frankfurt/M.: Wochenschau.

Koopmans, Ruud. 1995. *Democracy from below. New social movements and the political system in west Germany*. Boulder: Westview.

Koos, Sebastian. 2012. What drives political consumption in Europe? A multi-level analysis on individual characteristics, opportunity structures and globalization. *Acta Sociologica* 55:37–57.

Kornberger, Martin. 2017. The visible hand and the crowd: Analyzing organization design in distributed innovation systems. *Strategic Organization* 15:174–193.

Koslowski, Peter, and Birger Priddat, eds. 2006. *Ethik des Konsums*. München: Fink.

Kraemer, Klaus. 2002. Konsum als Teilhabe an der materiellen Kultur. In *Nachhaltiger Konsum. Auf dem Weg zur gesellschaftlichen Verankerung*, eds. G. Scherhorn and C. Weber, 55–62. München: ökom-Verlag.

Kuhlmann, Eberhard. 1990. *Verbraucherpolitik. Grundzüge ihrer Theorie und Praxis*. München: Vahlen.

Lamla, Jörn, and Ansgar Klein. 2005. Verbraucherpolitik als Querschnittsaufgabe profilieren! Ein Interview mit Edda Müller. *Forschungsjournal Neue Soziale Bewegungen* 18:98–105.

Lamla, Jörn, and Sighard Neckel, eds. 2006. *Politisierter Konsum – konsumierte Politik*. Wiesbaden: VS Verlag.

Lübke, Volkmar. 1991. Verbraucherverbände: Ansprüche, Wirkungen, Perspektiven. *Forschungsjournal Neue Soziale Bewegungen* 4:60–67.

Marshall, Thomas S. 1950. *Citizenship and social class and other essays*. Cambridge: CUP.

Micheletti, Michele, Andreas Føllesdal, and Dietlind Stolle, eds. 2004. *Politics, products, and markets. Exploring political consumerism past and present*. London: Routledge.

Micklitz, Hans-W, Andreas Oehler, Michael-Burkhard Piorkowsky, Lucia A. Reisch, and Christoph Strünck. 2010. *Der vertrauende, der verletzliche oder der verantwortungsvolle Verbraucher? Plädoyer für eine differenzierte Strategie in der Verbraucherpolitik. Stellungnahme des Wissenschaftlichen Beirats für Verbraucher- und Ernährungspolitik beim BMELV vom Dezember 2010*. Berlin: Bundesministerium für Ernährung, Landwirtschaft und Verbraucherschutz.

Müller, Edda. 2001. Grundlinien einer modernen Verbraucherpolitik. *Aus Politik und Zeitgeschichte B* 24:6–15.

Nessel, Sebastian. 2016. *Verbraucherorganisationen und Märkte. Eine wirtschaftssoziologische Untersuchung*. Wiesbaden: Springer VS.

Newman, Benjamin J., and Brandon L. Bartels. 2011. Politics at the checkout line: Explaining political consumerism in the united states. *Political Research Quarterly* 64:803–817.

Oehler, Andreas. 2013. Neue alte Verbraucherleitbilder: Basis für die Verbraucherbildung? *Haushalt in Bildung und Forschung* 2:44–60.

Raschke, Joachim. 1985. *Soziale Bewegungen. Ein historisch-systematischer Grundriß*. Frankfurt: Campus.

Rick, Kevin. 2018. *Verbraucherpolitik in der Bundesrepublik Deutschland. Eine Geschichte des westdeutschen Konsumtionsregimes, 1945–1975*. Baden: Nomos.

Riesman, David, and Howard Roseborough. 1964. Careers and Consumer Behavior. In *Abundance for what? And other essays*, ed. D. Riesman, 107–130. New York: Garden City.

Roth, Roland. 1994. *Demokratie von unten. Neue soziale Bewegungen auf dem Wege zur politischen Institution*. Köln: Bund.

Scherhorn, Gerhard. 1975. *Verbraucherinteresse und Verbraucherpolitik*. Göttingen: Schwartz & Co.

Schmidt, Imke. 2016. *Consumer Social Responsibility. Gemeinsame Verantwortung für nachhaltiges Konsumieren und Produzieren*. Wiesbaden: Springer VS.

Schmidt-Kessel, Martin, and Claas Christian Germelmann, eds. 2016. *Verbraucherleitbilder – Zwecke, Wirkweisen und Maßstäbe*. Jena: Jenaer Wissenschaftliche Verlagsgesellschaft.

Schrader, Ulf. 2007. The moral responsibility of consumers and citizens. *International Journal of Innovation and Sustainable Development* 2:79–96.

Selter, Gerhard. 1973. Idee und Organisation des Konsumerismus. Eine empirische Untersuchung der Konsumerismusbewegung in den USA. *Soziale Welt* 24:185–205.

Stolle, Dietlind, and Marc Hooghe. 2011. Shifting inequalities. Patterns of exclusion and inclusion in emerging forms of political participation. *European Societies* 13:119–142.

Stolle, Dietlind, Marc Hooghe, and Michele Micheletti. 2005. Politics in the supermarket. Political consumerism as a form of political participation. *International Political Science Review* 26:245–269.

Stolle, Dietlind, and Michele Micheletti. 2013. *Political consumerism. Global responsibility in action*. Cambridge: Cambridge University Press.

Ullrich, Wolfgang. 2008. ‚Gewissen ist geil' – Konsumkultur und Moral. *Utopiablog*. https://utopiablog.files.wordpress.com/2008/12/moralkonsum.pdf. Accessed 6 Febr 2020.

Verbraucher Initiative. 1996. Manifest Die Verantwortung der Verbraucherinnen und Verbraucher. In *Welche Dinge braucht der Mensch Hintergründe, Folgen und Perspektiven der heutigen Alltagskultur Gekürzte Fassung*, ed. D. Steffens, 216–222. Frankfurt: Anabas.

Wahlen, Stefan, and Mikko Laamanen. 2015. Consumption, lifestyle and social movements. *International Journal of Consumer Studies* 39:397–403.

Zald, Mayer N., and Bert Useem. 1987. Movement and countermovement interaction mobilization, tactics and state lnvolvement. In *Social movements in an organizational society*, eds. M.N. Zald and J.D. McCarthy, 247–272. London: Routledge.

Kai-Uwe Hellmann Prof. Dr., born 1962, teaches consumer and economic sociology at the Institute of Sociology at the Technical University of Berlin and heads the consumer sociology working group together with Prof. Dr. Dominik Schrage.

Ansgar Klein, Dr., born 1959, Managing Director of the Federal Network for Civic Engagement (Bundesnetzwerk Bürgerschaftliches Engagement (BBE)). The habilitated political scientist and graduate sociologist has been co-editor of the "Forschungsjournal Neue Soziale Bewegungen" since 1988. After working for several years as a scientific author, freelance publicist, editor and lecturer in political education, he worked from 2000 to 2002 as the scientific coordinator of the SPD parliamentary group for the Enquete Commission on the Future of Civic Engagement. The editor of several book series and private lecturer at the Humboldt University in Berlin has been the (founding) executive director of the Federal Network for Civic Engagement (BBE) since 2002.

The Informed Consumer as an Obsolete Model?

The Mature ('Mündige') Consumer: A Misunderstood Ideal?

Christoph Strünck

Abstract

The guiding principle of the mature ('mündige') consumer attracts criticism. Consuming maturely remains a goal that is not in question. But other questions arise: What does maturity ('Mündigkeit') mean in the context of consumption, what conditions must be met for this, what function can and should a guiding principle fulfill at all? The article critically engages with the scientific discussion about consumer guiding principles. It is discussed how sharply the proposed alternative guiding principles are differentiated from the mature consumer, and what soft flanks they have. At the same time, it is discussed what function the consumer guiding principles can have, whether the concept of the guiding principle is useful, and what misunderstandings there may be in the debate about it. The guiding principle of the mature consumer—so the conclusion—is more of an ethical orientation than an explanatory model. The recently proposed alternatives, on the other hand, serve as a kind of behavioral typology.

Keywords

Maturity · Consumer model · Rationality · Behavioral economics · Mind-behavior-gap

---

C. Strünck (✉)
Fakultät I, Seminar für Sozialwissenschaften, Universität Siegen, Siegen, Germany
e-mail: christoph.struenck@uni-siegen.de

K.-U. Hellmann et al. (eds.), *Consumer Policy from Below*,
https://doi.org/10.1007/978-3-658-44478-5_2

1 What does Maturity ('Mündigkeit') Mean Here?

Since the Enlightenment, maturity has been the lofty goal of every educational reform. It is one of the great promises and at the same time the prerequisite of liberal democracies, which rely on mature citizens. It is therefore not surprising that the ability to act maturely has been extended to just about every social role that people are ascribed in modern societies.

To be mature means to act responsibly. Maturity is close to the idea of rationality, but it is not identical to it. It is the will to act rationally. People can fundamentally be rational, but do not want to use their reason themselves, instead leaving the decisions to others. Then they renounce an important ability and thus act immaturely. The central philosophical commentary on this comes from Immanuel Kant (1784):

> "Enlightenment is man's emergence from his self-imposed immaturity. Immaturity is the inability to use one's understanding without guidance from another. This immaturity is self-imposed when its cause lies not in lack of understanding, but in lack of resolve and courage to use it without guidance from another."

When consumer policy and consumer research talk about 'mature consumers', there is a lot of conceptual baggage attached to it. Self-critically, one must admit that this baggage was perhaps too hastily discarded in the debate about consumer role models. Maturity, understanding, reason and rationality are related, but they are not the same. Also, the guiding principle of the mature consumer is not identical with the ideal-typical scientific model of 'rational consumption', which is increasingly being questioned by behavioral economic research.

In the political, science policy and partly intra-scientific discussion about consumer policy role models, actually little has been said about the idea of maturity. Instead, consumer sciences are grappling with the limits of rationality when it comes to consumption decisions. The idea of 'bounded rationality' is somewhat dated (Simon 1959). But the experiments of behavioral economics have given this concept, originally related to organizations, human proportions. And they have redirected the focus back to routines, habits and norms, which are not opposed to rationality, but embed it socially (Reisch and Oehler 2009).

To use one's understanding without guidance from another, i.e. to act maturely: What does this mean in terms of consumption? With our consumption decisions, we pursue certain purposes. These purposes are individually different, and they are also shaped by milieus, norms and social communication. Purposes define the space of the act of consumption, which can last a long time and during which the purposes can also change: First I buy a bicycle for excursions, then I use it for commuting and actually it is also a status symbol.

Purposes can also be emotionally charged, they are not 'rational' or utility-oriented in the strict sense. The economic theory of democracy by Anthony Downs (1965) captures this logic of purpose-means rationality, as Max Weber had already developed: Voters can prefer parties that advocate altruistic goals. This is not irrational. But if they then do not vote for these parties because they have not dealt with the program, then they do not act rationally.

Reason must guide the choice of means to achieve the respective purposes: money, time, sources of information. There are many restrictions here, both individual and structural. If I don't think about which means I can use how, then I act immaturely. But if I come to the conclusion that my means are limited and therefore I need substitute solutions like test results or experience reports, then this is entirely in line with mature consumer behavior. Trusting test reports is also not the 'guidance of another'. Because the actual decision to trust, I have to make myself.

What ultimately motivates me to make such decisions is empirically anything but clear. Possibly, the mentioned or apparent motives are only retrospective rationalizations, while the actual impulse remains undiscovered. The needs and motives for consumption are still a blind spot in research, a kind of black box (Bauer and Gegenhuber 2015).

Even if it should be the case that we construct motives only when we justify ourselves, maturity as the essence of an important social role is not superfluous. Consuming maturely means thinking about my decision-making options and their limits. However, how much responsibility I can take for the decision depends on the framework conditions and my life situation.

In fact, mature consumers must attribute self-responsibility or attribute it to themselves. However, I can only take responsibility for things that I can influence. Or in the words of Hans Jonas (1984, p. 172): "The condition of responsibility is causal power".

Limits of self-responsibility were the impetus for the recent discussion about consumer role models. However, they are not automatically antipodes of the mature consumer. It could also be argued that the guiding triad of 'trusting, vulnerable and responsible consumers' is not an antithesis, but rather variants of the mature consumer. This is especially true for responsible consumers, whose active role sharpens the idea of the mature consumer. Perhaps, however, the three new guiding images are not guiding images in the true sense, with their own ethical foundation. But more on that later.

2 The Trusting, the Vulnerable, the Responsible Consumer: Alternatives or Differentiation?

Does it make sense to oppose the normatively established guiding image of the mature consumer with new guiding images in a critical intention? The semantics of guiding images themselves require (self-)criticism. The new consumer guiding images also suggest that there are different ideal types of consumers or consumer groups. However, from a sociological point of view, consumers are not a social group, but a role that is perceived differently. Guiding images therefore rather describe ideal types of consumer behavior or consumer situations.

In the statements of the former scientific advisory board at the Federal Ministry of Food, Agriculture and Consumer Protection (BMELV), in which the author was also involved, this sometimes sounds different. Here it is said that most people behave like 'trusting consumers': "They do not want and cannot take too much time for a consumption decision" (Micklitz et al. 2010). This group would be dependent on a minimum level of protection, among other things. This statement is only partially empirically verifiable. It is also not far-fetched that quite a few people also behave like 'ignorant consumers' (Klug 2015). The 'mind-behavior-gap' widely proven in research suggests this. Attitudes do not automatically lead to corresponding behavior.

At other points in the text, the 'group of vulnerable consumers' appears, who should be able to rely on a special level of protection. The latter is also officially represented by politics, for example when the EU demands from the member states to define the group of consumers worthy of protection in the energy market in order to prevent power cuts (Strünck 2017b).

Such understandable political necessities, however, make only limited sense scientifically, as consumers are not a social group, but describe a social role. A cognitively impaired older person may be vulnerable when making health-relevant decisions. However, he does not necessarily have to be threatened by power cuts. If he also seeks help from independents, he rather acts as a trusting consumer.

Consumers can act responsibly in the fields where their political interest in change is greatest. However, those who buy fair trade clothing or organic food can also consume a lot of energy through digital consumption. And even 'average' consumers can be particularly active, informed, and responsible in certain areas of consumption.

The three new types of consumer (behavior) models therefore overlap. At the same time, they have different points of contact with the model of the enlightened consumer.

The 'trusting consumers' essentially rely on meta-rationality: They trust third parties, which they have to identify themselves and for which they have criteria for trustworthiness. Thus, the trusting consumers also use their intellect by acting in a way that saves efficiency, a classic form of means-rationality.

The vulnerable consumers (or vulnerable consumer behavior) are most likely to conflict with the model of the enlightened consumer. However, it is not necessarily a lack of 'will or courage' to use one's own intellect. Either their cognitive abilities are limited, or the conditions limit their options for action. The latter can be demonstrated again using the example of energy markets: Those in debt cannot easily switch to a cheaper electricity tariff, but are stuck in the expensive basic tariff (Strünck 2017b). Here, alternative solutions are needed to overcome the limits of enlightenment.

Do I also have to oversee the consequences of my consumption to be enlightened? This expectation is associated with the model of the 'responsible consumer'. Here, enlightenment means implementing one's own convictions through consumption in the sense of political consumerism: Negative external effects of consumption should be avoided, socially fair, ecological or other goals should be consciously promoted with consumption (Baringhorst 2007; Koos 2011). However, particularly active consumers in particular depend on receiving sufficient information about supply chains, product characteristics, and the consequences of consumption decisions. If this is difficult, they can only take limited responsibility for themselves.

Even this sketchy analysis suggests that the three models are not a replacement for the model of the enlightened consumer, but rather a differentiating supplement. Accordingly, the relevant statement concludes: "If one sticks to the model of the 'enlightened' consumer, consumer policy strategies must be more strongly oriented towards different behavior patterns". And the three new models are supposed to provide information about these behavior patterns. Are they then models in the true sense? In any case, they are based on assumptions that they share with the model of the enlightened consumer. And these assumptions are subject to criticism.

3 Are Consumer Models Too Individualistic?

One criticism that hits the model of the enlightened consumer as hard as its differentiations is that of individualistic narrowing. Consumption can fundamentally be seen as an act of community formation, embedded in larger societal consumption cultures and smaller communal consumption styles and habits. Even the needs themselves are not purely individual, but always socially constructed, not to mention the structuring of needs by industry, advertising, and media. Above all, however, consumption is a kind of network of social relationships.[1]

The act of purchase alone does not reflect consumption as a social principle. Both the reflection on the origin of products and the use and application of goods and services, for oneself, in households or in community, shape the act of consumption with its economic and social prerequisites and subsequent effects. Preferences arise and change in these social relationships, while they are assumed to be given in neoclassical economic models.

Although they critically oppose orthodox models, the newer consumer models also largely follow an individualistic approach inspired by behavioral sciences. Behavioral economics does reflect classic sociological concepts such as milieus or norms, but considers them as external factors that shape individual behavior. Purchase and consumption acts are socially embedded, they are primarily communication between various participants, and supposedly individual motives can be constructed retrospectively (Hellmann 2013). These social phenomena can only be partially reconstructed in experiments.

Therefore, the alternative models of recent times must also accept the criticism that they are thought too individualistically, even though they draw attention to the limits of rationality. However, a critically constructive view of the model discussion should also consider the context.

4 Understandings and Misunderstandings of Consumer Role Models

It would be worthwhile to reflect sociologically on the recent discussion about consumer role models. For it is a small part of a long developmental series in consumer research, in which consumers have been conceived “first as an animal, then as a computer, later as a tourist, and finally as a tribe member” (Hellmann 2017, p. 145). Consumer role models, when they also serve as a backdrop for scientific models, always reflect the zeitgeist in politics and public life, and the

[1] The author recalls that the discussions in the former scientific advisory board for consumer and nutrition policy of the Federal Ministry for Food, Agriculture and Consumer Protection (BMELV) got stuck on this fundamental point and could not be resolved: Do we start from a person-centered decision model, or do we consider consumption at least as household economics, if not even as a community-shaped network? And how much personal responsibility is legitimate or even necessary?

controversies woven into it. They transport scientific paradigms, fashions, norms, but also political mood swings. Even when they are intended as an analytical model, as an ideal type in the Weberian sense, they carry a normative core within them. Even jurisprudence is not immune to the vicissitudes of role models with their respective contestable assumptions (Strünck 2015).

The mature consumer, whom everyone wishes to be the target image, has come under fire from two directions: From a consumer policy perspective, as role models are always also politically instrumentalized, and from a consumer science perspective, as role models also inspire scientific models (Strünck 2010).

The bridge between the two is the growing criticism of the 'information approach' in consumer policy and consumer sciences (Kenning and Wobker 2013). For in addition to information asymmetry, there is also a power asymmetry between producers and consumers. Besides, choice and transparency do not automatically ensure that substantial choices exist. In the field of mobility, for example, this requires infrastructural changes (Strünck 2017a).

Since the financial crisis at the latest, there has been increasing criticism of the dominant paradigm of neoclassical economics, according to which self-regulating markets optimally promote consumer welfare. The explanatory value was questioned and at the same time criticized that political decisions would have been oriented too one-sidedly towards this model. In this climate, the role model of the mature consumer increasingly appeared more as an ideology than as an idea.[2]

If it was understood in the 70s as a normative act of emancipation of self-confident consumers and as an active part of overall economic control, today the role model is suspected of being a distorted and deceptive image instrumentalized by the industry (Strünck 2015).

But what were and are the motives for new role models being and having been opposed to the normative pole star of maturity? The following is a highly subjective conjecture, solely attributable to the author, without any evidence. It is more of a self-reflection than a systematic analysis.

5 Reminiscence and Self-Reflection

Firstly, there was the desire for scientifically based support for consumer policy, in order to enhance its status as a policy field compared to established departments (Hagen et al. 2013). From the perspective of some, not all protagonists,

[2] Here another discussion in the former scientific advisory board started: Why doesn't competition automatically create sufficient transparency for informed consumer decisions? Competition policy therefore cannot replace consumer policy.

"based" meant more empiricism in the form of evidence. And this empiricism should not be based on a behavior model criticized as being detached from reality. It should start with specific consumer problems and provide evidence for the effectiveness of certain consumer policy regulations. However, the methodological problems were ignored. Because here paradigms would have clashed. Associated with this motive was by no means a critique of capitalism, but a belief in the political balance ideas of the social market economy: Anyone who wants to promote the social effects of the market economy must not turn a blind eye to the behavior of people that is far from textbook. And he must not ideologize personal responsibility, but must enable its realistic implementation.

Associated with this motive was the interest in implementing the approaches of behavioral economics into political measures, for example in the form of 'nudging' and new decision architectures. The role models of the Obama administration and the British government offered the opportunity to stimulate consumer policy with innovative approaches. However, this required the importance of the enlightened consumer as a starting point for political measures to be relativized.

Another, highly controversial motive was skepticism about the reach of consumer education. Without better decision architectures, consumer education would fall flat in increasingly complex markets.

Another motive was to make the self-responsibility of the enlightened consumer more visible as social responsibility. This gave rise to the desire to independently frame the responsible consumer. From the outset, however, there was criticism that all other types of behavior would thereby be implicitly caricatured as irresponsible. But ultimately, sustainable consumption should also be reflected in a corresponding consumer model. Added to this was a certain dissatisfaction with viewing consumption as purely economic activity. The social participation through consumption up to the political responsibility of consumer citizens should not be ignored.

In addition to other motives, concerns were mixed in from the beginning, as they were also expressed in the advisory board. Models must have a normative core, otherwise they are not models. Therefore, shouldn't there be a much clearer semantic and analytical distinction between the functions of political models and scientific models?

Basically, we expect ethical orientation from models. However, developing these is not an inherently scientific task. Political organizations primarily see themselves as responsible for this and also have their own models. So why should a new model discussion originate from science? Isn't it presumptuous to propose new homogeneous models when the existing ones are interpreted very differently, depending on the interest situation?

6 Differentiated Consumer Role Models

Fundamentally, there is a central misunderstanding in the role model discussion. If a significant impulse was to cast an evidence-based, realistic view on consumer behavior, then it may not be appropriate to propose new role models. On the other hand, politics should be sensitized not to confuse role models with reality. Interest-driven interpretations of role models should be replaced by evidence-based decision architectures. One might attribute political naivety to this intention.

However, the three new 'role models' should direct attention to different variants of realistic consumer behavior. Because the statement 'Consumers should decide for themselves' obscures the demanding requirements for mature consumers. How realistic these requirements are is secondary when the role model of the mature consumer is understood as ethical orientation and less as an explanatory model.

The fact that such a role model is instrumentalized or scientifically narrowed does not mean that it has to be discarded. On the contrary: The contradictions between real action possibilities and ethical commandments only make visible where consumer policy can be effective and where its limits lie.

The new consumer role models are more of a typology of behavior and situations than an ethical-normative guide rail. Their value lies in putting the empirical fiction of the 'average consumer' to rest. And they also provide clues on how the gap between consumer behavior and consumer role model can be reduced. Thus, they also pay their respects to the role model of the mature consumer. But they do not take it at face value.

References

Baringhorst, Sigrid. 2007. *Politik mit dem Einkaufswagen. Unternehmen und Konsumenten als Bürger in der globalen Mediengesellschaft*. Bielefeld: Transcript.

Bauer, Robert M., and Thomas Gegenhuber. 2015. Crowdsourcing: Global search and the twisted roles of consumers and producers. *Organization* 22:661–681. https://doi.org/10.1177/1350508415585030.

Downs, Anthony. 1965. *An economic theory of democracy*. New York: Harper & Row.

Hagen, Kornelia, Hans-W Micklitz, Andreas Oehler, Lucia A. Reisch, and Christoph Strünck. 2013. Check Verbraucherpolitik und Verbraucherbeteiligung: Empfehlungen für eine evidenzbasierte Verbraucherpolitik. *Journal für Verbraucherschutz und Lebensmittelsicherheit* 8:61–66. https://doi.org/10.1007/s00003-012-0800-1.

Hellmann, Kai-Uwe. 2013. *Der Konsum der Gesellschaft. Studien zur Soziologie des Konsums*. Wiesbaden: Springer VS.

Hellmann, Kai-Uwe. 2017. Die akademische Konsumforschung aus soziologischer Perspektive. In *Verbraucherwissenschaften. Rahmenbedingungen, Forschungsfelder und Institutionen*, eds. P. Kenning, A. Oehler, L.A. Reisch, and C. Grugel, 141–165. Wiesbaden: Springer Gabler.

Jonas, Hans.1984. Das Prinzip Verantwortung. *Versuch einer Ethik für die technologische Zivilisation*. Frankfurt am Main: Insel-Verlag.

Kant, Immanuel. 1784. Beantwortung der Frage: Was ist Aufklärung? *Berlinische Monatsschrift* 12:481–494.

Kenning, Peter, and I. Wobker. 2013. Ist der ‚mündige Verbraucher' eine Fiktion? *Zeitschrift für Wirtschafts- und Unternehmensethik* 14:282–300.

Klug, Martin. 2015. Der ignorante Verbraucher als Leitbild der Verbraucherpolitik. In *Abschied vom Otto Normalverbraucher. Moderne Verbraucherforschung: Leitbilder, Information, Demokratie*, eds. C. Bala and K. Müller, 79–92. Essen: Klartext.

Koos, Sebastian. 2011. Explaining ethical consumption behaviour in Europe. A comparative analysis. In *Economy in changing society: Consumptions, markets, organizations and social policies*, ed. M. Nawojczyk, 17–44. Newcastle upon Tyne: Cambridge Scholars.

Micklitz, Hans-W, Andreas Oehler, Michael-Burkhard Piorkowski, Lucia A. Reisch, and Christoph Strünck. 2010. *Der vertrauende, der verletzliche oder der verantwortungsvolle Verbraucher? Plädoyer für eine differenzierte Strategie in der Verbraucherpolitik. Stellungnahme des Wissenschaftlichen Beirats Verbraucher- und Ernährungspolitik beim BMELV*. Berlin: BMELV.

Reisch, Lucia A. and Andreas Oehler. 2009. Behavioral economics: eine neue Grundlage für die Verbraucherpolitik? *Verbraucherpolitik zwischen Markt und Staat,* 30–43. Berlin: Duncker & Humblot.

Simon, Herbert A. 1959. Theories of decision-making in economics and behavioral science. *The American Economic Review* 49:253–283.

Strünck, Christoph. 2010. *Wollen wirklich alle den ‚mündigen Verbraucher'? Wie Interessengruppen ein Leitbild instrumentalisieren. Stellungnahme des Wissenschaftlichen Beirats Verbraucher- und Ernährungspolitik beim BMELV*. Berlin: BMELV.

Strünck, Christoph. 2015. Der mündige Verbraucher: ein populäres Leitbild auf dem Prüfstand. In *Abschied vom Otto Normalverbraucher. Moderne Verbraucherforschung: Leitbilder, Information, Demokratie*, eds. C. Bala and K. Müller, 19–28. Essen: Klartext.

Strünck, Christoph. 2017a. Energie und Mobilität. In *Verbraucherwissenschaften. Rahmenbedingungen, Forschungsfelder und Institutionen*, eds. P. Kenning, A. Oehler, L.A. Reisch, and C. Grugel, 235–259. Wiesbaden: Springer Gabler.

Strünck, Christoph. 2017b. *Energiearmut bekämpfen. Instrumente, Maßnahmen und Erfolge in Europa*. Bonn: Friedrich-Ebert-Stiftung Abteilung Wirtschafts- und Sozialpolitik.

Prof. Dr. Christoph Strünck teaches political science with a focus on social policy at the University of Siegen. His focus is on consumer research, social policy and health policy, as well as interest groups and interest politics.

Mature ('Mündige') Consumers—A Practice-Theoretical Revision

Thomas Cannaday

Abstract

The guiding principle of the mature ('mündige') consumer has fallen into disrepute. However, the criticism is based on the socio-theoretical caricature of a *homo oeconomicus*, which rather idealizes the consumer role than revealing the problem: Along the premises of utility maximization and by succumbing to rational choice assumptions of complete information, the mature consumer is constructed in such a way that its questioning must necessarily follow. The aim of the article is to provide a critique that both reveals one-sided determinations and explores the socio-theoretical possibilites of a practice-theory alternative. In order to identify the enabling mechanism of this political-economic principle, it is necessary to sensitize to the limits of personal responsibility and to redefine concepts such as responsibility, self-determination, co-determination, and transparency within the consumer discourse.

Keywords

Maturity · Political Philosophy · Practice Theory · Social Philosophy · Consumer Policy

T. Cannaday (✉)
Berlin, Germany
e-mail: Thomas.Cannaday@outlook.de

K.-U. Hellmann et al. (eds.), *Consumer Policy from Below*,
https://doi.org/10.1007/978-3-658-44478-5_3

1 Introduction

When we discuss consumer models, we are always already articulating a difficulty: The *sujet* of the discussed model needs to be both described and, regarding its political engagement, be addressed. A consumer model is therefore not only the subject of theoretical debate, but is shaped by practical expectations. The consumer model that this text is about is that of what is known in Germany as the 'mündige' consumer, i.e. the mature consumer.[1]

As much as the concept is invoked, it remains difficult to define what exactly is meant by "mündig". This is all the more true as it is associated with a whole range of diverse conceptual pairings. Maturity ('Mündigkeit') is sometimes understood as self-determination and assumption of responsibility (Eidam and Hoyer 2006, p. 7). Sometimes the term is equated with adulthood (Blatter 2007, p. 11 ff.). Autonomy and the ability to politically participate belong also to the vicinity of being mature (Habermas 1996, p. 277 f.). Finally, it is associated with complete information acquired through education (Fridrich et al. 2017, p. 121 f.). The obviousness that such *ad hoc* attributions seem to imply is lost when looking more closely at the offered conceptual constellations. Maturity suffers from being both over- and under-determined (Ebersold 1980, p. 150 ff.). It is under-determined because not only is the semantic content seemingly "left largely to the discretion of each individual" (ibid., p. 157), but also hidden theoretical traditions predecide the context within which maturity is to be understood (thus leading to different conceptualizations of "world") (Cannaday 2018, p. 11). On the other hand, maturity is over-determined insofar as it is simultaneously associated with perfectionist ideals of a transcendental decision-making power, from which perspective one can at best be 'semi-' or 'partially mature'. A critique of the term is therefore obvious, or as Strünck et al. (2012, p. 9 f.) complain:

[1] There is a vacancy in the English language when it comes to translating "Mündigkeit". For the latin-based term "maturity" the German language has reserved "Maturität" maintaining the meaning of a certain stage of development. What it profoundly neglects in comparison to the Germanic term "die munt" – from which "Mündigkeit" stems – is the implied ability to take care of others making "Mündigkeit" a genuin social practice. Lacking an adequate substitute, the text will proceed with the insufficient translation as the development for an acceptable term would lead astray from the initial enterprise. For further discussion see: Cannaday (2018, p. 10).

> "The figure of the münidge consumer [...] resembles that of the Loch Ness Monster. Some actors must or want to believe in it, others believe that it could exist under certain conditions, some doubt its existence and yet others describe what it should be like."

Nevertheless, maturity has been an integral part of the public discourse since the post-war period. Initially, it was predominantly discussed within pedagogy and in regards to legal issues. The increasing debate surrounding its function as a role model was picked up by sociological and economic thought. An 'education for maturity and responsibility' does not only concern the question of how to protect the masses from populist seduction. It is also a question of strengthening their will for democracy (Adorno 1971). Being a subject to economic considerations, maturity is associated with a capitalistic life-from in which individualization is expected: the individual is perceived as a self-responsible actor.[2] This dual perspective is neither temporally nor spatially limited to the early post-war period. With the end of the Cold War, the Federal and State Agencies for Political Education repeat the political demand for maturity to become the primary educational task.

After all, a democratic constitutional state is dependent

> "on the mature thinking and participation of its citizens and their willingness to form self- and socially responsible judgments, to respect the rules and values written in the constitution and to commit themselves to them" (bpb and lpb 1997).[3]

Almost at the same time, the Court of Justice of the European Union (ECJ) extends the validity of the guiding principle not only for an international context, but also reinforces the connection to capitalism in the model of an 'average' and 'sensible', a 'mature consumer', which it reaffirms in 2005 (ECJ 1998, 2005; Ulbrich 2005, p. 1 ff.; Sack 2005, p. 462).

---

[2] For example, the economist Gerhard Scherhorn (1973, p. 7) sees in maturity "the ability and the freedom to make independent decisions and active participation", which should be promoted especially in "economic areas of life", in order to fulfil—and this is crucial—the "democratic order" and meet the associated societal requirement of free decision-making ability.

[3] Maturity is seen as the means of choice to ensure the transition in East Germany from dictatorship to democracy. Especially in view of accelerating globalization, an education towards maturity should organize the change from a centralized planned economy to a—at that time still desired—social market economy.

The basis of this understanding of maturity lies in the intertwinement of two aspects, which are significant for the guiding principle of the mature consumer all the while promoting several misunderstandings: the combination of the so-called "information model" and the "origin or internal market principle" (Schmitt 2018, p. 128 ff.).[4] While the first introduces the question of "sufficient information as a basis for [...] autonomous and responsible decisions" in the model of the mature consumer, the connection with the second principle clarifies in what way self-determination is to be understood. It serves the goal of promoting 'entrepreneurial freedom' and 'competition', in short: economic efficiency:

> "Because of its injunction and competition control function, the consumer is required to act informed, attentive, and understanding, in other words, self-responsible" (Schmitt 2018, p. 129).

In the subsequent discussion of the concept of maturity, those interpretations of its aspects that are aligned with the needs of a functioning global economic system (Oehler 2012) come to the fore. The mature consumer is put into the spotlight. This applies not only to consumer policy ideas in the narrower sense, but at least since the 1990s (and further intensified by the *Agenda 2010*), a fundamental paradigm shift 'from citizen to customer' (Zymek 2004) also takes place in social policy: The 'well-informed, responsibly acting and self-determined consumer' is supposed to seamlessly bring together capitalism and democracy as the smallest economic-psychological unit and shape politics through his consumption decisions (Strünck et al. 2012, p. 3 f.). In entrusting market events to the rational calculation of the consumer, the hope is that issues such as sustainability will no longer primarily fall within the jurisdiction of political institutions. Rather, the citizen becomes the central instance that is supposed to individually implement

[4] For the ECJ, at the heart of its jurisprudence and interpretation of the consumer model was essentially 'the consumer understood as mature'. This combines, on the one hand, the information model, i.e., "that sufficient information is available to the self-responsible consumer as a basis for his autonomous and responsible decision". On the other hand, a link is made to the 'origin or internal market principle', i.e., to the consumer's scope of action. In connection with the information model, it is about "creating more entrepreneurial freedom and competition [...] by imposing increased self-responsibility. To achieve this goal, the ECJ explicitly referred to the normative criteria of the Union's consumer model. Because of its injunction and competition control function, the consumer is required to act informed, attentive, and understanding, in other words, self-responsible." (Schmitt 2018, p. 128 ff.).

consumer policies. The key to his political power and legitimation is seen in the provision of information. Only well-informed consumers can make well-considered decisions. The assumption is that by independently making rational decisions, a laissez-faire model of consumerist participation can fulfill the legitimizing claim of socio-economic progress desired by politics.

The fact that the inherent control optimism of an economically guided political development, however, encounters conceptual problems, which inevitably lead to practical implementation difficulties, needs to be proven in the following. From a social philosophical perspective, it will be shown that this optimism is based on uncritically adopted assumptions that already arise in the problem of consumer role models and the conception of a consumer as such. The aim of this article will be to expose these problems in order to reformulate a concept of the *mature* consumer for a social science debate, which is practically observable and politically enforceable. But first to the difficulties:

2 Problems of a Transcendent Understanding of Maturity

The intertwinement of the two spheres—economy with politics, politics with economy—is already reflected in the catchphrase of the 'mature consumer'. He is supposed to politically control or at least co-determine the market through his consumption decisions. In order to implement this demand, his 'personal responsibility' becomes a prerequisite and this is where the outlined information model comes into play. Henceforth, policies are to support the consumer in "information procurement and use" (BDI 2014, p. 65). Although it is recognized that he can often only act with "limited information in the sense of a weak rationality principle", this does not change the fact that maturity is determined by the degree of one's own information (Strünck et al. 2012, p. 3). Furthermore, the theoretical basis of (complete) informability is often derived from an 'economic behavior model', at the center of which, in terms of disciplinary history, a *rational agent* is located (BDI 2014, p. 65). Regarding this agent, expectations are formulated when conceptualizing the mature consumer which hardly can be met in practice.

There are mainly four difficulties that need to be highlighted in the implementation of this consumer role model: a) the information model itself, b) the practical implementation of self-determination, c) the range of responsibility and finally d) the fundamental conceptual problems in assuming a rational agent.

3 Limits of Informability

The first problem concerns the availability of information. If maturity is tied to responsible decisions and only well-informed consumers can make effective decisions, i.e., decisions that are supposed to meet a politically legitimizing claim, then only those consumers can be 'mature' who have sufficient information available. This problematizes the chance for informability in two respects: structurally, insofar as it concerns the provision and transparency of information, and individually, in the sense of how far it is possible to acquire sufficient knowledge about the entirety of one's consumption. The condition of being mature becomes problematic when maturity depends on having a complete overview of one's consuming practices and its consequences (both individual and social). For the mature consumer to also become a qualified co-governor of the economy, which means determining not only which products should exist, but also how production conditions are shaped, he must have sufficient knowledge about these and henceforth consume consciously and conscientiously. After all, every consuming act has become a political-economic statement, on which the future of society as a whole seems to depend.

The insistence for such conscious consumption, even if it were reduced to purchase decisions, seems preposterous when confronted with reality: the consumer will never be able to inform himself sufficiently and thus never succeed in becoming mature. Or in the words of the historian Günther Ebersold (1980, p. 153): Maturity as "mental penetration of the entire reality" lacks the insight that "man's consciousness is not equal to the complexity of his world." Consumers can "only act responsibly and self-determined to a limited extent" (Strünck et al. 2012, p. 3). This understanding of maturity is overloaded with expectations of perfectibility that are ultimately unattainable.

4 Failing Self-Determination

Even a reduced information principle not only puts a possible implementation of maturity at risk, but becomes also hinderance when it comes to putting knowledge into consume practices. This takes us to the second problem: self-performance, i.e., the question of how I must realize myself in order to be considered 'mature'. Perfectionistic requirements of this 'maturity model' let authors like Andreas Oehler (2012, p. 51) detect a significant danger: "It creates the illusion that everyone could always know and do everything. Yet it cannot be denied that not everyone can or wants to achieve this." Representatives of the Frankfurt School also feel compelled by these imposed normative settings to liberate themselves from maturity. Trying to fulfil the ultimate objective of being mature generates a constant, overwhelming pressure for the active consumer. The subject is put into a position to openly and reflexively realize itself in an 'authentic self-discovery' through consumption. In order to be recognized as an independent and responsible person, mature as it were, the consumer is expected to actualize himself in more and more potential self-aspects, unfolding in increasingly more consume practices. He is then left, as Axel Honneth summarizes, with the alternative between "staged originality" or "escape into depression" (Honneth 2002, p. 156).[5] This demand for maturity thus perverts a liberalizing self-realization into compulsion, which undermines individuality rather than promoting it.

5 The Inversion of Responsibility

The difficulty of self-actualization leads us to the third problem: the form of responsibility. If sustained reflexivity is required, everyone becomes the immediate addressee of accountability for the practices in which he or she is involved. This is accompanied by the constant demand, as Klaus Günther writes, to actively shape one's environment. Because if self-determination is politically postulated as co-determining social reality, it also means that the consumer, in order to assert himself, is always responsible for everything. Instead of giving the subject the means to empower himself, the dictum of self-responsibility thus turns into powerlessness. The subjectivation of responsibility not only leads to a state in which the "experienced contradictions, conflicts and ambivalences [...] are internalized" and endanger a coherent self-concept, but these tensions and the "failure to take responsibility can be attributed to the individual himself: everyone is responsible for his or her own failure" (Günther 2002, p. 117 ff.). In the course of this individualization of the "responsibility discourse", the failure of an all-encompassing self-responsibility towards the world, and how it turned from enabling to obstructing self-assertion, an "abolishment of responsibility" (ibid., p. 136) suddenly appears as liberation.

[5] This normative pressure can also be observed in the use of social media platforms such as Instagram, Youtube or Facebook, see Cunningham (2013).

6 The Failure of the Self

Beside the problems of being overtly informed, the inherent failings of the self-realization and co-determinacy expectations, other conceptual difficulties arise that are caused by the assumption of an independent actor shaped only by rationality. While committing to the idea of individuality, the focus on the individual as the smallest social unit initially seems to have *ad hoc* plausibility. By uncovering the individual's underlying need and preference structure it appears possible to identify and explain one's decisions. However, to exemplify the difficulties surrounding the social-ontological status of such a rational self-constitution especially in regard to maturity, the adjacent discussion based on *personal autonomy* can be utilized. It also grounds its conceptualization on an individual with a need and preference structure, in order to bring out and protect 'authentic' desires and needs.[6] It is based on a rather weaker principle of rationality, in which reason acts like a 'traffic cop' directing our actions and decisions in a way that seems important for us.[7] Rationality is in this sense a tool to express the actual will and to establish actionable options: the own preferences give the decisive impulse to follow a course of action.[8]

The burden of assuming such an 'authentic will' or any other 'I-container' is that it faces at least three challenges. Firstly, constructions of this kind are always bound to the identification of properties—such as preferences, characteristics and needs or what Charles Taylor (1971, p. 118 ff.) simply calls 'brute data'—which

[6] The inherent connection between *rational choice* and *personal autonomy* is emphasized among others by: Dan-Cohen (1992). See also the overview work on personal autonomy by Christman (1989).

[7] See Feinberg (1989, p. 40): "[R]eason is like a traffic cop directing cars to stop and go in an orderly fashion so that they might get to their destinations all more efficiently, without traffic jams and collisions.".

[8] See Schatzki (2002, p. 252 f.): "Many thinkers believe that a person is 'determined' to perform, or 'steered' toward, an action by her or his desires, beliefs, hopes, fears, preferences, expectations, and the like. Before discussing the specific sense in which this is true, it is necessary to set aside an important but misleading conception of the work of mentality. It cannot generally be the case that mental conditions, as opposed to the qualifications of paths, steer people toward one or another particular path. At least in most cases, these conditions are already implicated in the qualifications of paths. [...] An individual does not, so to speak, stand self-contained over against a landscape of qualified paths. Rather, she or he is present, or implicated, in the contours and textures of the landscape. Consequently, in most cases it cannot be that desires and ends, as opposed to the qualifications of paths, were responsible for the person's acting as she or he did. The action of the one is the action of the other."

are in turn challenged by questions of processualism (Casper 2019, p. 94). Not only does the determination of reidentification features lead to arbitrary assumptions about the extent to which these must be present at two different points in time in order to be able to say that it is the same person.[9] Every self-change is thus meet with suspicion of leading to a loss of self (Jaeggi 2005, p. 143 f.). More seriously, however, is the assumption of an 'authentic' core (Dworkin 1988, p. 129), as it leads us directly into two other challenges. The self, which determines itself autonomously, is assumed to have an essentialistic structure, which, in addition to problems of regression, i.e. the inability to determine a final reference point, also contains the idea of a kind of homunculus. The assumption of an all-decisive 'vessel of myself' leads us to the most significant test: the social constitution of self. Within individualistic theories such as rational choice approaches, the emergence of decisions from personal preferences, beliefs, plans, and other motives is already explained in such way, that predetermine the awaited action before its situational outcome has come to pass. Actions are thus determined *ante eventum* (Schatzki 2002, p. 262). With regard to the question of self-determination, however, this modeling leads to the fact that actions *ex post* can only be evaluated in the dichotomous categories of autonomy and heteronomy. To put it bluntly: any outcome that does not correspond to the expectations, any change must either be thought of as evidence of unfree or irrational processes or integrated as an unintended side effect within the social competition for the fulfillment of individually different needs. The efforts of behavioral economics to meet this uncertainty are no different (cf. Lamla 2018, p. 150). Apart from natural hurdles such as a physical world, the social context is therefore often reduced to an obstacle that stands in the way of satisfaction. Theories of pure individuality thus perpetuate the idea of a 'rationalizing super-ego' that is removed from its social context and let social relations generally appear arbitrary and exchangeable (Christman 2009, p. 128 ff.). Even if there are attempts within rational choice discussions to include the social, sociality presents itself as a choice and remains an arbitrarily exchangeable characteristic that one can possess or set aside.[10] The call to align the 'responsible consumer' with models like that of a *homo oeconomicus*

---

[9] In this sense, Maya Schechtman (1996, p. 78 f.) criticizes Derek Parfit's and Perry Lewis' assumptions of a necessary continuity of certain properties.

[10] For example, Mateusz Stachura (2017) has tried in this sense to build a bridge to Frankfurt recognition theory. However, he misunderstands recognition as merely an appreciation that has no effect on self-constitution as such and thus misses the principle of recognition theory.

can therefore lead to experiences of alienation, i.e., of a 'fractured self': As long as the socially constitutive conditions of the self are declared a residual category, self-determination becomes increasingly difficult, if not impossible (ibid., p. 148).

The implied assumptions and conclusions, which were developed through the critique of the previous consumer model, make it inevitable that those who are to be described are always misrepresented. The failure of the self as a rational actor is based on the idea that she has clear preferences, her existing values guide her through unknown or uncertain situations, and finally she chooses to the best of her knowledge the most useful action in a decision-making situation. However, considering the anticipation for predictable consumption, one must ask oneself to what extent this is not about a fetishization of decision-making power. If the 'sovereign consumer' is already overburdened with responsibility towards himself and society, he is now confronted with the task of living up to the 'one-dimensional' self-understanding of an always reflexively conscious, self-centered and above all judging actor (Fridrich et al. 2017).

To conclude the critique with Hegel at this point: Especially in the misrecognition of the social-ontological status of the self and the associated external conditions of constitution, it remains unclear how such an 'absolute interiority', as set by Kantian and also rationalist theories, should be realized. For 'due to its abstraction', i.e. only for-itself and thus not something in-the-world, it is "unable to develop anything out of itself or to generate any determinations in the way either of knowledge or of moral laws", because it "refuses categorically to acknowledge as valid or let take effect in it anything that has the character of something external" (Hegel 2010, §60).[11] The discrepancy between the consumer model and the

[11] See also Hegel (2010, pp. 34 f.):

"But the severance of actuality from the idea is popular particularly with that kind of understanding which takes the dreams of its abstractions for something true, and which insists pretentiously on the 'ought' which it likes to prescribe especially in the sphere of politics – as if the world had been waiting for this to learn how it ought to be, but is not. Were it as it ought to be, what would the precociousness of such 'ought' come to? When its 'ought' is directed against trivial, superficial and transitory objects, arrangements, situations, and so forth (that is to say, what may perhaps be of relative importance to certain circles for a period of time), then this understanding may indeed be right to find many things that are not in accord with universal and correct standards. Who would not have enough good sense to see much around him that is indeed not as it should be? But this cleverness is in the wrong when it fancies itself to have the interest of the philosophical science at heart with such objects and their 'ought'. Philosophical science deals solely with the idea which is not so impotent as to demand that it merely ought to be actual without being so and, hence, it deals with an actuality of which those objects, arrangements, situations, etc., are only the superficial exterior."

consumer as such including all the problems of perfectibility and the disregard of the social-ontological status of the self is thus a continuation of the subject-object split.[12] Not only do such views forfeit self-efficacy, they also promote ideology: The previous ideal is removed from practical actualization and remains unattainably transcendental beyond a horizon of expectancy. Instead of accounting for the plasticity of the material entanglement of human existence and understanding the self as a processual, changing, and adapting relation, the social situatedness as an essential moment of self- and world-relation is overlooked and the mature consumer is transfigured into an atomistic information and preference processing machine. It is therefore not surprising that the ideal of the mature consumer has come under criticism. It would be easy at this point to abandon this ideal. However, the more theoretical challenge lies in a shift of assumptions: Can maturity not also be understood without a remnant of a transcendental claim, which can never be achieved and therefore condemns us to constant failure? In the following, a social-theoretical revision of the previous consumer ideal 'mature consumer' is proposed, which avoids the outlined challenges and reveals the inherent potentials of the concept, referring to what is understood as *practice theory*.[13]

---

[12] To meet this demand for self-realization, one must, as Ulrich Bröckling (2007, p. 146 f.) formulates, practice a "mode of governing one's own person". As an entrepreneurial self, the individual disciplines himself to be a "reliable contract partner of himself" and thus comes into conflict. Anyone who wants to enter contracts as an equal must disregard what distinguishes one from another. Maturity therefore demands two irreconcilable assumptions, a 'self-duplication', at the end of which the surrender of one's own individuality stands:

"The individual demonstrates his maturity not least by appearing as a reliable contract partner of himself, who coordinates his disparate interests and needs, sets clear goals and makes binding self-commitments, instead of making good resolutions today under the pressure of reason and driven by passions, only to discard them tomorrow. The exploration of one's own desires and abilities, the commitment to self-set goals, the regular examination of whether they have been achieved, and finally the securing of contract compliance through self-imposed sanctions constitute a mode of governing one's own person, in which self-discipline and self-mobilization merge and the individual has to understand himself equally as a contracting party (more precisely: as a totality of contracting parties) and as an object of the contract.—Self-commitment as a continuation of living stoically through contractual means". This 'self-duplication' has been a recurring problem since Rousseau and Kant, see Menke (2015).

[13] In this sense, an immanent critique flanks practice-theoretical analyses: The starting point of the investigation is the explication of a practice and its constitutive norms, as well as the overcoming of norms of a practice (with Hegel: sublation), which are responsible for the formation of crises. It is not about an "adaptation of the practice to the norms, but rather a revision of both, norms and practice" (Stahl 2013, p. 46).

7 From a Theoretical to a Practical Self-Relation

The critique of the 'mature consumer' shows above all one thing: The problems of the guiding principle do not arise only in the implementation of the 'ought', they already begin in the fact that the self-understandings articulated in them miss the consumers themselves. In other words: The 'mature consumer' is in a crisis.

In regard to the critique and its exposition of necessary aspects like processuality, materiality, and sociality, practice-theoretical considerations seem to offer an approach to confront the crisis. But what is to be understand as 'practice theory'? Practice theory is about the explication of the constitutive elements of a single observable practice or a context of practices (praxis) within the social world. Practices are enactments in which the actors have an implicit practical knowledge. For them, it is about retrieving a "correct, habitualized script" that is crucial for the success of a practice (de Boer 2019, p. 25; Reckwitz 2003, p. 284). Practices tend towards a certain 'routine', which gives the social world a relative 'structuredness, comprehensibility and 'orderliness''. At the same time, they are forced into a certain openness by the materiality and unpredictability, by contingency, through which they change, adapt. While practices are thus subject to constant transformation, this happens not arbitrarily. They are bound to the context of meaning (with Heidegger: 'wholeness') of the participants and the plasticity of the practice itself. They often form loose complexes of practice, as

> "'social fields', in which practices are related 'in terms of the matter' and are coordinated with each other—for example in an institution, an organization or in so-called 'function systems'—*and* as 'forms of life', in which practices in a cultural class, a milieu or a cultural movement are so interconnected that they structure the entire life and everyday activities of the involved subjects" (Reckwitz 2003, p. 295; Jaeggi 2014).

Through the practices themselves, self-constitution processes occur, which provide information about desires, motivations, roles, and materialistic structural conditions. Practices are always situated in time and space and form 'the smallest social units of meaning in human action', the conditions of their success are inscribed in the inherent norms, rules, and laws of the respective practice itself.[14]

[14] Cf. De Boer (2019, p. 25): "From the perspective of third-order observers, practices are the smallest social units of meaning in human action. These are always situated in time and space. A practice is carried out in certain communicative situations and under specific socio-spatial conditions."

At this point the social-theoretical difference to an individualistic approach of the responsible consumer becomes apparent: We make

> "our decisions and 'identify' ourselves with desires, goals, etc. not as independent inner actors like a person in the person, but we *are* the complex totality to which the process belongs, in which our decisions, identifications, etc. are made" (Pothast 2002, p. 644 f.; Tugendhat 1979, p. 34; Schechtman 1996, p. 143).

This process belongs to the practice itself. Actions are thus not *ante eventum* already determined, but it remains open which and how actions are to be carried out:

> "For human activity is fundamentally indeterminate. [...] Until a person acts, it remains open just what he or she will have done. No matter how strongly his or her ends, desires, hopes, preferences, and the like 'point toward', or even 'single out', a given path of action, nothing guarantees that it or any other particular action is performed" (Schatzki 2002, p. 262).

This is due, among other things, to the social structure of practices, within which the manner of self-assertion is subject to a certain contingency. At the same time, however, this constitution is made possible through the social moment: world relations—and this includes especially those of care—are essential social-constitutive factors of self, namely through how one relates to oneself and one's world.[15]

The advantage of this theoretical foundation for our problem is obvious: Neither do we have to make arbitrary assumptions of a self detached from its reality, nor is the individual overwhelmed with unattainable expectations. Instead, maturity is made the subject of investigation as an observable practice. So, what is 'mature consumption' and how does consumption relate to maturity? Before we investigate these questions further, we must first understand what consumption can look like in a practice-theoretical conception.

[15] Cf. Barclay (2000, p. 53 f.): "A procedural notion of autonomy—which envisions a person critically reflecting on her desires and aspirations—could be thought to presuppose that the self can somehow simply transcend the influence of all of these factors and make oneself anew, to become a fully 'self-made (wo)man'. But this denies the obvious reality that none of us is self-made in this fashion for we are all, inescapably, 'a product of our environment.' This is the claim that the self is socially determined".

8 Practices of Consumption

Consumption is not just about critically examining individual decisions to consume something. Consumption as such is part of the practical reality of our existence, whether it is the food we eat, the air we breathe, the space we occupy—our practices are already characterized by a dimension of consumption because they involve a material interaction: in use, i.e., in the utilization of things or objects, consumption is inscribed in the form of wear and tear.[16] Even in the appropriation and co-creation of culture, it plays a role because it expresses the materiality and processuality of being-in-the-world. As much as consumption permeates being, so little is this *facticity of consumption* an end in itself—one does not consume for the sake of consumption. Instead, it is a by-product or side effect, a concomitant of practices that are themselves directed towards an inherent purpose (de Boer 2019, p. 35); for example, to ensure survival on a biological level, to produce something for further use, or simply to allow a new forms of self-expression through a change in wardrobe.

At this point, the political relevance of the concept of consumption comes into play. As a concomitant of practices the fact of consumption *in* practices can bring about a normative stance *towards* the practices themselves. For one, there are usually different variants for the same practice, such as different ways to shop, and these variants can entail different levels of material intensity. For two, consumption itself can be valued differently in different practices. To give an example: in certain activities a high expenditure may be desired, such as when it comes to the elimination of toxins, whereas an increase in pollutants seems not warranted.

By being able to normatively react to consumption it has become a political matter and has subsequently received attention: We can take a stance towards our practices. In this sense, consumer policy cannot be limited to consumption as such. Rather, it becomes a practice in which societal structures and inherent roles are negotiated in their economic, social, and cultural contingency (Reckwitz 2003, p. 290).[17] In other words, it must include the question of what forms

---

[16] With Marx, the transformation process could be expressed as follows: "The act of production itself is therefore in all its moments also an act of consumption. […] Production as immediately identical with consumption, consumption as immediately coinciding with production." (MEW, 13, p. 622).

[17] As Reckwitz (2008, p. 113) clearly outlines the relationship structure: "This is exactly what a 'social practice' is: a practice of negotiation, a practice of dealing with a tool, a practice of dealing with one's own body, etc."

of consumption exist, what they aim at, and how the associated goals and desires can be realized or not.[18] This "deregulation" makes it "difficult to reduce consumer research to a special area of social or economic practices or decision situations" (Lamla 2018, p. 148).

Even only focusing on what we could call consumer policy, i.e., on the aspect of a practice's consumption, the question is raised of how realization of one practice affects other practices. This applies to the practices of others, for instance, when it comes to different options of transportation, urban planning, or even event organization. Aspects such as health, sustainability, social compatibility, and future viability demand revisions of practices. But this also pertains to one's own practices: Within practices, spheres of life overlap, and with them different roles, expectations, and objectives. In addition to the internal conflict potential over personal priorities, a possible conflict arises as to which aspects of the self should be realized. For the practice of eating, the mere act of grocery shopping can testify to such an overlap. Here, for example, the role of the parent, who wants to provide sufficient food for the family, meets the role of the environmentalist, who focuses on locality and sustainability. If another role is added, such as that of the hobby cook who wants to try out exotic and expensive ingredients, the conflict potential increases with the rise in opposing objectives. With the buzzword 'consumption' self-realization processes—on an individual as well as societial level—are being questioned when it comes to their possibilities as well as incured exclusions. This is the moment when consumer policy had turned towards maturity. Considering the revision of consumption via practice theory, the effects of this grouping must be re-examined.

[18] The assumption that a stimulating consumer policy is necessary for the economic structure should not be misunderstood as being about mere consumption, but must understand in its demand that consumption as such remains empty without the practices and inherent norms associated with it. A consumer policy that demands mere consumption without including the purposeful orientation of practices and their negotiation not only refuses to discuss what should be consumed, but ultimately promotes meaningless structures, social pathologies, and experiences of alienation: "The less the culture industry has to promise and the less it can offer a meaningful explanation of life, the emptier the ideology it disseminates necessarily becomes.." (Adorno and Horkheimer 2002, p. 118).

9 The Practice of Maturity

The previous image of a mature consumer corresponds to the idea of a 'sovereign consumer', "a fundamentally rational and independently deciding individual who steers the economic processes according to his preferences" (Müller 2019, p. 83). Although the question of self-realization is also at stake here, it has been shown that such a preference approach leads to constructional problems of a realistic understanding of self and self-constitution as such falls prey to the snares of an individualized 'rationalizing super-ego'. Instead of making maturity dependent on an extensive amount of information, an essentialist core of rationality or a transcendental state of consciousness—and thus risking the chance of practical 'self-thinking'—a practice-theoretical approach circumvents these difficulties and asks how maturity is realized as a practice. This inevitably provokes a whole complex of questions. How is such a practice to be understood? What is its relationship to other practices? How does practice theory understand 'self', especially in view of Kant's imperative 'to think for oneself'? What about the formation of opinions and responsibility? And where are the limits of such an approach?

By understanding maturity as a social practice, the focus lies less on moral legislation than on existential expressivity. Personal self-realization does not take place qua moral freedom in which only general structures can be articulated (Honneth 2011, p. 83 ff.), but in the practical answer to the question: In what way do I understand myself in-the-world and how do I want to continue understanding myself, who do I want to be? Here, the freedom to choose between alternatives plays a rather subordinate role. Rather, the question of maturity is set prior to this: it is about being able to question oneself and one's actions, or to put it in the words of Ernst Tugendhat (1979, p. 193 f.): to take a fundamental stance towards oneself. One could also say that maturity thus becomes the reflective practice of dealing with one's practices (Cannaday 2018, p. 246).

For questions of self-constitution, a shift in perspective begins here. This take on being and world cannot aim at finding an 'authentic core'. Rather, every concept of 'self', including its motives, is inevitably dynamized; the self is held as the reference in which 'I' is expressed. This act is characterized by an organizational structure in which the concern for the relationship to oneself and the world is conveyed. The 'organization' of this relationship is always evaluative and takes place in pre-linguistic as well as narrative ways. It offers 'me' a self-image in regards to what is good, better, best for 'me'. On the other hand, this dynamic form is genuinely social. It not only eludes atomistic notions of authenticity, but also any dichotomous categorization of autonomy and heteronomy.[19] Instead of a private sphere of pure self-reference (as with Fichte), the described dynamization of self from a practice-theoretical perspective always originates in a reciprocal social relation. A (pure) self-relation without an external perspective suffers not only in the absence of a corrective, but in a mere *for-itself* every standard of self-relation becomes unfathomable. In other words: Only qua relation to others can 'relationability' assert itself as self-relation. Whether it is about the 'other self-consciousness' as with Hegel, Heidegger's 'Man', Mead's 'generalized other' or also the 'super-ego' in Freud's conception—only via other and others relating 'I' and 'world' gain plasticity.[20] The identification and criticism potentials inherent within this sphere not only give the self-relation a powerful opportunity to ques-

[19] If we think of 'mature consumers' from the concept of autonomy, then the social context and its dynamics are often left out or considered in a very limited form. In the case of *moral autonomy* the consumer becomes a kind of ethicist of conviction. Along ultimate principles, he faces the problem of atomistic conformity: Regardless of his circumstances, he seeks what everyone should do and forfeits any chance of dynamic individuality. *Personal autonomy*, on the other hand, often declares the consumer to be an individual hedonist: In his pursuit of authenticity alignment—be it with an inner substance like the soul or any other essence—it overlooks that social circumstances remain crucial for successful self-realization, no matter what his or her 'inner' attitude is. If others are considered within these variants, then often as antagonists in a competition in which everyone only strives for their own preference fulfilment. Not to instrumentalize other or somehow subjugate them, only is circumvented through the supposed insight, of not wanting to be subjugated either. Even in the discussions about *social* and *relational autonomy*, the conditions of self-constitution and independence are often underestimated. Either my relationships to others and to our consumption practices are understood as a kind of property that appears arbitrarily exchangeable. Or, consumer relationships completely elude availability and stand as a kind of fixed star in the rigid structure of one's own private interpretation (Cannaday 2018).

[20] The point should of course not be misunderstood to mean that every relating from others to oneself — be it internalization of expectations, criticism or alien experiences—should be taken as a fixed "matter of fact". It is and remains an opportunity to engage and this is how reality shows itself. With Hegel (2015, p. 389):

"It has its actualization in this opposition's movement, for this opposition is instead itself the *indiscrete continuity* and *equality* of the "I = I." Each of the I's, *for itself* just through the contradiction of its pure universality which at the same time strives against its *equality* with the other and separates itself from it, sublates itself in its own self. Through this relinquishing, this knowing, which is estranged in its own existence, returns back into the unity of the *self*. It is the *actual* I, the universal *self*-knowing in its *absolute opposite*, in the existing knowing that has *taken the inward turn*, which, according to the purity of its separated inwardly-turned-being, is itself the completed universal."

tion one's current practices: 'To what extent is the way others and things relate to me, concerning me?'. Through these, one's own form of actualization as well as possible contingencies of these practices become accessible (Adorno 1971, pp. 93, 97, 99). Only within the context of our own practices do roles, expectations and rules concern us. When we are confronted with identification and criticism potentials, we can constitute and actualize ourselves in the process.

To avoid misunderstandings: This form of self-constitution is initially pre-reflective in its everyday occurrence. That is, mediated by implicit "schemas of understanding and interpretation", by "*script*-like procedures of competent behavior" and an immanent orientation towards meaning, it remains mostly unthematic (Reckwitz 2004, p. 44; Tugendhat 1979, p. 213). Therefore, one could also say: Practices and the associated self-constitutions happen to us.[21] However, practices can become problematic, and this is where maturity comes into play. As a practice of dealing with one's practices, reflexivity is inevitably part of its implementation, through which the preconscious self- and external relations are elucidated.[22] The question remains as to what is meant by problematic. The fact that the implementation of a practice becomes thematic for the participant does not automatically mean that it is a problem in the sense relevant to maturity. The difference becomes clear when, for example, we suddenly have a flat tire while riding a bicycle. Although the practice becomes thematic as a problem—we can't keep on riding—none would invoke a "mature tire changer" to solve the problem: changing a tire does not necessarily require maturity, because we usually do not want to change the practice of cycling. It is different, for example, when the practice of waste disposal into surrounding waters affects practices of swimming at a lake or heating with oil is threated by the limitation of that resource. In these instances, a behavior towards the practice as a whole can be adopted. That is, with the problematization, the question of the changeability of the practice itself inevitably comes to the fore. This is what an active appropriation of a practice means: It leads to a change in the practice, because the inherent constitutive relations change through the behavior towards it. How the mature person realizes himself within this transformation is already predetermined by the (new) constituting structure as well as the content of what is to be formed.

[21] If reflexivity is possible, the self can be based on the abilities for such.

[22] Again, the mistake must not be made that consciousness assumes a separate essence. Consciousness is seen here only as mode of awareness opposed to pure behaviour. In this sense, Robert Brandom (1994, p. 628 ff.) points out that *discursive* practices are also social practices.

Thus, by appropriating the relations, an active self-relation becomes possible, as now *reasons* can be introduced to oppose or confirm the inherent purpose of a practice. This reflexive stance corresponds to a situation of action, but again the individual does not withdraw himself from his social context, his actualization, through reflection to a point of nowhere; instead, criticism and identification are to be understood as access, as an approach to oneself and one's world. Conversely, if one of the two leads to the assumption of a supposedly external standpoint alienated from his world—such as a transcendental, purely rational or cynical one—self-realization fails because what it is supposed to refer to, the person, is missed in a social-ontological sense. This is neither a capitulation to a 'true', 'essentialist' self nor an arbitrariness in the sense of *anything goes* (Reckwitz 2016). Rather, in regard to maturity, the previous contingent but necessary processes of self-constitution become accessible on the basis of one's own social relatedness, and this makes their further course more open. As de Boer (2019, p. 26) notes: "Such experiences of contingency can be processed either performatively through the adaptation of practices or through reflexive references and the generation of new practical logics." By criticising and identifying, the 'mature consumer' thus maintains an openness for the adaptation, change or rediscovery of practices. This openness is also necessary in order to be able to carry out a self-actualization. If the self is processual, then there is a necessity that a self-image, which one makes of oneself and consults for decisions, must constantly renew itself precisely because of the underlying processuality.

At the same time, this self-actualization cannot take the form of a 'permanent reflexivity'. As much as otherness plays an important role for a continued critical actualization (Jaeggi 2002, p. 60 ff.), maturity still takes into account the necessity for self-*realization*. For all the emphasis laid on the processual self this means: being able to successfully realize 'myself' as mature also depends on how the reflexively elucidated practices can 'enmesh' the person again in a postreflexive way. Maturity thus aims at overcoming specific problems, not at lingering in critical reflexivity.

Remaining in a mode of critical reflexivity for a longer period may initially be helpful in implementing routines. However, if the aimed for practice cannot transition into a habitual behavior without putting reflexivity aside—without letting go, so to speak—, appropriation must ultimately fail because self-realization remains indefinitely delayed. This 'deficit' has already been critically pointed out by Heidegger (2006, § 18). Elsewhere, it is cautioned that an excessive obsession with overthinking tends to indicate neurotic behavior (Oshana 2006, p. 79). Beyond individual misunderstandings, societal neglect can also promote such forms of constant reflection and create a kind of 'social pathology'. This is the case, for example, when societal demands cannot be structurally solved by the subjects themselves, but they are nevertheless expected to do so, thus unfairly overburdening the affected individuals in their misrecognition (Stahl 2011, p. 741). Perhaps most significant for our considerations: Remaining in reflective mode would lead to understanding oneself again from a target state, i.e., "a complete, transparent practical appropriation of all practical relevancies" appears possible—and thus reintroducing the 'rationalizing super-ego' through the back door. In contrast, it can only be "about resolving context-specific hindrances that cause appropriation to be become pathological", i.e., "about a specific reaction to frustrations with legitimate expectations" (Stahl 2011, p. 743). A successful practice of maturity always overcomes the reflective engagement with one's own practices. It can do this when the problems that have led to a confrontation with oneself and the world have been resolved to the extent that they no longer disturb or block everyday routines.

To return to the 'limitless' field of consumer research: If research and politics want to take their guiding principle seriously, it requires an understanding of the mature consumer beyond the conceptual restrictions and individualized over-responsibility that economic models impose. Maturity is about practical self-realization through self-determination and co-determination within a social context. The mature consumer needs the opportunity to co-determine his practices if he wants to fulfill his role. At the same time, this does not mean that he must or even can co-determine every practice. Especially practices that combine themselves to a broader life-form produce self-understandings that, like the way of life itself, tend to rigidness and mundanity. This allows us to recognize how life-forms build the basis of our understanding, i.e., that through which we evaluate sense and purpose (Jaeggi 2014, p. 119 ff.). We are then dealing with self-understandings that have become 'second nature' (Menke 2010, p. 690 ff.). The concern to change these self-understandings, whether through problematization or the desire for something new, requires the availability of alternatives and the time to transform these changes into a habit—because in this case that would mean success. However, transforming one's motivational structures to establish new practices lastly depends on whether the alternatives resonate (Rosa 2016, p. 281 ff.) or at least exert a sufficient identificatory stimulus. Because even if practices with alternative value and recognition possibilities are found, this does not make them automatically compatible with others or free from problems, nor allows them to immediately become 'second nature'.

10 Maturity and Responsibility

The difficulty of deliberately adopting, transforming, or abandoning practices is one of the reasons why the question of responsibility remains difficult. Responsibility in a post-Kantian (not post-Hegelian) understanding would mean, for example, individually meeting the maxims found, or making decisions, like within rational-choice theory, according to one's own "authentic" preference order. With both, one is committed to an overtly rigid self-understanding. From a practice-theoretical perspective, such a concept of responsibility is not very convincing because it overlooks sociality and the dynamisms of self-constitution. For example, what would taking responsibility for previous, but in the meantime outdated practices look like if the paradigm of transformability applies?[23] To what extent are the structural and societal conditions, on which the self-constitution processes build, taken into account? How do practices change and who can be held responsible thereafter?

Even if a complete, practice-theoretical elaboration on the concept of responsibility must remain a desideratum here, initial answers for such an understanding can be given. Because the alternative, to completely drop responsibility, would just be like turning one's back on maturity. It would forfeit the enabling functions that responsibility has in a practice-theoretical conception of maturity with regard to accountability, independence, and solidarity.

Charles Taylor offers an interesting proposal for practice-theoretical considerations to understand responsibility in terms of a 'radical evaluation' (Taylor 1985, p. 42). In an interpretation of one's own life, the person can critically examine with what he or she identifies with. If these are still maintained as constitutive factors for self-realization or if one is ready to stand up for them, this in turn would mean the person is taking responsibility for them. Such an understanding incorporates accountability from post-Kantian conceptions. Unlike these, however, it is not about a comparison of maxims. Instead, accountability can only be a confrontation with the norms, rules, and attributions inherent in a practice. Responsibility therefore lies in taking a stance towards oneself and the world when one's own relationship to either one is problematized.

[23] A circumstance of "stagnant" transformability can be identified particularly in cases of injustice that have not been overcome, in which both victims and perpetrators suffer. In this sense, the perpetrator is also owed the punishment, i.e., the judgment necessary for transformation (an otherness-enabling relation, for Hegel this would be spirit), cf. Gadamer (1973, p. 125 ff.).

The question of such an understanding of responsibility refers to an self-engagement in a twofold manner: retrospectively, dealing with the consequences of the problematized practice is demanded, prospectively, it calls for stance to be taken towards future outcomes considering the practice (Schatzki 2013, p. 182 f.). With a radical evaluation, respectively a fundamental stance—Tugendhat's and Taylor's concept converge at this point—, a temporally-local statement can be made about how one relates to the previous practices in which one was involved, as well as who one wants to be, or whether one wants to maintain existing practices. In this sense, taking responsibility leads to an 'update' of the self-image.

By taking on responsibility the person's relation to the future appears as a game. Because neither are all consequences ever known nor the reach of one's own possibilities of influence, or in what way one will realize oneself (i.e., who one will become).[24] At this point, another difference to the post-Kantian problem of self-responsibility becomes apparent: As a process within the social world, practices are not unilaterally shaped by individuals, but take place between individuals and artifacts. To change, adapt, or abandon practices, precisely by desiring to realize oneself differently, requires a productive confrontation with others and things.

To call for responsibility, therefore, can neither mean self-responsibility in an atomistic sense of self-assertion against others nor a blunt rule to conformacy. Rather, it happens more accordingly to the principle of a Hegelian self-sufficiency in a social setting. In it, self-assertion is always in tension with self-restraint.

For a self-constitution to achieve self-sufficiency, i.e., for appropriating the criticism and identification potentials inherent in the relationship towards others, this very relation depends on the recognition of the other as self-sufficient. (Hegel 2018, p. 108 ff., 388 f.). Its success is expressed when the own self-relation is elucidated as a *relation* and thus self-restraint and consequently self-realization becomes possible. In this way, the relation gains the necessary authority, because it is assumed that the other's self-constitional practices have efficaciously dealt with reality (Brandom 2014, p. 28 ff.). In regards to an understanding of self-assertion relevant to self-sufficiency, a social aspect is inherent in the practice of self-restraint: one can relate to oneself and one's practices because this self- and world-engagement becomes possible with and through the other. Thus, the other becomes the basis of one's own self-sufficiency and self-responsibility takes on

[24] Kant already recognized this problem and expressed skepticism towards a viable concept of responsibility (Kant AA III, p. 373 and AA VI, p. 227; cf. also Vogelmann 2016, p. 273 ff.).

the empowering form of self-restraint as a mode of self-relation.[25] Responsibility in this sense means to examine the boundaries of one's own self-assertion where it impairs the other's self-assertion efforts and thus endangers the foundation for self-realization relevant to maturity. This self-realization usually happens pre-thematically and in the sense of how basic trust is formed: Both are based on a pre-reflective, appropriated conviction to be able to co-shape self and world (cf. Erikson 1987, p. 222 ff.). If these forms of realization are denied or undermined, they can become thematic as problems.

The question of self-responsibility thus conceptually refers to the third aspect of responsibility relevant to maturity: solidarity. From a practice-theoretical perspective, taking responsibility for oneself ultimately can only mean confronting others with one's own desires and needs while dealing with others and their self-assertion claims. In this sense, a call for articulation, discussion, and a common approach is inherent within the social setting.[26] In other words, it is about the responsibility for a 'productive conflict' (Bertram 2017, p. 248 ff.). This marks a significant difference from theories of 'self-interest'—or to put it with Adam Smith: instead of 'Selflove' we should focus on 'Self-care' which includes the 'well-being and woe of our entire world'.[27] Instead of perceiving others as mere

[25] The self-sufficiency that one promises oneself through the other presupposes that this other is *in-itself* and not *for-me:* His uniqueness is respected. Conversely, if he is only a mere means to me, I fail to recognize his self-sufficiency as such and obstruct my reference to him as an authority.

[26] By common approach, I do not mean a harmonious consensus. Rather, it is also about productively shaping differences, as these differences and exclusions can be considered as constitutive and dynamizing moments from a practice-theoretical perspective.

[27] Adam Smith's considerations are often mistakenly reduced to a pure perspective of self-interest, as in Hirschman (1987). Instead of being concerned about 'self-interest', Smith is concerned with highlighting the limited and harmful aspects of such a reduction. He sees the counter or extension model in the concept of 'selflove':

"Selflove not only includes the concern for one's own self, but also includes concern for the well-being and woe of our entire world [...] Not selfinterest, but selflove is the foundation of the division of labor society. Its irresistible power guarantees us that our fellow human beings will respond to our exchange offers. If the success of our exchange transactions depended solely on their favor or goodwill, we would never embark on the venture of cooperative society based on a division of labor. Only the reliable power of selflove makes the life-threatening contingency of economic exchange a manageable risk." (Ronge 2015, p. 257 f.). In this sense, there is an overlap between Smith and his contemporary Jean-Jacques Rousseau, when the latter distinguishes between *amour de soi,* self-love, and *armour-propre,* self-esteem. While *amour de soi* in Rousseau aims at finding rudi-

opponents, fellow mature individuals are at the same time understood as constitutive for one's own independence precisely in their difference. Having responsibility for oneself always includes caring for others. In solidarity, self-responsibility always comes to light as a mutual realization of independence.

To conclude the question of a practice-theoretical connection between responsibility and mature consumers for now: Responsibility invokes a self-actualization within a productive confrontation with others. This makes self-sufficiency possible which is founded on a structural solidarity and whose upkeep is maintained by challenging problematic practices. We now come to the programmatic outlook, because the revision of the 'mature consumer' also addresses current assumptions both in politics and research.

11 The Programmatic Question

Unfulfillable expectations regarding the consumer model necessitated a dismissal of previous considerations of maturity. Using a practice-theoretical approach, the consumer is instead understood in his practical, constitutive relationships and maturity is considered as self-realization inherent in life: Maturity is the social practice of engaging one's practices. Practical self-determination is always confronted with questions of co-determination, because the social context not only affects living as such, but has always been inscribed into the self-relation. To then relate to these inscriptions with others would mean to perform a practice of maturity. By explicating the immanent determinations that constitute 'mature consumption', i.e., the implementation of self-determination and co-determination, a way out of the prelevant crisis of the 'mature consumer' has been shown.[28]

With the revised consumer model, research and politics nevertheless face particular challenges, especially in contemporary societies, whose legitimacy is based on the formation of opinion and participation of their citizens. In them, plural views emerge about how life should be led, and the self-relationships that

mentary happiness, without being subject to a competition or other relata, *armour-propre* on the other hand, takes up a comparative view towards other society members, in which self-interest is at the centre of considerations. With Frederik Neuhouser (2012), this then becomes problematic, i.e., a 'social pathology', when it leads to oppression, discrimination or the loss of socially constitutive recognition structures.

[28] For the discussion of self-determination and co-determination as constitutive claims of maturity, see Cannaday (2018).

are realized within different practices are becoming more complex. But instead of seeing the societal tensions of competing and mutual exclusions as a loss of consensus or interpreting the apparent incoherence of the self-image as a loss of autonomy, a practice-theoretical concept of maturity is about considering these relationships in their dynamics as constitutive on both levels. Constitutive under the condition that the individuals are able to actively deal with these contradictions, ambivalences, and changes. This is what is meant by a successful self-realization: It is less about finding ultimate maxims, authentic coherence, or a final design of what society should be than about a productive conflict within the process of confrontation itself.

The strength of the practice-theoretical concept of maturity lies in the fact that at the center of the considerations we don't have to assume deficient subjects or 'naive consumers'. This charge would simply portray them as misperceiving reality due to false consciousness and constitute a victimhood as they are inevitable exposed to their environment or the manipulation attempts of producers (Müller 2019, p. 112 ff.). Instead, the inquiry is focused on a practice that is directed at the appropriation of practices—through an openness to criticism and the willingness to get involved with something and for something in the world—and that can thus be realized as an everyday practice in pluralistically oriented societies. A programmatical demand for maturity would then mean to change, avoid, or eliminate those processes, learning blockages, or transformation stagnations that lead to immaturity—i.e., to situations in which people can no longer actively relate to themselves and their environment.[29]

We have arrived at the difficulty of the proposition: Politically, maturity is about the ongoing elimination of a defective state of affairs. This is even more necessary when, due to excessive complexity, legal or social rigidity, as well as lack of education, mature individuals are prevented from engaging in the struggle for their self-assertion. Often, these aspects exceed the sphere of legal recognition and show the importance of articulating outrage and making processes of exclusion visible. If societies and institutions are not able to respond to these grievances, 'social pathologies', such as reification, solidification of relational spaces and even loss of self loom (Stahl 2011, p. 734 ff.). In order to identify these debilitating conditions, research, protection associations, as well as politics

[29] See Jaeggi (2014, p. 332): "If ways of life can now learn, then as supra-individual formations they can possess a rationality that goes beyond the individual; conversely, collective (structural) learning blockages stand in the way of the learning ability of individual individuals, without this always being attributable to their individual inability to learn.".

can examine the ongoing negotiation processes between the mature individuals and institutions by focusing on three criteria: transparency, the sphere of influence consumers have (Bala and Müller 2015), and the 'teleo-affective' processuality of practices (Schatzki 1996, p. 89; Honneth 2015).

12 Transparency

The call for transparency supports the mature individuals to elucidate the contexts of their existence. It aims at the disclosure of the constitutive conditions of practices. Within the nexus of practices, insight into possible consequences can become accessible, e.g., the connection between a product and its producer's aspirations for privatization can be made. It concerns uncovering manipulation and deception attempts, as well as coercive relationships. Circling back to the question of solidarity, production conditions or legislative processes in the field of politics that undermine the active self-reference of workers can thus be problematized. The elucidation of topics, such as those of production and working conditions or the influence of lobby interests, can therefore play a crucial role in a successful co-determination of world and therefore self-realization. They seem to play a rather weak role if they are merely understood as a fact, yet as something disparate to one's own life. The stronger position, as demanded in solidarity, follows the insight that this is also about the possibility of one's *own* self-assertion.[30] The consequences of this may indeed vary, but transparency is firstly concerned with uncovering to what degree one is involved with the matters at hand.

To avoid misunderstandings here: This isn't a demand for a constantly mature 'expert citizen' who is aware of *all* aspects of his consumption and voting decisions as well as the direct and unintended consequences of these. Rather, it is about the individual gaining access to those pieces of information that are crucial for him or her to take a stance towards the respective problematic practices and their implementation. Even if not all information is available, because necessary research is lacking or excessive complexity makes insight difficult, mature

[30] The second, strong argument, also takes honesty as a compelling factor for one's *own* independence: By deceiving, misleading, or imposing my will on the other, I forfeit the opportunity to assert myself not only based on an exchange of facts. Furthermore, my disregard for the other, turns against myself and I lose the opportunity of self-realization, cf. Brandom (2019, p. 582). In this sense, trust becomes crucial for recognition relationships in a mutual pursuit of transparency.

individuals must not be prevented from bridging these gaps. For maturity, the advantage or disadvantage of a product or proposition plays a rather subordinate role. If we take a dictum for maturity seriously, it is necessary to highlight those moments and contexts in which negotiations fail due to lack of disclosure—that concerns consumers as well as producers. The pursuit of transparency thus takes the form of an open endeavor in which society's problematic practices and their inherent structures of recognition become available.

13 Sphere of Influence

This also leads to the next aspect of the negotiation process: the sphere of influence. For a mature consumer, there must be co-determination opportunities. This can take on various forms: from practices of 'prosumption' such as urban gardening and crowd-funding, or through petition and boycott, from protest marches to forms of solidarity-based economization like the founding of a cooperative brewery. What remains important is that social relationships or institutions do not adversely curtail the practice of co-determination. Therefore, mature consumers first need the assurance that voicing their opinions will not have negative consequences (Oshana 2006, p. 87). Secondly, the question of a certain financial independence or a scope for action gains traction. If citizens are to co-determine politics through consumption in a sense that is also relevant for them, then they must also have the means and the opportunities that allow them to have influence. A family of five, who depend on the welfare state or whose income is earned in the low-wage sector, will probably find it difficult to make their household consumption animal-friendly and sustainable. And even if it is possible and the labeling of products and offers are transparent, not everything is offered everywhere. The festival-goer knows that he usually only gets drinks that are under a certain corporate umbrella. Late-night shops often only carry water from one major brand. Before the discussion drifts into the difficulty of wanting to explore a maximization of product pluralism while considering logistical limits all the while leading to overburdened decision situations: For maturity, the most important point is that in addition to the concrete negotiation about products and their production methods, the form of these negotiations themselves has to be addressable. For many alternatives that respond to this deficiency of co-determination, in addition to the politically common forms of subsidy and tax collection, the installation of new decision-making and value-creation structures seem worth pursuing. Whether direct referendums or redistributions: In the end, what is decisive is the extent to which mature consumers can repeatedly get involved in co-determining their society. In other words, maturity requires a certain effectiveness and therefore it is necessary to work out the conditions in which such negotiation processes are non-existent or have been previously rejected.

14 Processuality

This brings us to the third point, namely that of processuality: Maturity is a process of recognizing one's own practices, and this also implies that some matters of the individual are more important than others. This entails, of course, that not all individuals care about certain political consequences or at least not at all times. Leaving an issue to others can also constitute a mature decision, obstructing others while the issue at hand doesn't concern oneself, on the other hand, would speak to a form of misrecognition that would also put one's own maturity at risk. What remains important is that the renunciation can be reversed and the mature person can again participate in the co-determining processes (cf. Mill 2009, p. 175). Maturity thus presupposes a certain openness, the ongoing possibility to connect with others. The own practices are critically engaged when one or another recognizes problems as well as possibilities. Processuality must therefore not only do justice to a fluid self, but also to a dynamic practice of life. Maturity does not aim at consensus-capable, definitive societal objectives, such as a climate goal, or ultimate solutions. It is precisely these assumptions, such as that of a single voter's will, a necessary consensus or the immutability of certain institutional structures, that make a practice of negotiation crucial for maturity difficult. Institutions are thus faced with the challenge of constantly confronting the self-assertion claims of their members. They do this by relieving, enabling and being willing to initiate learning and transformation processes. In this sense, they would be, as Jaeggi (2009) put it, 'good institutions'. Maturity therefore first requires work on the part of politics: It faces the challenge of being open to the needs and suffering experiences of its members and constantly exploring practical solutions anew (Honneth 2015, p. 155). To this end, it relies, among other things, on consumer research, which faces now its central task of uncovering such 'stagnant' conditions—whether limited to individuals or extending across institutions.

By investigating societal conditions in terms of transparency, sphere of influence and processuality, conclusions can be drawn as to whether self-realization endeavors of 'mature consumers' are hindered. It has been shown that it is precisely through a dictate of complete information that over-responsibility and an atomistic understanding of personhood turns maturity into immaturity. However, it is equally important to avoid the reverse conclusion and to understand the consumer only from the perspective of 'vulnerability' or as a 'deficient being', as is often the case under the guise of libertarian or nudging paternalism (Simanowski 2019, p. 30). There is fundamentally nothing wrong with installing societal offers that can promote certain aspects for the well-being of their members or making those that are harmful difficult to access. However, the decision as to how and in what way this is implemented must fall within the scope of influence of those mostly affected by these. Only in this way can we continue to speak of maturity. Kant famously appealed for openness and the possibility of revision when conceiving maxims and laws (AA VIII, p. 39):

> "An epoch cannot conclude a pact that will commit succeeding ages, prevent them from increasing their significant insights, purging themselves of errors, and generally progressing in enlightenment. That would be a crime against human nature whose proper destiny lies precisely in such progress. Therefore, succeeding ages are fully entitled to repudiate such decisions as unauthorized and outrageous."

The discussion about a practice-theoretical conception of maturity goes beyond the construction of simple dichotomies: It is neither about the complete responsibility of the individual nor about a nanny state that determines everything. Rather, the confrontation of the mature individual reflects and shapes the state itself and thus includes the (sometimes tension-filled) self-assertion claims of its citizens. It may Serious doubts may be raised whether the task of implementing such self-determination and co-determination practices has now become easier. At the same time, however, with the revised form of maturity presented here, a different normativity comes into the practical scope of political addressing: openness and with it the possibility of failure. Instead of proclaiming the search for definitive objectives, it is necessary to allow the procedural self-movement of maturity. By recognizing constantly changing self- and world-relations, the focus rests now on obstacles to appropriation such as blockages, suppressions, and exclusions. Not a failure or a lack of knowledge as such is problematic for maturity, but notions of perfectibility in which the solutions are already predetermined.

In conclusion, one last point can be addressed: A demand for maturity requires a responsibility for openness and if a state makes this demand, it follows something like a 'negative paternalism'. In a way, it is an *inverted* form of nudging paternalism in which the abolition of such is urged. This is not about undermining practices of self-determination and co-determination, not about manipulation or deception, nor about suppression. In addition to protection and enabling measures, a negative paternalism aims to encourage people to engage questions of their self-sufficiency and thus achieve reflected self-relating. The difficulty the state encounters, however, is that it must always consider social reality, the context of those affected in its demand. This intervention is less concerned with what a person should or should not do, but it sets out to protect individuals and their abilities to make independent decisions, it protects their self-referentiality. On the other hand, the state, aiming for maturity, also treats immature citizens as potential mature ones—to use Hegel's words: Thus, it can offer them a connection to questions of self-sufficiency, as it addresses them from the perspective of the 'spirit', i.e., in a sense relevant to their self-relation. This is what is understood by maturity as a practice. To put it in a formula: It is less about whether institutions or the state have authorization or receive decision-making powers, but about how flexible and willing they are to return these to sphere of influence of the people affected by them. In this sense, a consumer model must not only guide the consumer, but be guided by who and how the consumer has become.

References

Adorno, Theodor W. 1971. *Erziehung zur Mündigkeit*. Frankfurt a. M.: Suhrkamp.

Adorno, Theodor W., and Max Horkheimer. 2002. *Dialectic of enlightenment*. Stanford: Stanford University Press.

Bala, Christian, and Klaus Müller, eds. 2015. *Abschied vom Otto Normalverbraucher*. Essen: Klartext.

Barclay, Linda. 2000. Autonomy and the social self. In *Relational autonomy*, ed. M. Catriona and N. Stoljar, 52–71. New York: Oxford University Press.

Bertram, Georg. 2017. *Hegels 'Phänomenologie des Geistes.'* Stuttgart: Reclam.

Blatter, Harry. 2007. *Coming of age in times of uncertainty*. New York: Berghahn.

Brandom, Robert. 1994. *Making it explicit*. Cambridge: Harvard University Press.

Brandom, Robert. 2014. A hegelian model of legal concept determination. In *Pragmatism, law and language*, ed. G. Hubbs and D. Lind, 19–39. New York: Routledge.

Brandom, Robert. 2019. *On the spirit of trust*. Cambridge: Harvard University Press.

Bröckling, Ulrich. 2007. *Das unternehmerische Selbst*. Frankfurt a. M.: Suhrkamp.

Bundesverband der Deutschen Industrie e. V. 2014. Verbraucherleitbild und Positionsbestimmung zum ‚Mündigen Verbraucher'. https://e.issuu.com/embed.html#2902526/58123202. Accessed 27 Sept 2023.

Bundeszentrale für politische Bildung und Landeszentralen für politische Bildung. 1997. *Demokratie braucht politische Bildung – Münchner Manifest*. Bonn: Bundeszentrale für politische Bildung.

Cannaday, Thomas. 2018. *Mündigkeit*. Frankfurt a. M.: Campus.

Christman, John, ed. 1989. *The inner citadel, essays on individual autonomy*. Brattleboro: Echo Point Books.

Christman, John. 2009. *The politics of persons*. Cambridge: Cambridge University Press.

Cunningham, Carolyn, ed. 2013. *Social networking and impression management, self-presentation in the digital age*. Plymouth: Lexington.

Dan-Cohen, Meir. 1992. Conceptions of choice and conceptions of autonomy. *Ethics* 102: 221–234.

de Boer, J.-H. 2019. Praktiken, Praxen und Praxisformen. In *Praxisformen*, ed. J.-H. de Boer, 21–43. Frankfurt a. M.: Campus.

Dworkin, Gerald. 1988. *The theory and practice of autonomy*. New York: Cambridge University Press.

Ebersold, Günther. 1980. *Mündigkeit*. Frankfurt a. M.: Lang.

Eidam, Heinz, and Timo Hoyer, eds. 2006. *Erziehung und Mündigkeit*. Münster: LIT.

Erikson, Erik. 1987. *Childhood and society*. London: Paladin Grafton Books.

Europäischer Gerichtshof. WRP 1998, 848, 850, Rn.31 (‚Gut Springenheide').

Europäischer Gerichtshof. GRUR Int 2005, 44, 45, Tz. 24 -Sat.1.

Feinberg, Joel. 1989. Autonomy. In *The inner citadel, essays on individual autonomy*, ed. J. Christman, 27–53. Brattleboro: Echo Point Books.

Fridrich, Christian, Renate Hübner, Karl Kollmann, Michael Burkhard Piorkowsky, and Nina Tröger, eds. 2017. *Abschied vom eindimensionalen Verbraucher*. Wiesbaden: Springer VS.

Gadamer, Hans Georg. 1973. Verkehrte Welt. In *Materialien zu Hegels ‚Phänomenologie des Geistes'*, ed. H.F. Fulda and D. Henrich, 117–140. Frankfurt a. M.: Suhrkamp.

Günther, Klaus. 2002. Zwischen Ermächtigung und Disziplinierung. In *Befreiung aus der Mündigkeit*, ed. A. Honneth, 117–140. Frankfurt a. M.: Campus.

Habermas, Jürgen. 1996. Drei normative Modelle der Demokratie. In *Die Einbeziehung des Anderen*, ed. J. Habermas, 277–292. Frankfurt a. M.: Suhrkamp.

Hegel, Georg Wilhelm Friedrich. 2010. *Encyclopedia of the Philosophical Sciences in Basic Outline, Part I: Science of Logic*. Cambridge: Cambridge University Press.

Hegel, Georg Wilhelm Friedrich. 2015. *Phenomenology of the Spirit*. Cambridge: Cambridge University Press.

Heidegger, Martin. 2006. *Sein und Zeit*. Tübingen: Max Niemeyer Verlag.

Hirschman, Albert. 1987. *Leidenschaften und Interessen. Politische Begründungen des Kapitalismus vor seinem Sieg*. Frankfurt a. M.: Suhrkamp.

Honneth, Axel. 2002. Organisierte Selbstverwirklichung. In *Befreiung aus der Mündigkeit*, ed. A. Honneth, 141–158. Frankfurt a. M.: Campus.

Honneth, Axel. 2011. *Das Recht der Freiheit*. Berlin: Suhrkamp.

Honneth, Axel. 2015. *Die Idee des Sozialismus*. Berlin: Suhrkamp.

Jaeggi, Rahel. 2002. Aneignung braucht Fremdheit. *Texte Zur Kunst* 46: 60–69.

Jaeggi, Rahel. 2005. *Entfremdung*. Frankfurt a. M.: Campus.

Jaeggi, Rahel. 2009. Was ist eine ‚gute' Institution? In *Sozialphilosophie Und Kritik*, eds. A. Honneth and R. Forst, 528–544. Berlin: Suhrkamp.

Jaeggi, Rahel. 2014. *Lebensformen*. Berlin: Suhrkamp.

Kant, Immanuel. Akademische Ausgabe. https://korpora.zim.uni-duisburg-essen.de/kant/verzeichnisse-gesamt.html. Accessed 27 Sept 2023.

Kant, Immanuel. AA III, Kritik der reinen Vernunft. https://korpora.zim.uni-duisburgessen.de/kant/verzeichnisse-gesamt.html. Accessed 27 Sept 2023.

Kant, Immanuel. AA VI, Metaphysik der Sitten. https://korpora.zim.uni-duisburg-essen.de/kant/verzeichnisse-gesamt.html. Accessed 27 Sept 2023.

Kant, Immanuel. AA VIII, What Is Enlightenment? http://www.columbia.edu/acis/ets/CCREAD/etscc/kant.html. Accessed 27 Sept 2023.

Lamla, Jörn. 2018. Entgrenzter Konsum und Konsequenzen für die Verbraucherforschung. In *Entgrenzungen des Konsums*, ed. P. Kenning and J. Lamla, 147–153. Wiesbaden: Gabler.

Marx, Karl, and Friedrich Engels. 1971. *Zur Kritik der Politischen Ökonomie*. Berlin: Dietz.

Menke, Christoph. 2010. Autonomie und Befreiung. *Deutsche Zeitschrift Für Philosophie* 58: 675–694.

Menke, Christoph. 2015. *Kritik der Rechte*. Berlin: Suhrkamp.

Mill, John Stuart. 2009. *On Liberty*. Auckland: The Floating Press.

Müller, Robert Casper. 2019. *Konsumentenbilder als produktive Fiktion*. Wiesbaden: Springer Gabler.

Neuhouser, Frederick. 2012. Rousseau und die Idee einer, pathologischen' Gesellschaft. *Politische Vierteljahresschrift* 53: 628–645.

Oehler, Andreas. 2012. Neue alte Verbraucherleitbilder: Basis für die Verbraucherbildung? *Haushalt in Bildung Und Forschung* 2: 44–60.

Oshana, Marina. 2006. *Personal Autonomy in Society*. Cornwall: Routledge.

Pothast, Ulrich. 2002. Selbstbestimmung durch die Formung des eigenen Willens? *Deutsche Zeitschrift Für Philosophie* 50: 641–647.

Reckwitz, Andreas. 2003. Grundelemente einer Theorie sozialer Praktiken. *Zeitschrift Für Soziologie* 32: 282–301.

Reckwitz, Andreas. 2004. Die Reproduktion und die Subversion sozialer Praktiken. In *Doing Culture. Neue Positionen zum Verhältnis von Kultur und sozialer Praxis*, ed. K.H. Hörning, 40–53. Bielefeld: transcript.

Reckwitz, Andreas. 2008. *Unscharfe Grenzen. Perspektiven der Kultursoziologie*. Bielefeld: transcript.

Reckwitz, Andreas. 2016. Zwischen Hyperkultur und Kulturessenzialismus. Soziopolis. http://www.soziopolis.de/beobachten/kultur/artikel/zwischen-hyperkultur-und-kulturessenzialismus/. Accessed 27 Sept 2023.

Ronge, Sebastian. 2015. *Adam-Smith-Projekt*. Wiesbaden: Springer VS.

Rosa, Hartmut. 2016. *Resonanz*. Berlin: Suhrkamp.

Sack, Rolf. 2005. Die neue deutsche Formel des europäischen Verbraucherleitbilds. *Wettbewerb in Recht Und Praxis* 51: 462.

Schatzki, Theodore. 1996. *Social practices*. Melbourne: Cambridge University Press.

Schatzki, Theodore. 2002. *The site of the social*. University Park: The Pennsylvania State University Press.

Schatzki, Theodore. 2013. Human activity as indeterminate social event. In *Wittgenstein and Heidegger*, ed. D. Egan, S. Reynolds, and A.J. Wendland, 179–194. New York: Routledge.

Schechtmann, Marya. 1996. *The constitution of selves*. New York: Cornell.

Scherhorn, Gerhard. 1973. *Gesucht: Der mündige Verbraucher*. Düsseldorf: Droste.

Schmitt, Lennart. 2018. *Das unionsrechtliche Verbraucherleitbild*. Baden-Baden: Nomos.

Simanowski, Roberto. 2019. Zauberformel Nudging. *Lettre* 125: 27–31.

Stachura, Mateusz. 2017. Bewertungsspiele – Von der Handlungs- zur Koordinationstheorie. *Kölner Zeitschrift Für Soziologie Und Sozialpsychologie* 69: 1–26.

Stahl, Titus. 2011. Verdinglichung als Pathologie zweiter Ordnung. *Deutsche Zeitschrift Für Philosophie* 59: 731–746.

Stahl, Titus. 2013. *Immanente Kritik*. Frankfurt a. M.: Campus.

Strünck, Christoph, Ulrike Arens-Azevédo, Tobias Brönneke, Kornelia Hagen, Mirjam Jaquemoth, Peter Kenning, Christa Liedtke, Andreas Oehler, Ulf Schrader, and Marina Tamm. 2012. *Ist der, mündige Verbraucher' ein Mythos? Auf dem Weg zu einer realistischen Verbraucherpolitik*. Berlin: Bundesministerium für Ernährung, Landwirtschaft und Verbraucherschutz.

Taylor, Charles. 1971. Interpretation and the sciences of man. *The Review of Metaphysics* 25: 3–51.

Taylor, Charles. 1985. *Human agency and language*. Cambridge: Cambridge University Press.

Tugendhat, Ernst. 1979. *Selbstbewußtsein und Selbstbestimmung*. Frankfurt a. M.: Suhrkamp.

Ulbrich, Sebastian. 2005. *Irreführungs- und Verwechslungsgefahr im Lauterkeits- und Markenrecht*. Berlin: Dr. Köster.

Vogelmann, Frieder. 2016. Drei Gefahren philosophischer Begriffsanalysen von Verantwortung. *Deutsche Zeitschrift Für Philosophie* 64: 273–286.

Zymek, Bernd. 2004. Vom Bürger zum Kunden, Der Strukturwandel des Bildungssystems und der demokratischen Kultur in Deutschland. *Schweizerische Zeitschrift Für Bildungswissenschaften* 26: 121–140.

Thomas Cannaday, Dr., is a philosopher and sociologist. He works as an editor in Berlin. His research interests include social ontology, critical theory, political philosophy and practice theory.

Political Consumption and Political Participation

Protest—Participation—Propaganda: What is Political about Political Consumption?

Karsten Fischer

Abstract

Starting from the understanding of political consumption prevalent in the literature, a multi-level model of politics is developed that allows the various manifestations of political consumption to be classified and in particular to distinguish between 'top-down' incentivized and 'bottom-up' initiated boycott or 'buycott' actions, as well as to determine some future research desiderata.

Keywords

Boycott · Buycott · Participation · Politics · Political consumption

It is characteristic of sociocultural reality, in contrast to natural phenomena, not to have a subject area that can be determined once and for all, but rather to owe itself to a societal construction of reality (Berger and Luckmann 2003), so that it lies in the eye of the beholder whether something appears as a political, legal, economic, religious, or otherwise classifiable problem. Such classifications are

For comments and criticism, I would like to thank Kai-Uwe Hellmann, Sophie König, Stefan Matern, Vincent Rost, and Lorans El Sabee

K. Fischer (✉)
Geschwister-Scholl-Institut für Politikwissenschaft, Ludwig-Maximilians-Universität München, München, Germany
e-mail: karsten.fischer@gsi.uni-muenchen.de

K.-U. Hellmann et al. (eds.), *Consumer Policy from Below*,
https://doi.org/10.1007/978-3-658-44478-5_4

by no means purely theoretical; they have far-reaching consequences, especially for politics, which is constantly wrestling with desires for control and alternately, facing hopes of design or fears of repression- or even being perceived as obsolete. Thus, even the use of the term politics can become superfluous, as was the case in the early and high Middle Ages. During this period, characterized by theological dominance until the emergence of scholastic Aristotle reception in the thirteenth century there was no need to describe sovereign decisions using the term politics, which originated from antiquity and carried connotations of autonomy (Struve 1993, p. 189).

The question of what should be classified as a political phenomenon is therefore always of both theoretical and practical importance, and it is of correspondingly great interest that at the beginning of the twenty-first century, political consumption has been redefined as a domain that challenges the distinctions between politics and economics as well as between privacy and public life developed successively in modern Western politics.

Finally, the concept of civil society is characterized by the substitution of the old European-republican idea of a political community (κοινωνία πολιτική, societas civilis) in favor of the separation of a political-state from a privatistic-societal, bourgeois sphere. In this sphere, citizens may legitimately remain apolitical in order to pursue their economic self-interest alone, while the state ensures the peaceful framework conditions for this competitive order. Consequently, modern society believes that it can replace the social-moral intentionality of actors with an institutional framework, designed to balance self-serving interests.

In accordance with the categories of Niklas Luhmann's systems theory, this development can be typologized as shown in Fig. 1 (Fischer 2005, p. 21 f.).

In view of this complex constellation, a multi-level model of political action is first developed (1). This model subsequently facilitated the classification of forms of political consumption, distinguishing between those primarily based on consumer initiatives and those set by political institutions as incentives for political

	Social structure (primary differentiation)	Semantics	Self Description
Old European Republicanism	segmental	Political Virtue	Political community (κοινωνία πολιτική , societas civilis)
Modern liberalism	functional	rational self-interest	State vs.bourgeois society

Fig. 1 Old European Republicanism and Modern Liberalism. *Source*: own illustration

consumption (2). From here, it can then be determined what potentials and problems lie in political consumption and what further research perspectives arise from this (3).

1 A Multi-Level Model of Political Action

Against the backdrop of the brief historical sketch of political understandings, it is noteworthy that political consumption is understood in the relevant research as an ensemble of

> "Practices that are more explicitly than implicitly politically motivated and with which consumers, by using the exit, voice, and loyalty options of the market, consciously and intentionally refer to a policy behind the products. These are consumption decisions where not only private concerns are taken into account, but also attention is paid to injustices in the orders of global trade […]. Compared to participation in collective interest organizations or social movements, political consumption is more sporadic, closer to everyday life, more cost-efficient for the actors, and predominantly carried by women. […] Participation in boycotts, buycotts, or both also underlies the measurement of political consumption in the context of survey-based research, which notes a growing popularity of this market-based form of political engagement" (Lamla 2006, p. 12 f.).

This understanding is remarkable because it seems to posess a universally recognized and firmly established idea of what constitutes the political aspect in political consumption, even though the very notions of politics have not only changed over the course of history, as indicated above, but are also highly contested in the present. The latter is evident alone in the comprehensive controversy over Carl Schmitt's concept of the political. In his eponymous work, Schmitt argued in 1932 and republished in 1963 that the end of the era of statehood was a result of liberalism's failure to comprehend that the essence of the political lay in distinguishing between friend and foe and recognizing the enemy as existentially different (Schmitt 1963). In contrast, liberal political theory argued that the evolution of the modern state involved the monopolization of the politicalsphere encapsulating its latent potential for violence in the framework of a state monopoly on violence. Therefore it had no requirement for an existentialist politicization that operated outside the confines of the constitutional boundaries (Holmes 1995). In response to this, there is resistance from an affirmative reception of Schmitt on the part of a radical-democratic theory that does not want to see the political limited in its creative potentials by liberal constitutionalism (Mouffe 2007).

Beyond all these differences, the described concept of political consumption defines the motivation for political action, even if it is 'implicit', a sufficient criterion for a political character of consumer behavior. The question of a relation to the state or the fulfillment of a general political criterion is not posed, which is consistent within such a voluntaristic understanding of politics. In its pure form, it can lead to the paradox of the women's movement and the student protest movement at the end of the sixties, declaring the private as political, while at the same time claiming political responsibility for private matters such as the familial and professional equality of women, provided the formula did not remain a mere 'Sponti' slogan, as in Commune 1.

From the perspective of political science, which has remarkably and perhaps negligently hardly dealt with the phenomenon of political consumption, and has delegated to the fields of consumption, brand, and political sociology, it is doubtful whether it is a sufficient reason to classify social action as political because actors make a corresponding self-description, with the political lying solely in the eye of the beholder.

Thus, even in the realm of religion, the liberal state refers to the self-description of religious communities, as this is the only guarantee that the human right to freedom of religion, protected in the case of the Federal Republic of Germany by Art. 4 GG, is not undermined by a state determination that definitionally excludes undesirable groups. This has led to bizarre phenomena such as that of the Church of the Flying Spaghetti Monster, which claims the status of a philosophical community and has lodged a constitutional complaint with the Federal Constitutional Court and filed a lawsuit with the European Court of Human Rights. Even though the Federal Constitutional Court has consistently derived the recourse to the 'self-understanding of religious and philosophical communities' from the principle of neutrality, meaning that what considers itself or declares itself to be a religion is considered a religion,[1] the court has on the other hand emphasized that it must ultimately be up to the courts to examine whether it is "actually, in terms of intellectual content and external appearance, a religion and religious community"[2] and secular criteria may also be used in this examination.[3]

[1] BVerfGE 24, 236 (247 f.)—Aktion Rumpelkammer; BVerfGE 42, 312 (334 ff., 344)—Incompatibility/Church Office; BVerfGE 53, 366 (391 ff.)—Confessional Hospitals; BVerfGE 108, 282 (298 f.)—Headscarf at the Workplace.

[2] BVerfGE 83, 341 (353)—Bahá'í.

[3] BVerfGE 102, 370 (394)—Corporate status of Jehovah's Witnesses; BVerfGE 105, 279 (294)—Osho.

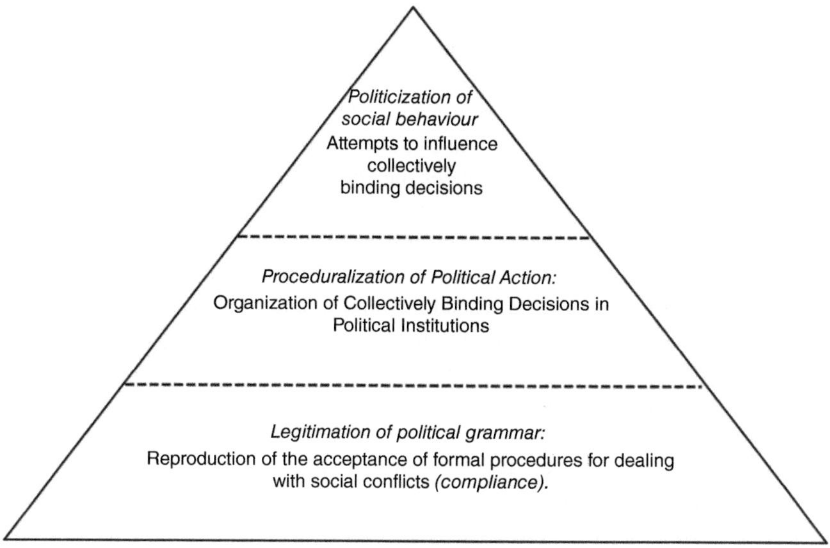

Fig. 2 Three-level model of politics. *Source*: own illustration

The case of political consumption presents a similar fundamental challenge when it comes to making a definitive determination beyond mere self-description: What belongs to the 'politics behind the products' mentioned in Lamla's definition, and in what way is consumption capable of affecting this political dimension?

If one layers the various understandings of politics, three levels can be differentiated, which vary the usual distinction in political science between 'polity' as the institutional structure of the political system, 'politics' as the content of political conflicts, and 'policy' as the individual political processes of conflict resolution (from debates to elections to wars) (Böhret et al. 1988, p. 7), see Fig. 2.

At the foundational level, there is therefore a need to legitimize the 'Political Grammar' (Meier 1997, p. 7 ff., 162 ff.), in the form of a reproduction of the acceptance of formal procedures for addressing social conflicts. This 'compliance', i.e., the voluntary willingness to follow, whose motives range from insight into the meaningfulness to the assumption of even more undesirable alternatives, is the prerequisite for a proceduralization of political action. This proceduralization enables, at the intermediary level the organization of collectively binding decisions within political institutions. This is especially relevant when these insitution, such as in the case of liberal democracies, are organized with a separation of powers. In this context, 'compliance' pertains to the adherence to decisions in which the parliament elected by the people, i.e., the legislature, has been corrected by the judiciary in the form of a constitutional court, as for example in 2006 in the case of the Air Security Act.[4]

With this level differentiation, one can also modify the formulation of Fritz W. Scharpf (1971, p. 1), politics guarantees the "possibility of collective action without presuming consensus". While the lack of guarantee of consensus at the level of proceduralization of political action through separation of powers is formally institutionalized and thus increased, insofar as control rather than consensus is desired between the legislature, executive, and judiciary, this model requires all the more consensus regarding the Political Grammar. In this regard, the acceptance of formal procedures as legitimate means of conflict resolution is crucial, especially when individuals or social groups do not realize their own interests and preferences. At the same time, the consensus regarding the Political Grammar cannot be reproduced by concrete procedures. This holds true for a liberal-democratic constitutional state, which, according to the famous dictum of Ernst-Wolfgang Böckenförde, lives from prerequisites that "it cannot guarantee itself" (Böckenförde 2007, p. 71), because it would give up its freedom with authoritative commands, nor in the Roman Republic, which failed in a "crisis without alternative" (Meier 1997, p. 203) to the existing, when its Political Grammar no longer worked. The same applies to authoritarian regimes, as the system transformations of 1989/90 and the 'Arab Spring' have proven, regardless of whether and with what stability liberal political systems could be established.

Precisely because the consensus on the Political Grammar can always only remain a silent 'tacit consent' (Locke 1764, p. 301 f.) that is institutionally solidified, it can only be read at the level of the politicization of social action, which is yet to be distinguished, how the Political Grammar stands. This level includes all attempts to influence collectively binding decisions, whether they arise from individual motives or organized interests, and regardless of their resonance at the level of proceduralization of political action.

At this specific level of the social functional system of politics, a politically scientifically sustainable sense can now also be given to the idea of consumer decisions, which, as a market-based form of political engagement, aim at a 'politics behind the products' and thus practice a consumer politics 'from below'.

---

[4] BVerfGE 115, 118—Air Security Act.

Therefore, political consumption refers to conscious and deliberate attempts to influence political decisions or to compensate for political decisions through consumption or abstention from consumption. On the one hand, it is about establishing a connection to the political system (Stolle and Hooghe 2003, p. 278 ff.), with the aim "to convince state actors to impose regulation" (Dubuisson-Quellier 2019, p. 828; Stolle and Micheletti 2013, p. 229 ff.), i.e., an indirect strategy to create incentives for democratic politicians beyond election cycles and re-election motives. Due to the decidedly moral orientation behind political consumption, it is typically not reflected upon whether the political institutions are even responsible and capable of solving, for example, an ecological or human rights problem in a far-off world region. This shows that politics is seen and treated "as a suction system for all residual problems that arise elsewhere but remain unsolved" (Hellmann 2003, p. 358).

On the other hand, political consumption can also extend to the attempt to compensate for the refusal or inability of political institutions to regulate alleged problems by constructively or destructively influencing company revenues, thus not only setting consciousness-raising and motivating incentives through indirect, symbolic and also cost-effective action, but achieving direct effects and incentivizing behavioral changes in this way (Andersen and Tobiasen 2004, p. 216; Hysing 2019, p. 835 ff.).

In both cases, the action or omission is market-based, but its primary orientation is political and not consumerist, with abstention from consumption being referred to with the common term boycott, and consumption with the neologism buycott.

2 Facets of Political Consumption

Despite all the heterogeneity of boycott and buycott campaigns and some common features, which remarkably include non-violence (Pezzullo 2011, p. 125, 135), both forms of political consumption are typically distinguished in an ideal-typical way. Thus, boycott is considered "more protest- and punishment-oriented, while buycotts are reward-oriented and therefore may appeal to different individuals with varying motivations for participation" (Katz 2019, p. 529 with reference to Copeland 2014).

This distinction treats both boycott and buycott as similar, namely morally 'good' motives, taken from minority positions and therefore directed against power elites, ranging from protest to participation.

This is indeed the case for boycott actions such as the protests against the Nestlé corporation regarding baby food, water policy, and coffee capsules, which have been ongoing since the 1970s, and for buycott campaigns such as the Fairtrade movement and the Carrotmob initiative, which organizes flash mobs to support businesses that have pledged ecological activities and donations (Pezzullo 2011, p. 135 ff.). All these initiatives have arisen 'from below' and are supported by broad, anonymous groups, i.e., they have not been incentivized by organizations or political institutions, and even if one does not share the specific goals and practices of these actions, there are hardly any fundamental objections to their motives.

The situation is different, for example, with the 'Boycott, Divestment and Sanctions' campaign against the state of Israel, which, in the alleged commitment to Palestinian concerns, turns against Israeli goods and products, but has thus also exposed itself to the accusation of exploiting and reinforcing anti-Jewish resentments, and thus crossing the threshold from protest and participation to propaganda (Micheletti and Oral 2019, p. 705 ff.).

Above all, the widespread focus on grassroots campaigns 'from below' needs correction. Because when one expands the view to campaigns of political consumption that have been incentivized by public organizations and political institutions, thus 'from above', remarkably similar patterns emerge.

For example, the supposedly civic engagement appearing Buycott actions have even been practiced by US presidents, such as when George W. Bush, following the terrorist attacks of September 11, 2001, advocated for increasing private consumption (Zieger 2004, p. 92 ff.) to send a political signal of undaunted optimism against terrorism, or when Donald Trump demanded to buy American products to support his protectionist-isolationist course. And the instrument of war bonds, which during the First World War not only had a military and an SPD-dividing, domestic political significance in Germany, but also in the USA was able to acquire 17 billion US dollars in the form of Liberty Bonds (Kang and Rockoff 2015), is also to be classified as a Buycott incentivized by political institutions.

In the area of 'top-down' incentivized boycott measures, the greatest diversity can finally be observed. On one hand, it includes the boycott of the Berlin S-Bahn, which was under the responsibility of the Deutsche Reichsbahn and thus brought in foreign exchange for the GDR, which was no longer acceptable for the West Berliners after the construction of the Wall in 1961, advocated by the then Governing Mayor of West Berlin, Willy Brandt (Jacob 2011).

On the other hand, it was also a 'top-down' incentivized boycott when the National Socialist regime called for the boycott of Jewish businesses, which was only a short campaign in 1933 with little immediate resonance in the population,

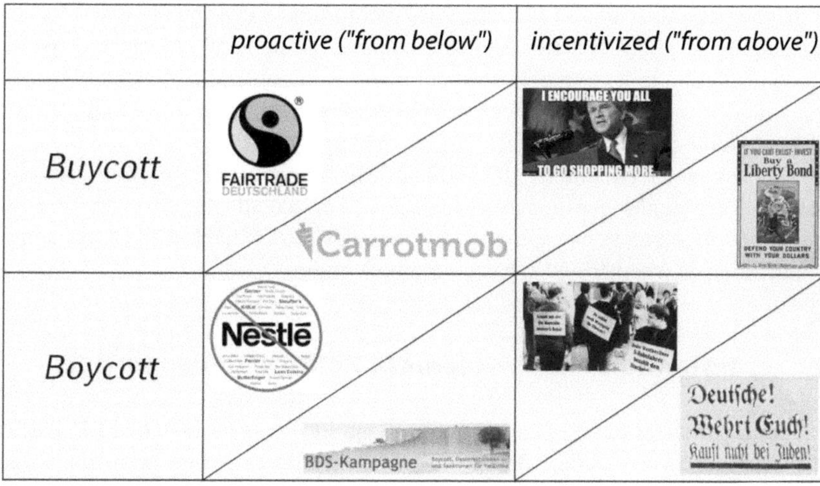

Fig. 3 Variants of Buycott and Boycott. *Source*: own representation

but undoubtedly subtly contributed a lot to the societal mood, to the National Socialist self-confidence (Ahlheim 2011; Stolle and Huissoud 2019, p. 629) and represents a low point in a series of racist, nationalist, sexist, homophobic and religious-fundamentalist campaigns of this kind that has continued ever since (Affeldt 2019; Lekakis 2019; Park 2019).

This complexity of political consumption oscillating between boycott and buycott can be schematically illustrated with Fig. 3, making it clear that buycott and boycott are equally popular in different political camps.

In this regard, the differentiation established earlier between attempts to influence collectively binding decisions and their procedural organization in political institutions can be heuristically valuable. This is because the attempts to incentivize political consumption can not only be understood as governmental forms of consumer mobilization (Lamla 2013, p. 376 ff.). There appears to be a reciprocal observation and resonance relationship between the political levels in such a way that both political institutions react to buycott and boycott activities, and consumers use such activities to respond to actions or omissions of political institutions. This also explains the political interest in consumer role models, whether this is "the ethical, the fleeting, the transparent, the informed or informable, the ignorant, the moral, the mature, the vulnerable, the responsible, the (appropriately) sensible or the trusting consumer" (Hellmann 2018b, p. 22).

In this regard, it is also necessary to avoid a one-sided intentionalist misunderstanding of political action and to recognize the political relevance of political consumption in its interplay with political institutions, which decides whether and when consumer behavior becomes political or remains an individual decision without public consequences.

The relevance conditions of political consumption are therefore obvious; however, it remains questionable whether it can actually be attributed a positive political potential, as exemplified in Lamla's (2013) book title of 'consumer democracy', or whether it also has problematic traits.

3 Potentials and Problems of Political Consumption

The term participation refers to the interest and involvement in public debates up to the influence on political decisions, which in turn can range from mere voting participation to the exercise of passive voting rights or other forms of direct engagement, such as in parties, associations and social movements. Accordingly, the idea that political consumption is a 'politics in the supermarket' (Stolle et al. 2005) and as 'politics with the shopping cart' (Baringhorst et al. 2007) a form of political participation, unfolds the paradox that the—per definition: public—sphere of politics could be affected by private consumption behavior.

This can be interpreted as a reaction to increasing self-referentiality of politics, which makes it attractive to use the higher degrees of freedom of consumption to "individually deviate, try something for oneself, get to know something new and reinvent oneself through and by one's individual consumption" (Hellmann 2019, p. 188 f.).

In any case, this shows the completion of the development described at the beginning from the virtue-possessed, demanding engagement in the political community, old-European republicanism to the trust of liberalism in the rationality of legitimate self-interests in a civil society distinguished from the state. Thus, the traditional contrast between the selfishly economically interested bourgeois and the virtuously politically active citizen in the debate about political consumption has finally been abolished by the pair of terms 'citizen' and 'consumer', in which no irreconcilable contrast is seen anymore (Schudson 2006; Hellmann 2018a).

This includes the fact that political consumers are attributed with a "postmaterialist outlook" (Stolle and Micheletti 2013, p. 84) in the sense of Ronald Inglehart's famous theory (1977) (Katz 2019, p. 526; critically, however, Andersen and Tobiasen 2004, p. 211). It is also known that in political consumption, women who are underrepresented in conventional forms of participation are overrepresented, and there is a predominance of educated, wealthy urban residents of middle age who are already engaged in about two-thirds of other activities, including in political organizations, where they are represented twice as often as average consumers, even though they are critical of political institutions and show an above-average trust in their fellow citizens (Stolle and Micheletti 2013, p. 68 ff.; cf. Baek 2010). Compared to participation in collective interest organizations or social movements, political consumption is more individual, sporadic, closer to everyday life, and more cost-efficient for the actors (Haenfler et al. 2012, p. 15; Forno 2019).

However, even such a form of political participation based in the private sphere cannot avoid inequalities of participation, as they also occur in other forms of participation. Thus, political consumption is "only within reach for those groups of the population who already are (because of their cognitive, financial, and other resources) highly active in social and political life" (Stolle and Micheletti 2013, p. 94).

In light of this, the question arises as to what problem political consumption is supposed to solve, and the answer that becomes clear in the referenced state of discussion is that political consumption represents a rational commitment based on moral convictions within market economic and representative democratic structures, aiming at compensating for the collective control deficits of functionally differentiated societies.

From a political science perspective, however, this understanding raises as many problems as it offers potential solutions. Because any civil society engagement is not only fragile due to the risk of frustration and disappointment (Hirschman 1984), but also tends towards thematic singularity. And while state institutions at least claim to operate complexly, far-sightedly, and sustainably, for example in environmental and welfare policy, civil society engagement is usually a particular 'one-issue-movement' (against environmental pollution and arms exports and for climate protection and childcare etc. pp.). Consequently it tends towards a NIMBY attitude ('Not In My BackYard'), meaning that protest is regularly only articulated when directly affected (Fischer 2005, p. 28) and can lead to phenomena of consumerist double morality, when certain corporations are boycotted because of questionable human rights production practices, while at the same time other corporations with comparable practices are not boycotted, be it out of ignorance, or be it out of higher prioritization of their products for one's own lifestyle, or simply out of everyday practical constraints.

This not only raises the question of how to reconcile the rationality of political consumption with its tendency towards emotional moral motivations, but also how to avoid a societal division that has arisen in the USA from the fact that exclusive and doctrinaire moral self-righteousness has solidified in different political camps (Haidt 2012). Particularly when political consumption is characterized by supplementing democratic decision-making processes with the use of market mechanisms (Micheletti 2003) to achieve the aforementioned indirect or direct political effects, such "counter-culture thinking" (Lamla 2013, p. 133) creates tension with liberal-democratic constitutionalism, which in times of increasing anti-liberal populism could provoke the problem of unintended side effects of political consumption.

It is all the more important, therefore, to pay due attention to the party preferences and voting behavior of political consumers, in addition to their socio-demographic characteristics and moral orientations, an area that is still insufficiently researched. While there are initial studies on the emergence of new institutions for political consumption (Gulbrandsen 2019), political attitude research in this area is as deficient as analyses of which forms of political consumption develop greater or lesser compatibility for political institutions and what consequences this can have for various policy areas, from environmental policy to international trade relations.

National and regional differences must also be taken into account, such as those evident in the East-West divide within Europe (Pellandini-Simányi and Gulyás 2019) and the difference between the OECD world on the one hand and Africa and the Middle East on the other (Oosterveer et al. 2019). These differences raise the particularly significant question of what role political consumption can play in a neo-totalitarian dictatorship with market-liberal economic practices, such as the People's Republic of China (Lei et al. 2019).

In this global perspective, one should not prematurely ask for the reasons for the lack of political consumption and thus make the still young Western development a heuristic benchmark (as exemplified by Boström et al. 2019, p. 896). Instead, where its occurrence is rather in need of explanation and the conditions of its possibility outside of societies, for which the ambiguous acronym WEIRD (*W*estern, *E*ducated, *I*ndustrialized, *R*ich, *D*emocratic) according to Henrich et al. (2010) applies, must be precisely determined. All these open questions show, in any case, that political consumption is a significant research field that is in need of considerable further development, especially from a political science perspective.

References

Affeldt, Stefanie. 2019. ‚Buy White—Stay Fair': Racist political consumerism in Australian history. In *The Oxford handbook of political consumerism*, eds. M. Boström, M. Micheletti, and P. Oosterveer, 643–663. Oxford: Oxford University Press.

Ahlheim, Hannah. 2011. *‚Deutsche, kauft nicht bei Juden!' Antisemitismus und politischer Boykott in Deutschland 1924 bis 1935*. Göttingen: Wallstein.

Andersen, Jørgen Goul, and Mette Tobiasen. 2004. Who are these political consumers anyway? Survey evidence from Denmark. In *Politics, products, and markets*, eds. M. Micheletti, A. Follesdal, and D. Stolle, 203–221. New Brunswick: Transaction Publishers.

Baek, Young Min. 2010. To buy or not to buy: Who are political consumers? What do they think and how do they participate? *Political Studies* 58:1065–1086.

Baringhorst, Sigrid, Veronika Kneip, Annegret März, and Johanna Niesyto, eds. 2007. *Politik mit dem Einkaufswagen. Unternehmen und Konsumenten als Bürger in der globalen Mediengesellschaft*. Bielefeld: transcript.

Berger, Peter L., and Thomas Luckmann. 2003. *Die gesellschaftliche Konstruktion der Wirklichkeit. Eine Theorie der Wissenssoziologie*, 19th edn. Frankfurt a. M.: Fischer.

Böckenförde, Ernst-Wolfgang. 2007. Die Entstehung des Staates als Vorgang der Säkularisation (1967). In *Der säkularisierte Staat. Sein Charakter, seine Rechtfertigung und seine Probleme im 21. Jahrhundert*, 43–72. München: Carl Friedrich von Siemens Stiftung.

Böhret, Carl, Werner Jann, and Eva Kronenwett. 1988. *Innenpolitik und politische Theorie. Ein Studienbuch*, 3rd edn. Opladen: Westdeutscher Verlag.

Boström, Magnus, Michele Micheletti, and Peter Oosterveer. 2019. Political consumerism: Research challenges and future directions. In *The Oxford handbook of political consumerism*, eds. M. Boström, M. Micheletti, and P. Oosterveer, 879–898. Oxford: Oxford University Press.

Copeland, Lauren. 2014. Conceptualizing political consumerism: How citizenship norms differentiate boycotting from buycotting. *Political Studies* 62:172–186.

Dubuisson-Quellier, Sophie. 2019. From moral concerns to market values: How political consumerism shapes markets. In *The Oxford handbook of political consumerism*, eds. M. Boström, M. Micheletti, and P. Oosterveer, 814–832. Oxford: Oxford University Press.

Fischer, Karsten. 2005. ‚Zivilgesellschaft' als Problemindikator – Semantik und Perspektiven einer Begriffskarriere. In *Zivilgesellschaft auf dem Prüfstand. Argumente – Modelle – Anwendungsfelder*, ed. J. Inthorn, 20–32. Stuttgart: Kohlhammer.

Forno, Francesca. 2019. Protest, social movements, and spaces for politically oriented consumerist actions – Nationally, transnationally, and locally. In *The Oxford handbook of political consumerism*, eds. M. Boström, M. Micheletti, and P. Oosterveer, 69–89. Oxford: Oxford University Press.

Gulbrandsen, Lars H. 2019. Globalization, governance gaps, and the emergence of new institutions for political consumerism. In *The Oxford handbook of political consumerism*, eds. M. Boström, M. Micheletti, and P. Oosterveer, 227–249. Oxford: Oxford University Press.

Haenfler, Ross, Brett Johnson, and Ellis Jones. 2012. Lifestyle movements: Exploring the intersection of lifestyle and social movements. *Social Movement Studies* 11:1–20.

Haidt, Jonathan. 2012. *The righteous mind. Why good people are divided by politics and religion*. New York: Penguin.

Hellmann, Kai-Uwe. 2003. *Soziologie der Marke*. Frankfurt a. M.: Suhrkamp.

Hellmann, Kai-Uwe. 2018a. Ein Casting der besonderen Art: Zum Menschenbild der Verbraucherwissenschaften. In *Multiperspektivische Verbraucherforschung. Ansätze und Perspektiven*, eds. S. Nessel, N. Tröger, C. Fridrich, and R. Hübner, 53–81. Wiesbaden: Springer VS.

Hellmann, Kai-Uwe. 2018b. Leitbilder, Erlebnisse und die mentale Dimension des modernen Konsums. Zum Menschenbild der akademischen Verbraucherforschung. In *Jenseits des Otto Normalverbrauchers. Verbraucherpolitik in Zeiten des ‚unmanageable consumer'*, eds. C. Bala and W. Schuldzinski, 19–51. Düsseldorf: Verbraucherzentrale.

Hellmann, Kai-Uwe. 2019. *Der Konsum der Gesellschaft. Studien zur Soziologie des Konsums*, 2., erweiterte Aufl. Wiesbaden: Springer VS.

Henrich, Joseph, Steven J. Heine, and Ara Norenzayan. 2010. The weirdest people in the world? *Behavioral and Brain Sciences* 33:61–135.

Hirschman, Albert O. 1984. *Engagement und Enttäuschung. Über das Schwanken der Bürger zwischen Privatwohl und Gemeinwohl*. Frankfurt a. M.: Suhrkamp.

Holmes, Stephen. 1995. *Passions and constraint. On the theory of liberal democracy*. Chicago: University of Chicago Press.

Hysing, Erik. 2019. Government engagement with political consumerism. In *The Oxford handbook of political consumerism*, eds. M. Boström, M. Micheletti, and P. Oosterveer, 833–855. Oxford: Oxford University Press.

Inglehart, Ronald. 1977. *The silent revolution. Changing values and political styles among western publics*. Princeton: Princeton University Press.

Jacob, Manuel. 2011. *Endstation Mauerbau. Wie das S-Bahnnetz am 13. August 1961 getrennt wurde*. Berlin: VBN Verlag Bernd Neddermeyer.

Kang, Sung Won, and Hugh Rockoff. 2015. Capitalizing patriotism: The liberty loans of world war I. *Financial History Review* 22:45–78.

Katz, Meredith A. 2019. Boycotting and buycotting in consumer cultures: Political consumerism in north America. In *The Oxford handbook of political consumerism*, eds. M. Boström, M. Micheletti, and P. Oosterveer, 515–538. Oxford: Oxford University Press.

Lamla, Jörn. 2006. Politisierter Konsum – konsumierte Politik Kritikmuster und Engagementformen im kulturellen Kapitalismus. In *Politisierter Konsum – konsumierte Politik*, eds. J. Lamla and S. Neckel, 9–37. Wiesbaden: VS Verlag.

Lamla, Jörn. 2013. *Verbraucherdemokratie. Politische Soziologie der Konsumgesellschaft*. Berlin: Suhrkamp.

Lei, Zhang, Wenling Liu, and Peter Oosterveer. 2019. Institutional changes and changing political consumerism in China. In *The oxford handbook of political consumerism*, eds. M. Boström, M. Micheletti, and P. Oosterveer, 583–603. Oxford: Oxford University Press.

Lekakis, Eleftheria J. 2019. Political consumerism and nationalist struggles in Europe. In *The Oxford handbook of political consumerism*, eds. M. Boström, M. Micheletti, and P. Oosterveer, 663–681. Oxford: Oxford University Press.

Locke, John. 1764. *Two treatises of government*, ed. T. Hollis. London: A. Millar.

Luhmann, Niklas. 2000. *Die Politik der Gesellschaft*. ed. A. Kieserling. Frankfurt a. M.: Suhrkamp.

Meier, Christian. 1997. *Res publica amissa. Eine Studie zu Verfassung und Geschichte der späten römischen Republik*, 3rd edn. Frankfurt a. M.: Suhrkamp.

Micheletti, Michele. 2003. *Political virtue and shopping. Individuals, consumerism, and collective action*. New York: Palgrave Macmillan.

Micheletti, Michele, and Didem Oral. 2019. Problematic political consumerism: Confusions and moral dilemmas in boycott activism. In *The Oxford handbook of political consumerism*, eds. M. Boström, M. Micheletti, and P. Oosterveer, 699–721. Oxford: Oxford University Press.

Mouffe, Chantal. 2007. *Über das Politische. Wider die kosmopolitische Illusion*. Frankfurt a. M.: Suhrkamp.

Oosterveer, Peter, Laurent Glin, and Michele Micheletti. 2019. Tracing political consumerism in Africa and the middle east. In *The Oxford handbook of political consumerism*, eds. M. Boström, M. Micheletti, and P. Oosterveer, 559–583. Oxford: Oxford University Press.

Park, Bo Yun. 2019. Racialized political consumerism. In *The Oxford handbook of political consumerism*, eds. M. Boström, M. Micheletti, and P. Oosterveer, 681–699. Oxford: Oxford University Press.

Pellandini-Simányi, Léna, and Emese Gulyás. 2019. Political consumerism in central and eastern Europe. In *The Oxford handbook of political consumerism*, eds. M. Boström, M. Micheletti, and P. Oosterveer, 479–515. Oxford: Oxford University Press.

Pezzullo, Phaedra C. 2011. Contextualizing boycotts and buycotts: The impure politics of consumer based advocacy in an age of global ecological crises. *Communication and Critical/Cultural Studies* 8:124–145.

Scharpf, Fritz W. 1971. Planung als politischer Prozeß. *Die Verwaltung* 4:1–30.

Schmitt, Carl. 1963. *Der Begriff des Politischen. Text von 1932 mit einem Vorwort und drei Corollarien*, 3rd edn. Berlin: Duncker & Humblot.

Schudson, Michael. 2006. The troubling equivalence of citizen and consumer. *The Annals of the American Academy of Political and Social Science* 608:193–204.

Stolle, Dietlind, and Lucas Huissoud. 2019. Undemocratic political consumerism. In *The Oxford handbook of political consumerism*, eds. M. Boström, M. Micheletti, and P. Oosterveer, 625–643. Oxford: Oxford University Press.

Stolle, Dietlind, and Marc Hooghe. 2003. Consumers as political participants? Shifts in political action repertoires in western societies. In *Politics, products, and markets*, eds. M. Micheletti, A. Follesdal, and D. Stolle, 265–288. New Brunswick: Transaction Publishers.

Stolle, Dietlind, and Michele Micheletti. 2013. *Political consumerism. Global responsibility in action*. Cambridge: Cambridge University Press.

Stolle, Dietlind, Marc Hooghe, and Michele Micheletti. 2005. Politics in the supermarket: political consumerism as a form of political participation. *International Political Science Review* 26:245–269.

Struve, Tilman. 1993. Regnum and Sacerdotium. In *Pipers Handbuch der Politischen Ideen*, Bd. 2, eds. I. Fetscher and H. Münkler, 189–242. München: Piper.

Zieger, Robert H. 2004. ‚Uncle Sam Wants You … to Go Shopping': A consumer society responds to national crisis, 1957–2001. *Canadian Review of American Studies/Revue canadienne d'études américaines* 34:83–103.

Karsten Fischer is Professor of Political Theory at LMU Munich, https://www.gsi.uni-muenchen.de/personen/professoren/fischer/index.html.

Consumer Participation through Digital Valuation Practices? On the Sociology of the Infrastructures of Consumer Participation

Jörn Lamla

Abstract

Digital (e)valuation practices are a widespread phenomenon today. Consumers participate in them, sometimes directly, through stars and comments, sometimes indirectly, by training machine-learning recommendation systems through data traces. The article puts the question as to which opportunities consumers receive by this for articulation. Do these valuation practices support a consumer policy from below? Or is it consumer activation that intensifies post-democratic decay, insofar as it merely simulates political participation? To answer this, the article draws on the sociology of infrastructures and contends that evaluation practices take place in pre-curated, steering or nudging decision architectures. These contribute to post-democratic change when they hinder the retrieval of critical competencies through conventionalizing framing and strong simplification of valuation problems, thus endangering their reproduction.

Keywords

Consumer Citizen · Digital Evaluation Practices · Decision Architecture · Infrastructure · Ability to Criticize · Platform Economy · Post-Democracy

J. Lamla (✉)
Universität Kassel, Kassel, Germany
e-mail: lamla@uni-kassel.de

K.-U. Hellmann et al. (eds.), *Consumer Policy from Below*,
https://doi.org/10.1007/978-3-658-44478-5_5

1 Introduction

Almost 20 years ago, when I began to deal with consumer policy during the BSE crisis, the Federal Government spoke of 'politics with the shopping cart', a protest movement against transnational brand corporations was conjured up on the globalization-critical stage—'No Logo!' (Klein 2002)—and with a view to the internet, the age of the 'Citizen-Consumer' was proclaimed (Scammell 2000). The internet seemed to provide an infrastructure for civic engagement by consumers and to mobilize new forms of participation in the form of lifestyle politics (Bennett 2004). I began with initial empirical studies, which resulted in an essay co-authored with Christoph Bieber for the research journal Neue Soziale Bewegungen. We wanted to appreciate which opportunities for innovation the internet holds for 'consumer politics from below' and we contrasted various forms of networking and the activation of consumers—at that time still with students in a joint research project (Bieber and Lamla 2005).

The spectrum of initiatives we looked at ranged from top-down enlightenment campaigns by the new green Federal Ministry of Consumer Protection—for example, the website 'really fair—clever shopping' (echt gerecht—clever einkaufen) to attempts at bottom-up activation, such as the Attac consumer network. The ministry's website also included participatory proposals such as self-tests or a limited comment function and was later abolished under the new leadership of the CSU Minister Seehofer. In contrast, the Attac mailing list still exists, but is only very sporadically served. In between were, on the one hand, initial formats for involving consumers in critical market observation, such as Foodwatch or Greenpeace, and on the other hand, commercial marketing platforms like ciao.de, yopi.de or dooyoo.de, which co-developed the crowdsourcing of product reviews and trust generation through consumer testimonials, which has now become ubiquitous through Amazon, YouTube, various travel and hotel booking sites, and much more. The old shopping and opinion platforms have mostly been shut down, but have had interesting careers and have not least flowed into the infrastructure of search engines. A little later, sites like utopia.de or karmakonsum.de were added, which aim to network and mobilize the LoHaS, i.e. consumers who strive for a 'Lifestyle of Health and Sustainability', with similar forms of community building. And the Federal Consumer Association (vzbv) has broadly set up a Market Watchdog for the Digital World with the consumer associations of the federal states, which continues the idea of outsourced detective work by consumers.[1]

Of course, the forms of engagement and participation of consumers are not limited to such digital participation offers and opportunities. What is very visible in the digital examples and to which I shall turn my attention in the following, is the connection to the development of (technical) infrastructures. My thesis is that a perspective on the infrastructures of consumer participation is needed to diagnose and assess the societal and political significance and problem content of consumer participation in social science terms.

This perspective is by no means limited to phenomena of digitalization, but can also in an enlightening way be applied and transferred to analogue aspects of (political) consumer participation—although the separation of these areas in times of ubiquitous computing, smart environment and the internet of things is becoming increasingly difficult anyway. However, it is important for me to emphasize that the (political) participation of consumers encompasses an extremely broad and confusing complex of phenomena, which includes initiatives of urban gardening as well as various cultures of self-service from ethically motivated—or merely exaggerated?—repair practices in the repair café to the heroization of DIY in the commercials of large DIY store chains. The inclusion of consumers in the practices and symbolic worlds of consumption is multifaceted, and the boundary between consumer political articulation and private everyday economy is fluid and dynamic.

This does not make it easy to arrive at general statements about the state and relevance of consumer participation in contemporary society, which are at the center of scientific and consumer political interest here. I do not want to evade this task by defining the phenomenon; rather, my view of digital valuation practices serves to introduce and make plausible the theoretical perspective on a paradigmatic aspect of today's consumer participation. Only a change of perspective from the diverse practices to the evolutionary dynamics of the change of infrastructures of consumer participation, according to my argumentation, facilitates an achievement of substantial hypotheses and time-diagnostic generalizations about the 'consumer politics from below'.

[1] For older, partly already shut down websites, see the information in Bieber and Lamla (2005). The Market Watchdog Digital World can be found at https://www.marktwaechter.de/digitalewelt. Accessed: January 7, 2020.

2 Post-democracy? Infrastructures of the Consumer Citizen

Before going into more detail about consumer participation through digital valuation practices, I would like to define the horizon for such general statements a little more precisely. As I have explained in more detail elsewhere (Lamla 2013, p. 86 ff.), it seems to me useful to first briefly refer to a hypothesis that is widespread in the scientific literature on democratic change. This null hypothesis links the growth of consumer engagement, participation and cooperation with a fundamental change in the form of democracy. It deserves thorough examination and is by no means easy to dismiss, even if, in my opinion, it does not fully do justice to societal developments and therefore needs to be revised. According to this null hypothesis, the political or politically charged consumption phenomena—especially in their diversity—are an expression of a post-democratic turn in politics, in which they primarily serve to simulate democratic participation (Blühdorn 2013). This interpretation contains a generalizing statement that the expansion of consumer participation and its political upgrading ultimately reflects the societal devaluation of democratic procedures. Paradoxically, the political gain in the relevance of consumers is thus to be valued as a loss of relevance of citizens, as the political game as a whole emancipates itself from democratic controls and participations. By creating and serving the illusion of democratic self-determination, consumer democracy even decisively helps to replace state action and governance from a public will formation and control and thus to legitimize and secure the transition to a technocratic administration of growing social and political inequalities, of ecological side effects of systemic imperatives and of economic constraints and capital interests.

Now, this strikingly elegant and radically sobering post-democracy hypothesis should not be adopted without scrutiny. Rather, several assumptions come into play in this diagnosis that need to be questioned. For example, the shift of commitment to the private sphere of consumption is explained by Ingolfur Blühdorn (2013, p. 134) with Sennett and Bauman through a general and profound change in the subject form of the consumer citizen. This demands and supports, with its characteristic flexibility and volatility, a democracy of non-commitment and superficiality, which should convey the feeling of participation, but should please not disturb the accustomed freedoms of private consumption. But Albert O. Hirschman (1984) has already interpreted such changes in his treatise on commitment and disappointment less as long-term cultural shifts of the subject form than as 'Shifting Involvements', i.e., as fluctuations resulting from the institutional conditions and participation opportunities of functionally differentiated societies. And perhaps such an interpretation, which does not contrast consumer democracy with a glossed-over image of real civic participation, but also takes its inadequacies into view, comes closer to today's reality of democracy and participation. Perhaps the pendulum will also swing back in the other direction and mobilize the consumer citizens to participate more in political institutions. Then the generalizing interpretation of consumer participation practices as post-democracy or simulative democracy would be exaggerated and inaccurate.

I also refer to Hirschman because he shifts the focus from the actors to the infrastructures in which the consumer citizens need to unfold their commitment in order to participate in consumer politics. With the concept of infrastructure, I should like to distance myself from interpretations that prefer to speak of subsystems of functionally differentiated society at this point and thus sharply separate the communication contexts of the economy and politics. The theory of social systems also helps to relativize and question the actions of and self- or external attributions of a subject status to the consumer citizens. However, it grants this status to the autonomously operating functional systems, which also generates too much theoretical ballast weight and is likely to reflect an unacknowledged subject-philosophical legacy of the systems theory itself (Habermas 1985, p. 426 ff.).

The concept of infrastructures refers to other social science schools, especially to the Science and Technology Studies (Bauer et al. 2017) and here e.g. to the Actor-Network Theory (Latour 2007), which have learned a lot from the analysis of technical infrastructures about society. Infrastructures do not act as substitutes for actors, but they act with them. They are not only enabling and limiting conditions of the actions of human subjects, but together with these, they first constitute the agency, i.e., in our case, the participation practices and political engagement of consumers. They are not only co-responsible for whether and how consumers can take responsibility and develop into a stable disposition. Rather, they also intervene in the consumer cultural processes of value attribution and evaluation, which the newer 'Sociology of Valuation and Evaluation' addresses (Lamont 2012). I would like to elaborate on this in the following using the example of digital valuation practices.

The sociology of infrastructures directs the analysis towards the production of infrastructures and not just their action- or behavior-stabilizing effect. It considers these as potentially controversial and examines their capacities for securing cooperation, without having to presuppose a consensus among all the different actors involved in maintaining the infrastructure and/or using it.[2] It strips infrastructures, so to speak, of their infrastructural, i.e., solidified and unquestioned, conventional character, in order to work out differences, contingencies, power distributions, and subsequent problems of infrastructures. If I subsequently discuss political consumer participation exemplarily based on infrastructures of digital consumer participation, it is also due to the implication or conclusion that consumer politics (from below as well as from above) could also be infrastructure politics. In the conclusion of my paper, I will try to justify why consumer policy actors should take on the challenges of infrastructure design and no longer leave them in the background. It will be crucial for this argument that the way infrastructures of consumer participation are designed today has changed significantly due to digitization and behavioral economics.

3 Digital Valuation Practices and their Infrastructures

An important aspect of consumer participation are valuation practices. They give consumers a voice and open up opportunities for them to influence the future design of offers, cultural trends, or pricing. With digitization, requests for the (e) valuation of consumer goods, services, peers, providers, etc. have been significantly expanded. Sociology increasingly diagnoses a shift in society towards an evaluation society.[3] Valuation practices range from clicking on like buttons and awarding stars to writing detailed reviews and experience reports. Participation in valuations also takes place via automated or semi-automated data collection and valuation processes, such as when purchasing profiles or statistics are included in recommendation algorithms ('Customers who bought this also bought that' or even more anonymously 'Jörn, you might like this'). Even purchasing acts them-

[2] An important contribution to the sociology of infrastructures from the field of Science and Technology Studies was made by Susan Leigh Star and colleagues with their work on boundary objects and boundary infrastructures, see Star (2017). The facilitation of cooperation, without having to demand difficult consensus-building from the heterogeneous actors involved beforehand, is a special characteristic of (especially technical) boundary objects. Infrastructure research focuses on these objects, not least because they can be linked to socio-technical control interests.

[3] Examples of this are the works of Mau (2017) and Reckwitz (2017), but also the establishment of a DFG network under the title 'On the way to the evaluation society?'.

selves are thus interpreted and processed as valuations. At the same time, social media and networks play a major role: valuations are staged by influencers on YouTube or Instagram and become a way to achieve cult status or advertising contracts. On various platforms, mutual feedback up to the communalization of peers becomes an important aspect of market practices, be it to prove one's own trustworthiness or that of other market participants (Airbnb, eBay) or be it to be encouraged or corrected in one's own self- and consumption practices through approval or evaluation by others, following the model of Facebook, Runtastic or Weight Watchers (Lamla 2013, p. 270 ff.). It is obvious that digital technologies and infrastructures have a significant share in this expansion and change of consumer participation. However, it is unclear what exactly this share is and to what extent it is relevant to consumer policy.

Digital valuation practices secure certain opportunities for participation for consumers beyond private consumption. Their opinion is sought. They are given a voice and not just exit options, to enable them to influence markets and market developments. The audience of these articulations is in many cases not limited to providers, it is not about complaints or claims, about evaluable user knowledge, error corrections or anonymous evaluations that are reported back to the manufacturers in individual cases or systematically. These communication channels have not disappeared, but digital evaluation practices go beyond this and approach a 'consumer policy from below' mainly because they take place in a larger public sphere. They are more similar to the reader's letter sent to the local newspaper, or the anonymous vote count in the 'Sunday Opinion Poll' than the direct confrontation with manufacturers or sellers. The influence is based on public and collective pressure—consumer policy from below. Various platforms have openly advertised this pattern for themselves and emphasized the new, increased power of consumers, which brings participation in public valuation practices (Lamla 2008). Consumers are apparently empowered by digital participation opportunities. And the boundaries of their influence appear fluid: Like hotels or PC games, political parties can also be rated in relevant networks. Rezo has shown how it's done.[4] And already some people yearn for the limitation and control of free expression of opinion.

The Valuation Studies of the new sociology of (e)valuation now take a closer look at such practices (Kropf and Laser 2019). They first strip them of their apparent naturalness and openness, which they are given by the (not least con-

[4] See https://www.youtube.com/watch?v=4Y1lZQsyuSQ. Accessed: January 7, 2020.

stitutionally protected) interpretation framework of free expression of opinion. This is not yet about the role of infrastructures, but first and foremost about distinguishing and typifying the valuation practices themselves more precisely. They are considered as actions that require certain conditions, which mobilize specific conventions and registers of valuation. For example, comparative evaluations can be distinguished from singularizing ones, quantitatively measuring from qualitatively curating or layman-like from those that claim a certain expert knowledge for themselves. Important for my argument here is the respective reference to certain conventional orders of justification, which provide the evaluators with standards, formats and criteria for evaluation (Diaz-Bone 2011). The sociology of (e) valuation always emphasizes the contingency and plurality of such orders, which, for example, significantly co-decide whether bargains are particularly positively rated or social status symbols, whether fun and private well-being or competitive performance measurements are in demand, whether ecological sustainability plays a role or only the aesthetic appearance is in the foreground, whether politically correct attention is paid to diversity or culturally different thinkers are ostracized.

For consumers to be able to evaluate at all, they must carry out certain determinations regarding such conventional orders of valuation. In the preliminary decisions about which valuation order is appropriate in a particular evaluation situation, which register they therefore draw on each time, their practical or pragmatic valuation competence and judgment power is expressed (Boltanski and Thévenot 2007). The plurality of possible valuation orders becomes a school of civil society's ability to criticize, insofar as it allows such judgments of appropriateness to be put under justification pressure: Is it right or wrong to largely neglect the ecological consequences when evaluating holiday trips? Can subjective taste experiences justify the renunciation of objective numbers? Is it okay to place the aesthetic appeal far above any financial comparison calculation? Within once set orders, such questions no longer arise and the execution of evaluations is not a great difficulty. It achieves a routine character and can potentially be carried out by algorithms (as in an electronic exam, the addition of points and ranking of exam results).

This is where the infrastructures of consumer participation come into play: In the area of valuation practices, technical infrastructures do not limit themselves to general enabling conditions such as electricity, digital protocols, hardware, etc. Rather, they involve complex platform architectures and specifically shaped interfaces, with which they secure certain valuation orders, thus setting a more or less narrow conventional framework for the execution of valuations. Consumer participation threatens to degenerate into a mere auxiliary algorithm that feeds the machine rankings and ratings with manual training data (Engemann 2018; Mühlhoff 2019), unless consumers are also required to engage with questions and problems of appropriateness and weighting of different orders and registers of valuation, which demand and activate their critical competencies in a special way. Valuation could indeed develop into a convenient post-democratic simulation of participation. Certainly, not all infrastructures of valuation can be tarred with the same brush. However, some worrying trends can be identified, which I will briefly list below:

- Infrastructures are designed by private companies in the digital economy, without public debates or participation by consumers or their political representatives during the pre-determinations made about valuation orders.
- During the pre-determination, opaque criteria come into play that take into account the business models of the infrastructure providers. These can be scaling, network and trust effects of social media activities, for which the idiosyncrasy of valuations becomes secondary, or profits from contracts entered into with third parties on data trading markets (Zuboff 2018). These interest-bound criteria selectively influence the design of valuation infrastructures, which then, for example, target certain generations or predominantly tend to 'applaud' (Lamla 2008).
- Behavioral psychology and economics provide knowledge about the behavior-guiding power of decision architectures, which is applied in the design of valuation orders to 'nudge' certain evaluations unnoticed, for example by pre-determinations on subjective testing of purchased products (Lamla 2013, p. 285). The mode of nudging (Thaler and Sunstein 2011) allows to officially uphold freedom of opinion (libertarian paternalism). Selective pre-determinations thus apparently no longer require public justification.
- Infrastructures of digital valuation practices also change rapidly without informing consumers, by observing their valuation practices and, for example, continuously improving their infrastructure through A/B testing and usage measurements—not to mention the possibilities of increasingly diversifying and adapting architectures in real time (Zweig et al. 2019).

If evaluations take place largely without an overlap in bubbles, no critical competence can develop for the appropriate mediation between and the separation of different orders and registers of valuation, although their plurality is present across different platforms. Their segmentation gains infrastructural character. Criticism remains abstract and sterile; the democratic public becomes fragmented.

Finally—and this is probably the most serious—such designed rating systems have socialization effects for humans and machines: Human and artificial intelligence converge and develop into a single, hybrid intelligence if valuation and criticism only move in predetermined paths and these valuation data are used to train IT infrastructures such as recommendation algorithms and other AI elements (Lamla 2019). The new editions of the old cybernetic dream of the universal integration of all information flows (Wiener 1952) are developing into a democratic nightmare, as they help to withdraw the friction surfaces necessary for the development of critical competencies from societal practice (Nassehi 2019).

4 Consumer Policy from below Beyond Post-Democratic Participation

I should like to come to a conclusion. My remarks have revealed some aspects that should be considered if consumer policy from below is not to be exhausted in post-democratic participation. I have certainly only looked at a small part of consumer participation with digital valuation practices. However, these participation practices touch on something crucial with the (medium-term) development of critical competence: It is about the question of preservation or loss of abilities in the population to judge the situational appropriateness of certain normative registers of valuation and justification and not to dismantle valuation into inflationarily expected and at the same time maximally complexity-reduced click routines. Where participation in pre-stamped, partly algorithmic valuation practices is still given the nimbus of a consumer policy from below and thus the good feeling of political participation is deliberately reinforced, this consolidates the post-democratic turn of politics and indeed turns participation into a mere simulation.

State consumer policy is also not immune to encouraging consumer participation in a way that reinforces post-democratic tendencies. It pursues with the nudging approach partially similar infrastructural settings—albeit with different normative objectives than the platform economy. However, it cannot easily reject or fundamentally modify their design paradigm by law. With the analytical perspective on the design of infrastructures of digital valuation practices, however, it also becomes apparent that such a post-democratic development is not inevitable. It does not necessarily have to lead to a fundamental dispute about behavioral economics, insofar as it does not want to deny the role of behavior-supporting infrastructures, but rather acknowledges them. But it shows that for democratic participation and the reproduction of critical consumer competences, two things are important, namely that consumer participation is not cut off from the design decisions about digital valuation architectures and orders, but consumer participation must extend to the infrastructural settings for their own engagement and their control. And secondly, the reproduction of critical competence itself should be a criterion for the design of orders in which consumers can and should make their voice heard (Lamla 2019, p. 53). This means that contrary to the tendency towards algorithmization and hybridization of digital evaluation practices, the infrastructures of consumer participation should be designed in the future in such a way that the plurality and conflictuality of different orders and registers of valuation remain tangible and thus maintain the pressure for public criticism and justification.

In the article mentioned at the beginning regarding the network of consumers, Christoph Bieber and I finally also looked at such initiatives that have actively turned to the design of digital infrastructures and did not just want to use them passively, namely the Wikipedia community, which has always thought and debated about its own criteria and procedures of (e)valuation, as well as the initiative of the 'Freifunker', who advocated for non-commercial, open WLan networks and a culture of broadband sharing (Bieber and Lamla 2005, p. 71 ff.). Their enthusiasm for infrastructure appropriation seems to have largely evaporated in consumer policy from below today. But in the area of valuation practices, such design enthusiasm is more necessary than ever.

References

Bauer, Susanne, Torsten Heinemann, and Thomas Lemke, eds. 2017. *Science and Technology Studies. Klassische Positionen und aktuelle Perspektiven*. Berlin: Suhrkamp.

Bennett, Lance W. 2004. Branded political communication: Lifestyle politics, logo campaigns, and the rise of global citizenship. In *Politics, products, and markets. Exploring political consumerism past and present*, eds. M. Micheletti, A. Follesdal, and D. Stolle, 101–125. New Brunswick: Transaction Publishers.

Bieber, Christoph, and Jörn Lamla. 2005. Das Netz der Konsumenten. Innovationschancen der Verbraucherbewegung im Internet. *Forschungsjournal Neue Soziale Bewegungen* 18 (4): 65–77.

Blühdorn, Ingolfur. 2013. *Simulative Demokratie. Neue Politik nach der postdemokratischen Wende*. Berlin: Suhrkamp.

Boltanski, Luc, and Laurent Thévenot. 2007. *Über die Rechtfertigung. Eine Soziologie der kritischen Urteilskraft*. Hamburg: Hamburger Edition.

Diaz-Bone, Rainer, ed. 2011. *Soziologie der Konventionen. Grundlagen einer pragmatischen Anthropologie*. Frankfurt a. M.: Campus.

Engemann, Christoph. 2018. Rekursionen über Körper. Machine Learning-Trainingsdatensätze als Arbeit am Index. In *Machine Learning – Medien, Infrastrukturen und Tech-*

nologien der Künstlichen Intelligenz, eds. C. Engemann and A. Sudmann, 247–268. Bielefeld: transcript.

Habermas, Jürgen. 1985. *Der philosophische Diskurs der Moderne. Zwölf Vorlesungen*. Frankfurt a. M.: Suhrkamp.

Hirschman, Albert O. 1984. *Engagement und Enttäuschung. Über das Schwanken der Bürger zwischen Privatwohl und Gemeinwohl*. Frankfurt a. M.: Suhrkamp.

Klein, Naomi. 2002. *No Logo! Der Kampf der Global Players um Marktmacht. Ein Spiel mit vielen Verlierern und wenigen Gewinnern*, 2nd edn. Pößneck: Riemann.

Kropf, Jonathan, and Stefan Laser, eds. 2019. *Digitale Bewertungspraktiken. Für eine Bewertungssoziologie des Digitalen*. Wiesbaden: Springer VS.

Lamla, Jörn. 2008. Markt-Vergemeinschaftung im Internet. Das Fallbeispiel einer Shopping- und Meinungsplattform. In *Posttraditionale Gemeinschaften. Theoretische und ethnographische Erkundungen*, eds. Ronald Hitzler, Anne Honer, and Michaela Pfadenhauer, 170–185. Wiesbaden: VS Verlag.

Lamla, Jörn. 2013. *Verbraucherdemokratie. Politische Soziologie der Konsumgesellschaft*. Berlin: Suhrkamp.

Lamla, Jörn. 2019. Selbstbestimmung und Verbraucherschutz in der Datenökonomie. *Aus Politik und Zeitgeschichte* 24–26:49–54.

Lamont, Michèle. 2012. Toward a comparative sociology of valuation and evaluation. *Annual Review of Sociology* 38:201–221.

Latour, Bruno. 2007. *Eine neue Soziologie für eine neue Gesellschaft. Einführung in die Akteur-Netzwerk-Theorie*. Frankfurt a. M.: Suhrkamp.

Mau, Steffen. 2017. *Das metrische Wir. Über die Quantifizierung des Sozialen*. Berlin: Suhrkamp.

Mühlhoff, Rainer. 2019. Menschengestützte Künstliche Intelligenz. Über die soziotechnischen Voraussetzungen von ‚deep learning'. *Zeitschrift für Medienwissenschaft* 21:56–64. https://doi.org/10.25969/mediarep/12633.

Nassehi, Armin. 2019. *Muster. Theorie der digitalen Gesellschaft*. München: Beck.

Reckwitz, Andreas. 2017. *Die Gesellschaft der Singularitäten. Zum Strukturwandel der Moderne*. Berlin: Suhrkamp.

Scammell, Margaret. 2000. The internet and civic engagement: The age of the citizen-consumer. *Political Communication* 4:351–355.

Star, Susan Leigh. 2017. *Grenzobjekte und Medienforschung*. Bielefeld: transkript.

Thaler, Richard H., and Cass R. Sunstein. 2011. *Nudge. Wie man kluge Entscheidungen anstößt*. Berlin: Ullstein.

Wiener, Norbert. 1952. *Mensch und Menschmaschine. Kybernetik und Gesellschaft*. Frankfurt a. M.: Alfred Metzner Verlag.

Zuboff, Shoshana. 2018. *Das Zeitalter des Überwachungskapitalismus*. Frankfurt a. M.: Campus.

Zweig, Katharina A., Bernd Lachmann, Christian Montag, and Marc Herrlich. 2019. Kontinuierliches A/B-Testing zur Optimierung von Spielerbindung und Monetarisierung bei, Freemium'-Spielen. In *Paradoxien des Verbraucherverhaltens. Dokumentation der Jahreskonferenz 2017 des Netzwerks Verbraucherforschung*, eds. B. Blättel-Mink and P. Kenning, 43–57. Wiesbaden: Springer Gabler.

Jörn Lamla, born 1969, is Professor of Sociological Theory at the University of Kassel. He is also Director at the Research Center for Information System Design (ITeG) there and one of the founding directors of the Hessian Competence Centre for Responsible Digitalisation. In addition to digitalisation and recent developments in pragmatist sociological theory, one of his main areas of research is the political sociology of the consumer society and its significance in the transformation of democracy. In this context, he has been involved in consumer (policy) research for many years. He is currently the spokesperson for the coordination committee of the Federal Network for Consumer Research, which has its office at the Federal Ministry for the Environment, Nature Conservation, Nuclear Safety and Consumer Protection, and is a member of the scientific advisory board of the Competence Centre for Consumer Research in North Rhine-Westphalia.

Responsibility and Responsibilities

Political Science Perspectives on Consumer Responsibility

Kathrin Loer

Abstract

Consumers regularly make choices about specific products or services that have a range of consequences such as production conditions, environmental damage, or climate impacts. Responsible consumer decisions could therefore be politically desirable, raising the question of the role of responsibility in consumer policy. To systematically approach various facets of consumer responsibility, this chapter first deals with concepts of responsibility that may be relevant for consumer policy. On this basis, the chapter is dedicated to the concrete assumption of responsibility by the consumer, as this can ultimately lead to political action. It also focuses on consumer responsibility as an expectation for political decisions. The chapter concludes that even responsible consumers in complex consumer societies are dependent on support and provides arguments as to why government interventions in the market are still—or perhaps increasingly—necessary.

Keywords

Sustainable development · Political instruments · Regulation · Consumer responsibility · Behavior · Behavioral policy · Civil society

---

K. Loer (✉)
Fakultät für Wirtschafts- und Sozialwissenschaften, University of Applied Sciences, Osnabrück, Germany
e-mail: k.loer@hs-osnabrueck.de

K.-U. Hellmann et al. (eds.), *Consumer Policy from Below*,
https://doi.org/10.1007/978-3-658-44478-5_6

1 Introduction

'Finally, young people are taking responsibility again' could be a spontaneous reaction when someone hears about the 'Fridays for future'[1] demonstrations, which have been taking place in many major cities initially in Europe, now worldwide since 2018. They are about demands for political, economic, and sometimes also social change, necessary to implement and adhere to the goals formulated in the Paris Climate Agreement through appropriate measures. However, often the praising reactions or generally positive comments meet criticism and doubt, beyond the question of what specific motivation (absence from school) is behind the commitment, there are doubts concerning the lifestyle of the demonstrators: Does their lifestyle match what they demand? Are they truly sustainably living consumers? Do the demonstrators take responsibility for their purchases in their everyday decisions as consumers?

But what is consumer responsibility, actually? Does it mean that the consumer takes responsibility for his or her actions voluntarily or out of individual need? Or does it mean that responsibility is transferred to the consumer so that certain (consumer) political goals can be achieved? The first question leads to a consideration of how individual and intrinsic consumer behavior affects the market, and in what forms it can develop into political action, a 'consumer policy from below'. From the second perspective on the consumer, the immediate subsequent question arises about the appropriate instruments for political actors, but also about the extent to which providers of products and services can or should ensure that the consumer can fulfil the responsibility attributed to him or her and thus initiate a 'consumer policy from below'. In this case, political measures of varying bindingness are available. Less in the sense of general (consumer) policy goals, but starting from the state's duty to protect, the question also arises as to how far

---

[1] Starting as 'Skolstrejk för klimatet', a protest action by Swedish student Greta Thunberg, it is now regularly organized by students worldwide, including in Germany. During the usual school hours on Friday mornings, students demonstrate, with participation levels varying greatly, but shaping a comprehensive discourse primarily in Europe. This discourse, based on universal dimensions of responsibility (Banzhaf 2016, p. 4), can be classified as the next step towards taking responsibility for nature and future generations. Even though "Fridays for future" is a current movement of the late 2010s, its concerns correspond to what Banzhaf describes as the demands of Rawlsian responsibility ethics (Rawls 1975), on the basis of which he concludes that "[c]ontinuous destruction of the basis of life, unchecked global warming or millennia-long radioactive waste […] cannot be justified towards future generations" (Banzhaf 2016, p. 4).

the responsibility of the consumer extends or can extend when it comes to risky products or services, or when it comes to the consumer or citizen contributing his share to a collective good (Loer 2016).

These initial questions already suggest that a spectrum of political options opens up, that can contribute to the further development of consumer policy in the sense of 'consumer policy from below'. The following will illustrate the paradoxes, perspectives, and problematizations (and problem structures) that occur in political action when it comes to consumer responsibility. The focus is not only on consumer protection policy or an explicitly so-called consumer policy. Because a politically relevant responsibility of the consumer (both intrinsically motivated and addressed by state measures) can be identified very fundamentally for a multitude of political issues in different policy fields. In doing so, the claim to consumer responsibility encounters challenges and generates a number of contradictions, especially in free market economies where consumers are accustomed to certain lifestyles and comfort.

Collective goods such as a high level of environmental protection, the reduction of CO_2 emissions, or even free traffic routes through reduced traffic can only be created if a critical mass of consumers behave in a certain way as continuously as possible. If there is a deficiency, such as a significant amount of environmental pollution, too high CO_2 emissions, or congested traffic routes, consumers may have to break familiar and popular routines to contribute to the political goal. In particular, the broad field of sustainability[2] covers a wide range of issues such as ecology, environment, climate, health, animal welfare, transport, trade and much more. In addition, other areas can be outlined in which consumer responsibility comes into play in its various dimensions; even social policy always requires an element of responsibility from each individual in order to function and especially to remain functional in systems designed for solidarity. In social policy, consumer responsibility can also be essential when the state withdraws from its responsibility and increasingly takes the individual into responsibility, who has to or must provide for his (social and financial) security privately. The transitions between

[2] The 'Oslo Roundtable on Sustainable Production and Consumption' (as one of the follow-up conferences to the 'Earth Summit', which took place as a summit of the United Nations on Environment and Development in June 1992 in Rio de Janeiro) formulated a definition for sustainable consumption in 1994: "goods and services that respond to basic needs and bring a better quality of life, while minimising the use of natural resources, toxic materials and emissions of waste and pollutants over the life cycle, so as not to jeopardise the needs of future generations" (https://enb.iisd.org/consume/oslo004.html, last: 02.01.2020).

expressly assigned responsibility, the protective function of the state with regard to risks for the consumer (products and services) and individually borne consumer responsibility, out of self-interest or altruistic motives, are often fluid, as will be explained below. In addition, although forms of a 'consumer policy from below' can be systematically differentiated within the political system and outside this system, i.e. exclusively in the market. However, the two spheres are so intertwined that the exercise of responsibility in each can also condition or at least influence the other.

In concrete terms, it becomes apparent that consumer behavior and thus the responsibility of the consumer for his or her actions play or should play an important political role, but at the same time faces challenges and contradictions in a complex field of action. Not only the complexity of political fields of action provokes paradoxes. In addition, guiding motives for action that go beyond a value-oriented assumption of responsibility for consumer behavior are likely to be very influential. These include in particular economic motives (price) and loss of comfort, but also cultural influences, habits and behaviour patterns that are difficult to break.

In order to systematically approach the various facets of consumer responsibility as a 'consumer policy from below', the following explanations first deal with a concept of responsibility as it can be relevant for consumer policy. After this introduction, the following subchapters are dedicated to the concrete assumption of responsibility by the consumer, as it can ultimately become political action. On the other hand, the focus is on consumer responsibility as an expectation for political decisions. Both facets of consumer responsibility in the sense of a 'consumer policy from below' are illustrated and explained by means of concrete examples, this serves as a basis for highlighting problematic structures, paradoxes and perspectives.

2 Concepts of Responsibility: What does Responsibility Mean in Consumer Policy?

Very fundamentally, consumer responsibility can be understood as part of the comprehensive responsibility of humans for economic, political, and social developments in the spheres of life that are essentially shaped by market logic. However, the responsibility for the character, development, and effects of global market events, starting from such a fundamental perspective, does not lie exclusively with the consumer. He shares it with governments, which can regulate markets to varying degrees, and market actors, i.e., the companies that are active in the markets (Schmidt 2016, p. 9; Schoenheit 2009; Luchs and Miller 2017, p. 261). Consumers can then take responsibility when they make certain consumption decisions, which they do voluntarily and consciously, depending on their personal values and beliefs (Luchs and Miller 2017, p. 255).

Values and beliefs, in turn, can change and vary individually. Even though the discourse on sustainability and the environmental impact of consumption have been shaping the values and beliefs of consumers since the 1990s at the latest, and especially since the 2010s the discussion on climate change, values and beliefs (normative background) can also be identified as guiding action, for example, in relation to individual and collective health, human rights, or cultural aspects. Consumer science outlines a broad spectrum of phenomena in which consumer responsibility can be observed, these are not sharply distinguishable from each other, which is why we can also speak of 'global consumer responsibility' (Beck 2018). Given global value chains, working conditions, social injustice and economic inequality, the consequences of climate change manifested in environmental damage and natural disasters, but also various forms of violence in production processes are interconnected and ultimately also condition health and cultural developments along the entire value chain (Beck 2018, p. 54).

Ultimately, it is always a matter of the individual consumer assuming responsibility for the purchase of a product or service and being accountable to an external or internal authority (Schmidt 2016, p. 6), this can be one's own conscience (internal authority) or the social community, a court, a state authority, etc. (external authorities). In this respect, common concepts of consumer responsibility are completely rationally shaped; they assume a consciously acting actor and exclude intuitive action.

However, for this form of conscious assumption of responsibility to become political action, further conditions must be met. The fact that responsibility can be assumed at all can be linked to prerequisites, as Heidbrink and Schmidt explain, citing Auhagen 1999: "People are then willing to take responsibility when they have freedom, identify with their intentions, and can influence their actions" (Heidbrink and Schmidt 2009, p. 29). With regard to consumer behaviour, it should be added that there must be a basic willingness and a non-threatening possibility to abstain, or, depending on the product or service and life situation, consumption and action alternatives must be available. Schmidt (2016) also points out that in order to take responsibility there must be hope that responsible consumer behavior can actually make a difference. This spectrum of criteria, which can ultimately also be applied for the attribution of responsibility, corresponds with Aristotle's concept of responsibility, to which Schmidt also refers (2016, p. 7): causality, freedom, knowledge, and intentionality.

This attribution of responsibility proves to be extremely difficult in relation to consumer behavior. Given global value chains and a confusing selection of different products and services in many areas, the transfer of such a responsibility model is tied to many factors: There must actually be a causal connection between the consumer decision and the product, which means that the consumer must be able to effectively influence production, sales (conditions), use, and disposal[3] with his purchase decision. For this influence, there must be suitable channels and refusal action. The consumer must have the freedom and privilege to decide against the product or service, so there must be options for renunciation, reduction, or substitution. They must also have information and, ultimately, an interest in change.[4]

The idea that the consumer alone shapes these conditions in order to take responsibility for his or her consumption behavior is likely to be unrealistic in complex consumer societies. In this respect, collective actors, both government organizations, companies, and non-governmental organizations, share a responsibility to shape these conditions. Individuals, civil society organizations, market actors, and state actors are always in a reciprocal relationship: State actors can be called upon by individuals (see Sect. 3) to regulate market actors, for example, impose information or transparency obligations on them and control these (Baringhorst et al. 2007, p. 14). Market actors can voluntarily become active in the sense of a prospective or retrospective attribution of responsibility, which they fulfill for example for reasons of reputation (Beck 2018, p. 56 f.).

Interestingly, consumer research shows that it is primarily in recent times that there has been a shift towards forms of 'responsibilization' of the consumer, i.e., a shifting of responsibility onto the consumer by state and market actors. Evans points out that there is an individualization of responsibility and consumers are simultaneously held accountable (Evans et al. 2017, p. 1399). In this context, Giesler and Veresiu (2014) identify four processes (based on Shamir's P.A.C.T.

[3] Systematically, different aspects can be differentiated for each product and service for which the consumer can be (co)responsible: the effects 1) of production or provision 2) of sales and use and 3) of disposal that are inherent to a product, see also Luchs and Miller (2017, p. 261); these aspects can have economic, social, and environmental impacts.

[4] See also Young (2013) on influence and power, privileges, interest, and collective capabilities.

concept 2008) that are intended to contribute to the creation of a 'responsible consumer subject' (Giesler and Veresiu 2014, p. 841): Personalization (P), Authorization (A), Capabilization (C), and Transformation (T). Personalization means that the consumer must make a responsible decision in relation to a social, economic, or ecological problem as a morally enlightened individual, as opposed to an irresponsible consumer. Authorization means that market actors and state institutions economically and morally justify the transfer of responsibility to the consumer by demonstrating that he can assume this responsibility because economic, psychological, and other scientific findings prove these abilities in studies and thus relieve state actors and market actors of responsibility. To ensure that the assumption of responsibility is successful, consumers should be empowered (this corresponds to the Foucauldian concept of governmentality), so that a market of products and services for such self-management emerges. Finally, it also requires the transformation of the individual into this responsible subject, which adopts a, possibly new, moral self-understanding suitable from a higher perspective (sustainability, economic efficiency, health, etc.) and can align its actions accordingly (Giesler and Veresiu 2014, p. 841). The two authors criticize this development and confront it with realistic consumer behavior (ibid., 854).

Notwithstanding this criticism, the demands on the responsible consumer in many political and economic contexts are likely to be shaped by the ideas in the sense of the P.A.C.T. concept. This is because many government organizations and especially companies have an interest in holding the consumer accountable and thus avoiding political disputes about responsibility. This is particularly the case when, for political reasons, be they national policy objectives or international agreements, certain patterns of behaviour are expected in order to achieve certain policy goals that would otherwise only be achievable through strict regulation, which in turn is politically unattractive and would be attacked by market actors (e.g., for effective climate protection). This brings to mind the idea of the 'bottom-of-the-pyramid' (bop), i.e., the integration of previously neglected population groups into certain market concepts and value chains, which can be marketed as "poverty reduction" but serves in a special way to tap into labor potential and sales markets in the interests of internationally active companies. Other goals are likely to extend to ecology in the sense of the 'green' consumer, if this can have not only environmental but also economic benefits from the perspective of government organizations and companies. Furthermore, it can be about strengthening health awareness or 'financial literacy', which can also serve the well-being of the individual, but is often associated with the dismantling of social security systems and their shift to the private market. Attributions of responsibility are therefore often politically charged and are likely to be particularly interest-driven by market forces in the cases described. Empirical studies will have to show to what extent the active assumption of responsibility by the consumer, which is provoked by the processes described, can be transformed into a 'consumer policy from below' that pursues opposing interests and even resists this burden of responsibility. However, contradictions can already be identified conceptually. On the one hand, there is talk of responsibility in the sense of P.A.C.T. logic; and the various concepts, from 'bop' to 'green' or health-conscious consumer to 'financial literacy', presuppose a certain degree of personal responsibility. But these concepts ignore the need for an individual moral background, which is crucial in general concepts of responsibility, because shifting responsibility ultimately makes it necessary to influence the moral background of the individual.

However, the fact that consumers can in principle develop the ability to take responsibility in complex product and service markets also depends on companies and, in particular, on political actors who can and must provide support and influence, even without such a conscious and interest-driven shift of responsibility as described above. Only in this way can consumers be empowered and authorized to take responsibility (Schmidt 2016, p. 15). Ideally, this should happen independently of specific corporate interests, which, however, is likely to be a criterion that is hardly feasible in political practice. To enable consumers as acting subjects to take responsibility, state actors and organizations have various instruments at their disposal (see Sect. 4). Empirical studies would also have to show to what extent the choice and design of the instruments is politically charged and thus shapes attributions of responsibility politically.

Consumers themselves can act in a number of ways to express their sense of responsibility, even without being prompted to do so by political action: They can migrate, i.e. not buy the product or service (boycott), or behave loyally as a consumer (buycott) in order to strengthen a certain product or market segment and thus weaken another. They can also express their opinions about products and services, which can even lead to political pressure on companies (Beck 2018, p. 64 f.). They can also support NGOs so that they can act effectively by pooling resources. In addition, traditional forms of political influence in democracies are available to them: elections, lobbying political representatives, and active political engagement, for example in political parties. Consumers can also exert some influence through appropriate response behaviour (related to their normative background) in consumer surveys for market research (Luchs and Miller 2017, p. 255 in modification of Devinney et al. 2006, p. 3).

Conceptually, the consumer operates in an area of tension: in a free market economy, the consumer still has almost complete freedom to consume products and services. They are free to choose to abstain or to buy, and to link this action to their individual values and beliefs. However, external influences are likely to play an important role in the transmission of information, the availability of choices and, ultimately, the emergence of moral and ethical reference points (media, etc.). However, they must have access to appropriate and reliable information. He must be able to process it and actually abstain or abstain, which requires financial resources and sometimes even the availability of an alternative. Especially when consumer responsibility is linked to a higher political interest, appropriate policy instruments are needed to strengthen this consumer responsibility (see Sect. 4). In addition to responsible consumption, consumers can also become politically active (see Sect. 3)

This conceptual view of consumer responsibility gives an impression that the discussion about consumer responsibility is always political; it is always a balancing act between attributing responsibility to the consumer, his active responsible consumer behavior, and the assumption of responsibility by the state or government organizations (regional, national or international), especially when there are information and power asymmetries in the market between companies and consumers. The question of to what extent consumers can assume responsibility on the one hand, but also which instances (internal and external) consumers refer to, determines the character of a 'consumer policy from below'.

3 Responsibility: Assumption of Responsibility by the Consumer

In order not to anticipate the following chapters on consumer participation and consumer policy actors, an overview will be given here of the basic forms of action that are conceivable for the assumption of responsibility by consumers in the sense of a "consumer policy from below", the paradoxes to which this action can lead and the perspectives that result from it: The choice of coffee in the morning, the way it is prepared, the choice of transport to work, the shopping for food and clothes, the heating of the apartment or house, the use of digital services, all these have a direct or indirect impact on what resources will be available in the future, under what conditions products and services will be produced or provided, and how living conditions in a community or region will develop. When a critical mass of consumers makes the use of a product or service dependent on overarching goals, when they recognize their own responsibility in it,[5] that their own market activity has an influence and they consistently align their market actions with it, this form of responsibility becomes political action and can be classified as 'consumer politics from below'. This responsible market action can take various forms.

Consumers can, theoretically, take responsibility on their own every day, without governmental impetus, to achieve certain goals in which they believe. In a free market, this is direct political influence on the market when consumers, out of conviction, make their purchasing decisions dependent on overarching values in order to consciously take responsibility. However, this is likely to become politically significant only if it is not just individual consumers, but rather a market-relevant number of consumers, and if the respective consumers make their actions noticeably (media-wise) public. Consumer science refers to this as discursive political consumption. An example of this is culture jamming, which Stolle (2018, p. 7) describes as a technique to "use a company symbol and humorously draw attention to problems in the production process." In addition, the use of social media (Instagram, Twitter, Facebook) offers a wide range of opportunities for discursive political consumption. However, these platforms are always also areas of action for market providers (companies).

Political consumption has a concrete impact on the market when reduced demand (as a result of a boycott) has an economic impact on suppliers of products or services or, conversely, increased demand (as a result of a boycott) leads to the market success of certain suppliers. This then leads to the "bundling of consumer power" (Lamla 2018, p. 28) to bring about changes in companies. This differs from traditional forms of political participation within the political system where consumer interests become political activity in the sense of taking responsibility. Political consumption can thus be understood as a 'consumer politics from below', which in turn is closely linked to the question of which reference points (moral background) consumers orient themselves towards in the sense of their assumption of responsibility. This does not necessarily have to lead to a confrontation between consumers and market providers, where the state may then act as a mediator or supporter (see Sect. 4). Consumer forces can also, together with market actors, exert political power through their economic actions. This form of

[5] In principle, it is also conceivable that there could be uniform market behavior by chance, which in turn has an effect on market events. However, in this case, it is not clear to identify to what extent this is more of a fashion or whether responsibility in a normative sense is actually guiding action.

political rationality of market actors, who act consciously, can under certain circumstances lead to the destabilization of established power relations, as Giesler and Veresiu (2014) describe in an example. They refer to early forms of consumer responsibility in the sense of political activity in the coffee houses of the Ottoman Empire. There, coffee house consumers had formed an alliance with market institutions to politically challenge state and religious authorities (Giesler and Veresiu 2014, p. 853). Other forms of political consumption that are directed against state authorities are also conceivable. However, especially in current market situations (including subtle forms of advertising and 'consumer information'), the question quickly arises as to how independent consumers actually are from market actors and on what basis they ultimately act (can) in the sense of their responsibility. Research that deals with the construction of new consumer identities and reveals how advertisers, marketing and brand experts consciously choose strategies to convey certain narratives to consumers about products and brands, which they may use in their political consumption in line with their good conscience or conviction, possibly also in contradiction to state authorities, points to this.[6] Not only as a demonstration of certain political interests towards state actors, but also in the sense of sales promotion, marketing strategies of companies can trigger an expected sense of responsibility to motivate the consumer to consume certain products or services. This has recently been observed in the food sector in particular ('regional', 'healthy', 'local', 'controlled growing conditions' etc.).

Another facet of 'consumer politics from below', which goes beyond a narrow focus on consumer politics, is described by Stolle (2018). She classifies political consumption as a new form of political participation or civic engagement, which stands in contrast to the talk of 'political apathy'. This development, according to Stolle (2018, p. 5),

> "is often, but not exclusively, associated with […] a sense of responsibility. We therefore see in it a kind of transformation of how people participate in politics. Political consumption is thus part of this transformation, which takes political challenges into its own hands, without waiting for help from the government or political parties."

Such forms of responsibility-taking can also form the basis for political participation in civil society organizations. In addition to the form described above, expressing consumer responsibility through market action, it can therefore

[6] An overview of this research can be found in Giesler and Veresiu (2014, p. 853).

happen that consumers consciously and purposefully organize as a social group with the aim of taking responsibility, in order to express their own interest either towards political actors and/or to exert sufficient (market) power. When a critical mass of consumers behaves in a certain way for a certain (possibly not clearly recognizable from the outside) motive, i.e., consciously avoids (boycott) or consciously chooses (buycott) products or services, they can thus generate a (market) political effect. Micheletti (2003) speaks in this context of the 'politics behind products' and emphasizes that a value-driven consumer behavior in the market expresses a certain understanding of social and normative conditions that are associated with the respective product. This is likely to be the case when sufficient information about the product is available and this information does not provoke contradictory options for value-driven behavior. For example, one might consciously choose regional agricultural products with an eco-label, but it may not be known to what extent the products also meet social requirements, for example with regard to working conditions in production, transport or trade and sales. This example shows that, for value-driven consumer behaviour, it is often necessary for an independent body to ensure that the relevant information is available. (see Sect. 4).

In order to provide enlightenment, to persuade producers to release information or to oblige them to certain production methods, consumer policy organizations can in turn influence political actors.[7] However, the civil society formation of consumer interests represents a particularly challenging undertaking. As Claus Offe pointed out in the 1980s, the heterogeneity of consumer interests (diversity of issues, diversity of interests in individual issues) makes it difficult to organise them (bottom-up) (Offe 1981). Finally, even individuals can have conflicting interests, which makes their formation more difficult. Moreover, it can be assumed that citizens, and thus consumers, are less likely to join formal and traditional civil society organisations in recent times, preferring instead informal, fluid and personal, sometimes even individualised forms of social relations (Putnam 2002, p. 411). This can be useful in terms of a 'bottom-up' consumer policy. For example, such activities of consumers can be observed as informal groupings; they appear as spontaneous organisation of protest actions or flash mobs and lead to the mobilisation of networks that may initially have been formed only virtually (Stolle et al. 2005, p. 250). To what extent participation in such actions can actually be traced back to a conscious assumption of responsibility by individu-

[7] For the options for action for political actors, see Sect. 4.

als and depends on it, however, remains ultimately open. It is conceivable that a certain social cascade (Sunstein 2019) is triggered and individual consumers within a group of like-minded people or peers join a narrative that then shapes the emergence of a certain action. The supposed reference to certain values and convictions that unite this group from an external perspective (narrative) could demonstrate common consumer responsibility without actually examining and consciously aligning values and beliefs. However, future research still has to show to what extent such active consumer political action ultimately constitutes more than the appearance of responsibility-taking, and which (other) forces influence the mobilization (herd instinct, desire for social inclusion regardless of consumer-relevant values, etc.).

Interestingly, the emphasis, that is, a public articulation, of responsibility can also be thought of directly or indirectly from (at least) two directions; both can unfold high potential for politicization. Either the problematization of a certain consumer behavior originates from consumers themselves, who identify connections, perceive their responsibility and want to generate pressure for action by rallying more consumers to their cause. This can be the case, in particular, when consumers are personally affected by a problem (environmental pollution, health damage, etc.) or they have good access to certain information that points to the discrepancies between their own moral background and the properties of a product or service. Or the appeal to consumer responsibility comes from outside, for example from market providers, who may also use this as a marketing factor; addressing the responsible consumer can strengthen the bond to a product or service because it may generate a 'good feeling' in the consumer. This could lead to a power play between market actors with comparable products or services, if the providers convey to the consumer that he can only fulfill his sense of responsibility with their own products, but not with those of the competitor. The call to take responsibility can also come from state actors, as discussed in the following chapter (see Sect. 4).

Regardless of whether it is a random, spontaneous or targeted, permanent formation of consumers who want to express their sense of responsibility through certain activities in the market or in the political space, the question arises to what extent this is actually political participation, i.e., whether one can speak of a 'consumer politics from below' in this way. Arguments can be found in research that recognise activities beyond traditional forms of participation as politically relevant, but this is countered by the warning that this could lead to any form of participation being labelled 'political'. Stolle et al. (2005, p. 250) demand empirical evidence in this context through research that shows how forms of participation in different spheres, the political sphere on the one hand and other spheres on the other, can be distinguished from each other. Recent research suggests that the (new) forms of participation, in which private and public-political spheres as well as the roles of citizens and consumers are blurred, are a sign of a certain development that needs to be critically assessed. Thus, Thompson and Kumar (2018, p. 2) classify "these market-oriented redefinitions of social activism" as "emblematic of an ongoing neoliberal colonization of the political field." In this way, there is a stylization of the ethical, sustainably acting consumer, who, however, moves in a market that in turn serves the 'carbon intensive consumer lifestyles'. The fact that market providers create an "ethical aura" (ibid., p. 3) leads to the seemingly responsible consumer believing to support a certain political goal with his consumption, without advocating for sustainable conditions for production and trade (e.g., development and successful implementation of standards) (ibid., pp. 2 f.). This can even degenerate into an 'alternative hedonism'. Thus, Caruana and Eckhardt (2019) have worked out the example of alternative tourism, which is ultimately enjoyed as a special expression of sustainable living, but is then contrasted with 'mass tourism', but also follows market logics and causes negative effects. The anti-capitalist argument of Thompson and Kumar (2018) points to the generally fundamental paradox that the logic of market economies, as they are now constituted, causes certain consequential effects along the entire value chains. In terms of certain values or beliefs, the only way to consistently assume consumer responsibility is often to abstain from consumption, combined with political influence to change the conditions of production etc.

The extent to which these consequences are problematised depends on political power relations and the conditions for articulating and disseminating certain information in democratic market economies. Ultimately, the problematisation of these consequences must be understood and classified politically when it is or is to be transported to a (wider) public. For it always has a (market) political effect when it meets the appropriate recipients. The use of media often plays a decisive role in this. The speed of information dissemination and its penetration is particularly intensified by the influence of social media (Twitter, Facebook, Instagram, relevant blogs or forums, etc.); (social) media are also likely to contribute to the fact that contexts are constructed in a particularly politicized form when the senders of the messages promise themselves better political penetration. More or less concretely, the authors and senders of such information must have an understanding of which values and norms can actually have guiding effects for consumers. This can always lead to manipulation, as it is used, for example, in company marketing strategies. An external impetus for further problematization can also be triggered by other factors: spontaneous events that lead to scandalization (e.g., food scandals), scientific findings, or the exposure of grievances by journalists, for example, can be triggers for consumers to change their market activities.

For Germany, the in-depth study by the Federal Environment Agency points to the challenges that even responsible consumers face:

> "For many people, there is an increasing impression of "complicated mixtures" […], in which citizens hardly know their way around and can increasingly hardly recognize what should be done and what should be left on the individual and everyday level. Many people in the population are exposed to growing material, temporal, and psychological pressure in everyday life. This contributes to the fact that cost and convenience aspects play a larger role. Sustainable and ecologically correct behaviors often conflict with the requirements of immediate everyday coping." (Schipperges et al. 2016, p. 16 f.)

Even though this study is dedicated to environmental awareness in Germany, similar findings are likely to apply to other fields of consumer policy, in a broad sense; this applies to individual health care, i.e., health-conscious behavior to avoid chronic diseases, which ultimately have not only individual but also collective effects (cost burden in the health care system, loss of work, etc.) (comprehensive Ewert and Loer 2019). This also applies to issues of leisure time behaviour and mobility (e.g. private transport). The assumption of consumer responsibility through everyday consumer behaviour in the sense of an effective "consumer policy from below" is therefore subject to certain limits. It is therefore not surprising that there are calls for incentives for both consumers and entrepreneurs (suppliers) to be designed in such a way that change actually occurs (for the example of carbon emissions comprehensive Zaks et al. 2009).

4 Interim Conclusion I

In terms of active responsibility taken by consumers, it can be concluded that the individualization of lifestyles, the strong focus on markets and consumption, conflicting responsibilities and new forms of communication often result in a diffuse and often unpredictable 'consumer policy from below'. This takes a different form than one would expect from traditional forms of civil society engagement. Digital platforms and forums may not be clearly identifiable in their intention. The complexity of reference points and the ambiguity of consumption effects can be addressed and exploited in different ways by the various actors (consumers, companies and state actors). It can be expected that 'consumer policy from below' will not always develop in a targeted manner in the future. Forms of a 'consumer policy from below' can be expected to emerge whenever consumers can align their responsibility with other factors influencing their market behavior (e.g., prices (economic resources), availability of options in the political sphere and/or product or service alternatives, as well as the ability to break certain habits, accept comfort losses). Such a balance in the sense of consumer responsibility is highly conditional for the reasons outlined above. Ultimately, all variants of responsibility-based 'consumer policy from below' always depend on the information available to consumers and their resources for action.

The information that ultimately leads the consumer to responsible market behaviour is now supposedly more readily available, especially digitally, but is also subject to the risk of manipulation or at least uncertainty as to source and quality.The consumer needs to be able to distinguish between reliable and unreliable information and to independently process relevant or appropriate information in order to relate it to his or her own beliefs and values. Even without manipulative action, contradictions arise because certain values and beliefs cannot be found in relation to all factors (resource extraction, working conditions, environmental impacts, economic, social and health consequences in relation to production, trade, purchase and disposal) that affect products and services throughout the value chain. Ultimately, public authorities in particular can help to ensure that markets are regulated in the interests of consumer responsibility, that companies provide certain information and that publicly available information is made available to consumers.

5 Responsibility: Expectations of the Consumer in the Political Sphere

When political actors refer to consumer responsibility, they do so in the context of their own political interests. It may be politically opportune and attractive to appeal to consumers' sense of responsibility of consumers in order to achieve certain goals, such as in climate and energy policy, public health issues (vaccination) or social policy issues (solidarity community). In this context, certain expectations of the consumer play a role in how they should ultimately behave, which in turn can affect the assumption of responsibility for their own behavior. Conceptually, two variants of consumer responsibility can be distinguished with regard to the political sphere: On the one hand, there can be a, more or less, diffuse idea of how consumers assume or can assume responsibility. This idea can be influenced by how political actors wish consumer responsibility to be (normative, ideological). The situation is different with the perception of how citizens as consumers actually behave in the market or in their everyday life, which can deviate from the political wish. This is particularly evident, for example, in mobility behaviour: In many urban areas, political actors would like to see fewer cars used for private transport and a successful switch to alternative means of transport (public transport, bicycles, etc.). In reality, despite much discussion about individual responsibility, the actual behaviour of individuals often runs counter to this, which is why not only are roads overcrowded, but many urban areas also suffer from poor air quality.

Political actors can attempt to identify the extent to which responsibility, i.e., a connection between purchasing and consumption decisions with individual values and beliefs, plays a role in at least three different ways: 1) as everyday, possibly anecdotal perception and observation of consumer behavior, which is then interpreted by political actors in terms of corresponding values, 2) as obviously recognizable or conveyed responsible consumer behavior (e.g., buy-cotts or boycotts) or 3) scientifically determined as a study result of consumer sciences, which prove that certain beliefs and values shape consumer behavior. The first variant, i.e., what political actors perceive as everyday and anecdotal consumer behavior, can be a subjective impression that mixes with the idea of how political actors would like consumer responsibility to be. It is an interpretation of observations and considerations about motives for consumer behavior, which can deviate from the actual motives underlying decisions. So far, there is no systematic research on the extent and manner in which concrete ideas of and demands for responsible behaviour influence political action and lead to the selection and combination of different political instruments.

A number of policy instruments can be distinguished, addressing both consumers and businesses. These instruments can be related to consumer responsibility. The spectrum ranges from prohibitions and mandates as instruments with the greatest depth of intervention, where the authority of the state is fully exercised, through incentive control (economic and social) to a broad portfolio of informational instruments (provision of information, labeling, education, etc.) and organizational instruments (round tables, initiation of voluntary agreements, organization of consulting services, expert groups, etc.), which can also include infrastructure measures (Loer 2019a). If the state uses prohibitions or mandates, it assumes responsibility, possibly also on the basis of normative considerations. This can be the case, in particular, when it is expected that neither market actors in the design of their offers, nor consumers on their own will change their decisions, but these are politically desired. An example of this are the non-smoking protection laws.[8] If it were about the protection of non-smokers, the expectation could prevail that every individual smoker is aware of the harm to non-smokers in their presence (at least when the effects of passive smoking are known to the respective smokers) and therefore refrains from tobacco consumption out of responsibility towards non-smokers. However, the example shows that the state does not expect such a sense of responsibility, but introduces clear rules to protect non-smokers. At the same time, state actors do not assume that private institutions (restaurants, etc.) would, without legal regulation, i.e., out of pure responsibility towards non-smoking customers (consumers), impose a smoking ban in their premises.

The use of incentives as a control instrument can have different characteristics. It can involve social incentives, which can also appeal to, generate, or utilize a sense of responsibility. An example of this can be found in Germany at many traffic lights: In addition to the color signals (red and green) of pedestrian lights, there are signs that read 'Only on green, setting an example for children'. Although this is an initiative by the traffic watch as an association (civil society organization), it takes on a socio-political function here and specifically uses social incentives as a control instrument.[9] The traffic watch assumes that there is a shared moral understanding that one's own behavior has an impact on other people (especially children in this case). Another form of incentive are taxes or subsidies, which are based on economic rationality. In terms of consumer responsibility, it is conceivable that an existing sense of responsibility should be supported, or that consumers lack a sense of responsibility, which is why an economic incentive should be set. This would be conceivable, for example, in terms of energy use in private households. In this case, existing responsibility (conviction to contribute individually to resource conservation, etc.) could be used, and a lack of responsibility could also be compensated for.

Government measures involving the provision and communication of information represent the starting point for consumer responsibility to arise at all. This should involve as neutral and transparent a communication of information as possible, for example about the conditions for the production of certain goods,

---

[8] In Germany, these are non-smoking protection laws with varying detailed regulations at the federal state level.

[9] The traffic watch is supported in its activities by state organizations, cf. https://www.muenchen.de/rathaus/Stadtverwaltung/Kreisverwaltungsreferat/Verkehr/Verkehrssteuerung/Nur-bei-Gruen.html (Accessed: 02.01.2020).

about usage options that are environmentally friendly or promote health, or also about disposal issues. If a certain sense of responsibility is expected, the form of presentation of information could also be crucial in helping consumers align their everyday decisions with their own values and beliefs in the sense of consumer responsibility.

Organisational tools can also be designed to encourage responsible consumer behaviour. A prominent example of this are the consumer advice centres in Germany, which offer a comprehensive range of services. Less permanent are individual campaigns, such as the German government's 2004 campaign to "activate the citizen consumer", which was carried out by the then consumer minister Künast (Alliance 90/The Greens) (detailed in Kneip and Niesyto 2007). Another example would be the initiation of voluntary commitments or agreements, e.g. by the food industry, which then ensures the certification and labelling of products to facilitate consumer responsibility (e.g. through appropriate labels). In this context, there is an increasing use of behaviourally informed policies that can increase the effectiveness of traditional instruments (Loer 2019b), such as changes in default values, the use of heuristics, anchoring effects or simplifications (Reisch and Zhao 2017).Finally, an important role in the assessment and evaluation of policy instruments is that they are always linked to a policy objective, which is preceded by a specific construction of the respective problem structure. Some examples will illustrate how expectations of consumer responsibility are dealt with in the political sphere.

6 Assistance in Taking Responsibility: Consumer Protection

A very close examination of consumer protection policy would likely include concepts of responsibility when it comes to the question of when or to what extent the state must fulfill its protective responsibility through appropriate action because the consumer cannot take on this responsibility themselves. The expectations of consumers are then indirectly or directly reflected in the contexts in which state regulations of products and services occur and how comprehensive these regulations are. For consumer protection policy, the initial decisive factor is likely to be in what context the responsibility of the consumer is problematized and thus becomes part of the political agenda. The fact that individual responsibility from the perspective of state actors reaches its limits can be illustrated by the institutionalization of organizations that ensure the introduction, review, and monitoring of product or service standards. Examples include the Technical Inspection Association (TÜV) or the Federal Institute for Drugs and Medical Devices (BFARM), which provide fixed routines for each product to ensure consumer protection. In a certain sense, the TÜV could also be understood as 'consumer policy from below', even if its members are not consumers, but companies that take responsibility for the consumer in this case. As a classic corporatist body, the various TÜVs in Germany fulfill state tasks in the sense of self-administration also in the sense of consumer protection and are closely linked with state control. Institutions like the TÜV are examples of the fact that the independent assumption of responsibility by the consumer reaches its limits and he would therefore be exposed to the risks of products or services without appropriate regulatory measures. The participation and support of consumer protection organizations could be classified as intermediary: Here, too, the state takes on responsibility, which is expressed, for example, in the financial support of institutions, these, however, should not completely relieve the consumer of responsibility, but enable him.

7 Problematic Consumer Behavior: Product Counterfeiting

The example of product counterfeiting illustrates a special area of consumer responsibility: Especially with certain brand products and a corresponding brand affinity of consumers, counterfeits can have a great appeal to price-conscious consumers. A study by Large (2015) discusses how the consumer can be held accountable in this context. She distinguishes two variants: One approach aims at educating the consumer through awareness campaigns. This approach is sometimes mixed with the idea of stigmatizing the purchase of counterfeits, it remains questionable whether there is actually a change in values and convictions that then trigger a change in behavior, or to what extent even the change in attitudes as a moral background can replace the primacy of the attractive price, so that consumers refrain from buying counterfeit products. Alternatively, the purchase of counterfeits could also be criminalized, i.e., result in criminal prosecution. This approach is likely to be effective when the respective values and convictions of consumers are actually in conflict with the price-conscious purchase of the counterfeit and he just needs support to stop buying counterfeit products. However, both variants assume that the consumer knows about the counterfeit. Therefore, the demand for consumer responsibility goes even further when it comes to every consumer having enough information to distinguish legal from illegal products (Large 2015, p. 182). A 'consumer policy from below' would be discussed in this case if consumers, in turn, based on corresponding values and convictions, ensure the stigmatization of counterfeit purchases (e.g., through peer-to-peer information in digital media, reference to providers who offer counterfeits, establishment of internet forums etc.).

8 Contradictory Consumer Behavior: Sustainable Development

Current debates about climate protection and more economical resource use often revolve around a few individual market activities, such as air travel or the purchase or use of cars (especially those with high CO_2 and/or particulate matter emissions). Ultimately, however, this discussion can be extended to an incalculable spectrum of products, each associated with a specific resource consumption for material, transport, marketing, and trade. The more differentiated the product, the more remote the production sites, the higher the price pressure in world trade, the more questions arise from ethical, environmental or climate-relevant as well as social perspectives. Responsible consumer behavior then presents itself as a crucial pillar in many policy areas in a free market economy when sustainability goals are to be achieved. In a study on environmental policy, Soneryd and Uggla (2015) have worked out how expectations from green governments can be directed at the individual to behave in an environmentally friendly manner and in line with sustainability goals, and what effects this has. They point out that there is even an emphasis on the consumer role in the first place (and secondary to the appeal to the citizen) to initiate responsible consumer behavior (Soneryd and Uggla 2015, p. 925 f.). The study comes to the interesting result that the state's encouragement to take responsibility even brings those consumers to active participation, to change everyday practices, whose moral background only partially corresponds with the conveyed values and can also partially contradict certain dimensions of responsibility. The direct address and formulation of expectations to the responsible consumer can also, as Soneryd and Uggla show, lead to rejection, criticism, and "anti-consumption" (Soneryd and Uggla 2015, p. 926). In liberal democracies, however, this also generates counter-positions, so that consumers, for example, in response to those who reject green consumption as a path to a sustainable society, organise themselves in NGOs and try to exert pressure on companies and government organisations. (Soneryd and Uggla 2015, p. 926). The example is intended to show how state measures on the one hand direct expectations at responsible consumers, this can simultaneously be the impetus for a double "consumer politics from below": On the one hand, the multiplication of individual behavior changes as a reaction to the state's impetus, which has market policy effects and on the other hand, the provocation of a societal discourse, which is expressed in active political participation.

9 Interim Conclusion II

Expectations of consumer responsibility by political actors can be identified in many policy areas, which go beyond the examples given. It can be expected that they will become more comprehensive, on the one hand, due to the importance of individual consumption, especially in matters of climate protection and sustainable development, and on the other hand, due to political interests in reducing state responsibility. At the same time, many consumer policy discussions, such as those on data protection, show that the state's claim to consumer responsibility can collide with the realistic conditions for responsible consumer behavior, even if these should be in the consumer's own interest. Accordingly, there are also doubts about the extent to which the provision of data protection-related information and education, in order to empower the consumer and transfer responsibility to him, is meaningful and ultimately effective in terms of consumer protection (e.g., Kamleitner in Kenning et al. 2018, p. 132). In addition, habits (especially in the context of a certain lifestyle level) and economic rationalities can conflict with values and convictions that would be necessary for responsible consumption. What Isenhour (2010) points out about consumer behavior in Sweden is likely to apply to many industrial and service societies: Only a small group of consumers consistently orient themselves in the sense of consumer responsibility and reduce the consumption of goods and services for sustainability policy reasons. Even for this group, the switch to more efficient products or the reduction of energy consumption encounters hurdles, for example, because no corresponding alternatives are available. These barriers, which are already difficult to overcome for responsible consumers in the sense of a sustainable policy, are probably insurmountable for those with less pronounced sense of responsibility (Isenhour 2010, p. 466). Therefore, Isenhour doubts to what extent the appeal or challenge of consumer responsibility by governments is sufficient to pursue effective sustainability policy. Efforts to promote a sustainable lifestyle and consumption behavior thus depend not only on appeals to consumer responsibility, but on very fundamental structural decisions to politically regulate markets in the interest of sustainability (ibid., p. 466). This corresponds with the demands of the 'Fridays for future' and other civil society climate policy organizations, which are active in the sense of a "consumer policy from below" and partly also applies to discourses in the political space: The everyday temptations and consumption options in the market economies as they are currently constituted, but also complexities 'behind' products and services provoke demands for more state regulation, so that consumers can act in accordance with their values and convictions.

10 Conclusion

When activists of 'Fridays for future' are confronted with demands that they should consume responsibly and not demonstrate, they could point to the many dimensions that consumer responsibility in the sense of a 'consumer policy from below' entails and fully justify that demonstrations and demands on governments and companies are necessary in any case and that it is not enough to wait for intrinsically motivated responsible consumption. The mutual conditions of responsible action by companies, government organizations, and consumers (citizens/society) in a complex consumer world require a look in all directions: Each group of actors can take responsibility in both the market and the political space, depending on the political goal, however, power asymmetries have an effect, which can often only be balanced by comprehensive state regulation if the goal is to be seriously pursued (for example, environmental or health protection).

Political consumption includes not only traditional forms of participation but also extends to various forms of participation in the market as well as political contexts. The conceptual considerations on consumer responsibility lead to the initial condition that values and beliefs must be in line with political goals if these goals are to be achieved, at least harmony is necessary if the beliefs are to act as an internal instance (moral background). Individual responsibility by consumers would be possible under this condition, but requires further framework conditions: Adequate resources for action (information, material resources) must be available, either abstention is existentially possible or an alternative exists, and from the consumer's point of view there must be a realistic probability that his own action will be effective. Apart from these influencing factors, behavioural science can tell us what other mechanisms can reinforce certain patterns that may even contradict individual beliefs, preferences or goals, if even the belief that one wants to take care of one's health is repeatedly thwarted by health-damaging behaviours (lack of exercise, unhealthy diet), this can be expected to be even more so in other areas (energy use, mobility behaviour, choice of products and services, etc.). In this case, the individual's reference to values and beliefs, which may also be mentioned in surveys or influence voting decisions, is not or only to a limited extent successful.

If there is no individual reference to values and beliefs, or if the individual lacks the strength to align his or her own actions with them, only an external authority can effectively contribute to a change in consumption; then prohibitions and commands or possibly also economic incentives would be the means of choice. In particular, the realisation that habit or even individual enjoyment often overrides possible references to responsibility, and that there is an abundance of consumer offers in free market economies, leads to the question of how comprehensive state measures are necessary to encourage consumers to act responsibly. However, it is always interdependent with 'consumer policy from above'. Responsible consumers in complex consumer societies need support: If the claim to consumer responsibility is extended in view of political goals of sustainability, climate protection and health promotion, insights from behavioural and consumer sciences should also provide important arguments why state intervention in the market is still, or perhaps increasingly, necessary.

References

Banzhaf, Günter. 2016. Der Begriff der Verantwortung in der Gegenwart: 20.-21. Jahrhundert. In *Handbuch Verantwortung*, eds. L. Heidbrink, C. Langbehn, and J. Loh, 1–19. Wiesbaden: Springer VS.

Baringhorst, Sigrid, Veronika Kneip, Annegret März, and Johanna Niesyto, eds. 2007. *Politik mit dem Einkaufswagen. Unternehmen und Konsumenten als Bürger in der globalen Mediengesellschaft*. Bielefeld: transcript.

Beck, Valtentin. 2018. Globale Konsumentenverantwortung – Überlegungen zu ihrer Konzeptualisierung und Begründung. In *Entgrenzungen des Konsums*, eds. P. Kenning and J. Lamla, 53–65. Wiesbaden: Gabler.

Caruana, Robert, Sarah Glozer and Gianna M. Eckhardt. 2019. ‚Alternative Hedonism': Exploring the role of pleasure in moral markets. *Journal of Business Ethics*, online first: 1–16.

Devinney, Timothy M., Pat Auger, Gianna M. Eckhardt, and Thomas Birtchnell. 2006. The other CSR: Consumer social responsibility. *Stanford Social Innovation Review* 4:30–37.

Evans, David, Daniel Welch, and Joanne J. Swaffield. 2017. Constructing and mobilizing 'the consumer': Responsibility, consumption and the politics of sustainability. *Environment and Planning A* 49:1396–1412.

Ewert, Benjamin, and Kathrin Loer, eds. 2019. *Behavioural policies for health promotion and disease prevention*. Cham: Palgrave.

Giesler, Markus, and Ela Veresiu. 2014. Creating the responsible consumer: Moralistic governance regimes and consumer subjectivity. *Journal of Consumer Research* 41:840–857.

Heidbrink, Ludger, and Imke Schmidt. 2009. Die neue Verantwortung der Konsumenten. *Aus Politik und Zeitgeschichte* 32–33:27–32.

Isenhour, Cindy. 2010. On conflicted Swedish consumers, the effort to stop shopping and neoliberal environmental governance. *Journal of Consumer Behaviour* 9:454–469.

Kenning, Peter, Ellen Enkel, Birgit Blättel-Mink, Bernadette Kamleitner, and Walter Blocher. 2018. Was steht im Fokus der Verbraucherforschung angesichts der Entgrenzungen des Konsums? Podiumsdiskussion. In *Entgrenzungen des Konsums*, eds. P. Kenning and J. Lamla, 127–144. Wiesbaden: Gabler.

Kneip, Veronika, Niesyto, Johanna. 2007: Politischer Konsum und Kampagnenpolitik als nationalstaatliche Steuerungsinstrumente? Das Beispiel der Kampagne Echt gerecht. Clever kaufen. In *Politik mit dem Einkaufswagen Unternehmen und Konsumenten als Bürger in der globalen Mediengesellschaft*, eds. S. Baringhorst, V. Kniep, A. März, and J. Niestyo, 155–180, transcript.

Lamla, Jörn. 2018. Entgrenzter Konsum und Konsequenzen für die Verbraucherforschung. In *Entgrenzungen des Konsums*, eds. P. Kenning and J. Lamla, 147–154. Wiesbaden: Gabler.

Large, Joanna. 2015. ‚Get real, don't buy fakes': Fashion fakes and flawed policy–the problem with taking a consumer-responsibility approach to reducing the 'problem'of counterfeiting. *Criminology & Criminal Justice* 15:169–185.

Loer, Kathrin. 2016. Gesundheitspolitik zwischen Schutzpflicht und Eigenverantwortung. Das Beispiel der Impfpolitik in Deutschland. In *Risiko und Katastrophe als Herausforderung für die Verwaltung. Schriften der Deutschen Sektion des Internationalen Instituts für Verwaltungswissenschaften*, eds. H. Pünder and A. Klafki, 81–104. Baden-Baden: Nomos.

Loer, Kathrin. 2019a. Approaches and Instruments in Health Promotion and the Prevention of Diseases. In *Behavioural policies for health promotion and disease prevention*, eds. B. Ewert and K. Loer, 11–28. Cham: Palgrave.

Loer, Kathrin. 2019b. The enzymatic effect of behavioural science. In *Handbook on behavioural policy making*, eds. S. Silke and H. Straßheim, 180–194. Cheltenham: Edward Elgar.

Luchs, Michael Gerhard, and Rebecca A. Miller. 2017. Consumer responsibility for sustainable consumption. In *Handbook of research on sustainable consumption*, eds. L.A. Reisch and J. Thøgersen, 254–266. Cheltenham: Elgar.

Micheletti, Michele. 2003. *Political virtue and shopping: Individuals, consumers, and collective action*. New York: Palgrave.

Offe, Claus. 1981. Ausdifferenzierung oder Integration – Bemerkungen über strategische Alternativen der Verbraucherpolitik. *Journal of Consumer Policy* 5:119–131.

Putnam, Robert, ed. 2002. *Democracies in Flux*. Oxford: Oxford University Press.

Rawls, John. 1975. *Eine Theorie der Gerechtigkeit*. Frankfurt a. M.: Suhrkamp.

Reisch, Lucia A., and Min Zhao. 2017. Behavioural economics, consumer behaviour and consumer policy: State of the art. *Behavioural Public Policy* 1:190–206.

Schipperges, Michael, Maike Gossen, Brigitte Holzhauer, and Gerd Scholl. 2016. *Umweltbewusstsein und Umweltverhalten in Deutschland 2014. Vertiefungsstudie: Trends und Tendenzen im Umweltbewusstsein. UBA-Texte, 59*. Dessau-Roßlau: Umweltbundesamt.

Schmidt, Imke. 2016. Konsumentenverantwortung. In *Handbuch Verantwortung*, eds. L. Heidbrink, L. Langbehn, and J. Loh, 1–30. Wiesbaden: Springer VS.

Schoenheit, Ingo. 2009. Nachhaltiger Konsum. *Aus Politik und Zeitgeschichte* 32–33:19–26.

Shamir, Ronen. 2008. The age of responsibilization: On market-embedded morality. *Economy and Society* 37:1–19.
Soneryd, Linda, and Ylva Uggla. 2015. Green governmentality and responsibilization: New forms of governance and responses to 'consumer responsibility'. *Environmental Politics* 24:913–931.
Stolle, Dietlind. 2018. Kaufen, um die Welt zu retten: Wie Verbraucherinnen und Verbraucher globale Probleme lösen wollen. In *Entgrenzungen des Konsums*, eds. P. Kenning and J. Lamla, 3–14. Wiesbaden: Gabler.
Stolle, Dietlind, Marc Hooghe, and Michele Micheletti. 2005. Politics in the supermarket: Political consumerism as a form of political participation. *International Political Science Review* 26:245–269.
Sunstein, Cass. 2019. *How Change Happens*. Cambridge: MIT Press.
Thompson, Craig J., and Ankita Kumar. 2018. Beyond consumer responsibilization: Slow food's actually existing neoliberalism. *Journal of Consumer Culture* 2018:1–20.
Young, Iris Marion. 2013. *Responsibility for justice*. Oxford: Oxford University Press.
Zaks, David, Carol Barford, Navin Ramankutty, and Jon Foley. 2009. Producer and consumer responsibility for greenhouse gas emissions from agricultural production – A perspective from the Brazilian Amazon. *Environmental Research Letters* 4:1–12.

Prof. Dr. Kathrin Loer has been teaching political science at Osnabrück University of Applied Sciences since July 2020. Previously, she worked as a research assistant at the FernUniversität in Hagen, where she led a research project on 'Instruments in Consumer Policy' from 2017 to 2020. From 2007–2012, she devoted herself to research and teaching activities at the University of Osnabrück, where she received her PhD in 2010. In 2012, she switched to policy consulting at a consulting firm in Berlin (focus: health policy) and returned to academia in 2013. Since then, she has been intensively involved in consumer policy, social policy issues, including health policy in particular, and policy field analysis including theory development across the board.

Responsibility Design. Consuming as Moral Action

Wolfgang Ullrich

Abstract

Consumption has been increasingly interpreted as an action for some time now, thus elevating it to something that is subject to the 'principle of responsibility' just like other forms of action. However, this understanding of consumption initially threatens to lead to even more resource consumption and environmental pollution. Because the better social, political or ecological responsibility can be demonstrated—as particularly valuable—especially through (often newly developed) variants of consumption, the more is also consumed. The article discusses what an alternative responsibility design could look like. It is discussed whether a duty ethics in the sense of Hans Jonas is not superior to the value ethics prevailing in today's consumerism.

Keywords

Hans Jonas · Consumerist imperative · Duty ethics · Principle of responsibility · Value ethics

Few things have likely changed as much in recent decades as the experience of consumption. Long dismissed as problematic—as superficial, manipulated, infantile—it is increasingly seen as something that can also be pursued with

W. Ullrich (✉)
München, Germany
e-mail: ullrich@ideenfreiheit.de

K.-U. Hellmann et al. (eds.), *Consumer Policy from Below*,
https://doi.org/10.1007/978-3-658-44478-5_7

commitment and high standards. Consumption is no longer equated with having been seduced by an advertisement, but is supposed to mean having made a conscious decision based on criteria. Accordingly, packaging provides information about ingredients or production processes, and buzzwords such as 'sustainable', 'regional', 'fair trade' or 'vegan' mark the respective products as ambitious; they can be used to articulate and negotiate entire worldviews. This is all the more true as values—such as family, home, health, freedom, naturalness—are discussed whenever consumption is involved. And it will probably soon become common to obtain additional information about product characteristics, supply chains, and company philosophies at the 'point of sale' via smartphone, information provided by the manufacturers themselves or by consumer initiatives and independent institutes, making every consumption decision even more of a judgement.

Today, consumption is considered more than ever before as a significant, important form of action—as something that can change the world. 'Consumption', charged with values, is almost naturally equated with 'taking responsibility'; with one's own consumption behaviour, one can, should, wants to prove oneself more than with many other things as smart, foresighted, sensitive to problems and morally integral.

Marketing today is therefore not least about responsibility design. Popular are product concepts where consumers are first made to feel guilty by vividly presenting a problem to them, then offering the respective product as a solution or at least alleviation of the problem and portraying its purchase as active engagement and thus as an act driven by responsibility. Indications that parts of the company's profits are used or donated for ecological, social, infrastructural or other projects also serve to give consumers the reassuring and uplifting feeling that their consumption has far-reaching—positive—effects, and thus takes place from the outset in a sphere of responsibility. The same feeling is possible when causalities are made transparent. Then consumers, often uplifted by large numbers, see the prerequisites and consequences of their actions and how complexly they are networked.

However, they are usually only shown what good they can do by purchasing the respective product—such as providing work for people in another part of the world. But it would probably also mean asking too much of the manufacturers if they were to portray the act of purchase not as responsible, but as negligent, harmful behaviour. If they were to associate consumption primarily with negative associations and make consumers feel guilty and remorseful, they would risk deterring them and earning less themselves. The customer would then no longer feel like a king, elevated to a prudent bearer of responsibility, but like a scapegoat onto whom everything is shifted—and who accordingly turns away sooner or later or hides behind resentments.

Manufacturers therefore have good reasons to design consumption as responsible action and to put consumers in a flattering position. By attributing competence, professionalism, value awareness and judgement to them, companies also relieve themselves to some extent of responsibility. However, they also contribute to increasing pressure on consumers. It is precisely through marketing that the image has become entrenched that the future of the world largely depends on consumers. Parts of politics often confirm this image, as it allows them to rave about the responsible consumer in analogy to the responsible citizen—and also to shift responsibility.

The invocation of responsible consumption is not only one-sided, but even dangerous—especially for ecological concerns. The more consumers are suggested that their consumption behavior is responsible, the easier they deceive themselves about the consequences of their actions, overestimate their merits, and trigger rebound effects, as they believe in the exuberance of their shopped good conscience, that they can occasionally be negligent or excessive. This may be good for the company's sales; however, presenting responsibility as a beautiful thing with quick successes is irresponsible in relation to the respective overarching goals.

But regardless of how much the merits of consumers are glorified, there is an even more fundamental problem. If responsibility is closely tied to consumer behavior, the idea arises that nothing else can prove as responsible as—correct—consumption. And the more consumption decisions a person makes associated with values, the more responsibility is also attributed to them. The option that responsibility could be demonstrated precisely by refraining from consumption, however, is not even considered.

Even NGOs propagate the same responsibility design as companies. Just one example: On the website of the internationally active initiative 'Parley', which is committed to saving the oceans and fights primarily against plastic waste in the world's oceans, it is stated that they are convinced that "the power to change lies in the hands of the consumer" ('we believe the power for change lies in the hands of the consumer'). However, they are not called for boycotts or frugality. Rather, the initiative focuses on encouraging the development of new, more environmentally friendly products and also finding prominent supporters who should present these products and the problem of plastic waste as influencers.

The fact that morally responsible action is primarily interpreted as a question of consumption is only conceivable in an affluent society. However, since not everyone participates equally in this, not everyone can equally freely decide what and how much they consume. However, this means that the poorer have fewer opportunities to prove themselves as responsible. By limiting their consumption behavior, they are more likely to be labeled as indifferent and insensitive—or even perceive themselves as too weak to demonstrate responsibility.

This creates the paradoxical situation that some are wealthy, consume a lot—ideologically elevated—and are therefore considered responsible, while others are not wealthy, consume much less—and not refined by values—and therefore cannot profile themselves morally. To put it bluntly: those who consume the most, i.e., use the most, have the best chances of being considered exemplary, while those whose consumption barely goes beyond necessity are assumed to be irresponsible. And the more emphatically consumer products are charged with values, the more emphatically consumption is portrayed as responsible action, the more an idea of ethics that is inegalitarian in its design and ties moral action to economic prerequisites is established overall.

By the way, it is not surprising that this value ethics is primarily an ethics of consumption. Originally, values were material goods such as a house, jewelry, or a good dowry, which were also ideologically charged as they embodied tradition, diligence, or social status. Since the late nineteenth century, the accents have shifted. Now, values are primarily something ideal—family, health, sustainability—but they still have at least a material foundation. Without money, one cannot afford a sufficiently large apartment and time for children and thus live the value 'family' credibly. And to meet the value 'sustainability' and live responsibly for future generations, one equips one's own house with additional technology—from insulation to solar cells—or upgrades household appliances such as refrigerators to more ecological models.

Indeed, in the case of sustainability, it could also be about renunciation—limiting flights or car trips—but the association of values with something material is so strong and common that most people only renounce as long as there are alternatives that, in terms of time or money, are often even more demanding. In other words: People prefer to fly on vacation and make a compensation payment for the CO_2 emissions rather than spending the vacation at home. Especially since the additional payment can be presented much better as a commitment to values, as a conscious decision, than mere renunciation, which could also be due to convenience or poverty. The recognition of values is therefore very closely linked to economic conditions, which is why material inequalities in the form of unequal opportunities for moral qualification continue to reproduce and intensify in a society grounded in value ethics.

The value-ethical linking of responsibility with consumption is also facilitated by the fact that consumer products serve as evidence of attitudes. Products from brands with strong value and responsibility design act as moral status symbols—and are booming, not least thanks to social media. Thus, some purchases are made today only because one wants to demonstrate on one's own Instagram account what a responsible and value-conscious person one is. To put it polemically: In some milieus of high earners, the work on one's own moral qualification now mainly consists of posting photos of valuable products, supplemented with appropriate hashtags.

As a result of the prevailing value ethics with its variants of responsibility design, not only is more consumed than ever before, but there is also a risk of accelerating consumption cycles. Those who express their sense of responsibility primarily via consumption do not use many things until they are broken, but only as long as they want to demonstrate responsibility in another variant or find something with which they can bring responsibility and value consciousness to bear more currently, more pointedly, more humorously or more stylishly. So you might buy new sneakers without environmentally harmful plastics, even though another pair from the fair trade shop is only a few months old and actually still flawless. Their prosperity tempts consumers into strange forms of competition, the main rule of which is that more moral authority is gained by those who consume more and always take into account further criteria and values, so after the shoes produced without child labor, the next pair is also vegan. Thus, the race for responsible consumer behavior—at least in ecological terms—ends in a high degree of irresponsibility.

Therefore, nothing less than a new design of responsibility is needed. Instead of continuing to stage consumer products as a manifestation of values and thus constantly fueling consumption and at the same time forcing forms of social inequality, the criteria for responsible action should fundamentally be achievable by all people equally; moreover, it should not exacerbate the problems it claims to alleviate. Responsibility should therefore no longer be integrated into a value ethic, but should be thought of from a virtue or duty ethic, which are egalitarian in character. They may not be as attractive as a value ethic, which offers many opportunities for self-realization and satisfaction to the better-off milieus of society. But they may offer the only way out in a situation where the 'Fridays for Future' movement has brought an urgency to the debates that makes the previous efforts for an ecological design of responsibility appear insufficient or even wrong. Therefore, from the perspective of the 'Fridays for Future' movement, the following will outline what a new—more radical—design of responsibility could look like.

Indeed, there is already a detailed duty-based ethics that assigns a central role to responsibility in the context of the ecological crisis. The philosopher Hans Jonas published in 1979—during a first wave of ecological fears of doom—under the title 'The Principle of Responsibility' the 'Attempt at an Ethics for

Technological Civilization', which was also vigorously discussed in the years that followed. Jonas further develops Kant's Categorical Imperative, starting from the conviction that human action has never been as consequential and responsible as it is today, as it can have an unprecedented impact due to technologization. Instead of mostly only affecting the direct environment and the present, it can even have global consequences and influence the living conditions of future generations, in the extreme case leading to an end of humanity. Since "no previous ethics [...] took into account the global condition of human life and the distant future, even the existence of the species" (Jonas 1979, p. 28), philosophy faces a great new task, but above all, each individual must first learn to estimate the possible scope of their own actions. Kant's imperative 'Act in such a way that you can also want your maxim to become a general law' does not exclude the possibility of self-destruction of humanity according to Jonas, therefore it must be supplemented by a new imperative: "Act in such a way that the effects of your actions are compatible with the permanence of genuine human life on earth." (ibid., p. 36)

In order to be able to comply with this imperative at all, "knowledge becomes an urgent duty" (ibid., p. 28)—namely knowledge about the possible consequences—thus about the effects—of the respective actions. It must become a general claim to be able to at least estimate the dimensions in which one's own actions stand. Jonas further specifies the duty of knowledge and sees a 'first duty' of man in the 'procurement of the idea of remote effects'. Instead of only paying attention to the immediate effects of an action, one should mobilize the imagination with as much knowledge as possible about the causalities in which it stands, and above all imagine 'worst case' scenarios. Only then does one properly engage with the new Categorical Imperative. Jonas describes the 'second duty' with the words 'mobilization of the feeling appropriate to the imagined'. So it is not enough to imagine unpleasant consequences of actions; rather, one must also be 'affected' by them, i.e., already feel the fear that only becomes quite real for those who have to deal with the consequences of an action (ibid., p. 64 f.).

As much as Jonas imposes responsibility translated into duties on all people equally, he is also aware that the new Categorical Imperative is less egalitarian than its Kantian predecessor. The more knowledge becomes the basis for judging an action and thus itself a duty, the greater the danger that only a few are qualified enough to fulfill this duty. However, the problem is relativized insofar as "the new imperative is much more directed at public policy than at private behavior, which latter is not the causal dimension to which it is applicable" (ibid., p. 37). While it is desirable for the individual to know as much as possible about the contexts in which his actions stand, lack of knowledge does not discredit everything, it is much more crucial for the future of humanity that the elites of direct and indirect decision-makers—legislators, entrepreneurs, but also scientists or journalists—declare knowledge maximization to be their highest duty.

Jonas' duty-based ethics is therefore less directed at consumers than at institutions; he does not want to shift the responsibility for the future onto those who often have the hardest time acquiring the necessary knowledge and whose actions are less consequential. Nevertheless, his duty-based ethics does not absolve anyone from responsibility. Within the realm of the possible, everyone must try to obey the duties of the new imperative. But what does this mean for consumption, for consumer products, for responsibility design?

Educating about production processes, trade routes, pollutant balances or other causal chains fits well with the concept of a duty to know, but should then no longer primarily take place on packaging and manufacturer websites, where it is more likely to encourage consumption rather than force abstinence. However, in the case of product types where complete or extensive abstinence would not be possible, information is desirable that makes consumers aware of their responsibility for as long a use and complete consumption as possible, or that transparently shows how the resources bound in it can be reused.

To convey the often abstract product knowledge in a more sensual and emotional way, a reformed responsibility design should also include the aesthetic experience. If the acquisition and first use of a product is associated with it being irreversibly changed, injured in its flawless novelty, then not only does a feeling of ownership and thus obligation arise, but it also becomes palpable how much consumption overall is an intervention and thus a responsible—or irresponsible—matter. Ecological sensitivity can be increased in this way, and consumers are then more likely to feel obliged to take care of their products and dispose of them properly.

Similarly, designers could work more intensively on developing effects of good aging of products and deliberately using them. If, in earlier centuries, patina was considered a status symbol because it demonstrated tradition-consciousness, reliability, conservatism in the best sense, then in the future it could testify to developed ecological awareness if one mainly had objects around oneself that have been in use for a long time and show it. Therefore, materials that become more interesting through signs of use should be preferred: more individual or striking. The new, smooth, flawless would appear in contrast as nouveau riche and obscenely wasteful, indeed as a sign of lack of responsibility.

However, it would also be worth considering how a general awareness of taking responsibility arises. For example, the ritual of signing—the act of signing a contract—serves to create a threshold experience in which one specifically feels to take on an obligation and to determine one's own future to some extent. Accordingly, it could be conceivable that individual labels only sell a product when consumers not only pay for it, but also sign or perform a similar ritual. They would thereby commit themselves to using the product carefully, to recycle its materials, or to become a member of an initiative that has committed itself to certain goals.

A duty-ethically motivated responsibility design could even go further. In this context, strong brands that have cult status and fans could play a significant role. They could move to regulate supply and demand not only through money—a commodity price. Rather, they could tie the sale to further conditions, such as how much CO_2 the person interested in a product has saved, how they eat, or how much charitable work they have done. The acquisition of the product would then have the character of a reward, so that the motivation to abstain from something or to do something would not necessarily be moral in the sense of Kant, but at least behaviors would be practiced that are considered socially responsible. The brands that change their business model accordingly could become even more desirable through these forms of exclusivity and increase their cult status. Their products would be unbeatable as moral status symbols and would make all previous 'valuable' products appear as embarrassing indulgences. (This is comparable to parts of the art market, where galleries also do not sell works of particularly prominent artists to those who offer the most money for them, but to those who have done a lot for the art world or have behaved fairly in the market.) (At the same time as establishing a second currency—a duty fulfillment or virtue currency—scoring techniques would be established, because everyone would have to be able to prove that they have behaved in a certain way and thus meet the criteria for acquiring a product. In the extreme case, this could lead to an eco-dictatorship run by companies with cult status.)

Finally, one could also arrive at reformulating Kant's Categorical Imperative once again, this time specifically addressing consumers, to help them transition from a value-ethical to a duty-ethical motivated behavior, but also to provide orientation and stimulation for a 'consumer policy from below'. Such a reformulation is not only close at hand, as long as and insofar as consumption is considered an excellent form of action. With it, one could also avoid the mortgage that Hans Jonas takes on himself. After all, his imperative presupposes the conviction that the permanent survival of humanity is absolutely desirable. However, as he himself admits, this can "ultimately only be justified metaphysically" (ibid., p. 35, which puts him in argumentative difficulties within his book).

The new consumeristic imperative could therefore—less presumptuous—be: 'Consume only that which you can at the same time want everyone to consume.'

At first, this imperative would probably make it clear how often a supposedly purely value-oriented consumer behavior is driven primarily by the need for distinction. After all, the idea that everyone would suddenly make the same value commitments with the same products would hardly be perceived as a victory for the corresponding values, but rather lead to disappointment about no longer being able to distinguish oneself so well from others. This alone is likely to prevent some consumption in the future.

Above all, however, the idea launched by the consumeristic imperative that everyone lives at the same standard as oneself would often lead to a shock. With knowledge of ecological factors, it would become clear when this would not be possible or only with dire consequences. The fear of the future, which Hans Jonas elevated to a duty, would therefore be abruptly and repeatedly awakened with the new imperative.

Once one has started to no longer see consumption as a good and responsible form of action in itself, but rather tries to avoid it, one will also compare it with other forms of action. Instead of responding to every problem with a value-conscious consumption of new product types—i.e., new, additional offers—one will consider whether one might prefer to join a party or an organization that wants to combat the problem through legislation. Or could one not support an NGO that organizes demos, protests, and boycotts against companies that are more responsible for the problem than others? Could one not simply do without something—and donate the saved money?

Perhaps today's practices of consumption will soon seem absurd and above all irresponsible. What were those times—one will ask—when people believed that with even more consumption they could solve even more problems—and especially ecological problems? A consumeristic imperative and a duty-ethically designed responsibility design, on the other hand, could give momentum to a 'consumer policy from below' and set a new competition in motion, which would be characterized by developing more and more ideas for forms of action that replace or at least minimize the consequential damage of consumer action. Equating consumption with morally responsible action would then be a thing of the past.

References

Jonas, H. 1979. *Das Prinzip Verantwortung. Versuch einer Ethik für die technologische Zivilisation*. Frankfurt a. M.: Suhrkamp.

Parley 2019: *Parley for the Oceans*. https://www.parley.tv/#fortheoceans. Accessed: 14 Aug. 2019.

Wolfgang Ullrich, born 1967, lives as a freelance author and cultural scientist in Leipzig. Publications on the history and critique of the concept of art, on topics related to the sociology of the image and on consumer theory. Publications on the history and critique of the concept of art, on topics related to the sociology of the image and consumer theory.

Consumer Morality—Bright and Dark at the Same Time

Between Self-Change and Social Change: On the Present of the 1970s Alternative Consumption Discourse

Marianne Heinze

Abstract

Starting from the currency of ecological attitudes and protest phenomena in the course of the so-called climate debate, the essay asks about their cultural and historical specificity. Three peculiarities of ecological criticism can be identified: firstly, the focus on action alternatives in the immediately available everyday life, secondly, a turn towards the self and its potential for change as a precondition for societal change, and thirdly, a temporal determination of social action as pointing towards the future. Consumer behavior and consumer ideas repeatedly move into the center of the ecological search for solutions, also in the West German alternative milieu of the 1970s, where critical consumption began, so the assumption. Using contemporary magazine material from the historical discourse, the historicity of the three peculiarities will be made clear, but also how the culture and attitude of the alternatives of the 1970s differ from today's consumer criticisms.

Keywords

Alternative milieu · Critical consumption · Sustainability · Ecological criticism · Political consumption · 1970s

M. Heinze (✉)
Berlin, Germany
e-mail: marianne.heinze@posteo.de

K.-U. Hellmann et al. (eds.), *Consumer Policy from Below*,
https://doi.org/10.1007/978-3-658-44478-5_8

1 Do Something! But What?

In the current debate on the climate crisis, public appeals a radically change in environmental policy and individual lifestyles are as present as they have not been for 40 years, when the left-alternative avant-garde, fueled by ecological criticism, had reached its peak. There is an urgent call to act now and immediately, to do something, in order not to be guilty of a looming 'climate collapse'. It is noteworthy that in the new climate protest movements, the fear is not that individual concrete people could die from the consequences of unsustainable economic activity, rather than the 'human species' could become extinct. With its name the new political initiative 'Extinction Rebellion', which distinguishes itself from the 'Fridays for Future' movement through its choreographed protest aesthetics and its professional handling of the media, programmatically carries this out. Occupations of squares and streets or skipping school, various forms of civil disobedience, are experiencing a renaissance in the wake of recent protests. This can be attributed on the one hand to the police's pre-emptive definition of danger and the expanded possibilities of prosecution and arrest in the context of changes to police laws in recent years (Janisch 2019; Amnesty International 2019). On the other hand, those involved in civil disobedience actions experience a high degree of self-efficacy: "A coal excavator that stops because people are in the pit is a success that the participants can immediately see" (Weiermann 2019).

2 'Politicization' of Consumption, Value and Structural Change in the 1970s

The crisis scenario that the climate debate sketches out raises socially relevant questions about how a sustainable society can secure not only survival, but the dignified life of many. This requirement of sustainable societal development is also affirmed in the discourse of critical consumption, where capitalistic consumption is problematized with regard to its consideration of socio-ecological boundaries. For example, questions are asked: How is and how can societal prosperity be earned and distributed in the future? How can utopian questions about a good life be asked? What scope for action do experiments and models have in the given socio-economic structures? What could a beyond look like?

In the phenomenon area of contemporary critical consumption, which is labeled under the keyword 'sustainability' and discursively includes both market and non-market practices, the appeal to the individual to do something *now* for the environment and society reappears. The attraction lies in the alternative consumption and acting opitions associated with this appeal, making it easy to achieve sustainability in everyday tasks at a low level. The ideal of an at the same time responsible and pleasure-oriented consumer appears here which is invoked by marketing and politics, but also widely accepted by consumers and integrated into their own self.

Critical consumption phenomena such as 'zero-waste', 'zero-plastic', 'Degrowth' or solidarity-based economy (Zajak 2018, p. 99) and the new forms of knowledge exchange and community building enabled by websites and social media are often interpreted in social and historical science as 'politicization of everyday practices', which includes a contemporary historical judgment. Thus, Sigrid Baringhorst (2015, p. 24) wrote about the emergence of 'political consumption':

> "Questions of societal and individual consumption and general lifestyle have been increasingly negotiated in the media public and subjected to norms of social responsibility since the 1980s."

Regarding the international professional debate, Dietlind Stolle and Michele Micheletti (2013, blurb) problematize the phenomenon similarly: "Political Consumerism captures the creative ways in which citizens, consumers, and political activists use the market as their arena for politics." The possibilities of establishing political participation through consumption and the consequences for democracy and political theory are as well research subjects of German political sociology (Lamla 2013). Stolle and Micheletti substantiate their politicization perspective—initially for the USA but with a similar development for the Western countries—with a change in political culture between the mid-1970s and the 90s. This is marked by an increase in unconventional forms of political actions, such as participation in demonstrations and boycotts. In contrast, so-called conventional forms, for instance involvement in parties and classic political institutions, are tending to decrease (Stolle and Micheletti 2013, p. 32 ff.).

The socio-economic and cultural context for these developments since the 70s, as the authors also point out, is formed by the change in value orientation of Western societies analyzed by Ronald Inglehart (1977), from the primacy of socio-economic security and social recognition through performance to post-material values such as quality of life, leisure, and meaningfulness. This becomes apparent in the area of consumption only when a certain level of material saturation exists in society. However, in Germany the boom phase that began after the Second World War ended in the 60s. The hitherto assumed level of prosperity and the belief in the growth model that made this possible were shaken. The collapse of the Bretton Woods international monetary system in 1971/72 and the resulting devaluation of money, the oil crisis in 1973 and the distress of the already declining industrial production, the economic policy change from Keynesianism to monetarism, which laid the foundation for neoliberal politics and today's financial market capitalism, and the increase in unemployment were perceived as threatening by the population (Doering-Manteuffel and Raphael 2012, p. 24, 48 ff.). Against this background, Detlef Siegfried, who studies the youth pop and protest culture of the 1960s, notes that, in the 70s the consciousness of the young generation would have reached a high political sensitivity while economically "the limits of economic growth were reached" (Siegfried 2006, p. 13). The latter is also underlined by the report of the Club of Rome on the 'Limits to Growth', published around the same time, which is considered the initial spark for the current discussion on sustainability (Meadows et al. 1973).

3 Historicity and Culture of Critical Consumption

The current problematizations of non-sustainability and the designs of possible solutions have themselves undergone a historical development, which I would like to illuminate in the following chapters based on my case study on the consumption discourse of the alternative milieu from the 1970s. My thesis is, that the nowadays virulent idea, that one can bring about decisive social changes through alternative shopping and consumption behavior, was first coined in a West German left-wing alternative milieu. The environmental protests of the 80s and the anti-globalization movement in the following decade developed publicly effective campaigns, such as the boycott of Shell petrol stations in 1995 in response to the sinking of the Brent Spar oil platform by the company (Idies 2015). During this time, the model of the 'ecological footprint' was also introduced into the debate, by which—interpolated from the resources available worldwide on average—the appropriate consumption per capita can be measured and thus illustrated. With the help of calculators available on the Internet, every private individual can determine for themselves, whether and in which of the areas such as mobility, housing, energy consumption or food consumption, they can still 'do something' to bring the size of their footprint closer to the average. With the turn of the millennium, in the course of new growth and globalization-critical debates and organizations, but at the latest with the financial crisis of 2008, critical consumption experienced a final breakthrough, on which the current demands for sustainable and responsible consumption in the context of the climate debate are being built.

The depicted historicity of critical consumption makes it clear that the discourse produces and further develops a knowledge of sustainability, which includes social and ecological aspects equally. In doing so[1] the problematization of an undesired societal state is often combined with the projection of a future, different society (Wendt 2017).

In view of this, I would like to take a closer look at the crossroads for the 'politicization of consumption' in the 1970s: How were self-change and societal change thought and practiced in this field? To this end, I will present magazine material on three strands of the alternative consumption discourse: 1) self-help, 2) self-supply and life reform, and 3) international solidarity and peace groups.[2] The selection of the material cannot be traced back to individual political groups or ideologically clearly delineable sub-milieus. In addition to the preselection by secondary literature (Büteführ 1995; Pasterny and Gehrets 1982; Huber 1980), the strategy of a motif-guided condensation to the cross-sectional topic 'consumption, everyday life and supply' was chosen, with a view to ecological and solidary problematizations of another economy and politics.

4 Three Characteristics of Critical Consumption in the Present

As a backdrop for the further analysis of the historical discourse in the 70s, three characteristics of the current debate on sustainability and climate crisis should be considered. Firstly, that one's own lifestyle and consumption style is declared a significant field for political action. It is suggested that one cannot (only) do something about climate change on the street, in clubs and neighborhoods, but that practical and manageable solutions to societal and global problems also lie in one's own everyday life, in the area of consumption. These can be experimental

[1] The Club of Rome report initially defined sustainability by stating, that only as much should be consumed, as can regrow. The social dimension of sustainability was only added with the Brundtland report of 1987 to the definition, on which the current conception of sustainability and the use of the term in this essay is based.

[2] This material is taken from my ongoing dissertation project titled 'Commodity-Aesthetic Subjectivity—Shifts and Renewals of Discourses of Alternative Consumption' at TU Dresden. The sources/discourse fragments, cited in chapters 7 and 8 for the sake of clarity only with short titles, are from the holdings of the Archive for Social Movements in Freiburg, the Archive for Alternative Culture of HU Berlin, and the Papiertiger Archive in Berlin.

fields such as self-managed businesses or agricultural projects, but also the everyday choice of means of transport, the purchase of food, appliances and services, economical energy use and household management. The second characteristic, which is related to the development described as the politicization of everyday life, is, that the focus of social criticism is increasingly placed on the moment of self-change. The identification with the political goals and demands takes up more space, and related to this, the conviction of others through the personal exemplification of a different behavior (persuasion). The third characteristic is the temporal order of the debate: Action must be taken now to avert a future, very soon possible catastrophe. This mode of prevention or pre-emption seems to merge with the concept of prefiguration, the search and promotion of approaches to the new within current society (Boggs 1977, p. 100). The exemplification of alternatives, i.e., persuasion, and prefiguration are interdependent, as the realization of prefigurative ideas encourages imitation and thus the path to their generalization or socialization can be imagined (Baringhorst 2015, p. 22).

5 The Consumption Discourse of the West German Alternative Milieu around 1970

The alternative milieu existed in West Germany between the years 1968 and 1983 and emerged parallel to the protest movements of the New Left (Reichardt 2014, p. 13). It can best be described with Dieter Rucht (2010, p. 65) as a

> "conglomerate of people, groups, places, institutions and infrastructures" that can be defined "by physical and symbolic presence marking a certain social space, which is reproduced by strongly inward-focused communication and especially by direct interaction".[3]

A crucial condition for the emergence of this historically specific milieu was the founding of the first communes and shared living communities during the anti-authoritarian phase between 1967 and 1969/70 (Glaetzer 1978). The second pillar were the alternative projects, i.e., democratically run businesses, self-sufficient farms, left-wing bookstores and pub collectives, most of which were founded between the years 1970 and 1975. The following five years, 1976 to 1980, which

[3] Cf. Büteführ (1995, p. 119), who has conducted extensive magazine research on the alternative milieu.

also includes the Tunix Congress at the TU Berlin in January 1978, then form the high phase of the milieu (Büteführ 1995, p. 133). Sven Reichardt estimates the number of the hard core of the alternatives at the end of the 70s at 300,000 to 600,000 activists, with a circle of sympathizers of about 5.6 million (Reichardt 2014, p. 14).

6 What is 'alternative'?

The question of what an alternative is or might look like was much discussed and argued among the participants themselves in the 70s. At this point, there is no claim to unravel the various positions within the debate. Instead, with a few spotlights, an impression of the 'alternative' self-understanding should be given. For example, Gerda Kurz (1979, p. 56 f.) writes in her book 'Alternative Living? On the Theory and Practice of the Counterculture' from a sympathizing-participating attitude:

> "Alternative literally translates as: born differently. According to Duden, it means: the choice between two possibilities. In this context, the choice is meant between the existing system with its prosperity and progress and all its weaknesses and deficiencies and a society with more freedom and self-realization and less alienation."

This state of 'being born differently' names the critical intention to deal with the dissatisfaction with the found social environment, with what is supposedly natural, in order to create something new. Here, the utopian or prefigurative claim of the alternativists is indicated, to anticipate a state that is not (yet) of this world and to live it in self-experimentation. Another external assessment is given by a reporter in ZEIT (Gerste 1978) about a scene meeting[4] 1978 in Hamburg:

> "Thinking alternatively, acting alternatively, living alternatively, 'doing projects', 'developing target perspectives', 'doing something concrete'—the language clichés are already coined—that's what they all want, those who traveled from their rural communes, shared apartments and self-managed small businesses to Hamburg. They brought a flood of literature—about 'bio-energy' and 'eco-diet', 'Zen-cooking' and rural communes—and their own products: bread from the alternative bakery and self-spun wool."

[4] Presumably, the 'Great Council' on alternative economy, organized in Hamburg in the fall of 1978 by the Sozialistisches Büro, an organization of the New Left founded in 1969, is meant.

In the anthology 'Counterculture' from 1985, an article headline nonchalantly states: "Green and Strong—We didn't necessarily want to be 'alternative', but it was fun, and that's why it seemed alternative" (Pletsch 1985, p. 32). More combative, however, another contemporary argues in the same volume (Röder 1985, p. 153):

> "'We want it differently' is the slogan, which includes a clear and self-confident rejection of the given. Long ago, the point has been passed to postulate rejection exclusively and only to demonstrate against something. Feasible approaches to overcome the old and live the new can be found to varying degrees in almost all areas of life and work: in living together, in consumer behavior, in media work, in the use of technology and energies, in medicine, in production and distribution forms."

7 Alternative to What? 'The Crisis—an Attack'

An example of the formation of alternative social criticism is the founding manifesto of the European cooperative Longo Maï, which was founded by a Swiss association of apprentices and an Austrian youth group. It still exists today and maintains 10 cooperatively and self-managed farms in five countries, including Germany and Costa Rica. The 1972 manifesto can be read as a critique of power and ideology as well as of the societal narratives of prosperity and crisis of the capitalist social and economic system, as the title 'The Crisis—an Attack' already suggests. On the first page it says:

> "*The crisis is not a crisis*. Nor an economic setback. Just a simple economic adjustment. Decided above our heads. By high economic committees, strategists and politicians. They play our fate. We are supposed to be the executors. Without us!" (Gruppe Longo Maï 1972, p. 1).

Here, the drastic events of the decade are clearly referred to, which the aforementioned historians Anselm Doering-Manteuffel and Lutz Raphael (2012) have characterized as being affected by a profound structural change.

The 4-page manifesto also addresses reification and dehumanization as effects of the process of 'over-industrialization' as well as the increasing urbanization or desolation of the provinces. Interpersonal relationships would be disturbed by these processes, physical and mental health attacked ("Inhuman, stone giant neuroses, isolated robots in an dearly saved small car, on crowded streets"); there is a lack of 'use values' such as good education ("bad schools, lack of teachers") and healthy food ("Europe is becoming dependent on industrial food production. Natural foods are being replaced more and more by industrial preserves. The quality of food is getting worse"; "We breathe gasoline, we drink detergent, we hear machines. Our day is scheduled, our labor power precisely calculated"); there are "no or too expensive apartments" (ibid., p. 1).

A basic feature of the named crisis, which for the authors of the text is not an incidental effect, but systemic normality, is the imperialist competition between states—one must keep in mind the historical context with the so-called block confrontation—, which in their view would produce a thinking that would further divide the workers on the one hand, and advance the exploitation of countries of the global South on the other. The military and political conflicts that are allegedly fought out and mediated by the media between the industrialized states, would in reality amount to a sheer expansion, division, and securing of national sales markets. The text continues:

> "The apparent economic recession is tailor-made for such brainwashing. The workers are dissatisfied. So give them their inner and outer enemy—their Jews and Bolshevik subhumans. Now that the lure and sedative, the consumer society, is no longer there, enthusiasm becomes an economic necessity."[5]

Five years later, in the invitation to the Tunix Congress in Berlin, one finds the same foil of demarcation in a prominent place as in the manifesto. The aim is to develop alternatives that would clearly distinguish themselves from the Federal Republic, "described as 'factory society', 'technocracy', as a country covered by an ice shield or concrete" (Rucht 2010, p. 62).

8 So What to Do?

8.1 The So-called Self-help Projects

"Wir wollen's anders' (We want it different)", the slogan quoted by Röder, was also the proper name of an alternative newspaper, which can be considered representative of the first discourse strand of self-management companies and was published by the so-called Arbeiterselbsthilfe (Worker's Self Helf) Krebsmühle, abbreviated

[5] This coincides with Alexander Sedlmaier's historical study, according to which contemporaries saw the climate of military armament and threat of the block states as a cover-up of the 'real' battles that would be fought in the field of consumption and the (manipulation) of human needs, cf. Sedlmaier 2017, p. 8 f.

as 'ASH Krebsmühle'. The magazine name also indicates a political-strategic development, as it refers, obviously for contemporaries, to the preceding left-wing company newspaper 'Wir wollen alles'. If the authors of the latter were convinced, that company interventions and the criticism of wage labor should be essential to left-wing politics (Notz 2012, p. 79 f.), the ASH Krebsmühle and "Wir wollen's anders' (WWA)" (We want everything) exactly mark the transition to the construction of their own alternative project within the capitalist control mode.

In the first issue of the WWA, the following self-conception is given for the strand of self-help:

> "We have formed groups with which we try to make our own businesses, our own education, pedagogical and social work according to our own ideas" (Anonym 1977, p. 4).

The self-help projects' perspective on societal transformation through their activity is illustrated by a comic, captioned with the line "Create 1, 2, many self-help groups" and titeled "Geschichtsunterricht 1985 (History lesson 1985)" (Anonym 1977, p. 47). Depicted is a supposed teacher-figure with the typical alternative features such as long hair, beard, 'Jesus sandals', pointing with his stick at a map of West Germany, which is filled with city names. In a speech bubble he is quoted:

> "The movement of self-help groups in the FRG emerged in the mid-seventies. From about 1980, the economic situation of these groups was absolutely secure. At that time, about 2000 groups existed in a solidary association. In our current social system, this alternative way of living and working is probably unthinkable" (ibid.).

8.2 Self-sufficiency and Life Reform

A second strand of the consumer discourse is formed by magazines that deal with the possibilities of a different and more ecological way of life, production, and work. The focus is on community living, in communes in the city, and the establishment of self-sufficiency projects both in the city and province. The attitude of the first is represented by the 'Montagsnotizen—Zeitung für Wohngemeinschaften und andere Alternativen (Monday Notes—Magazin for Shared Living and Other Alternatives, abbreviated 'Mono')' from Hamburg, published by the Verein für Humanes Wohnen e. V. Under this title, the magazine aims to promote the exchange and networking of shared living projects, communes, and collective businesses, creating a theoretical and politically undogmatic exchange. In addition to practical information, announcements, and advertisements, an attempt is made to connect with the revolutionary ideas of the 68ies' movement, updating them. Reference is made, for example, to the Marxist sociologist Henri Lefèbvre, especially his ‘Critique of Every Day Life’.

The questions of self-change and self-sufficiency, but also the constant reflection on the societal effects of the decision to live and work individually or collectively, take up a large space. An overarching voice for those interested in rural projects is offered by the magazine ‘Kompost’ (1973–1980) around the publisher Werner Pieper. Without assignment to a specific project or commune, it covers topics such as biodynamics, spiritualism, loving nature, anti-repression, and anti-nuclear power protest. Like ‘Mono’, ‘Kompost’ is designed as a reader's magazine (everyone can submit and contribute) and contains a comprehensive classifieds section, travel reports to other communes, interviews, and instructions on how to make or organize various everyday items by yourself. For example, it deals with how to successfully manage a self-sufficient farm, build solar showers, tan leather, or spin wool. In defining what it means to be alternative, the newspaper goes well beyond the longing for more originality. It is more about gaining expertise in doing things yourself, as the article ‘Kleinbäuerliche Tierhaltung (Small-scale Animal Husbandry)’ in ‘Kompost’ no. 24 shows. Before the authors goes into the basics of agricultural management, they distance themselves from those who understand self-sufficiency only as a purely aesthetic decision (Runk and Culemann 1977, p. 18):

> “For some, it's enough to have long hair and live in the country, grow some weed and vegetables behind the house and feel like a country freak (and don't forget candle making). Becoming a real farmer and advocating for the peasant way of life as a fundamental alternative to our technocratic society is something else.”

8.3 International Solidarity and Peace

A third strand, contributing to the alternative consumption discourse, is formed by magazines and texts, that criticize the current (consumer) society in its global dimension by doing political grassroots work. The political and theoretical activity ranges from information and discussion offers on worldwide oppression and exploitation issues, calls for solidarity actions, to proposed models and solutions to fight injustices, for example, through cooperatives. This also includes the topic of solidarity or 'fair' trade, which emerged in the 1970s within the political spectrum of ecumenism, and (left-wing) internationalism, and was voiced by activists in the fields of Third World initiatives and development politics. On their agenda were the military conflicts between the North and the South, but also various struggles against a "cultural and economic imperialism" (Huber 1980, p. 23). A good impression of the ideological orientation and the range of topics is given by the still existing magazine 'Graswurzelrevolution (grass-roots revolution)' or the 'blätter des IZ3W' (notes of the Information Center on the Third World) in Freiburg.

The magazine 'gewaltfreie aktion (Nonviolent Action)', abbreviated 'GA', also gives a good impression of contemporary consumer criticism. Issue 5/6 from 1970 contains reports on solidarity campaigns, theoretical articles on the criticism of advertising and consumption, on distribution justice, and on the idea of boycott as a political protest tool. However, excessive consumption is also problemized. A political campaign, for example, is dedicated to the upcoming Christmas 1970. In the 'Call for Consumption Refusal' (Arbeitskreis Kritischer Konsum 1970, p. 42) it reads:

> "While 10 million people die of malnutrition every year, while the poor nations are increasingly lagging behind in their economic development […], we as consumers participate in a waste whose frightening extent the individual no longer understands. […] The turnover for luxury expenditures increases by about 110% in November and by about 280% in December."

In the further text, the 'Arbeitskreis Kritischer Konsum (Critical Consumption Working Group)' calls for "refusing wasteful consumption and the obligation to make gifts" and in doing so return the Christmas gift to its original sense, namely to give "attention and love". In this sense, it is suggested to invest in a "development project of your own choice" or to practice anti-consumption, that is, to (buy and) give *nothing*. At the same time, the activists with their call want to oppose the "outdated idea", "that the problem of hunger and exploitation in the Third World can be solved with only charitable means". In contrast to the established national development policy and religious charity, the authors of the text see their commitment as one 'from below': "Without us developing nonviolent power from below via personal commitment, a reorientation of government policy is not to be expected" (ibid., p. 43).

9 Alternative Consumption as History of the Present

Let's look at the presented material again with the question of how self-change and societal change were conceived and practiced in this field, specifically in terms of everyday life, self-conception, and temporality. The alternative projects and groups try different solutions and answers on how to deal with a society perceived as crisis-ridden.

Among the practices of everyday action that are subjected to revision, for example, is the redefinition of the formation of work. Inside the self-managed businesses and self-help groups, not only are their own standards and production processes tested, but also the ways in which education and learning can be organized non-hierarchically and without exploitation. The idea is that a redefined work as varied, voluntary, and collective, in both the service and manual sectors, can bring more meaningfulness, satisfaction, and social cohesion. But the 1970s discourse remains vague how these models can spread into society; the ideas of persuasion and prefiguration often remain implicit. This changes, however, in the early 80s, when questions of employee motivation, productivity, and the sales of the manufactured goods increasingly dominate the discourse and businesses' reality.

For those actors who deal with questions of self-sufficiency, the mode of production, often in the form of self-production of organic food, is central. In the urban communes, where the means for home-growing are limited, the communities therefore increasingly advocate for networking with projects in the countryside. This is how, for example, the articulations in 'Mono' can be interpreted, which also assign a high importance to the theoretical debate within the milieu. For the rural communes other questions are present: on the one hand, quite practically, how a permanent ecological self-sufficiency can succeed. On the other hand, self-education, the unfolding of creative potential in a corresponding lifestyle takes up a lot of space, as the many instructions according to the principles of 'do-it-yourself/learning-by-doing' illustrate. The regular reports in Kompost or Mono about oppressed peoples, liberation movements, North American hippies, community projects or occasional spiritual keynotes show the desire to participate in an emancipatory movement. Therefore, self-change and community are the central themes here.

In the discourse strand of international solidarity and peace, in the GA, the reference to the global protest movement also plays a role, but here the medium of action is not do-it-yourself and self-management, but internationalist politics. Although, one's own self-image and consumer behavior must be aligned with the political goals and values of a more just, violence- and domination-free world.

However, the offered informations and calls to support the international labor and liberation movements are superior. In this respect, everyday life plays a role more as a place of mobilization for symbolic actions and the awareness of global and systemic contexts of imperialism, militarism, natural ressources and financial markets. For this purpose, those protest means are applied and propagated that have determined the global dynamic of social movements since the 70s: demonstrations and happenings on the streets, rallies in front of local institutions, boycotts of companies, signature campaigns. The political goals and values are ultimately decided in public politics and on the streets, in public space.

10 Ambivalences of Critical Consumption

Critical consumption as a discourse combines various objectives. Broadly, one can distinguish between 'consuming less', 'consuming differently', and 'consuming better' (Binkley and Littler 2008, p. 525). It is legitimate to ask whether capitalistic consumption[6], which is merely continued under a different, namely sustainable, sign, is still maintaining its disadvantages. It is questionable, whether an action critical of consumption, which does not attack the capitalist system as such—that is, continuous growth, wage labor, private property, and capital concentration—can be called critical at all. Criticism of consumption, and the same can apply to ecological criticism, therefore faces a legitimatory, analytical, and effective dilemma: against the system or with it? Currently, it seems as if the question is being decided pragmatically. Because the current debate is not solely determined by polemics, revelations, and effectiveness analyses. The various ideas and practices of a more sustainable lifestyle are omnipresent. More and more citizens in Germany seem to be ready to change or at least reconsider their lifestyle, their consumption behavior, without having to forego a certain level of enjoyment (Uchatius 2019; Hage et al. 2019).

Social change through self-change: This basic tendency is also paradigmatic for the current political culture of the climate debate. The alternative consumption discourse of the 1970s created this narrative, which is still—or again—effective today. This is because the alternative projects aimed to change social reality on three levels.

[6] In my work I define consumption, which ist essentially based on the commodity form, according to Dominik Schrage as "the acquisition and use of consumer objects under the conditions of a money economy" (Schrage 2009, p. 19).

- Firstly, at the level of subjectivity: By searching for new forms of life 'here and now', there was an increasing politicization of everyday life. Reflections on alienation structures inside the own self led to the understanding, that needs and desires could now be seen as open to modification.
- Secondly, at the level of community and the 'forms of interaction': Within the projects and communes, the alternatives underwent a kind of post-socialization. The 'opened' alternative subjects here entered into negotiation and learning processes with the collective or the community, whereby the political activities, the way of working, the values, and also the consumption behavior were redefined.
- Thirdly, the alternative projects forced a change at the level of the economy: Foundations for an alternative economy were laid, in which activity, possession, and supply were organized according to the standards of use value, enjoyment, and common good.

11 Back to the Present

In the current debate about climate and critical consumption, the desire is expressed to have more power to act as a consumer and thereby as a citizen. In this turn consumer policy platforms like Utopia.de are increasingly popular. They offer public exchange and information about correct consumer behavior in everyday life, denounce misconduct of individual companies or questionable, because unsustainable, products, and make alternatives known. From collected purchase recommendations, calls for boycotts or even instructions on how to make things yourself, everyone can pick something out. In the sustainable consumer goods segment of the industry, but also from politics, this desire for alternatives is used to enforce other interests for profit, which many are aware of. There is skepticism about the meaningfulness (Dohmen 2014) of certain sustainable consumption alternatives in view of the unpredictable negative consequences (Naylor 2018), their potential to be co-opted by corporate or capital interests (keywords 'green washing', 'green economy'), or the social inequality and distinction that alternative consumption (re)produces on a national and global level (Wendt and Görgen 2018; Weller 2006; Kraemer 2007). There are also increasing voices criticizing one-sided appeals to individual responsibility and private initiative (Grunwald 2012) when it comes to consuming or living more sustainably. Finally, the governmental history of consumerism also includes "state deregulation policies, the associated reduction of state welfare services and the omnipresent appeal to personal responsibility" (Baringhorst 2015, p. 24).

How close the power to act and powerlessness, the feeling of losing overview, lie to each other, the political philosopher Slavoj Žižek (2019) elaborates on the climate change debate, under the provocative title 'The rainforest is burning—so what?' According to him, the overzealousness with which the immanent 'ecology of fear' demands sustainable everyday action reveals a redemptive function in an religious sense. About the connection between guilt and drive to act, he writes: "We like to be guilty, because if we are guilty, everything depends on us: We pull the strings of the catastrophe, so we can save ourselves by changing our lives" (Žižek 2019). To Žižek the activism of the climate protesters becomes sedative and anesthetic like a narcotic, which makes it understandable: In the face of global socio-economic and ecological complexity and the actually difficulty to predict the future, the feeling of powerlessness can be managed this way. While in his article Žižek aims to shift the focus away from everyday action and towards the grand vision of communism, in his book 'Shiftings Involvements' the social scientist Alfred O. Hirschman advises for more political pragmatism: "It is due to the limitations of our imagination that it paradoxically produces images of 'total' change instead of more modest expectations" (Hirschman 1988, p. 105). In other words, he sees the causes of unstable political engagement in the disappointments that regularly occur when goals are set too high and therefore impossible to achieve.

References

Amnesty International. 2019. Übersicht über die Änderungen der Polizeigesetze in den einzelnen Bundesländern. https://www.amnesty.de/informieren/positionspapiere/deutschland-uebersicht-ueber-die-aenderungen-der-polizeigesetze-den. Accessed: 19 Dec. 2019.

Anonym. 1977. Geschichtsunterricht 1985 [Comic]. *Wir wollen's anders* 0:47.

Anonym.1977. [Ohne Titel]. *Wir wollen's anders* 0:4.

Arbeitskreis Kritischer Konsum. 1970. Kampagne Christliche Weihnacht 1970 – Aufruf zur Konsumverweigerung. *gewaltfreie aktion* 5/6:42–43.

Baringhorst, Sigrid. 2015. Konsum und Lebensstile als politische Praxis. Systematisierende und historisch kontextualisierende Annäherungen. *Forschungsjournal Soziale Bewegungen* 28:17–27.

Binkley, Sam, und Jo Littler. 2008. Introduction. In *Cultural studies and anti-consumerism. A critical encounter*, eds. Sam Binkley und Jo Littler, 519–530. London: Routledge.

Boggs, Carl. 1977. Marxism, prefigurative communism, and the problem of workers' control. *Radical America* 11: 99–122. Online (23. Sept. 2010). https://libcom.org/library/marxism-prefigurative-communism-problem-workers-control-carl-boggs.

Büteführ, Nadja. 1995. *Zwischen Anspruch und Kommerz: Lokale Alternativpresse 1970–1993*. Münster: Waxmann.

Doering-Manteuffel, Anselm, und Lutz Raphael. 2012. *Nach dem Boom. Perspektiven auf die Zeitgeschichte seit 1970*. Göttingen: Vandenhoeck & Ruprecht.
Dohmen, Caspar. 2014. *Otto Moralverbraucher. Vom Sinn und Unsinn engagierten Konsumierens*. Zürich: Orell Füssli.
Gerste, Margrit. 1978. Was ist alternativ? *Die Zeit* 41. *Oktober 1978*. https://www.zeit.de/1978/41/was-ist-alternativ.
Glaetzer, Harald. 1978. *Landkommunen in der BRD Flucht oder konkrete Utopie?* Bielefeld: AJZ-Dr. u. Verl.
Grunwald, Armin. 2012. *Nachhaltiger Konsum—Das Problem der halbierten Verantwortung*. Karlsruhe: KIT Scientific Publishing.
Gruppe Longo Maï. 1972. *Die Krise - ein Angriff* [leaflet].
Hage, Simon, Anton Rainer, Thomas Schulz und Gerald Traufetter. 2019. Die Weltverbesserer. *Der Spiegel* 29.
Hirschman, Albert O. 1988. *Engagement und Enttäuschung. Über das Schwanken der Bürger zwischen Privatwohl und Gemeinwohl*. Frankfurt a. M.: Suhrkamp.
Huber, Joseph. 1980. *Wer soll das alles ändern. Die Alternativen der Alternativbewegung*. Berlin: Rotbuch.
Idies, Yusif. 2015. *Kritischer Konsum zwischen Selbsttechnologie und globalem Handeln. Zur Konstituierung ‚verantwortlicher' und ‚raumsensibler' Konsumsubjekte*. Leipzig: Universität Leipzig, Diss.
Inglehart, Ronald. 1977. *The silent revolution. Changing values and political styles among western publics*. Princeton: Princeton University Press.
Janisch, Wolfgang. 2019. Wenn schon die Gefahr einer Gefahr ausreicht. *Süddeutsche Zeitung*. https://www.sueddeutsche.de/politik/polizei-polizeigesetze-sicherheit-1.4333604-0#seite-2. Accessed 19. Dec. 2019.
Kraemer, Klaus. 2007. Umwelt und soziale Ungleichheit. *Leviathan* 35:348–372.
Kurz, Gerda. 1979. *Alternativ leben? Zur Theorie und Praxis der Gegenkultur*. Berlin: AHDE-Verl.
Lamla, Jörn. 2013. *Verbraucherdemokratie. Politische Soziologie der Konsumgesellschaft*. Berlin: Suhrkamp.
Meadows, Dennis, Donella Meadows, Peter Milling, und Erich Zahn. 1973. *Die Grenzen des Wachstums. Bericht des Club of Rome zur Lage der Menschheit*. Reinbek: Rowohlt.
Naylor, Tony. 2018. Ditch the almond milk. Why everything you know about sustainable eating is probably wrong. *The Guardian*. https://www.theguardian.com/food/2018/sep/05/ditch-the-almond-milk-why-everything-you-know-about-sustainable-eating-is-probably-wrong. Accessed 14 Febr. 2019.
Notz, Gisela. 2012. *Theorien alternativen Wirtschaftens. Fenster in eine andere Welt*. Stuttgart: Schmetterling-Verl.
Pasterny, Udo, und Jens Gehret. 1982. *Deutschsprachige Bibliographie der Gegenkultur. Bücher & Zeitschriften von 1950–1980*. Amsterdam: Verl. Azid-Presse.
Pletsch, Eugen. 1985. Grün und Kräftig. Oder: Wir wollen nicht unbedingt ‚alternativ' sein, aber es machte spaß, und darum wirkte es alternativ. In *Gegenkultur. Von Woodstock bis Tunix von 1969 bis 1981*, ed. J. Gehret, 32–34. MarGis: Asslar.
Reichardt, Sven. 2014. *Authentizität und Gemeinschaft. Linksalternatives Leben in den siebziger und frühen achtziger Jahren*. Berlin: Suhrkamp.

Röder, Klaus. 1985. Thesen zur Alternativbewegung. In *Gegenkultur. Von Woodstock bis Tunix von 1969 bis 1981*, ed. J. Gehret, 152–159. MarGis: Asslar.

Rucht, Dieter. 2010. Das alternative Milieu in der Bundesrepublik. Ursprünge, Infrastruktur und Nachwirkungen. In *Das Alternative Milieu. Antibürgerlicher Lebensstil und linke Politik in der Bundesrepublik Deutschland und Europa 1968–1983*, eds. S. Reichardt und D. Siegfried, 61–86. Göttingen: Wallstein.

Runk, Reinhard und Culemann, Roman. 1977. Kleinbäuerliche Tierhaltung. *Kompost* 24:18–25.

Schrage, Dominik. 2009. *Die Verfügbarkeit der Dinge: Eine historische Soziologie des Konsums*. Frankfurt a. M.: Campus.

Sedlmaier, Alexander. 2017. *Konsum und Gewalt. Radikaler Protest in der Bundesrepublik.* Berlin: Suhrkamp.

Siegfried, Detlef. 2006. *Time is on my side. Konsum und Politik in der westdeutschen Jugendkultur der 60er Jahre*. Göttingen: Wallstein.

Stolle, Dietlind, und Michele Micheletti. 2013. *Political Consumerism. Global Responsibility in Action*. New York: Cambridge University Press.

Uchatius, Wolfgang. 2019. Ich habe kein schlechtes Gewissen mehr. Der Mythos vom Verzicht. Warum es in Ordnung ist, Auto zu fahren, in den Urlaub zu fliegen, Fleisch zu essen und trotzdem für den Klimaschutz einzutreten. *Die Zeit* 29.

Weiermann, Sebastian. 2019. Ungehorsam statt militant. *Jungle World* 46.

Weller, Ines. 2006. *Mit Kaufentscheidungen die Krise bewältigen? Bedingungen für den Wandel von Konsum- und Produktionsmustern in Richtung Nachhaltigkeit*. Vortrag, 29. November 2006. FU Berlin.

Wendt, Björn. 2017. *Nachhaltigkeit als Utopie*. Dissertation. Münster: Universität Münster.

Wendt, Björn, und Benjamin Görgen. 2018. Macht und soziale Ungleichheit als vernachlässigte Dimensionen der Nachhaltigkeitsforschung. Überlegungen zum Verhältnis von Nachhaltigkeit und Verantwortung. In *Reflexive Responsibilisierung. Verantwortung für nachhaltige Entwicklung Sozialtheorie*, eds. A. Henkel, N. Lüdtke, N. Buschmann, und L. Hochmann. transcript: Bielefeld.

Zajak, Sabrina. 2018. Engagiert, politisch, präfigurativ—Das Selbstexperiment als transformative Bewegungsforschung. *Forschungsjournal Soziale Bewegungen* 31:98–105.

Žižek, Slavoj. 2019. Der Amazonas brennt—na und? *Die Welt*, 07.09.2019. https://www.welt.de/kultur/plus199865460/Slavoj-Zizek-Der-Amazonas-brennt-na-und.html.

Marianne Heinze is currently a research assistant working in the BMBF-funded project "De-escalating crises and conflicts through communication (K3VR)" at the Akkon University of Applied Sciences in Berlin. She is also a doctoral student at the Institute of Sociology at the TU Dresden. Research interests: Consumer culture, History of Social movements, Discourse research, Police forces and communication, Virtual reality and AI. Last publication: Verantwortung tragen—Schlaglichter auf die gegenwärtige Debatte um nachhaltigen Konsum, in: Nicole Burzan (ed.): Komplexe Dynamiken globaler und lokaler Entwicklungen. Proceedings of the 39th Congress of the German Sociological Association in Göttingen 2018. http://publikationen.soziologie.de/index.php/kongressband_2018.

Revolt Against Morality—Unintended Feedback Effects of Citizens

Daniel Kofahl

... Would it
not be easier to have the government
Dissolved the people and
elected another?
(from: The Solution by Bertold Brecht, first published in 1959 in Die Welt)

Abstract

As part of a sociological diagnosis of the present, it can be attested that there is a steady increase in different moral entrepreneurs who, through discursive strategies of so-called 'Political Correctness', work to morally contaminate disliked everyday practices and lifestyles. Allegedly unenlightened citizens and consumers are thus making decisions that deviate from the hegemonic ideas of the 'right mature' behavior. They are therefore negatively evaluated with moral and educational communication and classified as 'immature'. However, many of these consumption practices are unwanted, but they are indeed justified decisions, with which the citizen living in the age of moral pluralism wants to explicitly express his cultural preferences (e.g. 'Meat—now more than ever!') and demands societal participation through unintended, cybernetic feedback effects.

D. Kofahl (✉)
Büro für Agrarpolitik und Ernährungskultur – APEK, Kassel, Germany
e-mail: kofahl@apek-consult.de

K.-U. Hellmann et al. (eds.), *Consumer Policy from Below*,
https://doi.org/10.1007/978-3-658-44478-5_9

Keywords

Brexit · Democracy · Nutrition · Ethics · Consumption · Media power · Morality · Feedback effects · Sociology · Consumer · Trump

Undoubtedly, Bertold Brecht was not the first to come up with the—admittedly here subtly ironic—idea that it is a real crux for the ruling class, for the governing milieu, for the social apex of a population organized hierarchically in many cases, with the (remaining) people. The obstinacy up to the resistance of the mass against the ideas of an upper class—a kind of *floating establishment*—which imagines itself in possession of advanced knowledge, is known at many points in human history and in relation to the most diverse use cases.

It is also well known in this regard that certain functional structures emerge in such a constellation, how to deal with such a situation—that is, the ideal conception of a hierarchically superior class (ought) plus a mass behaving deviantly to these ideals (being)[1] —can be handled. Although it is always an option to simply sigh, lean back, take a sip of Crémant de Loire and let the whole matter rest. But this is empirically not the case in many instances. Instead, a kind of sociocultural organization of the situation is arranged, in which the deviant being is to be somehow brought into conformity with the norm of the ought.

1 The Moral Dilemma of Life After the Fall of Man

The idea that the world should be different than it actually is, and that this—not only, but to a not insignificant extent—is the result of the life and action practices of people or the population or the people, we already find in early religious conceptions. The biblical fall of man is the prime example of this. If Eve had better controlled her appetite and if Adam had not been so easily manipulated, we would all still be living in paradise.[2] The consequences are well known: The earth

[1] Cf. on the difference between ought and being also Luhmann 2008 (p. 27 ff.).

[2] Elsewhere, in a sociological (taste) search for meaning in religion, I have tried to argue that from the perspective of a sociologically inspired theology there is indeed reason to assume that the divine ecology of paradise contained a certain structural imbalance towards the fall of man, cf. Kofahl (2014b).

is cursed,[3] people can only eat with toil[4] and childbirth takes place in pain.[5] As a result, man, who is supposed to subdue the earth (Gen 1.28) as well as treat its resources with a certain consideration (Deut 22.6), is branded as an (eternal) sinner.[6]

This divine classification may initially seem harsh, but upon closer examination, it is quite human and understandable in the nature of man. Thus, it is clear that man is flawed in his existence and in all his actions. Error, so to speak, is part of the basic human constitution. This may be regrettable, but this is how the earthly, this-worldly world is. Although man is given, in addition to a number of non-negotiable laws to which he is subjected, a list of commandments (Ex 20, 1–17). Yet even here, Christian-Catholic doctrine will introduce procedures (confession, repentance, penance) to deal with the expected non-compliance. Also, man cannot free himself from his sinfulness and guilt in this life, but must trust in the postmortem, otherworldly life and possibly even wait until the Day of Judgment.[7] And above all: All people are sinners alike. There is no one who can escape this community of fate. Therefore, there is also no reason to look down on another person. Even the saints are not free from the stigma of sin, but they are above all isolated exceptions who have particularly contributed to the welfare of the world and others, possibly at their own expense. Saints are by no means people who have particularly cared for themselves or morally exalted themselves.

---

[3] Although it can be noted that the 'cursed earth' has proven to be quite generous throughout human history and the harvest yields in 2017 averaged a proud 3586 kg per hectare of land globally, cf. theglobaleconomy.com (2019).

[4] It should be noted that indeed even today 822 million people are starving and two billion suffer from malnutrition (Welthungerhilfe.de 2019), but the security of food supply (keyword *food security*) in relation to a steadily growing world population is now as good as rarely (perhaps even never) before in human history.

[5] Even for those women who choose to give birth without epidural anesthesia, there is now a whole range of options for pain relief, which is not to deny that the pain of childbirth is still a severe pain experience for the majority of birthing women, but even here there is a certain gradual relief.

[6] For several years now, there has been talk in church-related discussions of "preserving creation". In contrast to the clear statement about "ruling over the world", however, there is no such passage in relation to "preserving". In Gen 2.15 it is mentioned that man should 'cultivate and keep', but this actually refers to his position in the Garden of Eden, i.e. to the time and conditions *before* the fall of man. But these are theological, religious and communication sociological subtleties that need to be analyzed elsewhere.

[7] Which may eventually fall on the same date as St. Neverday.

It is clear: The mass of people will not become saints, but will move back and forth in worldly life, exposed to its toils and temptations, between trial and error and try again and again.

The Ten Commandments, with their normative guidelines such as 'You shall have no other gods before me', 'You shall not commit adultery' or 'You shall not bear false witness against your neighbor' are thus fundamentally to be understood as a kind of divine invention. Thus, in sociological systems theory, it has also been pointed out that "one can describe the cultural invention of normativity [...] as a doubling of reality—just as one can distinguish between play and seriousness" (Luhmann 2008, p. 231). Norms are simply not reality and the clerical sermons along with their very vividly embellished hellish notions from the Middle Ages, which often give the modern man the impression that there was a true virtue terror over the world, are in truth primarily an expression of a world in which the deviation from moral normativity could hardly have been greater. After all, all the sophisticated, panoptic surveillance and education mechanisms of modernity were missing to monitor, condition and regulate people influenced by drives and affects in everyday life.

At the center of the moral order of the post-paradise world, therefore, stood for a long time the scripture with the commandments and prohibitions, the spoken word of the sermon, which constantly reminded of the norms as a doubling of reality. This was flanked by the recognized sinfulness of man, who could only hope for a life truly free from sin after death (but he could indeed hope for that!) and by a violent demonstration of normative power from time to time, which aimed less at enforcing law and order than at reminding what was to be considered as normative doublings of reality and simply cemented worldly political power (Foucault 2008).

2 Training of Professional Moral Entrepreneurs

The normative doubling of reality through norms is not only functional as a sociocultural project to provide human collectives with a value-oriented superstructure to which they can commit as a community—at least through confessions[8]

[8] One does not necessarily have to align one's *actual* actions with normative values, prohibitions and commands. Not even in the present, cf. Wilk (2011). What is important is that one knows what to commit to and what to distance oneself from, and how to classify and evaluate the observable practice of others.

—and organize inclusions and exclusions of individuals. Elaborated as morality, formulated and narratively embellished normativity also creates the option to create differentiated positions in this sector and thus opportunities to demand a performance-based livelihood:

> "It is probably historically correct to say that already in ancient high cultures a moral interest in moral judgments could be differentiated in reference to either religion, education, and political rhetoric. Behavioral assessment thus becomes a moral achievement that brings respect and possibly disrespect. Prophets, literati, agitators, and other moral entrepreneurs appear" (Luhmann 2008, p. 149).

Those who act as moral entrepreneurs are those who dedicate themselves to the professional observation of the world under the binary-coded premise of respectable and contemptible actions. They derive the legitimacy of their existence from the fact that they classify, that they (pretend to) be able to judge, with which actions individuals, organizations, systems qualify for moral fame or at least for non-attention, and with which they disqualify themselves and must be labeled with operations of contempt.

With increasing internal differentiation of the overall society and the undeniable cultural contingency of normativity programs, a competitive situation has also arisen in the field of morality. It has become a kind of *moral market,* with different providers, offers, and indeed with the development of productive forces underlying the free market, as well as the emergence of innovations. Because even though it is popular to describe morality and cultural reaction as closely intertwined, this is too short-sighted in the analysis of expansive moral communications. Of course, there are moral entrepreneurs and moral programs that primarily refer to traditions or to things established in the past. But the moral entrepreneur often acts as an innovator.

A moral entrepreneur aiming to conquer the normative discourse hegemony "acts innovatively" when he "applies his morality, so to speak, against the truth, when he claims respect for the fact that he values bad behavior as good [...] or good behavior as bad [...]" (Luhmann 2008, p. 150). The truth of reality then consists in the fact that the world is bad in itself and the moral entrepreneur looks at the world as it currently exists and codes it morally-normatively. The better he succeeds in applying coding, the more cases of immorality he can identify, the more glaring the discrepancy between normative doubling of reality and the actually empirically found reality, the more likely he can succeed in developing a moral program that he can offer on the moral market as a concept for reducing complexity.

'We are all little sinners' wrote Heinz Korn in 1964 and the Rhineland Catholicism-influenced Willy Millowitsch made the phrase widely prominent as folk wisdom. The moral entrepreneur—or nowadays also the moral enterprises—sees in this recognition of anthropological sinfulness the field that he can cultivate. The modes in which this is done vary. The rule is that instead of 'We are all sinners', for practical purposes of communicative addressing, it is usually more 'You are all sinners'. This then also eliminates the need to always explain again why there are professional positions that are allowed to despise others' reality of life. Moreover, the wisdom that 'We are all little sinners' already contains, through the diminutive used, the plea for leniency towards the sinner.

It is interesting to see that there is currently a form of moral enterprise that equally says 'We are all sinners' and 'No mercy for the sinner'. A kind of *moral masochism* emerges from this. This moral masochism is found in political discussions about intergenerational collective war guilt ('perpetrator nation') and resulting—also intergenerational and collective—descriptions of contempt (self-) and demanded sanctions up to the moral negations of one's own existence.[9] But it is also found in recent topics of consumption and civilian life. Thus, with reference to the apparently still lacking self-control and emotional control of people, it is demanded to introduce state consumption bans or to make consumption more difficult and to mark consumption practices marked as morally incorrect with operations of contempt, in order to evoke a shame effect in the corresponding consuming groups of people.

As particularly striking and resonant empirical examples of this form of moral masochism, the comment 'Please, please more bans!' by Mely Kiyak in the weekly newspaper Die ZEIT in June 2019, the comment by WDR journalist Lorenz Beckhardt in the ARD-Tagesthemen on 29.07.2019 and the call for a 'ban party' by Sebastian Erb in the daily newspaper taz on 17.06.2019 can be cited.

With the hint that prohibition decrees are the instrument of politics par excellence, disliked everyday and widespread life practices are singled out from a pool of action options and the call for a strong, authoritarian, regulating state is justified to restrict them. Behind this form of order politics communicated as political self-evidence, however, it is obscured that there are indeed also opposing liberal, libertarian and individualistic political programs. Their focus is on dismantling existing regulations, lifting prevailing bans and even eroding processes against

[9] It is rightly pointed out again and again that while there is a certain tendency to confess to 'collective self-annihilation', this does not empirically correlate with a first step towards 'individual annihilation'—one might say: Fortunately!

not legally anchored, but exclusively cultural taboos. Liberal and libertarian politics weigh the complexity of the individual's or smaller collectives' life world higher than the complexity reduction of person- and group-wide regulations and taboos. It tries to reduce interventions by one group on the life reality of other groups.

At the same time as the new illiberal political programs, the mere demand for everyday cultural bans is now communicated not only politically, but primarily morally. The state-enforced bans do not yet exist, so they must be made plausible and prospectively legitimized. The legitimization of bans on consumption practices is also so delicate because in a global culture, which regulates the inclusion and exclusion of its members—the individual people—through participation in consumption, it directly intervenes in the most everyday identity constructions of individuals and groups: in the nutrition practice performed several times a day, in the possibility of being mobile in space in a globalized world, in the everyday living and living space, in the clothing worn by humans as a second skin and so on. Therefore, the general empirically given life with its qualitatively graded quality of life must be ordered and evaluated. It is not about extraordinary actions like murder, war or dealing with highly infectious life-threatening diseases like Covid-19. It is about the variables of everyday existence and decisions about which form of this everyday existence is still permissible. Decisions must therefore be made here because the matter is by no means so clear that no decision would be necessary and everything would simply result by itself. This is not the case.

Is it legitimate to eat meat, or not? How much meat is legitimate? How should access to meat be regulated? Should the wealthy be allowed to eat more meat, live in larger apartments, and heat them more than less well-off individuals, because the former can pay the now demanded higher consumption taxes and the latter have to budget? Should air travel become so expensive that it returns to the exclusive travel experience it was in the middle of the twentieth century, when not all the nurses, students, roofers, and precariously employed journalists were clogging the airports with their tickets from the inexpensive package tourism tariff? How do you deal with the fact that cheap mass consumption has always been a project of democratic participation (has been?)? (Kofahl 2018a, b)

Ultimately, this decision—if one really wants to enforce it—can only be made through morality, through a justified, but ultimately arbitrary coding of (still) respected and despised actions. These moralizations are now in the world, even if the prohibitions have not (yet) been issued.

Moral entrepreneurs, however, are found in the increasingly secularized world not only on the pulpits of churches, but they are found in paid positions elsewhere, preferably in the press, but also in universities and not infrequently even in organizations specifically founded for moral communications. From these positions, they can announce their selected moral programs with reach and access to the scarce resource of attention.

3 Controlled Observer and Evaluation Access

The ambiguity of the correctness of concrete norms and universal normativity in modern times, especially since the 1960s, has long been interpreted as a structural advantage of liberalism in terms of moral communications. Why should one adhere to a certain moral doctrine when one knows that others prefer completely different moral programs and are still human? The free market of morality would solve the problems with morality, according to the motto of supply and demand. Or science would provide rational arguments instead of moralisms. Or it was assumed that the better or at least the more practical morality would gradually assert itself in everyday actions. Unfortunately, morality is not that simple.

Morality works primarily through communicatively addressed classifications, assignments, judgments, and confessions, and not through actual actions. Morality sorts the world through the mentioned doubling of reality, but it is not a binding action program—then it would be legally enforceable law.

Because morality functions primarily through its linguistic formulations[10], it is extremely important for a successful, resonant morality to have the necessary distribution channels and the corresponding media competence to proclaim and preach the preferred normativity. Respect and disregard must be distributed in a way that attracts public attention. What used to be the pulpit of the church and the authority of the church-ordained priest, has become the gatekeepers in modern times, who select the messages at the interfaces of mass media: the editors. In a church, you reach—if things go well and that is becoming increasingly rare—perhaps 100 or 200 listeners.[11] With the right TV program, the national newspaper or a popular internet portal, you can potentially reach several million. Positions that can influence the programming here are particularly suitable for announcing normative innovations and communicating moral classifications.

---

[10] This also includes visual language.

[11] In St. Peter's in the Vatican, it is of course also possible to reach 20,000 people, Cologne Cathedral—with extra seating and standing places—can accommodate just over 5000 people.

Indeed, it seems that access to these positions in the mass media system is easier to achieve than a place on a church pulpit as a priest, cardinal, or pope, as no lengthy theological studies, no ordination, and no lifelong march through clerical institutions are necessary to become an editor at a radio station or sporadic commentator of a national weekly newspaper. However, this would be an analytical quick shot, overlooking the fact that there are indeed mechanisms of inclusion and exclusion that regulate access to journalistic positions with high reach. This includes everything that Pierre Bourdieu (1987) described as cultural capital in his main work 'Distinction'. It is the power of words and images, the vocabulary, the ability to reproduce hegemonic aesthetic practices, that enable a certain milieu of the population to occupy gatekeeper positions in the mass media system. If the right words or appropriate analogies and metaphors are missing, or if someone prefers an aesthetic that is considered anaesthetic, then access is blocked. With the new forms of institutionalized, partly already legalized language regulations, where one has to maneuver with particular care between the cliffs of politically correct and gender-sensitive word choice, access to the already established media narrows even further.[12]

In light of these restrictions, it can be stated that the ability to contribute to the hegemonic moral and to divide the world into good and worthy versus bad and contemptible is not equally distributed across all population milieus. Instead, only a part of the population with already very similar cultural similarities and in this sense also (application) knowledge of ethical-moral norms can professionally and entrepreneurially operate moral communication. A discourse that thus concerns the entire society and basically even the entire world—because nature too is morally observed and sorted—is therefore neither conducted in an equal opportunity manner nor consistently liberal. Instead, access to moral observation is regulated by implicit procedures, namely the availability of cultural capital, which can be more opaque and difficult to acquire for new competitors than the explicit rules of a professional-institutional hierarchy such as the formalized Catholic clergy.

It is in the nature of things that the condemnation of selected practices and life designs as bad and contemptible is generally perceived as degrading and unpleasant in the concrete life world of the persons to whom this practice is attributed.

[12] One does not even necessarily have to be a right-wing liberal to come to these analytical conclusions. The 'functionalization of language' that is evident here, which helps to 'suppress nonconformist elements from the structure and movement of speech', was also aptly addressed in critical theory under the heading 'The Language of Total Administration', cf. Marcuse 1994 (p. 104 ff.) Somewhat more modern still Robert Pfaller (2017).

Indeed, since the philosophy of the Marquis de Sade, it can be said that there can also be a well-founded pleasure in the immoral (Sade 1990, 1991). However, with regard to the overall society, these seem to be exceptions or an occasion for a truly meta-paradoxical sociology of morals.

Now, the term moral masochism was already introduced above, which characterizes that recently not only the life practices and lifeworld arrangements of others are classified as morally reprehensible, but also the actions cultivated by the professional moral entrepreneurs and those equipped with positions of moral observation themselves are marked as morally highly dubious. With moral masochism, it seems as if, even if the access to moralizing is not egalitarian or liberally accessible, at least the distribution of contempt is egalitarian. But this too is a half delusion.

Indeed, it may be the case from time to time that anyone wishing to obtain a moral position must bring a willingness to self-flagellate as a qualification requirement. However, the practices focused on sanction desires are then selected in such a way that they take effect where the moralizing milieu is prepared to practice the confessions to the good needed for a morally correct life. One can sharply criticize the (contrary to all vegetarian narratives) ever-increasing meat consumption[13] if one knows that one's own diet plan has long since been adjusted to consume meatballs only at home, excluding the public, while even praising the bizarre taste of a pea protein meatball in public, against one's own physiological-gustatory experience, if one knows that this stabilizes or even improves one's position in the social hierarchy. One can accuse New Year's fireworks as a noisy practice of aesthetic plebeians if one knows that it even saves money to refrain from participating in the fireworks and instead watch the quite pretty fireworks from the roof terrace of the (office) penthouse—knowing full well that those living in the lower floors of narrow streets only get to see the fireworks they set off themselves, because they lack easy access to the exposed spectator position. One can criticize the driving of the rural population and the CO_2 emissions that occur when one person drives alone, because one rides a bicycle in good weather in urban areas, takes the subway in bad weather, and takes a short taxi ride when sick. For someone who moves between various small towns in areas like the North Hessian Werra-Meißner district—Witzenhausen, Ringau, Großalmerode, Wanfried and all the others—for professional reasons and perhaps also wants

[13] See for sociological analysis Kofahl and Weyant (2016) and for statistical evidence of the recently increasing per capita consumption of meat in the FRG BMEL (2019) and worldwide FAO (2019).

to be involved in local politics on a voluntary basis, the car is indeed the only alternative. And if one stands as a professional moral observer in public and is observed in morally dubious life, then one has the narratives of the cultivated apology: 'It is an exception!', 'It is organic!', 'It should be banned!', 'A compensation certificate was purchased!', 'One must not completely distance oneself from the plebs!'

Through this elaborate practice of moral dissonances, the established moral observer ultimately distinguishes himself from the subordinate moral observed: The one knows how to name the right, decent practice and to condemn the bad one as well as to excuse the other exactly. The other does what he does, and names it as it is, and can only feel guilty because he has come under criticism from elsewhere, but suspects that he will not succeed in sincerely excusing his practice, because it is constitutive for him and his individual and social identity and the presented excuse would lack staged authenticity.

4 Heated Coolings—The Cybernetic Feedback Effect

It has been pointed out that with the philosophy of the Marquis de Sade there is a theoretically founded elaboration that vice and immorality exert a certain fascination, and that from time to time some selected individuals or collectives act not only amorally, but deliberately immorally. Here one must assume a very consistent, but not at all hegemonic lifestyle, which in the large macrosociological structure also relies exactly on what it rejects in the microsociological practice: a strict morality. For without such a restrictive moral program, there would be no sinful taboo break and therefore no pleasure in the immoral.

Something different, however, is the revolt of the citizen and consumer in everyday life against the impositions of still disputed norms, that is, against a still negotiable morality, which is communicated and attempted to be imposed from another position in society.[14] These waves of a revolt that is less *anti*moral than

[14] As an example of a morality that is undisputed in large parts of the civilized world and no longer negotiable, the commandment 'Thou shalt not kill!' can be cited. Of course, this rule is contingent and subject to numerous restrictions—for example, the police and the army are allowed to kill under certain conditions that are socially accepted—yet it currently does not seem observable that an individual right to decide who may kill whom and when is negotiable anywhere.

rather *a* moral can be traced back to the time of the modern, anti-bourgeois bohemia around Charles Baudelaire and Arthur Rimbaud in the nineteenth century (Schivelbusch 1997) and such revolts also reappear again and again in the cultural-aesthetic practices of the most diverse milieus, including that which is titled as the living area of the so-called 'little man' (with fluid boundaries). The fact that amorality is first and foremost a communicative, (image-)linguistic undertaking is also noted by the left-wing political (and not averse to moralization itself) Herbert Marcuse (1994, p. 105) when he writes:

> "It is as if the simple man (or his anonymous spokesman) asserts his humanity against the existing powers in his way of speaking, as if rejection and revolt, suppressed in the political sphere, emerge in a vocabulary that calls things by their name: 'head shrinker' (for the psychoanalyst) and 'egghead', 'boob tube' (stupid cylinder), 'think tank' (for the intellectual), 'beat it' (get lost) and 'dig it' (finally get it) and 'gone, man, gone' (I'm totally gone)."

So it is a 'calling things by their name' or rather a 'calling things by another name' that brings the experienced discrepancy between first-order everyday reality and the impositions of a morally propagated doubling of reality of the second order back into overall societal communication. In times of social media like Facebook, Twitter, Instagram, Reddit, Telegram etc., the amorally revolting milieu has even managed to bypass the restrictive gatekeeper positions of traditional journalism and thus the new moral enterprises, to the horror of the hegemonic cultural establishment.[15] Contrary non-hegemonic amoral narratives are thus again as present and as provocative in the twenty-first century as they have been in 'Confessions of an English Opium Eater', in Elvis Presley's hip swing perceived as obscene, or on the records of the Beatniks, Punks or Rappers time and again.

But it does not stop at the (image-)linguistic revolts, there are explicit action revolts. Citizens and consumers deliberately make decisions that deviate from the hegemonic idea of the 'right mature' behavior and which are then negatively evaluated with moral and educational communication and classified as 'immature' in order to rein them in again.

Two major, specifically political phenomena have emerged in recent history: Firstly, the election of Donald Trump as the 45th President of the USA on

[15] This is already being responded to by various legal-political regulations, as can be seen exemplarily in laws such as the one 'to improve law enforcement in social networks', the so-called *Network Enforcement Act*.

November 8, 2016, and secondly, a few months earlier, on June 23, 2016, the victory of the so-called Brexiteers over the Remainders in the 'Referendum on the United Kingdom's continued membership in the European Union'. In both cases, it can be seen how the decisions made in the run-up to and aftermath of the democratic, free and secret elections were negatively judged and condemned through moral communications. Cultural-aesthetic arguments always played a role, for example, comparing the nonconformist, undoubtedly also characterized by loud arrogance, but also affective spontaneity, habitus of Donald Trump with that of his predecessor Barack Obama, who moved elegantly and stylishly in the sense of legitimized cultural aesthetics.

In both cases—the election of Donald Trump and the Brexit referendum—the voter groups that emerged victorious from the election were repeatedly suspected of political immaturity, and this happened (or is still happening) primarily through established mass media formats.[16] The fact that a milieu with its moral positions ("the election of Donald Trump is contemptible"; "the decision for Brexit is normatively bad") is omnipresent in the mass media and yet could not win the elections can be partly explained by this omnipresence. As Jürgen Kaube, publisher of FAZ (2016), correctly points out in an election analysis published shortly after Trump's election, it was a protest vote, a vote of censure. There was a democratic feedback effect on the norm and an explicitly amoral revolt against the institutionalized norm of a mass media communicated moral normativity.

But it's not just major political events that show these feedback effects. Since the political discourse has tipped in favor of a—as already described above—deliberalization of everyday practices (language, consumption, mobility, sexuality) and no longer negotiates individual and collective struggles for freedom, but primarily morally introduced prohibition and paternalization strategies, the formerly private everyday life of citizens and consumers is indeed repoliticized (Lövenich and Richardt 2018).

5 Nutrition Culture as an Example

This can be particularly well illustrated by discussions about food culture, that is, in relation to the alimentary everyday practice of humans. Eating and drinking are among the universal basic needs of humans, but they are always culturally

[16] For a detailed analysis of the Brexit coverage, see Beppler-Spahl 2019, and for a review of Donald Trump's election, see O'Neill 2016.

shaped.[17] A moral thematization of the highly differentiated food culture in the global world society[18] and the practices found in it (culinary techniques, gustatory taste, food taboos, food production, table manners, consumption quantity, etc.) can indeed divide the entire population into good and bad, that is, into those who behave commendably and those who should be punished with contempt:

> "Thus, each collective, within its means, has its own morality, which not least affects the way in which forms of nutrition and eating are morally accepted, i.e., predominant in such collectives" (Hellmann 2008, p. 95).

The prime example in the alimentary field has become meat consumption or the renunciation of (selected) animal products (vegetarianism/veganism), which has somewhat pushed the long-dominant discussion about the product group of alcoholic beverages into the background.[19] The consumption of meat has indeed been stigmatized by individual smaller groups[20] through morally imposed prohibitions since antiquity—for example by the Pythagoreans—not least in the course of the emerging reform movement since the mid-nineteenth century (Fritzen 2016). But it is only with the beginning of the third millennium that one can say that in certain parts of the modern world, meat consumption is disparaged and the renunciation of meat is favorably judged. While Alliance 90/The Greens still stepped into

[17] This distinguishes nutrition, for example, from breathing. While all humans have to breathe, this usually happens almost automatically (i.e., naturally) and is hardly the subject of major debates. Major debates, for example, occur in the area of sexuality, but here it is possible to carry out these practices largely in a 'private', non-public space. Moreover, in the case of eroticism, as with mobility or any consumption beyond nutrition, it is indeed possible for individuals or entire collectives to practice complete abstinence or celibacy. However, humans must eat and drink something and somehow if they want to survive at least in the medium term, so complete abstinence without self-annihilation is not an option.

[18] The food culture of contemporary society is a food culture of food cultures and of food culture contact, cf. Kofahl (2014a).

[19] It should be noted here that the debate about alcoholic beverages is by no means off the table—Christina Berndt (2019) prominently advocated for 'more alcohol bans' in Germany in the Süddeutsche Zeitung under the headline 'The Last Glass', and in the wake of Islamic dietary morality, alcohol consumption is also increasingly being discussed in Europe. In addition to meat and alcoholic beverages, there are now many more product groups for which normative edibility or non-edibility is being debated with moral communications, such as sugar, fast food, convenience food or industrially manufactured food in general.

[20] The strongly vegetarian-influenced Indian-Hindu dietary culture must definitely be mentioned here as an exception.

a political pitfall in the 2013 federal election campaign when they called for a mandatory 'Veggie Day' in public canteens, this position is now hegemonic and the at least occasional renunciation of meat in the weekly menu of canteens is consistently articulated as desirable. However, even in the debate about meat-eating and the preference for plant-based alternatives, it can be observed that it is primarily a project of communication-strong moral entrepreneurs. While vegan and vegetarian cookbooks sell well and wherever others decide on the menu of the eaters (in canteens), the renunciation of meat flourishes, meat consumption overall stagnates or even increases (again)—as described above. So it is mainly about the aforementioned moral confession practice and staged symbols of the normatively doubled reality of the second order.

An illustrative blossom of this oscillation between normative paternalism and *amoral feedback effect* could be observed in the revolt that ignited over the 'Kassel sausage dispute'. The story is quickly told: An 'environmental and cultural festival' organized annually by the Kassel-based association 'Umwelthaus Kassel' and the city of Kassel was converted into an event with exclusively vegetarian catering by decree of the festival management in 2017. Since it is a well-attended festival in public space and financially supported with public funds, it must have been assumed in advance that this would at least meet with skepticism from a population that predominantly feeds according to the criteria of an omnivorous and carnivorous food culture. In addition, the consumption of sausages (made from the meat of animals) is an established tradition in the festival culture of a large part of the local population. And—to top it all off culinarily—hardly any dish is as closely associated with the identity of Northern Hesse as the *Ahle Wurscht* made from pork, the production of which is also dedicated to several artisanal businesses in the region. All in all, the decision-making organizers were not following a local movement, but had come up with the idea of restrictively limiting the possible menu of the festival visitors and symbolically disqualifying the consumption of meat as morally not permissible in the context of a major dietary moral climate. Instead of offering attractive alimentary alternatives and allowing consumers to choose between different products and thus possibly also between diverging concepts of normativity in individual, democratic market decisions, they resorted to a morally justified temporary and locally limited ban.

The *feedback revolt* in the nutrition feedback system did not take long to manifest. There were protests against the decision. A post by FAZ on Facebook from 22.01.2017 (under the headline 'The city is in uproar') with the corresponding reporting on the decision and the reactions from the population that had already occurred at that time generated over 1100 reactions in the form of specified emoticons and provoked over 1200 comments.[21] In a satirical report about the Kassel sausage dispute on NDR[22] the different nutrition-norming factions of the dispute were able to express themselves in the form of the chairman of the environmental house (pro meat ban) and two CDU city councillors (contra meat ban).[23] Here, the moral masochism that lay in the meat ban decree was once again clearly staged with verve. The chairman confessed frankly and freely that he himself was by no means a vegetarian, but for the symbolism of the festival, which he explicitly wanted to be understood not as a folk festival, but as a festival around sustainability and environmental protection, the meat renunciation was 'a sign'. In short, it was marked in a mass media orchestrated staging what was good and what was bad, on a direct material level (initially and causally) without consequences, but morally politically quite effective.

However, a moral communication and symbol strategy of this kind does not remain completely without consequences. In the comments on social networks, in various online newspaper articles, letters to the editor and in an agenda item of the city council meeting of the city of Kassel, it becomes clear,[24] that in a democracy with a free market economy, one cannot simply change everyday cultural changes by moral mass communication—no matter how elaborate and hegemonic in the establishment—and by symbolic decrees without expecting resistance.

Figure 1 illustrates the cybernetic process of cultural transformations. Accordingly, there is always an initial situation X, applied to the example given, i.e., a prevailing omnivorous-carnivorous food culture. This proceeds more or less unre-

[21] This single post by FAZ, which carried the article 'Dispute over Kassel street festival—It's all about the sausage', was shared over 130 times on Facebook, thus spreading and continuing the discussion.

[22] To be viewed on Youtube: https://www.youtube.com/watch?v=Vwwkl2J8WAw&feature=share Accessed: 01.02.2019.

[23] An interesting aspect of the film narrative of the rather short 2:32 min clip, which was shot in a clearly moralizing manner in favor of the sausage ban, is that it does not bring logical arguments, but merely tries to ridicule the meat-eating defenders of individual decision-making possibilities. As 'voices from the population', only three women (presumably taken in the pedestrian zone) are shown, and this is remarkable because socioculturally, it is easier for women to abstain from meat and the consumption of meat is more strongly linked to the construction of male identity, see Kofah and Weyant (2016). Thus, people are claimed for the plea for the ban of meat products who are structurally more likely not to be negatively affected by it in their everyday routines.

[24] And probably also in numerous personal conversations in offline interaction situations.

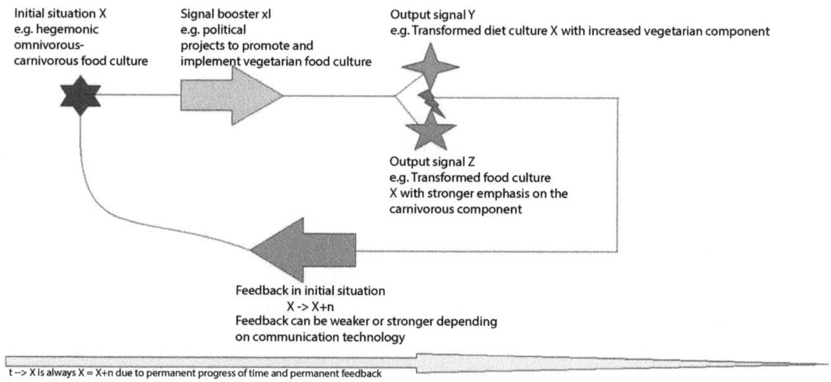

Fig. 1 Intended and unintended feedback effects in the feedback system of dietary culture. (Own illustration)

flected,[25] until someone takes issue with it and makes this food culture and its practice a topic of discussion. This draws attention to X and one must understand the thematization as a signal amplifier, just like the communication that strives to shift from an omnivorous to a vegetarian-vegan diet, where this shift does not primarily occur through an evolution of innovative products, but by morally ostracizing the omnivorous eating culture. However, as with the Kassler sausage dispute, there can always be (at least) two types of reactions to this moral-communicative signal amplifier. Of course, it would be conceivable that everyone simply abandons their previous habits, changes their habitus without a second thought, forgets learned traditions, and at the next observation point of cultural evolution, a transformed (dietary) culture Y stands. Y would mean that no meat or animal products are eaten anymore, simply because the moral communication was so convincing and awakening that everyone gladly agrees under the new doctrine. However, what is more likely is what happened in the first half of the twentieth century in the USA during the Prohibition era in relation to the relationship between alcohol ostracism, legal alcohol prohibition, and alcohol consumption: At the next observation point of cultural evolution, a (dietary) culture Z emerges

[25] In vegan dietary culture analysis, 'carnism' is spoken of as an unreflected and normalized form of meat-eating (Joy 2013).

as a signal, which has exactly the opposite, unintended effect. The signal amplification not only emphasizes the practice that has so far been barely noticed in everyday life, but even upgrades it. In confrontation with the counter-movement, good reasons are collected and new ones are found or invented as to why the previous, traditional action is not completely irrational, but meaningful. So there is a conservative and preserving reaction. In relation to the Kassler sausage dispute: Many, who might have simply eaten a pancake, a pretzel, or even an exotic vegetarian sausage that stimulates curiosity instead of a pork, poultry, or beef sausage, feel patronized, reflect on the value of eating meat, do not want to be morally devalued by those culturally not close to them, and now emphasize all the more how important meat and sausage are to them.

In sum, the moral communication has not achieved anything, but only created a heated divide between those on the (supposedly) good side and those on the (supposedly) evil side, between those who consider themselves morally superior and those who try to cool down the inflamed debate with an amoral revolt—which of course they cannot do, because they are undoubtedly heated themselves. This new (dietary) morally differentiated situation comes back as feedback into the initial situation X, which now presents itself as X + 1 and will undergo further developments (X + n) over the continuously ongoing time.

6 Concluding Remarks

Numerous consumers resist being perceived and defined as incapable in their decision-making processes. Undoubtedly not all. Allowing one's options to be limited by others, giving up freedoms, can also be a strategy for reducing complexity, relieving stress, and acceptance and asceticism can be tolerated, even welcomed in some cases (Auer and Kofahl 2018). However, for those who rise against the moral innovations and normative impositions, this accepting acquiescence does not apply. The concrete existence of their everyday life or an *articulated will against,* against the hegemonic morality of the moral entrepreneurs with a plan, represent their counter-morality. Decisions made through democratic elections or selected consumer practices may be unwanted, but they are still decisively made decisions. With these rebellious practices, consumers and citizens express their habitual or milieu-specific cultural preferences and demand societal participation. There may also be a latent awareness that in a non-egalitarian organization of coexistence, more security and advantages lie in a liberal or libertarian or conservative or traditional order than in a morally induced politics of the over-regulated postmodern. For the time of the aristocracy, Niklas Luhmann (1998, p. 689) could state: "No plebeian can become noble, solely through moral virtuosity". Something similar could also be said for the milieus and groups of people under constant moral fire today. No matter how much they feel obliged to moral masochism, practice self-flagellation and adapt to the politically correct renunciation of their everyday practices, they will not succeed in deriving personal gain from the new behavioral maxims. On the contrary, the experiences of loss of quality of life are assessed as more severe than the prospective promises of salvation that result from the new moral standard: One should eat less, but more expensive meat and knows that the individual effect on the climate and animal welfare globally tends towards zero.[26] One should refrain from air travel, well aware that one will then again watch the world travels of the financially well-equipped milieu with astonished eyes, only not as before at the slide evening, but on Instagram. One should leave the car and get into an overloaded public transport, which is overcrowded at peak times and does not operate at all or under increased security conditions at a later hour. One should normatively obfuscate one's language, developed from the milieu-specific life world, until there is only the way into the spiral of silence or the loss of the ability to satiate and the socio-economic siding threatens. One should renounce the small joys in everyday life and enjoy the joyless self-mortifications of the moral pioneers. But the negative effects of the feedback revolt are preprogrammed as long as there is both a welfare state democracy and market-economically organized selection options. And historically speaking, these are not such bad starting conditions to deal with the actual problems, which are either not solved by the moral communications or are tackled at the expense of many individuals with the paternalistic crowbar, in such a way that they do not even intensify from a protest action struggling for participation.

References

Auer, Rebekka, and Daniel Kofahl. 2018. Nutritive Genussaskese – Ein Beitrag über kulinarische Entschleunigung und Verzicht. *Epikur Journal*, Themenschwerpunkt ‚Genuss und Disziplin'. http://www.epikur-journal.at/interactivist/frontend/downloadDoc.asp?file=Auer%5FKofahl%2Epdf&typ=.pdf&id=00707&chk=1024443. Accessed 22 Dec. 2019.

Beppler-Spahl, Sabine. 2019. *Brexit – Demokratischer Aufbruch in Großbritannien*. Berlin: Parodos Verlag.

[26] Remarkably, the often demanded slogan 'Think globally, act locally' can be read and implemented in various directions.

Berndt, Christina. 2019. Das letzte Glas. https://www.sueddeutsche.de/leben/alkohol-deutschland-gesellschaft-sucht-1.4698085?reduced=true. Accessed 22 Dec. 2019.

BMEL. 2019. *Nach vorläufigen Zahlen sind Fleischerzeugung und Selbstversorgungsgrad 2018 erneut rückläufig*. https://www.bmel-statistik.de/ernaehrung-fischerei/versorgungsbilanzen/fleisch/. Accessed 10 Dec. 2019.

Bourdieu, Pierre. 1987. *Die feinen Unterschiede. Kritik der gesellschaftlichen Urteilskraft*. Frankfurt a. M.: Suhrkamp.

FAO. 2019. *Food outlook. Biannual report of global food markets*. Rome: CC BY-NC-SA 3.0 IGO.

Foucault, Michel. 2008. *Überwachen und Strafen. Die Geburt des Gefängnisses*. Frankfurt a. M.: Suhrkamp.

Fritzen, Florentine. 2016. *Gemüseheilige. Eine Geschichte des veganen Lebens*. Stuttgart: Steiner.

Hellmann, Kai-Uwe. 2008. Erst das Fressen, dann die Moral? Ein Beitrag zur Soziologie des Essens. In *Ernährung, Kultur, Lebensqualität. Wege regionaler Nachhaltigkeit*, eds. I. Antoni-Komar, R. Pfriem, T. Raabe, and A. Spiller, 93–111. Marburg: Metropolis.

Joy, Melanie. 2013. *Warum wir Hunde lieben, Schweine essen und Kühe anziehen: Karnismus. Eine Einführung*. Münster: Compassion media.

Kaube, Jürgen. 2016. *Die Irrtümer der Wähler-Beschimpfe – Motive der Trump-Anhänger*. https://www.faz.net/aktuell/feuilleton/debatten/motive-der-donald-trump-waehler-beschimpfer-irren-sich-14520799.html?printPagedArticle=true#pageIndex_3. Accessed 20 Dec. 2019.

Kofahl, Daniel. 2014a. *Die Komplexität der Ernährung in der Gegenwartsgesellschaft. Soziologische Analysen von Kultur- und Natürlichkeitssemantiken in der Ernährungskommunikation*. Kassel: Kassel University Press.

Kofahl, Daniel. 2014b. Religionssoziologische (Geschmacks-)Sinnsuche – Ein Gesprächsangebot über Essen, Gott und die Welt. In *Die Sprache verstehen. Interdisziplinäres zwischen Germanistik, Philosophie und biblischer Exegese*, ed. S. Müller, 115–134. München: Utz-Verlag.

Kofahl, Daniel. 2018a. Versöhnen statt Ampel. Wir sollten uns mit unserer modernen Esskultur versöhnen, statt anderen Menschen ihr Essen vorzuschreiben oder Lebensmittelampeln zu fordern. *Novo – Argumente für den Fortschritt*. https://www.novo-argumente.com/artikel/versoehnen_statt_ampel.

Kofahl, Daniel. 2018b. Hartz-IV-Menü und Feinkosttheke – Warum es beim Essen um mehr geht als ums Sattwerden. *LuXemburg – Gesellschaftsanalyse und Praxis*: 60–65.

Kofahl, Daniel, and Theresa Weyant. 2016. Halb vegan, halb vegetarisch, aber auch mal Huhn – soziologische Aspekte des Fleisch-essens und Fleisch- Verzichts in der Gegenwartsgesellschaft. *Zeitschrift für Agrargeschichte und Agrarsoziologie*: 77–92.

Lövenich, Christoph, and Johannes Richardt, eds. 2018. *Genießen verboten! Über die Regulierung der kleinen Freuden des Lebens*. Berlin: NOVO Argumente.

Luhmann, Niklas. 1998. *Die Gesellschaft der Gesellschaft*. Frankfurt a. M.: Suhrkamp.

Luhmann, Niklas. 2008. *Die Moral der Gesellschaft*. Frankfurt a. M.: Suhrkamp.

Marcuse, Herbert. 1994. *Der eindimensionale Mensch – Studien zur Ideologie der fortgeschrittenen Industriegesellschaft*. München: DTV.

O'Neill, Brendan. 2016. Trump ist nicht der Weltuntergang. https://www.novo-argumente.com/artikel/trump_ist_nicht_der_weltuntergang. Accessed 22 Dec. 2019.

Pfaller, Robert. 2017. *Erwachsenensprache. Über ihr Verschwinden aus Politik und Kultur.* Frankfurt a. M.: Fischer.
Sade, Donatien-Alphonse-François Marquis de. 1990. *Die 120 Tage von Sodom oder Die Schule der Ausschweifungen.* München: Orbis Edition.
Sade, Donatien-Alphonse-François Marquis de. 1991. *Justine und Juliette*, vol. 10. München: Matthes & Seitz.
Schivelbusch, Wolfgang. 1997. *Das Paradies, der Geschmack und die Vernunft – Eine Geschichte der Genussmittel.* Frankfurt a. M.: Fischer.
Theglobaleconomy.com. 2019. *Getreideertrag pro Hektar – Land-Rankings.* https://de.theglobaleconomy.com/rankings/cereal_yield/. Accessed 18 Dec. 2019.
Welthungerhilfe.de. 2019. *Hunger: Verbreitung, Ursachen & Folgen.* https://www.welthungerhilfe.de/hunger/. Accessed 2 Dec. 2019.
Wilk, Nicole M. 2011. Snack Talk – Wie (funktionalisierte) Lebensmittel mit uns "reden". In *Die Zukunft auf dem Tisch*, eds. A. Ploeger, G. Hirschfelder, and G. Schönberger, 253–268. Wiesbaden: VS Verlag.

Dr. Daniel Kofahl is a sociologist. He heads the Office for Agricultural Policy and Food Culture—APEK and is a lecturer at the University of Vienna and the University of Applied Sciences Mittelstand. His research focuses on the topics of nutrition, enjoyment, taste and consumption. He also works as a consultant for civil society organisations and entrepreneurs in the private sector. More information at https://www.apek-consult.de/team/dr-daniel-kofahl/.

Dark Sides of Consumption: How Consumers Trick and Deceive

Günther Rosenberger

Every person is like a moon: he has a dark side that he side that he shows no one.

Mark Twain

Abstract

Members of civil society often prove to be rude and egocentric in everyday life. For example, they lie to compensate for a disadvantage, or they cheat to gain an advantage. This is also the case in consumption: shoplifting, fare evasion, insurance fraud are common and rarely ostracized violations against decency, social norms, and criminal law. The causes of such misconduct lie in a web of internal and external, situational and structural conditions. Who can do what against 'criminal consumption'? New tasks for consumer science are proposed.

Keywords

Fraud · Consumer misbehavior · Consumer misconduct · Consumer images · Criminal consumption · Shoplifting · Norms · Consumer research · Insurance fraud

G. Rosenberger (✉)
Institut für Verbraucherjournalismus ifv, Berlin, Germany
e-mail: guenther.rosenberger@t-online.de

K.-U. Hellmann et al. (eds.), *Consumer Policy from Below*,
https://doi.org/10.1007/978-3-658-44478-5_10

1 Consumer Images in Consumer Research

1.1 The 'Ethical Consumer'—A Myth?

The image of the consumer fluctuates in the history of consumer research. Its primary interest lies in the rationality-limited, vulnerable, overwhelmed consumer: a potential victim of marketing, capitalism, globalization, digitalization, depending on the perspective. He is only seen as an actor when he appears as an ethically responsible consumer or as a 'prosumer' who acts participatively and collaboratively (Blättel-Mink and Hellmann 2010). Many consumers indeed acknowledge their responsibility for nature, society, culture, and economy. For some observers, such "consideration for the well-being of a distant human or non-human third party" (Fuentes and Sörum 2019, p. 131) has already become 'mainstream'. Not everyone sees it that way.

Ten years ago, Timothy M. Devinney, Pat Auger, and Giana M. Eckhardt (2010, p. 1 ff.) got the impression that the image of the ethical consumer had been evolving for some time: from a narrow environmental context to a comprehensive concept that encompasses a variety of conscience issues, they wrote in 'The Myth of the Ethical Consumer'. They saw a problem in combining debates about ethical consumer thinking with certain initiatives, such as the 'Product Red 2006' project (which was intended to raise money to fight AIDS, tuberculosis, and malaria). High-profile actions would disguise the fact that products with an ethical or social dimension are rarely purchased. Surveyed consumers would express a willingness to take responsibility, but not act accordingly. The gap between attitude and behavior is due to 'unpleasant empirical truths' (Devinney et al. 2010, p. 172 ff.). Their conclusion from surveys, observations, and experiments in various countries was formulated as follows: "We argue for, and support with research findings, the position that the ethical consumer is a myth, an idealized fiction supported by neither theory nor fact" (ibid., p. 9). The figure of the ethical consumer would be unrealistic and heroic, an unsuitable role model, and would only lead to disputes about 'faulty' behavior (ibid., p. 185).

Ethical consumption is narrowly limited because consumers also weigh factors in their decisions that are advantageous for themselves (Devinney 2011)—such a statement set against the zeitgeist was bound to provoke contradiction. It was criticized that the studies were not representative and did not include people who identified themselves as ethical consumers, that the argumentation around the myth was weak and apolitical (Vargha 2011). The ethical consumer would also appear as a one-dimensional figure; ethical behavior does not stem from a single source of moral values. Ethics is not a genetic trait like eye color, rather morality is acquired, multifaceted, contradictory, and imperfect (Kleinrichert 2012). Thus, "the ethical consumer [...] is multifaceted, fluid and elusive, subject to individual, contextual, cultural and emotional vagaries" (Carrigan 2017, p. 17).

Despite these objections, the latter text speaks almost exclusively of the 'ethical consumer', a fictional person, and not of ethical consumption as a process ('consumption'). The controversies are likely also due to a lack of awareness of the problem that the guiding principle of a fictional figure cannot do justice to the heterogeneity of consumption. It is hard to blame an abstract model for having little to do with reality. Such a myth proves to be a 'straw man' that is easy to dispose of with any methodological argument, without gaining empirical insight.

1.2 Ethical Consumption—A Volatile Variable

The fact that personalizations can be misleading is evident in the debate about consumer role models. In an effort to move away from the unrealistic image of the 'informed consumer' (Bala and Müller 2015), three behavioral patterns were conceived with the labels trusting, vulnerable, and responsible (Micklitz et al. 2010). This triad has enriched consumer policy concepts and at the same time led to misunderstandings, namely when the chosen adjectives were personalized; for example, when speaking of a 'trusting consumer', as if someone were only this one thing and not the other or the third (Bala and Schuldzinski 2019b, p. 9 f.). Fictional people were interpreted as one-dimensional and criticized misunderstandingly (ibid., p. 10). However, what was meant were behaviors or styles that can overlap or alternate within a person, that are situation-dependent, that can be learned and modified, precisely because they are 'multifaceted, fluid and elusive'. The consumer has many faces. Consumer research also personalizes and defines specific images of the consumer. It helps if such consumer images are recognized as 'productive fictions' (Müller 2019). Behind them, there can be images of people such as the human being as a rational dual being, as a creative symbol being, or as a deficient being. The latter, Müller (2019, p. 32 ff., p. 66) refers to as a skeptical-pessimistic image. The orientation towards consumer images has practical consequences for consumer policy and systematic consequences for consumer sciences.

Following Hellmann (2019a, p. 2), consumption should be understood as

> "the satisfaction of any needs, whether through goods or services, whether paid or not, whether consumed individually or collectively. Consumption, in turn, encompasses a multitude of activities that contribute (or are supposed to contribute) to the satisfaction of any needs."

This means that both the information and decision phases before a purchase are significant, as well as the use of goods and the utilization of services. This includes, for example, complaint behavior or exchange, as well as disposal. In this understanding, consumption practices also take place outside traditional markets, in sharing models, exchange markets, or in the household. Consumption is also the use of public goods, for example, public transport or the indirect use of security services from the fire department or police.

Consumption is a process and can take various forms. Its manifestations can be located on a continuum of ethical relevance. Therefore, instead of talking about ethical consumption, one should speak of 'ethically relevant consumption', because the extent of ethical content in consumption practices varies. Colloquially, ethical is used in a dual sense: If something is 'ethical', it is morally high-quality. One extreme position on the scale of 'more or less ethical behavior' would then be 'ethically high-standing' or 'very ethical'. The opposite position would have to be described as 'very unethical', which sounds pale. More vivid would be adjectives like irresponsible, dangerous to the community, criminal. If one imagines the scale as a thermometer, one could ask how deep then evil misconduct would be located, perhaps even on a scale open at the bottom. In these dark depths, the consumer appears as an unethical perpetrator, as a counter-figure of the bright ethical actor. For consumer policy, there may also be starting points here, 'from below'.

Is there a risk of exaggeration with such a view? Should we warn against a 'myth of the unethical consumer' (Hellmann 2019a, p. 42)? Every form of consumption is always embedded in a certain lifestyle, can only be understood systemically and is therefore, in the sociological sense, moral (ibid.). And by the way: When 'Crooked Tours in the Economy. On the History of Ethical Misconduct and its Combat' (Engels et al. 2015) are extensively presented, unethical consumption is not even considered: 'There are reasons for that, it shows the exaggeration!' one hears people shout.

1.3 Misconduct is Ubiquitous

The following is about consumers as perpetrators who violate norms in their consumption. This is not an expression of their lifestyle. Misconduct often occurs spontaneously, due to a combination of internal and external factors. 'Opportunity makes thieves' would be a plausible explanation for many forms of consumerist misconduct. The 'perpetrator profile' of an evil consumer will hardly be found. There is also no polarization between wrong and right consumption assumed; the practices described below are not opposed by a counter-model of 'correct' consumption. Thus, it is not about anomalies, deviations from the assumptions of the rational choice model. No stand is taken here for ideal-typical or idealistic behavior models.

It is also not about misconduct in the sense of Richard Thaler's (2015) 'Misbehaving', which refers to the limitations and bias effects in decisions, as he described them in 'Misbehaving: The Making of Behavioral Economics'. Also not meant are the 'errors' of the fictional Homo Oeconomicus: "In terms of traditional economic theory, Humans misbehave" (Thaler 2016, p. 5). Also not included are self-harming behaviors such as excessive eating, drinking too much, saving too little, smoking too much etc., which has also been referred to as 'consumer (mis)behavior' (Wertenbroch 2016). Finally, it is not about thinking errors: forgetting a name, miscalculating, misunderstanding something (Dobelli 2014). Such rather harmless missteps point to two peculiarities. First, there is nothing malicious in them. Second, someone suffers the damage themselves: If something has 'gone wrong', then for the person concerned. The misconduct discussed here involves the opposite, namely violation of norms for self-interest or malice and the harm of others.

That such misconduct is of an everyday nature is shown by examples in non-consumption-related areas of life. A representative survey by the Institut für Demoskopie Allensbach in July 2019 revealed the following: The societal development causes massive discomfort among people between 30 and 59 years ('middle generation'). Four out of five respondents note an increasing aggressiveness in societal interaction. 90% experience this in road traffic. Respondents confront reckless and aggressive behavior in public places (59%) and in public transport (51%), but also on the internet (54%) (Institute for Demoscopy Allensbach 2019).

The Cluster of Excellence 'Temporal Communities' at the Free University of Berlin finds it worth investigating whether Adolph Knigge's 'On Dealing with People' from 1788 can still help us today. "In times of hate speech, the question of how people interact with each other is of great societal relevance," it was explained (Herbold 2019). Students are becoming increasingly noticeable: "It can be observed […] that behavioral norms are deliberately violated because they are considered 'square' and outdated. Consideration seems to be an unknown phenomenon" (Turner 2019). And among children and adolescents, the incidents are piling up. A nationwide survey of 1200 school principals in 2018 revealed that almost every second school had experienced violence against teachers in the past five years; incredible disrespect had increased (Bachner et al. 2018, p. 7). Time and again, better grades that do not correspond to the performance level have to be given to avoid trouble and conflicts (Lehmann 2016, p. 3).

We all have our experiences with derailments and ugly confrontations in everyday life. They also find their representation. 'On Decency in Difficult Times and the Question of How We Interact with Each Other' is a telling book title. The writer Axel Hacke (2018, p. 10) is touched by everyday misconduct: "For a while now, not just a wave of indecency has been sweeping around the world, but an entire ocean is raging." A series of relevant book titles hit the same note: 'Behave Yourselves! A Pamphlet' (Gärtner et al. 2014), 'Screw It. The Culture of Rudeness' (Mießgang 2013), 'The Rude Republic. Why Are We So Unsocial?' (Schindler 2012), 'Manners for the twenty-first Century. Why We Have No Manners Anymore—How We Learn to Respect Each Other Again' (Weber et al. 2014), 'Avoid Your Neighbor. Observations of a City Neurotic' (Mohr 2010), 'Loss of Shame. On the Change of Emotional Culture', 'Hatebook. The Mob Democracy' (Hatebook 2017), 'Politeness. On the Value of a Worthless Virtue' (Erlinger 2016), 'I Object to This Tone, You Asshole! On the Decline of Manners' (Hock 2016). Conclusion: There is a general lack of "normal decency, which creates bonds between people and brings obligations for the individual." (Bude, quoted after Monath 2019)

More severe rule violations, which go beyond verbal jostling, are recorded in different areas. There is no need to even address the hate tirades on social networks, nor the interpretation of red traffic lights and speed limits as non-binding recommendations. Even blockades of public facilities by 'activists' are considered lenient by some, and the disruption of lectures by unpopular lecturers finds understanding. The following headlines come from current newspapers: 'Selfish and without a sense of wrongdoing. Wrong parkers show little insight', 'Lifeguards complain about aggression', 'I'll stab you—Emergency room staff in fear', 'Suppressed news: Crime scene church. The number of church break-ins and thefts remains high', 'Violence on football fields is increasing', 'Fiddling with professorships. Corruption at universities is an international phenomenon', 'Attack on doctors. Verbal and physical violence in clinics or practices is increasing' and 'Excrement-happy. More and more book titles rely on foul language'. Such and other things are "examples of everyday madness in the ranks of supposedly quite normal citizens." (Steinbrück 2018, p. 135)

Similarities in the examples are noticeable. Always at play are aggressions, low inhibitions, lack of empathy; social behavioral expectations are violated; often in a current incentive situation; a feeling of guilt or shame is not visible; there are also no immediate sanctions. All of this fuels initial suspicion. 'We are all consumers' is often said. But then norm-violating oversteps should also manifest in consumption. Then consumers would not be immune to loss of control, then they too would trick and deceive.

2 Dark Sides of Consumption

2.1 Consumers in the Shadows: 'Consumer Misbehaviour'

The 'dark sides' of consumption have long been the subject of American consumer research. For example, Solomon (2016, p. 143 ff.) includes various activities in 'consumer misbehavior'. He understands this to mean behavior that is harmful to individuals or society: consumer terrorism (when someone injects poison into a food product in the supermarket), consumer addiction and pathological buying compulsion, 'consumed' consumers (who are exploited to generate profits), illegal purchase and illegal product use, theft and fraud, and anti-consumption. Acts such as deliberately defacing products, spraying graffiti, releasing computer viruses, or destroying advertising signs fall under the latter term.

A influential definition of 'consumer misbehavior' was proposed by Fullerton and Punj (1997, p. 336): "Consumer misbehavior may thus be defined as behavioral acts by consumers which violate the generally accepted norms of conduct in consumption situations, and disrupt the order expected in such situations". Evans et al. (2013, p. 445 ff.) subsume the following facts: abnormal (excessive buying) or illegal actions (theft, black market, smuggling, brand piracy) when purchasing products, and addictive (drug abuse, gambling, binge drinking) and illegal behavior (drug purchase, misuse of services, underage drinking or smoking) when using products. Also considered norm-violating are aggressive behavior towards saleswomen or call center employees, refusal to pay, defacing posters, credit card fraud, vandalism, false statements in surveys. The term is used similarly by other authors: "Consumer misbehavior, within the context of this research, is defined as the extent to which a customer deliberately behaves in a way that violates the norms and unwritten rules of an individual service setting in a negative fashion" (Reynolds and Harris 2009, p. 321). Here, hidden behavior is also included, in contrast to Fullerton and Punj, who focus on observable actions (Fisk et al. 2010, p. 418).

An overview of alternative, sometimes synonymous terms for 'consumer misbehavior' can be found in Hailat (2016, p. 53 ff.): 'deviant behaviour', 'aberrant customer behaviour', 'problem customers', 'dysfunctional customer behaviour', 'inappropriate consumer behaviour' and 'direct and indirect customer revenge'. For the following, 'consumer misbehaviour' should be narrowed down: It is primarily about the peculiarities of 'fraud': "All types of fraud have in common that someone wants to gain a financial advantage by deceiving others." (Fetchenhauer et al. 2019, p. 101).

2.2 Tricks and Deceptions

A representative survey in 2017 wanted to know if people had ever lied before (markengold PR; Shoop 2017). These are the tricks German consumers use to gain their advantages:

- Extending vacation by calling in sick 44%
- Deducting private meals from taxes 20%
- Switching contract partners for new customer benefits 17%
- Fake accounts on eBay to drive up the price 16%
- Taking advantage of benefits with a fake student ID 16%
- Using the neighbor's Wi-Fi without their knowledge 15%
- False statements in job interviews 13%
- Slightly damaging clothing in the store to get a discount 11%
- Buying clothes for an event and then returning them 10%
- Using a friend's streaming service without their knowledge 9%

Thus, one thing is unmistakable: there is cheating and lying galore. "The temptations of consumer society thus promote—possibly flanked by the tendency towards hedonism—certain forms of crime." (Wiswede 2000, p. 64)

2.3 The Consumer: A Baron of Lies?

Lies have short legs, as the saying goes. That lies can take great leaps and grow into massive frauds was discovered by researchers from University College London. They prefaced their study with a simple statement: "Dishonesty is an integral part of our social world, influencing domains ranging from finance and politics to personal relationships" (Garret et al. 2016, p. 1). Cheating, deceiving, lying are part of life: 65% of Germans lie at least once a day, according to the aforementioned study (markengold PR; Shoop 2017).

The dishonesty of consumers is well researched, because "Consumers tell many lies" (Cowley and Anthony 2019, p. 180). In doing so, they run the risk of forgetting their content and revealing themselves; the memory of a lie is more accurate the riskier its exposure and the higher its arousal potential (Cowley and Anthony 2019). Emphatic statements ('I can swear it') are more truthful than purely factual ones; with 'weak' statements, the tendency to fib increases

(Gawn and Innes 2018). When it comes to dishonesty in a professional context (e.g. application), 32% of the German population seem to cheat for their own advantage, and there are hardly any differences between individual groups; only students cheat more than non-students (Djawadi and Fahr 2015). In market relationships, the tendency to lie is more pronounced than in personal relationships, where decisions are based more on intuition (Cappelen et al. 2013). And if there is no fear of being exposed and punished, many people lie quite significantly (Yaniv and Siniver 2016).

Is the tricking and deceiving consumer an oddball, a consumption alien, a modern baron of lies? Everyday misconduct such as white lies or tactical fibs have something banal about them. Benevolent observers of the times often perceive untrue claims as venial, small sins that can be helpful and do not really harm anyone: 'That's normal!'. Lying is very widespread and not limited to villains, the baron of lies à la Münchhausen would be an exaggerated metaphor. But the validity zones of market exchange are extended into shadowy areas.

2.4 The Consumer: an 'Average Joe'!

No one can tell by looking at a person's nose whether they have ever fibbed or lied or become aggressive. Even criminal behavior can easily elude the eye. According to the sociologist Wolfgang Sofsky (2016), perpetrators of violence, a more dramatic state of tricksters and deceivers, only become noticeable through their actions.

> "They are always inconspicuous, friendly, nice, balanced, some were considered a bit shy or inhibited. One greeted in the stairwell, the other did not. One seemed on the best way to 'integration', the other was on the way to 'disintegration', to Bulgaria. One prays, the other does not. One goes to the mosque, the other to school. [...] Some were mentally ill like millions of contemporaries. Others were not mentally ill like millions of contemporaries. But they were always quite inconspicuous".

The same can be assumed for consumers as perpetrators, although the norm violations of consumers weigh lighter compared to violent acts. One can only marvel at some tricks and stratagems, tantrums and frauds when they become known, especially when the culprits are well-liked neighbors, relatives, colleagues, sports comrades. Even people who stand out 'for the better' from the average of their fellow citizens are more likely to be noticed by their invisibility.

> "In a series of studies we found that it is nearly impossible to ascertain ex ante using observable measures such as gender, income, age, education and so on who is or is not more likely to possess certain social preference."

At least when comparing within a country; social responsibility of consumers is "more deeply embedded in the psyche of the individual" (Devinney et al. 2006, p. 8). Whether this applies equally to consumer misconduct remains to be seen. One might think of Bertolt Brecht's Threepenny Opera: "For some are in darkness/and others are in light/and you see those in the light/those in the darkness you do not see."

Misconduct in consumption is 'always and everywhere'. Consumers who—occasionally or often, a little or massively—misbehave are not social fringe existences or eccentrics with pathological peculiarities. This is about the maliciously egocentric behavior of citizen consumers, of 'average Joes'. About the rise of minorities, it was once said that their deviations from the usual expectations are now themselves assumed to be expectable (Kaube 2007, p. 9). Similarly, consumerist misconduct is not about unexpectedly extreme or bizarre: "But it's about quite normal deviations and the description of a society in which they have established themselves as normality." (ibid.)

2.5 Expansion of the Consumption Zone

A definition of consumerist misbehavior can be oriented towards a definition of 'dysfunctional customer behavior', which includes norm-based and damage-based approaches (Plein 2016, p. 11 ff.). Misbehavior in consumption is referred to in the following when a consumer behaves in relation to exchange processes on or off markets "- consciously or unconsciously, observable or unobservable—in such a way that his behavior violates an existing norm and is capable of impairing an achievement of objectives related to the behavior" (ibid., p. 13). Norms include laws, regulations, and generally accepted rules of conduct. Violations cause financial, physical, or emotional impairments. Achievement of objectives refers to one's own, selfish goals, not those of stakeholder groups, companies, authorities, or other consumers.

The 'misbehavior' corresponding to 'misconduct' is unclear, but it means nothing less than cheating, stealing, insulting, deceiving, disadvantaging, exploiting, taking advantage of, fooling—drastic terms that do justice to the intended norm violations in colloquial language. In this sense, one would like to call out to science in the spirit of the vernacular, it should also give the terms of research an object-appropriate color. In this sense, one can speak of 'criminal consumption', which is obvious in the case of shoplifting or insurance fraud. In Anglo-Saxon literature, 'criminal' is predominantly rejected for the misbehavior of consumers; reference is made to the unclear and misleading meaning of the term (Fullerton and Punj 1997, p. 339). In German usage, however, criminal has a more extensive meaning. According to Duden (https://www.duden.de/rechtschreibung/kriminell), criminal means 'tending to criminal, criminal actions' as well as "representing a punishable, criminal action"—both of which are serious. Colloquially, however, criminal also means, 'moving at the edge of what is allowed; irresponsible, bad; ruthless'. So you often hear in everyday life 'That's criminal!', even with banal occurrences.

With this meaning, we will continue to speak of 'criminal consumption' (CC). The concise formula does justice to the intended object: CC violates decency and manners, taste and values, acts aggressively and self-righteously, harms companies, authorities, and other consumers. CC is antisocial and weakens social cohesion. "CC" denotes objective misconduct, which is individually accountable and is not attributed decisionistically, as the labeling approach (Labelingansatz) assumes (Wiswede 1979, p. 142 ff.) However, precisely because of the colloquial meaning of 'criminal', one will ask oneself what is supposed to be so norm-violating about a criticized behavior and who decides about it.

2.6 Standards and Normality

The violation of social norms and/or 'unwritten laws' is constitutive for the definitions of 'consumer misbehavior'. This can be seen as their Achilles' heel. Because the vagueness of 'norms' raises questions about what exactly is to be criticized: "Indeed, behavior that is deemed 'dysfunctional' may differ according to individuals, contexts, cultures, and geographical locations." (Fisk et al. 2010, p. 422) Popular sayings to relativize normative expectations come to mind: 'Everyone does it', 'It's peanuts', 'Who's going to get upset?', 'You have to be a pig sometimes' or 'Once is not a time'. Some talk may even be based on firmly held beliefs. So what value-oriented behavioral demands are still clearly valid today? Hasn't it become normal to laugh at the decency criteria of a Knigge canon or to dismiss 'secondary virtues' such as politeness, diligence, discipline, duty, reliability, orderliness as outdated notions? Don't advocates of multiculturalism insist that cultural traditions are in principle equal, irrelevant in individual cases? Postmodernism advocates for arbitrariness of forms and contents. The demand for diversity claims general acceptance also of conflicting beliefs in societal, cultural, political, economic contexts. Group-specific diversity desire, however, necessitates the rejection of the standards of other stakeholders or the majority society. Diversity has its price also in the form of a disorienting value conflict.

As for norms and behavioral expectations that are understood under umbrella terms such as decency, only those value concepts that still find approval in the majority society and are sanctioned, more or less emphatically, should be meant here. As (at least probably future) majority-capable norms, the growing expectations for ethical, responsible, sustainable consumption should also apply. Whereas a 'moralization of consumption' is countered by the argument that it can lead to a self-righteous 'conscience prosperity' that stigmatizes all those who cannot (or do not want to) afford such a consumption style as 'consumption proletariat' and thus contributes to the exacerbation of social differences (Ulrich 2013, p. 140 f.). Finally, the norms of civil and criminal law should be given unrestricted validity.

2.7 Nothing Goes Without Norms

Any determination of deviant behavior presupposes certain ethical, moral, political, or theoretical considerations, which in turn are normatively oriented, which can lead to an infinite regress (Lamnek 2018, p. 33). The following assumes that economic exchange processes can only function successfully within an accepted set of rules, be it norms of decency, sustainability norms, contractual obligations, or criminal laws. The violation of such norms harms the trader, seller, craftsman, and other consumers at the micro level. In addition, it causes collateral damage: as a perceived shift in value orientations that still claim validity and are increasingly relativized:

> "People align their behavior with what they expect others to do or what others want from them. In certain situations, they are even able to change their behavior so drastically that they move far away from their values and beliefs. The more imperceptible this shift, the easier the change comes to us. In this way, even serious transgressions can appear to us as 'adjustments'" (Precht 2012, p. 264)

Such distorted perceptions of changed environmental conditions are referred to as 'shifting baselines': reference points of human perception shift (Rost 2014, p. 17 ff.). With the relativization of some traditional values, a loss of reputation of the model of the social and sustainable market economy is likely to be associated, which in turn should cause disorientations in consumer behavior. Further consequential damages are to be expected in social cohesion or respect for the state's monopoly on violence. It applies what was said in connection with Fair Trade: "Without justice, fairness, or decency, however, there are no stable exchange relationships. They form the foundation of the economy, which is always dependent on a certain amount of fairness." (Dohmen 2014, p. 145)

2.8 Variations of the Consumer Role

When CC takes extreme forms, the question arises whether, for example, repeated shoplifting or massive insurance fraud can still be referred to as consumer behavior, or whether criminal behavior would be more accurate. Otherwise, wouldn't the concept of the consumer role be overstretched? Expectations of a functioning market exchange include that performance is fairly exchanged for performance, goods for price, and in a mannerly form. Otherwise, the "elementary reason of the economy—a competitive value exchange—[…] would be turned into its opposite" (Kirchhof 2019). Social roles are constituted from behavioral expectations of the holder of a position. But should-expectations of CC, of intentional violations of the consumer role, are unimaginable in the majority society. Rather, such abnormal expectations exist in marginal fringe groups, sects, parallel societies, clans, gangs.

If one understands the role of the consumer with Hellmann (2019a, p. 3) as a public role (like that of the voter or the patient, i.e., a recipient of services), it becomes clear that it

> "equips the respective consumer with very own values, norms, role models. It is particularly important to emphasize that the individual consumer seems almost completely free in what is consumed and how it can be consumed." (ibid.)

In the understanding of this consumer role, self-responsibility towards the freedom moment would be of significantly less importance, both are only loosely coupled, which would have its consequences:

> "Despite the greatest degrees of freedom, consumers act astonishingly irresponsibly, as if the consumer role not only promises a maximum of freedom of action, but also largely absolves from appropriate self-responsibility!" (ibid.)

Under these circumstances, traditional rules of behavior and norms of decency are rather taken lightly. This also shows, as Hellmann (2019a, p. 261) points out, the dark side of often quite creative consumption: for example, 'burn-out' at motorcycle meetings or targeted modification of SUVs to consume particularly much fuel on public roads.

> "Less harmless, however, are shoplifting, rent nomads or electricity thieves; nonetheless, one cannot deny a certain creativity in their crimes to these consumers." (ibid., p. 262)

In the common conceptions of the consumer role, the possibility of indecent or criminal actions is not provided for. Nessel (2017, p. 37 ff.) for example, describes four dimensions of the consumer role: the interests of the consumer, his specific knowledge, the political-legal dimension, and the societal demands on consumers. One of the few exceptions is found in Fullerton (2007, p. 335), who refers to kleptomania, the pathological impulse to steal, as "an extreme form of consumer misbehavior characterized by impulse-control and obsessive-compulsive disorders". Here, extreme misbehavior is not separated from common consumer actions; this includes forms of criminal 'misbehavior'. But is the pickpocket also a consumer, with all his rights, or is he just a greedy villain? Is reaching into other people's pockets a market relationship? Probably not, but these are nominal definitions, their usefulness alone should decide their use. Violations of norms in exchange relationships are part of consumer reality. The functionality of communication and interaction in exchange processes is threatened by CC, but the role of the recipient of services is not invalidated. Faulty consumer behavior certainly implies a demoralization of the consumption zone and an expansion of the consumer role.

2.9 Typologies of Misbehavior in Consumption

A typology by Evans et al. (2013, p. 437) focuses on behavioral practices. The categories of misconduct in goods acquisition and product misuse are each assigned to abnormal and illegal consumer behavior. Thus, shoplifting falls into the combination of acquisition and illegal, excessive buying into the combination of acquisition and abnormal. Some authors systematize using overt and covert behaviors in financial motives (Harris and Reynolds 2004, cited in Hailat 2016, p. 42 f.) or define personal types such as 'model students', 'agitators', 'violators', 'role players' and 'arguers' (Jackel and Veres 2010, cited in Hailat 2016, p. 42). If less focus is placed on norm violation and more on the forms of action of 'consumer misbehavior', the term 'jaycustomers' is occasionally used, referring to problem customers, "who act in a thoughtless way, causing problems for the firm, its employees and other customers" (Lovelock 2001, p. 73). These are consumer images on a broad spectrum for Lovelock, which also includes criminal behavior: 'thiefs', 'rulebreakers', 'belligerents', 'cheats', 'family feuders' and 'vandals'

Along the dimensions of intensity and frequency of norm violations, behavior types of criminal consumption (CC) can be described. Figure 1 of such a domain-unspecific typology distinguishes four consumer images, which are named with slightly polemical wording:

For the CC 'little sinners' with few norm violations, micro-fouls against decency and manners would count, small cheats, such as 'overlooking' something in the shopping cart or white lies or the hoarding of toilet paper. These are practices that often arise from a current situation when a temptation is too great and self-control too low—peanuts for criminologists. With the 'slip-ups', one would also find irascible, unplanned short-circuit reactions, often also cunningly planned violations for one's own advantage, ugly attacks against salespeople or officials, which already hint at the psychological correlates. With very frequent norm violations, it looks different. Here one can assume a lack of empathy, insensitivity or even icy coldness, at least temporarily in the actions, probably also as a latent disposition. Speaking of 'consumer crooks' would be appropriate for habitual norm violations; here criminal law comes into play. This is exacerbated in the

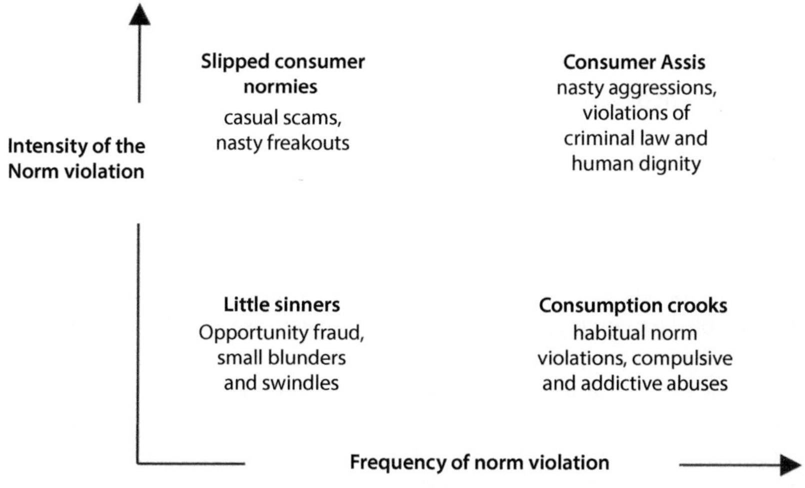

Fig. 1 A typology of criminal consumption (CC). *Source*: own illustration

'consumer louts', with their malicious aggressions, brazen frauds, contemptuous assaults on people, institutions and rights—a presumably small minority, to be expected in fringe groups, who are connected to the majority society in hostility; bizarre lifestyle and psychological anomalies would probably be disproportionately registered. The four categories overlap in reality, depending on the situation and current mood. Actions such as shoplifting or insults will probably be found in all four consumer images—John Q. Public is flexible.

3 Misbehavior in Everyday Consumption

3.1 Exemplary Keywords

Regarding minor invasive transgressions of 'little sinners', such as rudeness towards service staff or panic buying, reference is made to the everyday impressions of everyone. More severe are the civil or even criminally relevant practices: Returning used clothing to the sender, rental fraud by squatters, petrol theft at petrol stations, harassment of flight attendants, holiday complaints by means of false information, attacks on firefighters or police officers, physical assaults on doctors, downloading copyrighted files, payment with stolen debit or credit cards, theft in hotels. The following CC examples illustrate the often astounding combination of lack of guilt consciousness and mass prevalence in the so-called civil society.

3.2 Prototypical Examples

A lot is left by the wayside with Deutsche Bahn (DB) and public transport. Phone calls, loud talking, music in the quiet area of the DB are the least of it. Some reports on the DB information portal (bahnblogstelle 2019): 53-year-old man threatens train attendant in ICE; train driver spat on and attacked—federal police searching for suspect with photo; heavily intoxicated woman rampages in ICE. Attacks on DB employees also continued to increase in 2017 (faz.net. 2018). Security forces were particularly affected. "The tone in society is getting rougher, our employees feel it just like the police or fire brigade," a DB spokesman noted (ibid.). Two thirds of all offences occurred during ticket inspections and the enforcement of house rights at stations, especially during football matches and other major events. The increase in such cases, from almost zero a few years ago, is thought-provoking. Fraud against DB with the Bahncard 100 also seems to be increasing: Compensation payments are claimed for delayed trains that were not used at all (Ashelm 2019). With false information, one can swindle a quarter of the price. The low social ostracism is striking: Users exchange lively information on social media (ibid.).

Fare evasion is the colourful term for a "transportation by a means of transport in order to avoid paying the fare" (Bussmann 2016, p. 49). It is estimated that annually about 3.5% of all bus and train users travel without a valid ticket. Due to the minor consequences, 'fare evasion' is considered a petty offence, but is treated criminally. A downgrade to a regulatory offence is seriously discussed due to the effort for police and judiciary. The damage to the individual transport company is hardly noticeable, but the total lost revenue is estimated at 250 million EUR annually, which is missing from the overall deficit-ridden public transport. The perpetrators come from all age groups, men and teenagers are disproportionately noticeable. Motives are considered to be cost-benefit considerations (with low risk of detection) or the search for excitement, arousal.

This is also attributed to shoplifting. "One of the most impressive and typical phenomena of a modern economic and consumer society is shoplifting." (Bussmann 2016, p. 33) It too is considered a minor sin and falls under petty crime despite its widespread occurrence: It is estimated that approximately 23 million theft offenses are committed in retail each year, resulting in a total loss of 2.38 billion EUR (HDE 2019, p. 2). Besides suppliers, employees, and service staff, customers are the most frequent thieves. These are mainly teenagers and retirees, housewives and students, all from relatively low-income groups (Bussmann 2016, p. 41). According to police statistics, two-thirds are male, the proportion of repeat offenders is around 60%, the proportion of foreigners is above average, and every tenth person caught was under the influence of hard drugs (Spiegel online 2019). The causes mentioned include rising demands in consumer society, anonymity between customers and sales staff, and 'victim dilution'. This is a typical effect for shoplifting, which relieves the perpetrator's perception of a victimized victim because the damage is insured or spread over all buyers, especially in large companies (Bussmann 2016, p. 43). Additional factors were found in a Chinese study: a materialistic attitude, sensation seeking, and alienation, where perceived similarity with the staff rather inhibits and the impression of staff incompetence promotes the intention to steal (Bai et al. 2019). In general, the sigh of a security expert probably applies to all takeaway effects: "In retail, what is not nailed down is still stolen" (Spiegel online 2019).

Insurance fraud is considered the quintessential gentleman's crime, as every third insurance customer considers fraud largely acceptable and every second fraudster has told another person about it (Köneke et al. 2015, p. 5 f.): CC as a mass sport. About 20% of Germans have already submitted a false damage report

(Bussmann 2016, p. 86.) and obtained an unjustified cash or in-kind benefit from an insurance company. “A special investigation revealed that 45% of the submitted damage reports for laptops, smartphones, and flat screens were not justified” (ibid., p. 87). The damages in property and accident insurance due to fraud amount to approximately 4 billion EUR annually and increase the premiums for all insured. The perpetrators come from all social classes, younger policyholders, middle and upper bourgeoisie are somewhat overrepresented (ibid., p. 89). Causes and motives are similar to those of shoplifting and other wealth crimes. The main causes are the numerous opportunities for crime with an increasing number of insurance policies and ‘victim dilution’: One acts ‘rationally’ because the offense is considered normal, the insurance companies pay less than they should, the damages are abstract and distributed among many, the risks appear low; and one believes one can ‘avenge’ oneself because one has paid high premiums in the past or has been disappointed by insurance companies (ibid., p. 90 ff.). The result is a lack of awareness of wrongdoing, which further undermines the moral situation: the uncertainty about which values and norms actually apply, which are unclear or no longer apply.

> “In terms of insurance fraud, our society is certainly not yet in a state of anomie, in which the value of honesty towards insurers no longer exists, but possibly on the way there, or in other words somewhere between yellow and red.” (Köneke 2015, p. 148)

The civilizing veneer in the everyday consumption of civil society is obviously thin. Why is that?

4 Causes and Conditions

4.1 Present Notes

‘Victim dilution’ and a lack of awareness of wrongdoing, coupled with low social ostracism, appear to be key causes of criminal consumption (CC). Other causes and motives are mentioned in the literature on ‘consumer misbehavior’. Evans et al. (2013, p. 447) mention the following: temptation to satisfy unfulfilled aspirations when this is not legally possible; desire for thrill and adventure; a lack of moral inhibition; weak/strong group bonding; negative attitude towards capitalism or certain companies; situational circumstances; weighing of risks and benefits. In the case of unauthorized exchange of goods, they note a widespread lack of awareness of wrongdoing (ibid., p. 436). Fullerton and Punj (1993, p. 571 f.) distinguish between demographic and psychological characteristics, social influences, interaction effects, and the situation of the exchange. Fisk et al. (2010, p. 419 ff.) separate situational factors from personality factors and refer, among other things, to the role of psychological and triggering trigger factors. Other authors cite materialism, narcissism, or unethical attitudes, for example. A stringent system is not in sight, which is likely due to different research perspectives and disciplines.

4.2 A Framework Concept for Criminal Consumption

In addition to internal factors (personality traits), there are external, situational factors that become effective as triggers of the current setting. Added to this are situationally conditioned cognitive processes that result from the current decision-making situation, such as assessments of impending risks. External factors are based on cultural, social, or economic contexts. Figure 2 shows how the individual factors mentioned can be grouped into these four categories.

4.2.1 Internal Factors

Fullerton and Punj (2004, p. 1240 ff.) highlight five factors: the absence of binding moral convictions; opportunism as a result of weighing risks and benefits; 'thrill seeking' as a pursuit of excitement; unfulfilled claims that promote compensatory action and contribute to a 'claim audacity' (Botho Strauß); and pathological socialization that leads to 'misbehavior' as revenge on a disliked company. In this context, one can think of the 'Dark Triad' as a consequence of socialization, the collective term for Machiavellianism, psychopathology, and narcissism (Jonasson and Middleton 2015, p. 671 ff.). Machiavellianism is attributed a cynical, empathy-free instrumentalization of social relationships to gain, for example, selfish advantages in economic exchange relationships, tactically cunning. Machiavellians are considered skilled liars. Psychopathology characterizes reckless, aggressive individuals who tend to antisocial behavior. Narcissism refers to an egocentric lifestyle that places the self above the needs of others. With high self-esteem, narcissism tends to an aggressive attitude, risk-taking, and expectation of reward. Narcissistic students, for example, tend to cheat because they have no guilt (Brunell et al. 2011, p. 323 ff.). The three dimensions are likely to correlate closely with low self-control and low law-abidingness, which are mentioned in connection with 'misbehavior'. Increased values on the scale of the Dark Triad show materialistically minded people who also tend to escapist shopping and

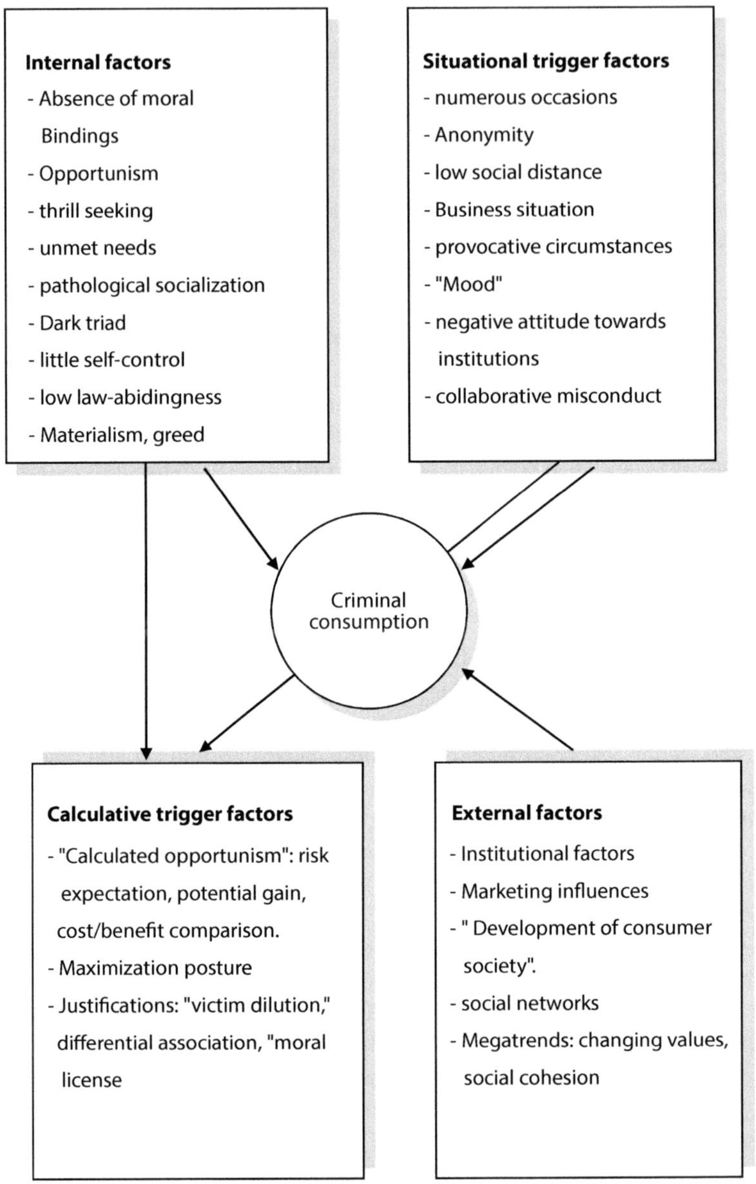

Fig. 2 A framework concept for criminal consumption (CC). *Source*: own illustration

impulsive buying (Richins 2017, p. 490). Materialism is seen as the belief that possession and acquisition are central to satisfaction and happiness (ibid., p. 481). The social relationships of materialists are weaker and the fears of threats greater than others. This and other characteristics of materialists such as lack of control, envy, and selfishness (Lee and Ahn 2016, p. 21) are likely to make them more susceptible to CC. Greed manifests itself in "excessiveness, grabbing without end, a never-ending dissatisfaction" (Edelbacher et al. 2015, p. 16). As an "excessive desire for more than is needed" (Razen and Stefan 2019, p. 164), it is based on dispositions or is situationally stimulated; feelings of a pronounced entitlement are often its background (ibid., p. 167).

4.2.2 Situational Trigger Factors

The likelihood of CC increases with the number of occasions, which is obvious, and with assured anonymity (Schitter et al. 2019). The situation in the business affects the type of products and services, the physical environment (size, displays, light, colors, scent, noises), the behavior of the staff, the security measures, the image, etc. (Fullerton and Punj 1993, p. 573). Dissatisfaction with these features can trigger dysfunctional customer behavior (Daunt and Harris 2012). According to Bude (2016, p. 45), a behavior-relevant 'mood' is "the affectation by the socio-spatial, time-historical and biographical situation, which invites me to get involved and play my role". This could be a description of the situation in which a consumer sees himself when the opportunity that makes thieves seems favorable. Provocative circumstances such as waiting times, heat, crowds, and noise are mentioned, which can trigger misconduct (Fullerton and Punj 2004, p. 1245). Negative attitudes towards companies, for example due to moral misconduct, can lead to 'consumer cynicism', a hostile attitude that promotes rebellious and manipulative behavior such as lying (Helm et al. 2015, p. 516): CC then appears legitimized. Also, harmful products can lead consumers to lie, steal, cheat in order to punish the brand (Rotman et al. 2017). Collaborative misconduct is possible when the respective need for connection and belonging is intense in a pair, with the common misconduct further bonding. Then the dyad behaves as a 'partner in crime' more unethically than comparable individuals (Nikolova et al. 2018).

4.2.3 Calculative Trigger Factors

'Calculated opportunism' involves selfish but rational considerations. It has been proven that fraud is easier when the risk of detection and reputation loss is low, as shown by the example of tax morale (Grundmann and Lambsdorff 2017). A decision to lie follows a weighing of potential advantage and the intrinsic costs of lying. The cost/benefit comparison then decides on truth or lie (Kajackaite and Gneezy 2017). The higher the probability and extent of disadvantages, the less is lied (Thielmann and Hilbig 2018); the higher the expected advantage, the more is lied (Brocas and Carillo 2019). Also, a maximizing attitude ('maximizing mindset') in the sense of 'only the best!' can promote immoral behavior (Goldsmith et al. 2017).

Victim dilution facilitates rationalizations. The assumption, for example, that the damage caused to the victim is minor, facilitates 'denial of injury' and 'denial of victim', i.e., the denial of misconduct (Dootson et al. 2014). Differential association means that the members of a group, whose values differ from those of the majority society, receive legitimation of their misconduct from the group (Fullerton and Punj 2004, p. 1245). Individuals issue themselves a moral free pass when they act without guilt because they have done good in the past. Also, the impression of having suffered injustice could cause a kind of feeling of revenge and strengthen the conviction to now compensate themselves through CC.

4.2.4 External Factors

Behind internalized attitudes and values, influencing factors at the meso and macro level are assumed, which work either in the short term or indirectly through socialization processes. The research situation on this is, as far as can be seen, extremely thin, so only a few, quite speculative keywords are appropriate. The importance of trust in public institutions for unethical behavior is shown using the example of India, which offers parallels to Western countries (Agnihotri and Bhattacharya 2019). Influences of marketing, which tend to reinforce a consumer ideology, can according to Fullerton and Punj (2004) also unintentionally be the cause of negative consumer behavior. Falk and Szech (2013) showed in an experiment how market interaction can erode moral values. The combination of market exchange and specific culture can also lead to a displacement of moral values and to offenses according to Irlenbusch and Villeval (2015, p. 89) when the marginal benefit of an action appears higher than its marginal costs, especially with a materialistic orientation and diluted sense of responsibility. The development of consumer society is taking a negative direction according to Schmidbauer (2017, p. 70 ff.): decreasing frustration tolerance, demand for quick satisfaction, renaissance of revenge, which brings narcissistic disorders and is likely to also promote tendencies towards CC. The problematic effects of social networks for value formation, identity ideals, and affirmation in the virtual bubbles with their excluding consonance offers could also be mentioned here. This should be linked to a debate about value change in the context of extremist cultural and political camp formations, which are characterized by increasing black-and-white thinking and the pleasure in enemy images. This certainly also has to do with the lamented loss of social cohesion—all factors that obviously facilitate, legitimize, and reinforce misconduct. Why not also in consumption?

The variables of the four categories can reinforce a tendency towards CC. With opposing characteristics, they can indeed have inhibiting, 'good' effects in favor of the consumer role. Can one agree, after all, when there is increasing talk of 'prosperity neglect', not only in children? It would make sense to argue about this with clear terms. CC is only limited evidence for the claim because the search for its occurrence has so far mainly taken place at the micro level. The notorious misconduct in many areas of behavior, the brutalization of civil society—does it still deserve its name?—are social, cultural phenomena, the personal aspects of which only represent a section of the interdependencies. Is this how the "Age of Extremes" continues, as Eric Hobsbawn (1995, p. 428) called the twentieth century? "The real drama took place rather in the dissolution of the old value systems, rules and conventions that once ordered human behavior." (ibid.)

5 What Could be Done?

CC has underlying causes that partially overlap, reinforce, and vary by area. Insurance fraud is committed with different motives and under different conditions than shoplifting in a supermarket. Victim dilution, lack of awareness of wrongdoing are widespread, the acceptance of some CC practices seems to be gaining popularity. A royal road to containing market-hostile and antisocial overreaches in consumption processes is therefore not to be expected from any of the following groups of actors.

5.1 Companies and Associations

Companies and business associations are noticeably reticent in their statements on CC. Apparently, they do not want to unnecessarily step on the toes of customers, whether loyal or potential. 'The Empire Strikes Back' is not a threat, just the title of a movie. The President of the German Bundestag, Wolfgang Schäuble, criticized the offering economy when he accused it of complacent contentment in connection with globalization: "There needs to be an awareness that the behavior of economic actors cannot be free of moral self-obligations [...] In short: We need more decency again" (author unknown 2019). This should also apply in relation to their customers, whom the actors of the economy have to face, confidently and with a sense of proportion. “For acts of economic crime, it is often the absence of reactions, the non-intervention of the authorities […], which encourages the actors to repeat or even increase their activities.” (Wiswede 1979, p. 47) Possible measures depend crucially on industries, types of companies, and forms of CC. A specific overview is not possible at this point. Differentiated presentations of measures for prevention and sanction can be found in Bussmann (2016, p. 44 ff.), for example for shoplifting, credit fraud, criminal use of new payment systems, insurance, violation of intellectual property.

5.2 Consumer Policy

“Consumer policy is about how consumers can be educated, informed, supported, and protected” (Reisch and Micklitz 2019, p. 94). It is not about preventing planned CC. The instruments of consumer policy are hardly suitable for addressing CC. At most, it is conceivable that the dark sides of consumption at the expense of third parties could be included in the human images underlying the instruments and, for example, be taken into account in advice. This could draw attention to the impropriety of false claims or warn of criminal risks. Towards companies and Schufa (General Credit Protection Agency), for example, one could show understanding for scoring measures and participate in their design. In policy advice, initiatives might need to be taken that target fraudulent customer behavior in the insurance industry. All not very convincing, ultimately CC remains a non-issue for consumer policy.

5.3 Politics and State

Politics and the state should be reminded of their duty to enforce law and order. Because consumer protection laws are the necessary one thing, sanctions from CC the complementary other. Against shoplifting, for example, facilitated video surveillance and increased interest from the police and judiciary would help, both of which obviously lack consistent law enforcement (HDE 2019, p. 3). The liberal state, which imagines itself to be defensive, finds it difficult to show edge: in the case of abuse of social systems or asylum law, anti-Semitism, criminal parallel societies, digital hate excesses. And with ‘minor offenses’ such as shoplifting or fare evasion, the urge to act against consumers, who also vote, is likely to be even lower. What has been noted about political radicalization should also apply to consumer aberrations:

> "Here one encounters what can be observed in politics and society since time immemorial: resentment and envy, hatred and contempt, anger and aggression, and one is reminded that the state order, with the monopoly of violence concentrated in it, was established to control these dispositions and behaviors and to prevent their expression—something that has often been forgotten under the impression of a society that has become liberal as a matter of course." (Münkler and Münkler 2019, p. 59)

So consequently

> "it is necessary to demand rule-compliant behavior and to strengthen the authority of the state enforcement and legal bodies. Anyone who rejects this as a 'law and order' course because they see behind it the danger of an illiberal, authoritarian state, has not understood the importance of the rule of law for social stability." (Steinbrück 2018, p. 137)

So far, so accurate. Only: Broken windows can no longer be cleaned.

5.4 Education and Upbringing

The debates about the education system "overwhelm schools with dozens of expectations they can only fall short of, which keeps the debate in a state of constant alarm" (Kaube 2019, p. 23). Schools are overwhelmed and complain about too little and inadequately trained staff, the premises are often worn out, bullying and indiscipline are rampant, pedagogical approaches are ideologically and practically distorted (Winterhoff 2019). In such a situation, an overloaded curriculum, limited time resources, and damaged motivation of the teaching staff set limits for further demands.

It remains unclear what schools could even achieve on the topic of consumer culture. They are hardly able to prepare the young consumers for their role as consumers. In a subject like 'Economic Education', a promotion of consumer competence (Bala and Schuldzinski 2019a, p. 149) and training to be a contractually reliable and fair consumer could be conceivable. The consumer interest anchored in the subject of consumer education in the schools of Schleswig-Holstein offers the chance to also address misconduct as a didactic orientation mark. However, this also depends on the individual inclinations of the teachers. This leads to the conclusion:

> "Anyone who wants to change something in the reality outside of school must turn to the adults. Because they create the circumstances of socialization and education, and if they partially withdraw from it, it makes the work of the school more difficult." (Kaube 2019, p. 266)

The possibilities of parents to influence the behavior-guiding norms of their children are considerable; adolescents perceive exactly how people in their immediate environment behave (Collado et al. 2019, p. 288). What parents suggest about correct consumer behavior, about contractual fidelity or civil dealings with sellers, is likely to be embedded in their own behavior. Personal values and norms conform—in the learning type of "do-feel-learn" (Moser 1997, p. 273)—to previous behaviors in such a way that they become consistent with them and prevent cognitive dissonances (Rosenberger 2005, p. 44). Thus, educational impulses for fair consumer behavior are actually only conceivable within the relevant ethical corridor of the older generation. It may not always be wide enough. The differences in consumption and behavioral norms between generations are therefore likely to be less significant than in other areas of life. If young and old are equally exposed to materialistic consumer temptations, it could be concluded, individual resilience also against temptations to cheat and deceive probably differs more between different families (households, partnerships etc.) than within a family. In addition, parents who believe that external circumstances control the outcome of an event more than they themselves can (with an external 'locus of control', LoC), for example in the case of the problem of children's advertising on the Internet, prefer state regulation and have less responsibility than parents with an internal LoC. People with an internal LoC see themselves as 'change agents', perceive their environment more consciously and strive to change it (Vijayalakshmi et al. 2018). They would be well suited to the task of educating for fair consumer behavior.

5.5 Media

One can feel a relative optimism when looking at the potential impact of radio, television, and magazines as traditional leading media. However, their socializing and orienting effects are shrinking compared to digital networks, influencers, and virtual worlds. Advice or information formats certainly offer the opportunity for exciting and informative contributions about peculiarities of CC: shoplifting, complaint fraud, vandalism, mail order fraud, assaults against service or security personnel. Pushing for such topics would also be a task for consumer representatives in the committees. Tricking and deceiving for the sake of an undeserved advantage without significant threat of sanction—this topic, however, seems unpopular in the editorial offices. Media executives do not want to unnecessarily offend their recipients, for whom there is indeed an initial suspicion of CC. There is no public bashing, the educational mandate remains non-binding.

5.6 Consumer Sciences

A significant part of consumer research sees itself as "consumer policy relevant research" (Ölander 2005, p. 23), oriented towards the interests of consumers. Socially harmful interests are not meant by this. The consumer only becomes the subject as a wrongdoer when he harms the environment or climate. "Otherwise, many works are dedicated to what is labeled in public discourse as ethical, moral, sustainable, or political consumption and now receives a lot of attention." (Hellmann 2019b, p. 441) This is sensible, but not enough. A decidedly realistic consumer image has not yet been won with this.

Future research should examine the factors mentioned in the framework for CC, their direct and indirect, CC-promoting and CC-inhibiting effects. Research funds could be hoped for from companies or associations affected by CC. For funding sources that are favorably disposed towards sustainability issues, initial presentations of the dark sides of consumption would be appropriate to raise awareness of this problem as well.

The Consumer Research Network of the Federal Ministry of Justice and Consumer Protection chose 'The Dark Sides of Consumption—Old Problems, New Challenges' as the theme of its annual conference in 2019. For a long time, consumer research has dealt with the bright sides: from the informed consumer to the 'information seeker' to the trusting, worthy of protection, participative, cooperative, ethical, sharing-driven consumer. This may be because a consumer image that depicts unethical or criminal behavior does not fit a friendly human image. 'Consumer misbehavior' "is an unpleasant aspect of a culture which does not like unpleasantness" (Fullerton and Punj 1997, p. 337). The conference agenda included topics such as addiction risks in gambling and media, new worlds of desire in mass art and self-optimization, consumers between old and new egoisms (immoral behavior and the 'hypocritical consumer'). The conclusion was that one should beware of over- and under-moralization in order to arrive at a differentiated view of the consumer; he is neither only good nor only evil. However, this increasing talk of dark sides of consumption has not yet gained the brand personality of a real narrative, where it may also remain. Nevertheless, every narrative requires an introduction.

5.7 Civil Society

Consumer citizens could also become active in favor of ethical consumption practices outside of their consumer role. Familiar with the dark sides of CC, they should be asked to share responsibility and participate. What would be required is a determined 'attitude' towards CC, an insightful and conflict-ready opposition. However, this would have to be able to rely on a socially binding norm for individual (and institutional) behavior, which is still little to be seen. What is required is an expansion of consciousness that CC is anti-social and anti-economic. The consumer citizens are far from this, also because of their opinion leaders and media. Social ostracism of CC practices should follow the problem awareness. This would also include an understanding of sanctions. Ostracism would mean: making it clear to the friend who boasts of insurance fraud that he is acting anti-socially; reminding the colleague that shoplifting requires video surveillance and breeds mistrust; dissuading the son from thinking that fare evasion is cool, etc. This would not be about paternalistic know-it-all or denunciation, but about the chance to set a credible impulse for attitude changes. In the best case as a guide for model learning and identification. All of this is still a desideratum in a convenience culture, because the talks about prosperity neglect point in other directions.

6 Consumer Images Reloaded

Trickery and deception in consumption, if it goes beyond the banal, testify to a damaged sense of responsibility. In the context of globalization, historian Ian Kershaw (2019, p. 764 f.) recognizes a strengthening of individualism. The individual choice of consumer goods and lifestyles would have immensely widened

> "But in the course of this development, the sense of responsibility for a community that goes beyond the individual has been weakened, and there is nothing to suggest that this trend will reverse." (ibid.)

One must probably realize "that consumer misbehavior is an ineradicable component of consumption culture itself" (Fullerton and Punj 2004, p. 1245). Consumption and culture is not a mésalliance.

Is such talk pessimistic? Education and intelligence, for example, do not exclude misconduct. Mental power and expertise, awareness of problems and insider knowledge, experience and empathy, competencies for this and that—everything is initially ambivalent and equidistant to compliance with norms and rule-breaking. Any human capital can also be instrumentalized in consumption for or against behavioral expectations, for or against law and order. Historical examples, cinema westerns or television crime dramas present us with ambivalent characters. Many a hero or heroine are often thieves/crooks/gangsters/fraudsters/killers—but they are also sympathetic, intelligent, self-confident and clever and often look dazzling. Regarding another figure demanding respect, that of the intellectual, the songwriter and poet Wolf Biermann disrespectfully formulates:

> "My grandmother always said: 'Through cleverness one becomes stupid.' That was a very wise sentence. It means that people who are a little cleverer in the head are very endangered because they can lie to themselves faster and better. The simple people can't do that so well. […] They can bend everything to fit their needs. That's the curse of the intellectuals. It's an occupational disease of the educated. They can deceive themselves elegantly and effectively." (Biermann and Szpilman 2014)

Our consumer images should also include such things and the possibility of CC.

Is such research a misanthropic science? That negative images of people have a tradition in economics is shown by a historical overview of ideas by Thieme (2013). He sees misanthropic basic patterns in the negative image of man in economic approaches, in their distance from reality of life as well as in the concept of competition/market (ibid., p. 56 f.). The talk of CC remains unaffected by this: Unbiasedly, consumer sciences should investigate the personal and cultural spectrum of the real existing consumer world, the bright *and* the dark sides of consumption. A behavior-relevant combination of human potential, socialization and opportunity decides how stable or unstable the endangered balance between mastering the consumer role and its violation is. Whether the effort for 'Consumer Social Responsibility' or for 'Mindfulness' helps significantly here remains open. This is not a misanthropic statement, but a plausible assumption about behavioral contingencies of man as a deficient being. Even through criminal consumption, he tries to compensate for some need deprivation. Trickery and deception is ubiquitous, therefore also in consumption. The work on the myth of the 'ethical consumer' is not yet finished.

References

Agnihotri, Arpita, and Saurabh Bhattacharya. 2019. Unethical consumer behavior: The role of institutional and socio-cultural factors. *Journal of Consumer Marketing* 36:124–135.

Ashelm, Michael. 2019. Betrugsmasche mit verspäteten Zügen. *Frankfurter Allgemeine Zeitung* 44:22.

Bachner, Frank, Sylvia Vogt, and Susanne Vieth-Entus. 2018. Schüler und Eltern im Kampfmodus. *Der Tagesspiegel* 23462:7.

Bahnblogstelle. 2019. Aktualisiert November/Dezember 2019. https://bahnblogstelle.net/2019/10/29/stark-alkoholisierte-frau-randaliert-im-ice

Bai, Yin, Wu Wie-Ping, and Millissa F.Y. Cheung. 2019. How personality traits, employee incompetence and consumer similarity influence shoplifting behavior. *Journal of Consumer Marketing* 36:379–392.

Bala, Christian, and Klaus Müller, eds. 2015. *Abschied vom Otto Normalverbraucher. Moderne Verbraucherforschung: Leitbilder, Information, Demokratie*. Essen: Klartext.

Bala, Christian, and Wolfgang Schuldzinski, eds. 2019a. *Der vertrauende Verbraucher. Zwischen Regulation und Information. Reihe Beiträge zur Verbraucherforschung*, Vol. 9. Düsseldorf: Verbraucherzentrale NRW.

Bala, Christian and Wolfgang Schuldzinski. 2019b. Einleitung: Der ‚vertrauende Verbraucher'. In *Der vertrauende Verbraucher. Zwischen Regulation und Information.* Reihe Beiträge zur Verbraucherforschung, Vol. 9. eds. C. Bala and W. Schuldzinski, 7–15. Düsseldorf: Verbraucherzentrale NRW.

Biermann, Wolf and Daniel W. Szpilman. 2014. Jeder Massenmörder ist menschlich. *Basler Zeitung*, 6. November.

Blättel-Mink, Birgit, and Kai-Uwe Hellmann, eds. 2010. *Prosumer Revisited. Zur Aktualität einer Debatte. Buchreihe Konsumsoziologie und Massenkultur*. Wiesbaden: VS Verlag.

Brocas, Isabelle, and Juan D. Carillo. 2019. A neuroeconomic theory of (dis) honesty. *Journal of Economic Psychology* 71:4–12.

Brunell, Amy B., Sara Staats, Jamie Barden, and Julie M. Hupp. 2011. Narcissm and academic dishonesty: The exhibitionism dimension and the lack of guilt. *Personality and Individual Differencies* 50:323–328.

Bude, Heinz. 2016. *Das Gefühl der Welt. Über die Macht von Stimmungen*. München: Hanser.

Bussmann, Kai-D. 2016. *Wirtschaftskriminologie I Grundlagen – Markt- und Alltagskriminalität*. München: Vahlen.

Cappelen, Alexander W., Erik Ø. Sørensen, and Bertil Tungodden. 2013. When do we lie? *Journal of Economic Behavior & Organization* 93:258–265.

Carrigan, Marylyn. 2017. Why are we still no ethical shoppers? Revisiting ‚The myth of the ethical consumer' – do ethics matter in purchase behavior? *Journal of Consumer Ethics* 1:11–21.

Collado, Silvius, Henk Staats, and Patricia Sancho. 2019. Normative influences on adolescents' self-reported pro-environmental behaviors: The role of parents and friends. *Environment and Behavior* 51:288–314.

Cowley, Elizabeth, and Christina I. Anthony. 2019. Deception memory: When will consumers remember their lies? *Journal of Consumer Research* 46:180–199.

Daunt, Kate L., and Lloyd C. Harris. 2011. Customers acting badly. Evidence from the hospitality industry. *Journal of Business Research* 64:1034–1042.

Daunt, Kate L., and Lloyd C. Harris. 2012. Exploring the forms of dysfunctional customer behavior: A study of differencies in servicescape and customer disaffection with service. *Journal of Marketing Management* 28:129–153.

Devinney, Timothy M. 2011. The myth of the ethical consumer. *The conversation.* https://theconversation.com/the-myth-of-the-ethical-consumer-204

Devinney, Timothy M., Pat Auger, Gianna M. Eckhardt and Thomas Birtchnell. 2006. The other CSR: Consumer social responsibility. *Stanford Social Innovation Review*, Leeds University Business School Working Paper, Nr. 15–04, 1–14.

Devinney, Timothy M., Pat Auger, and Gianna M. Eckhardt. 2010. *The myth of the ethical consumer*. Cambridge: Cambridge University Press.

Djawadi, Behnud Mir, and René Fahr. 2015a. ‚… and they are really lying': Clean evidence on the pervasiveness of cheating in professional contexts from a field experiment. *Journal of Economic Psychology* 48:48–59.

Dobelli, Rolf. 2014. *Die Kunst des klaren Denkens: 52 Denkfehler, die Sie besser anderen überlassen*. München: dtv.

Dohmen, Caspar. 2014. *Otto Normalverbraucher. Vom Sinn und Unsinn engagierten Konsumierens*. Zürich: Orell Füssli.

Dootson, Paula, Larry Neale, and Sam Fullerton. 2014. When size matters. Exploring perceptions and justifications of deviant consumer behavior. *Advances in Consumer Research* 42:298–301.

Edelbacher, Max, Valentina Bruns, and Elmar Weixlbaumer. 2015. *Die neue Gier. Warum wir immer maßloser werden*. Berlin: Goldegg.

Engels, Jens Ivo, Andreas Fahrmeit, Frédéric Monier, and Olivier Dard. 2015. *Krumme Touren in der Wirtschaft. Zur Geschichte ethischen Fehlverhaltens und seiner Bekämpfung*. Köln: Böhlau.

Erlinger, Rainer. 2016. *Höflichkeit. Vom Wert einer wertlosen Tugend*. Frankfurt a. M.: Fischer.

Evans, Martin, Ahmad Jamal, and Gordon Foxall. 2013. *Consumer Behaviour*. 2nd edn. Chichester, West Sussex: Wiley.

Falk, Armin, and Nora Szech. 2013. Morals and markets. *Science* 340:707–711.

faz.net. 2018. Aktualisiert am 19.03.2018. https://www.faz.net/aktuell/gesellschaft/kriminalitaet/deutsche-bahn-mehr-angriffe-auf-mitarbeiter-15501913.html

Fetchenhauer, Detlef, Anne-Sophie Lang, and Dominik H. Enste. 2019. Otto Normalbetrüger: Psychologie eines alltäglichen Delikts. In *Betrug in der digitalisierten Welt. Erkennen. Vorbeugen. Schützen*, ed. M. Freytag, 100–113. Frankfurt a. M.: FAZIT Communication GmbH.

Fisk, Ray, Stephen Grove, Lloyd C. Harris, Dominique A. Keeffe, Kate L. Daunt, Rebekah Russell-Bennett, and Jürgen Wirtz. 2010. Customers behaving badly: A state of the art review, research agenda and implications for practitioners. *Journal of Services Marketing* 24:417–429.

Fuentes, Christian, and Niklas Sörum. 2019. Agencing ethical consumers: Smartphone apps and the socio-material reconfiguration of everyday life. *Consumption Markets & Culture* 22:131–156.

Fullerton, Ronald A. 2007. Psychoanalyzing kleptomania. *Marketing Theory* 7:335–352.

Fullerton, Ronald A., and Girish Punj. 1993. Choosing to misbehave: A structural model of aberrant consumer behavior. *Advances in Consumer Research* 20:570–574.

Fullerton, Ronald A., and Girish Punj. 1997. What Is Consumer Misbehavior? *Advances in Consumer Research* 24:336–339.

Fullerton, Ronald A., and Girish Punj. 2004. Repercussions of promoting an ideology of consumption: Consumer misbehavior. *Journal of Business Research* 57:1239–1249.

Gärtner, Stefan, and Jürgen Roth. 2014. *Benehmt Euch! Ein Pamphlet*. Köln: Dumont.
Gawn, Glynis, and Robert Innes. 2018. Language and lies. *Journal of Behavioral and Experimental Economics* 74:167–176.
Garrett, Neil, Stephanie C. Lazzaro, Dan Ariely, and Tali Sharot. 2016. The brain adapts to dishonesty. *Nature Neuroscience* 19:1727–1732.
Goldsmith, Kelly, Caroline Roux, and Jingjing Ma. 2017. When seeking the best brings out the worst in consumers: Understanding the relationship between a maximizing mindset and immoral behavior. *Journal of Consumer Psychology* 28:293–309.
Grundmann, Susanna, and Johann Graf Lambsdorff. 2017. How income and tax rates provoke cheating – An experimental investigation of tax morale. *Journal of Economic Psychology* 63:27–43.
Hacke, Axel. 2018. *Über den Anstand in schwierigen Zeiten and die Frage, wie wir miteinander umgehen*. München: Goldmann.
Hailat, Khaled Qassem. 2016. *The influence of consumer misbehaviour on the perceived brand image of Jordanian higher education institutions*. PhD.Thesis, College of Business and Law University of Salford
Harris, Lloyd C., and Kate L. Reynolds. 2004. Jaycustomer behavior: An exploration into the types and motives in the hospitality industry. *Journal of Services Marketing* 18:339–357.
Hatebook. Die Pöbel-Demokratie. 2017. *Cicero Magazin für politische Kultur*, Nr. 3.
HDE Handelsverband Deutschland. 2019. *Forderungspapier. Forderungen zur Bekämpfung des Ladendiebstahls*. Berlin: BDI. https://einzelhandel.de/index.php?option=com_attachments&task=download&id=10309
Hellmann, Kai-Uwe. 2017. Die akademische Konsumforschung aus soziologischer Sicht. In *Verbraucherwissenschaften. Rahmenbedingungen, Forschungsfelder und Institutionen*, eds. P. Kenning, A. Oehler, L.A. Reisch, and C. Gugel, 141–164. Wiesbaden: Springer Gabler.
Hellmann, Kai-Uwe. 2019a. *Der Konsum der Gesellschaft. Studien zur Soziologie des Konsums*. 2., erweiterte Aufl. Wiesbaden: Springer VS.
Hellmann, Kai-Uwe. 2019b. Akademische Konsumforschung im Aufwind: multidisziplinär, kritisch, politisch. *Soziologische Review* 42:440–453.
Helm, Amanda E., Julie Guidry Moulard, and Marsha Richins. 2015. Consumer cynicism: developing a scale to measure underlying attitudes influencing marketplace shaping and withdrawal. *International Journal of Consumer Studies* 39:515–524.
Herbold, Astrid. 2019. Ein Knigge für heute. *Der Tagesspiegel* 23853:16.
Hobsbawn, Eric. 1995. *Das Zeitalter der Extreme Weltgeschichte des 20. Jahrhunderts*. München: Hanser.
Hock, Andreas. 2016. *Ich verbitte mir diesen Ton, Sie Arschloch! Über den Niedergang der Umgangsformen*. München: Riva.
Institut für Demoskopie Allensbach. 2019. *Generation Mitte 2019*. https://www.gdv.de/resource/blob/51046/99f507fd8da99911222384e62482c8fe/generation-mitte-2019—factsheet-data.pdf. Accessed 27 Sept. 2019
Irlenbusch, Bernd, and Marie Claire Villeval. 2015. Behavioral ethics: How psychology influenced economics and how economics might inform psychology? *Current Opinion in Psychology* 6:87–92.

Jackel, Katalin and Zoltan Veres. 2010. *Exploring Frontline Conflicts at Higher Education Institutions. A Complex Methodological Approach*. Apas Papers 166, Academic Public Administration Studies Archive – APAS.

Jonasson, Peter K., and P. Middleton. 2015. Dark triad: The ‚Dark Side' of human personality. In international encyclopedia of the social & behavioral sciencies. 2nd edn. 5:671–675.

Kajackaite, Agne, and Uri Gneezy. 2017. Incentives and cheating. *Games and Economic Behavior* 102:433–444.

Kaube, Jürgen. 2007. *Otto Normalabweichler. Der Aufstieg der Minderheiten*. Springer: Klampen.

Kaube, Jürgen. 2019. *Ist die Schule zu blöd für unsere Kinder?* 2nd edn. Berlin: Rowohlt.

Kershaw, Ian. 2019. *Achterbahn. Europa 1950 bis heute*, 2nd edn. München: DVA.

Kirchhof, Paul. 2019. Von Freiheit geprägt Das Grundgesetz enthält keine besondere Wirtschaftsverfassung, aber einen klaren Leitgedanken. *Frankfurter Allgemeine Zeitung* 188:6.

Kleinrichert, Denise. 2012. Review: The myth of the ethical consumer. *Contemporary Sociology* 41:191–193.

Köneke, Vanessa, Horst Müller-Peters, and Detlef Fetchenhauer. 2015. *Versicherungsbetrug verstehen und verhindern*. Wiesbaden: Springer Gabler.

Lamnek, Siegfried. 2018. *Theorien abweichenden Verhaltens I: Klassische Ansätze'. Eine Einführung für Soziologen, Pädagogen, Juristen und Sozialarbeiter*, 10. durchges Aufl. Paderborn: Fink.

Lamnek, Siegfried, and Susanne Vogl. 2017. *Theorien abweichenden Verhaltens II: Moderne Ansätze'. Eine Einführung für Soziologen, Psychologen, Juristen und Sozialarbeiter*, 4. überarb. u. akt. Aufl. Paderborn: Fink.

Lee, Michael S.W., and Christie Seo Youn Ahn. 2016. Anti-consumption, materialism, and consumer well-being. *The Journal of Consumer Affairs* 50:18–47.

Lehmann, Armin. 2016. Was Schule macht. *Der Tagesspiegel* 22967:3.

Lovelock, Christopher H. 2001. *Services marketing: People, technology, strategy*. Upper Saddle River: Prentice-Hall.

markengold PR; Shoop. 2017. *Kleine Lügen in der Not – 65 Prozent der Deutschen lügen jeden Tag. Geschrieben von markengold PR. Veröffentlicht in Internetportale, Pressetexte, Shoop*. Berlin. https://www.markengold.de/kleine-schwindelleien-erleichtern-das-leben-mit-diesen-tricks-verschaffen-sich-die-deutschen-vorteile/

Mießgang, Thomas. 2013. *Scheiss drauf. Die Kultur der Unhöflichkeit*. Berlin: Rogner & Bernhard.

Mohr, Reinhard. 2010. *Meide deinen Nächsten Beobachtungen eines Stadtneurotikers*. Berlin: wjs Verlag.

Monath, Hans. 2019. Ein heimatloser Antikapitalismus stiftet irre Allianzen. *Der Tagesspiegel* 23987: 3. https://www.tagesspiegel.de/politik/thueringen-wahl-2019-ein-heimatloser-antikapitalismus-stiftet-irre-allianzen/25159004.html

Moser, K. 1997. Modelle der Werbewirkung. *Jahrbuch der Absatz- und Verbrauchsforschung* 43:270–283.

Müller, Robert Caspar. 2019. *Konsumentenbilder als produktive Fiktionen. Eine theoretische und ethnographische Untersuchung*. Wiesbaden: Springer Gabler.

Münkler, Herfried, and Marina Münkler. 2019. *Abschied vom Abstieg. Eine Agenda für Deutschland*. Berlin: Rowohlt.

Nessel, Sebastian. 2017. Was macht Menschen zu Konsumenten? Dimensionen und Voraussetzungen der Konsumentenrolle in Geschichte und Gegenwart. In *Verbraucher in Geschichte und Gegenwart. Wandel und Konfliktfelder in der Verbraucherpolitik*. eds. C. Bala, C. Kleinschmidt, K. Rick and W. Schuldzinski, 35–54. Beiträge zur Verbraucherforschung, Vol. 7. Düsseldorf: Verbraucherzentrale NRW.

Nikolova, Hristina, Cait Lamberton, and Nicole Verrochi Coleman. 2018. Stranger danger: When and why consumer Dyads behave less ethically than individuals. *Journal of Consumer Research* 45:90–108.

Ölander, Folke. 2005. Die verbraucherpolitisch orientierte Forschung – allerorts ein Stiefkind. In *Verbraucherforschung in Deutschland*. Schriftenreihe des Verbraucherzentrale Bundesverbandes zur Verbraucherpolitik, Vol. 1. ed. Verbraucherzentrale Bundesverband e. V., 21–29. Berlin: VZBV.

ohne Autor. 2019. Schäuble liest der Wirtschaft die Leviten. *Frankfurter Allgemeine Zeitung* 224:17.

Plein, Katrin. 2016. *Dysfunktionales Beschwerdeverhalten. Ausprägungen, Entstehung, Auswirkungen und Managementimplikationen*. Wiesbaden: Springer Gabler.

Precht, Richard David. 2012. *Die Kunst, kein Egoist zu sein Warum wir gerne gut sein wollen und was uns davon abhält*. München: Goldmann.

Razen, Michael, and Matthias Stefan. 2019. Greed: Taking a deadly sin to the lab. *Journal of Behavioral and Experimental Economics* 81:164–171.

Reisch, Lucia A., and Hans-W Micklitz. 2019. Vertrauen ist insbesondere für digitale Märkte wichtig. In *Betrug in der digitalisierten Welt. Erkennen. Vorbeugen. Schützen*, ed. M. Freytag, 94–99. Frankfurt a. M.: FAZIT Communication GmbH.

Reynolds, Kate L., and Lloyd C. Harris. 2009. Dysfunctional customer behavior severity: An empirical examination. *Journal of Retailing* 85:321–335.

Richins, Marsha L. 2017. Material pathways: The process that create and perpetuate materialism. *Journal of Economic Psychology* 27: 480–499.

Rosenberger, Günther. 2005. *Risiken für Konsumkompetenz und Persönlichkeitsentwicklung in der Wohlstandsgesellschaft*. Frankfurt/M.: Peter.

Rost, Dietmar. 2014. *Wandel (ver)kennen. Shifting Baselines und die Wahrnehmung umweltrelevanter Veränderungen aus wissenssoziologischer Sicht*. Wiesbaden: Springer VS.

Rotman, Jeff D., Mansu Khamitov, and Scott Connors. 2017. Lie, cheat, and steal: How harmful brands motivate consumers to act unethically. *Journal of Consumer Psychology* 28:353–361.

Schindler, Jörg. 2012. *Die Rüpel-Republik. Warum sind wir so unsozial?* Frankfurt a. M.: Fischer.

Schitter, Christian, Jürgen Fleiß, and Stefan Palan. 2019. To claim or not to claim: Anonymity, symmetric externalities and honesty. *Journal of Economic Psychology* 71:13–36.

Schmidbauer, Wolfgang. 2017. *Jetzt haben, später zahlen. Die seelischen Folgen der Konsumgesellschaft*. Reinbek bei Hamburg: Rowohlt.

Sofsky, Wolfgang. 2016. Unauffällige Gewalttäter. Posted in Kommentare, Moralia, am 25.7.2016. https://holbachinstitut.wordpress.com/2016/07/25/unauffaellige-gewalttaeter/

Solomon, Michael R. 2016. *Konsumentenverhalten*, 11., akt. Aufl. Hallbergmoos: Pearson Deutschland.

Spiegel ONLINE. 2019. Diebstahl im Einzelhandel. https://www.spiegel.de/wirtschaft/unternehmen/einzelhandel-mehr-schaden-durch-ladendiebstaehle-a-1274159.html

Steinbrück, Peer. 2018. *Das Elend der Sozialdemokratie. Anmerkungen eines Genossen.* München: Beck.

Thaler, Richard.H. 2015. *Misbehaving. The making of behavioral economics*. New York: W.W. Norton.

Thaler, Richard H. 2016. *Summary of Misbehaving*. Instaread, Inc.

Thielmann, Isabel, and Benjamin E. Hilbig. 2018. Daring dishonesty: On the role of sanctions for (un)ethical behavior. *Journal of Experimental Social Psychology* 79:71–77.

Thieme, Sebastian. 2013. *Der Ökonom als Menschenfeind? Über die misanthropischen Grundmuster der Ökonomik*. Leverkusen-Opladen: Barbara.

Turner, George. 2019. Hochschulen sollten auch Benimmregeln lehren. *Der Tagesspiegel*. https://www.tagesspiegel.de/wissen/turners-thesen-hochschulen-sollten-auch-benimmregeln-lehren/24484696.html.

Ullrich, Wolfgang. 2013. *Alles nur Konsum. Kritik der warenästhetischen Erziehung*. Berlin: Klaus Wagenbach.

Vargha, Zsuzsanna. 2011. Review: The myth of the ethical consumer. *Journal of Consumer Culture* 11:392–394.

Vijayalakshmi, Akshaya, Meng-Hsien (Jenny) Lin., and Russell N. Laczniak. 2018. Managing children´s internet advertising experiences: Parental preferencies for regulation. *The Journal of Consumer Affairs* 52:595–622.

Weber, Ma Gyan Sevanti. 2014. *Umgangsformen für das 21. Jahrhundert. Warum wir keine Manieren mehr haben – wie wir einander neu respektieren lernen*. Norderstedt: Books on Demand.

Wertenbroch, Klaus. 2016. *Consumer (Mis)behavior and policy intervention*. Working Paper Series. 2017/14/MKT. Insead The Business School for the World. http://ssrn.com/abstract=2916152

Winterhoff, Michael. 2019. *Deutschland verdummt. Wie das Bildungssystem die Zukunft unsrer Kinder verbaut*, 7th edn. Gütersloh: Gütersloher Verlagshaus.

Wiswede, Günter. 1979. *Soziologie abweichenden Verhaltens*. 2.völlig neu bearb. Aufl. Stuttgart, Berlin, Köln, Mainz: Kohlhammer.

Wiswede, Günter. 2000. Konsumsoziologie – Eine vergessene Disziplin. In *Konsum: soziologische, ökonomische und psychologische Perspektiven*, eds. D. Rosenkranz and N.F. Schneider, 23–72. Opladen: Leske + Budrich.

Yaniv, Gideon, and E. Siniver. 2016. The (honest) truth about rational dishonesty. *Journal of Economic Psychology* 53:131–140.

Günther Rosenberger, Dr., has been a freelance market and consumer researcher in Berlin since 2008 with interests in consumer competence, consumer policy, consumer socialisation, compensatory and deviant consumer behaviour, lifestyles, consumer culture, freelancer at the Institute for Consumer Journalism (ifv) and author of the former newsletter 'Verbraucherforschung aktuell'.

Actors, Activists, Initiatives, Organizations, Associations

The Consumer Policy Landscape in Austria—With a Special Focus on Grassroots Movements

Nina Birkner-Tröger

Abstract

This article firstly provides an overview of the Austrian consumer policy landscape, introducing the main actors briefly. Secondly, it focuses on societal participation processes, presenting civil society consumption initiatives in Austria and elaborating on their similarities and differences. Finally, it explores the potential that such grassroots movements can have for socio-political strategies and processes.

Keywords

Grassroots movement · Consumer power · Consumer policy · Participation · Self-sufficiency

I would like to thank Sebastian Nessel, Gabriele Zgubic and Helga Birkner for the valuable comments on this article.

N. Birkner-Tröger (✉)
Abteilung Konsumentenpolitik, Arbeiterkammer Wien, Wien, Austria
e-mail: nina.birkner@akwien.at

K.-U. Hellmann et al. (eds.), *Consumer Policy from Below*,
https://doi.org/10.1007/978-3-658-44478-5_11

1 Introduction

Consumer protection organizations provide advice in problem cases, investigate markets, and advocate for the interests of consumers. In doing so, they create transparency and influence politics, as well as markets (Nessel 2016). This is particularly true for the 'large' organizations. In Austria, these are the Chamber of Labor, which is also legally authorized to comment on legislative decisions, or the Association for Consumer Information, which conducts model processes and class actions on behalf of the state. But also small civil society initiatives or grassroots movements, which are to be classified at the other end of the scale due to various factors such as financing, organizational structure, etc., have a certain potential for political design options, especially with regard to socio-ecological transformation processes (Seyfang and Smith 2007). These initiatives include forms of political consumption, which, however, go beyond politically oriented shopping in the sense of "individualized collective action" and rather represent specific forms of political participation in the sense of "collectivist collective action" (Lamla 2013, p. 45).[1]

This article investigates the question of what influence grassroots movements can have on politics in Austria. This requires an overview of existing initiatives and the identification of their similarities and differences. Since there are hardly any current structured sketches of Austrian consumer policy actors[2] or these only include a selection of consumer policy organizations due to very narrow definitions,[3] a presentation of the landscape follows first. The classification is based on the institutional structure of the organizations (external and self-organization) according to Kuhlmann (1990) and based on the policy fields processed by the institution (mono- and polythematic) according to Klug (2017). The basis was the websites of the respective organizations ('about us') as well as annual or activity reports. Since the article focuses on 'consumer policy from below', it can only be a shortened representation of the institutions, which is why, for example, the pursued strategies and goals of the individual organizations are not discussed. The

[1] Although the boundaries here can be fluid, as will be further explained using the example of sharing.

[2] Cf. older versions like Kollmann (1986) or L & R Social Research (2005).

[3] On the European Commission's website, https://ec.europa.eu/info/files/national-consumer-bodies-austria_en accessed 28.01.2020.

sketching of state consumer protection institutions in Austria can only be done graphically and not in detail.[4]

2 Actors of Consumer Policy in Austria

In order to structure the various Austrian consumer organizations and initiatives, the ideal-typical structure of consumer organizations according to Kuhlmann (1990), who distinguishes consumer-external organizations from consumer-self-organizations, is suitable. Consumer-external organizations (CEO) are usually founded and financed by institutions and not by individuals, and there are no individual memberships, but only associations are usually members (Klug 2017, p. 46 f.). The tasks of the CEO include consumer information, advice, education and comprehensive consumer protection (as legal, information, health and wealth protection) and the representation of consumer interests towards the legislature, the executive, companies and the public (Kuhlmann 1990, p. 418 f.). Another characteristic of consumer-external organizations is that they operate in several policy fields and are therefore polyvalent consumer organizations (Klug 2017, p. 48).[5]

Kuhlmann (1990, p. 416 f.) distinguishes consumer-self-organizations (CSO) from external organizations. Here, consumers join together of their own accord, negotiate their interests collectively and represent themselves or are represented by directly commissioned representatives; financing is mainly through membership fees. Self-organizations are usually characterized by a small number of members, and the costs of joining and leaving such an initiative are usually low (Kuhlmann 1990, p. 416 f.). Self-organizations are further divided into representative and cooperative forms (see Fig. 1).

In representative forms, consumers can be members, but apart from the usual annual general meetings, they have no say. The organizations are mainly operated by full-time employees; there are also sometimes voluntary supporters. According to this definition, initiatives such as automobile clubs, but also environmental

---

[4] For a more detailed presentation of the state institutions, see https://ec.europa.eu/info/files/national-consumer-bodies-austria_en accessed on 31.01.2020.

[5] Klug (2017) only speaks of polyvalent VFO, but the analysis for Austria shows that there are indeed also monovalent VFO, see Sect. 2.2.

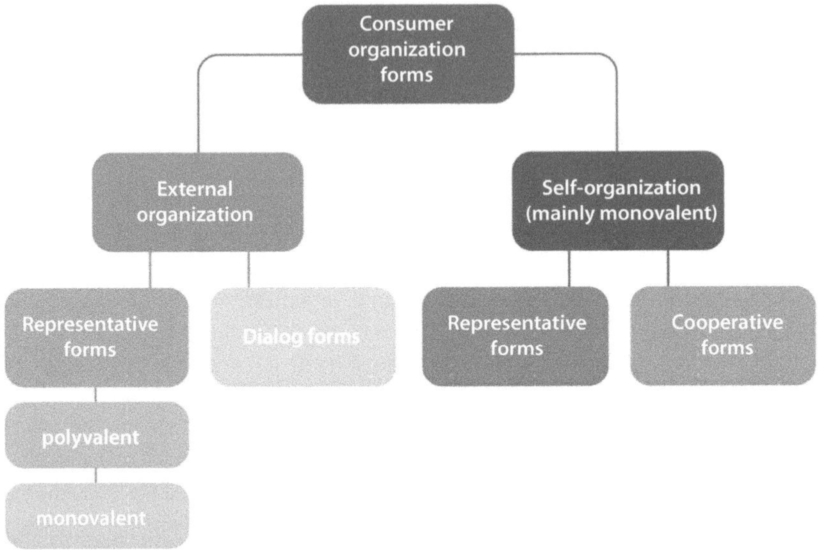

Fig. 1 Basic forms of consumer organizations. *Source* sketch according to Kuhlmann (1990, p. 420); Klug (2017)

NGOs, can be classified under this.[6] In cooperative forms, on the other hand, members can actively participate and influence the goals and tasks of the initiative and help shape them. Cooperative CSO are also expressed through "collectivist collective action" (Lamla 2013, p. 45); this 'consumer policy from below' is explained in more detail in Chap. 3.

The structure of Kuhlmann[7] with adaptations according to Klug (2017)[8] is well suited to sketch an overview of the Austrian landscape of consumer protec-

[6] However, according to Klug (Klug 2017), environmental NGOs are not direct consumer organizations, but "secondary interest groups", as they do not focus on consumption as a primary goal.

[7] The subcategory of dialogue forms mentioned by Kuhlmann refers to an offer from private and public companies to exercise a certain right to have a say, such as so-called consumer departments to which consumers can turn. However, this category is not relevant for this article and will not be further elaborated and specified.

[8] This structure is expanded by the differentiation made by Klug (2017) into polyvalent and monovalent forms. This results in the following structure: external organizations that are

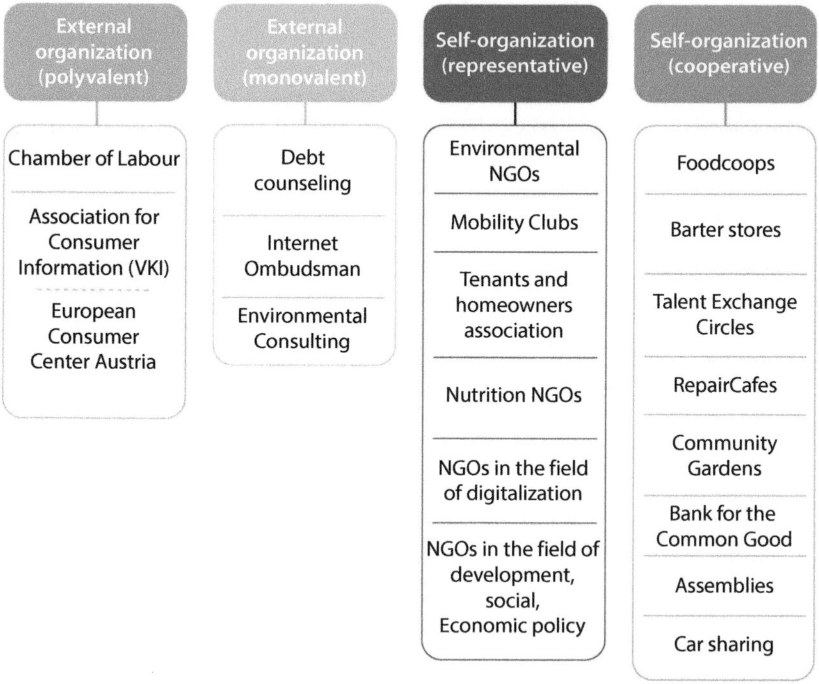

Fig. 2 Non-governmental consumer protection organizations and initiatives in Austria (overview without claim to completeness). *Source* own representation

tion organizations and initiatives. However, it should be taken into account that these are ideal types that may not necessarily be found in reality. In addition, there is more of a continuum than a clear line between representative and cooperative self-organizations.

The following chapter will now introduce individual organizations and initiatives of consumer protection in Austria (from Fig. 2). Since the focus of this

polyvalently positioned and external organizations that focus on one policy field. These are distinguished from (predominantly monovalent) self-organizations, which are divided into representative and cooperative forms.

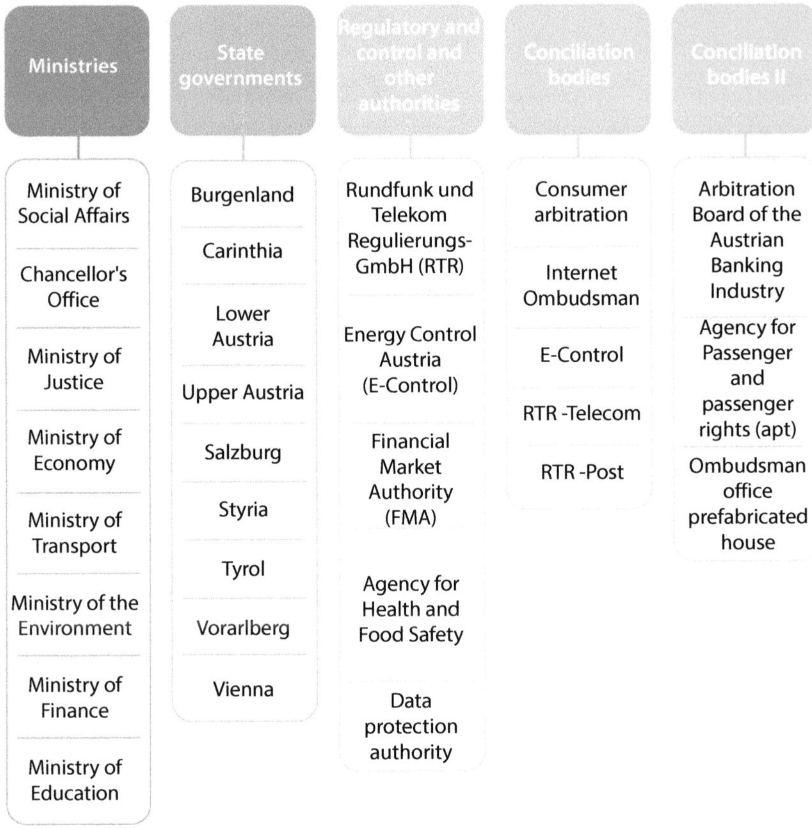

Fig. 3 State institutions in consumer policy. *Source* own representation [sketched after European Commission (see https://ec.europa.eu/info/files/national-consumer-bodies-austria_en, accessed on 30.01.2020) with own additions]

article is on 'consumer policy from below', this can only include a very reduced representation. The state institutions in which consumer policy is shaped and implemented, such as ministries, arbitration and regulatory bodies, and arbitration bodies, cannot be discussed in detail due to the scope, but can only be graphically sketched (see Fig. 3).

2.1 Polyvalent External Organizations

In Austria, there are two major consumer protection organizations: the Chamber of Labor (AK) and the Association for Consumer Information (VKI), which can be classified as polyvalent external organizations.

2.1.1 The Chamber of Labor (AK)[9]

The Chamber of Labour (AK) represents the interests of all non-self-employed workers as well as freelance employees and unemployed persons[10] based on the statutory compulsory membership in Austria.[11] In 2018, the Chamber of Labour thus represented approximately 3.8 million employees in Austria (Federal Chamber of Labour and Employees 2019). The AK is primarily financed through membership fees.

It is legitimized by the Chamber of Labour Act, which is anchored in the constitution; it has the statutory mandate to "represent and promote the social, economic, professional and cultural interests of employees" (Chamber of Labour Act 1992). This implies that it not only represents interests in labor law, but is also active in other fields such as social, educational, environmental, economic and particularly consumer policy.[12] The Chamber of Labour was established in 1920 as a counterweight and equal partner to the already existing Chambers of

[9] According to the ideal-typical classification by Kuhlmann (1990), the AK is more of a hybrid between VFO and representative VSO, as it is financed by membership fees and is only obligated to its members. However, due to its comprehensive tasks and its legal legitimacy (anchoring in the constitutional law), it is assigned here to the consumer external organizations.

[10] Excluded are: employees in the public administration, employees in agriculture and forestry (except Vienna & Burgenland), unemployed without benefits from unemployment insurance, executive employees.

[11] Cf. https://arbeiterkammer.at, accessed on 30.01.2020.

[12] For an overview of the various departments, see https://wien.arbeiterkammer.at/ueberuns/transparenz/Organigramm.html, accessed on 15.01.2020.

Commerce, thus laying the foundation for the social partnership[13] established in 1946.[14]

The Chamber of Labour is a self-governing body and thus only obligated to its members. The General Assembly (the so-called 'Employees' Parliament') is elected by its members every five years. The political objectives and contents for which the Chamber of Labour should commit itself are decided in the General Assembly (ibid., p. 62).

The tasks of the AK include representing interests towards state institutions, e.g. in the form of legislative assessments and statements or representation in committees and advisory boards. There is a wide range of services for members, especially advice and legal protection in the field of labor law. Another important area of responsibility is the scientific preparation of relevant topics (e.g. education, consumer, social policy), which serves as a basis for interest-led expertise internally as well as externally, e.g. as evidence-based support for trade unions.

In the field of consumer protection, the following activities are carried out at the Chamber of Labour: advice and service in case of problems in the general consumer area (e.g. problems in case of warranty, contract termination problems at fitness studios), in the financial sector (e.g. credit approval, account termination), in the field of telecommunications and data protection (e.g. in-app purchases, telephone bills), in the travel sector (e.g. problems with accommodation, flight delays). Price comparisons and food inspections serve to inform consumers and promote market transparency, and function as a market monitoring tool. In the field of data protection, the dark sides of digitization are highlighted and combated. In legal protection, class actions and sample lawsuits are conducted. Scientific preparation of studies on societal developments in the field of consumption serve as a basis for interest policy activities. Interest policy work is carried out in the areas of general consumer law, nutrition, digitalization and

[13] The Austrian social partnership is the cooperation between four major interest groups (Chamber of Labour, trade union, Chamber of Commerce and Chamber of Agriculture). Important political developments, particularly in the field of economic and social policy, are negotiated and coordinated in dialogue with each other. The aim is to avoid conflicts and to shape policy in a partnership-based manner, the social partnership is considered a guarantee of social balance. One of the most important political tasks of the social partnership is the annual negotiation of collective agreements, https://www.sozialpartner.at, accessed on 24.01.2020.

[14] Cf. https://arbeiterkammer.at/ueberuns/akundoegbgeschichte/index.html, accessed on 19.12.2019.

telecommunications, sustainable consumption, financial services, housing, environment, transport and energy.

2.1.2 Association for Consumer Information (VKI)

In addition to the Chamber of Labour, the Association for Consumer Information (VKI) is the second major consumer protection organization.[15] The association was founded in 1961 by the four Austrian social partners Chamber of Labour, trade union, Chamber of Commerce and Chamber of Agriculture, who were also ordinary members. In 1973, the Republic of Austria joined as an extraordinary, promoting member. The trade union, Chamber of Commerce and Chamber of Agriculture have left the association several years ago. The VKI is therefore supported by the Federal Chamber of Labour and the Republic of Austria, represented by the Federal Ministry of Social Affairs, Health, Care and Consumer Protection.[16] This continues to be an extraordinary member.[17]

The association is financed 75% from revenues from publications (KONSUMENT magazine, book sales), projects, consulting services and organizational contributions. 25% are covered by membership fees and subsidies (Association for Consumer Information 2019, p. 36).

The fields of activity are laid down in the association's statutes and include consumer information (e.g. via website or magazine), in particular the examination of consumer goods in the form of product and service tests or market observation, the results of which appear in the monthly test magazine KONSUMENT. In addition, the VKI offers legal advice, intervention and mediation. On behalf of the Federal Ministry of Social Affairs, Health, Care and Consumer Protection, the association also conducts class actions and association lawsuits as well as sample lawsuits. The formation of purchasing associations, especially in the energy sector, is another task that is very successful. The VKI Academy offers special professional seminars and a course in consumer law. In case of cross-border problems, consumers can turn to the European Consumer Centre (ECC), which has also been located at the VKI since 1999.

---

[15] Cf. https://vki.at, accessed 30.01.2020.

[16] Since January 2020, before that Federal Ministry of Labour, Social Affairs, Health and Consumer Protection.

[17] Cf. https://vki.at/wer-sind-wir, accessed on 30.01.2020.

2.2 Monovalent External Organizations

In Austria, there are several organizations that operate in only one policy field, but due to their structure and functions, they are more likely to be classified as external rather than self-organizations[18] . These organizations are largely funded by public funds and are generally accessible to all citizens (with Austrian residence) equally.[19]

2.2.1 Debt Counseling (Finance)

The 28 debt counseling services in Austria (ten state-recognized with 18 associated regional offices) are important actors in the consumer policy landscape, especially in the financial sector. They offer private individuals information and advice on payment problems, work out possible solutions with those affected, and support them before, during, and after a personal bankruptcy process. The debt counseling services are mostly organized as non-profit associations and are funded by the public sector (state, cities, AMS, other institutions). The advice is free, accessible to everyone (the respective federal state is responsible) and is primarily intended as help for self-help. The interests of the debt counseling services are represented by the umbrella organization ASB.[20]

2.2.2 Internet Ombudsman (Internet and Digitalization)

The Internet Ombudsman is an independent dispute resolution and advisory body and is funded by the Federal Ministry of Social Affairs, Health, Care and Consumer Protection and the Federal Chamber of Labor. Consumers with residence in Austria are advised on topics such as online shopping, data protection, personal rights, and copyright.[21]

---

[18] Klug (2017, p. 47) defines consumer external organizations exclusively as polyvalent and refers to monovalent VFOs as "secondary interest groups" that only act in consumer policy as a secondary priority, such as environmental associations. However, from the author's point of view, the assignment to VFOs is more sensible for the reasons mentioned above.

[19] The environmental consultation is funded by the Vienna City Council, so the focus of the activity is probably on the Vienna region, but this is not further described or limited by the organization itself.

[20] Cf. https://www.schuldenberatung.at/fachpublikum/organisation.php, accessed on 21.01.2020.

[21] Cf. https://www.ombudsmann.at/schlichtung.php/cat/7/aid/20/title/UEber_uns, accessed on 21.01.2020.

2.2.3 Environmental Consultation (Environment)

Since 1988, private households and businesses have been able to obtain information on ecological topics and consumer topics such as clothing, cosmetics, repair, nutrition, energy, living, climate protection, etc. from the environmental consultation. Various educational offers such as training as a nutrition provision coach or energy consultant can be taken up or obtained. The environmental consultation is an institution of the Vienna Adult Education Centers and is financially supported by the Vienna City Council.[22]

2.3 Representative Self-Organizations

In representative self-organizations, consumers are indeed members of the organization, but the activities and tasks are carried out by full-time employees. Members benefit from information and representation of interests, but also in the form of special member offers and discounts. In some organizations, members can also become volunteers (Kuhlmann 1990). In Austria, representative consumer self-organizations can be identified in the fields of environment, mobility, housing, nutrition, and digitization.

2.3.1 Environment

In Austria, the two environmental protection organizations Greenpeace and GLOBAL2000 are particularly dedicated to the topic of consumption from an environmental perspective. Greenpeace is financed exclusively by private donations or foundations and is known for its commitment in the area of classic environmental protection (protection of the seas, forests, landscape, climate). In the area of consumption, Greenpeace is particularly active in terms of sustainability and conducts campaigns (e.g., for the reduction of plastic), studies (e.g., on consumption habits in clothing), information offers (e.g., guides to quality seals), and also market checks (tests on various topics in supermarkets).[23]

GLOBAL2000 was founded in 1982 by six Austrian activists who aimed to actively shape Austrian environmental policy. This NGO is one of the most important environmental protection organizations in Austria, alongside Greenpeace and WWF. In this NGO, consumption plays a role particularly from an

[22] Cf. https://www.umweltberatung.at/ueber-uns, accessed on 23.01.2020.

[23] See https://news.greenpeace.at, accessed on 24.01.2020.

ecological perspective—waste, plastic, resource consumption, nutrition, and agriculture.[24]

2.3.2 Mobility

In the field of mobility, there are different players. The Austrian Traffic Club (VCÖ) is a non-profit organization and advocates for 'climate-friendly, oil-independent, and healthy mobility'. The VCÖ is financed by donations from private individuals, the public sector, and advertisements from companies. Various publications inform both experts and the public.[25]

ÖAMTC[26] and ARBÖ[27] are nationwide car and motorcycle clubs that offer their members services in case of problems and advocate for the interests of drivers. The equivalent institution for bicycles is called Radlobby,[28] and for pedestrians, it is Walk-Space,[29] the Austrian association for pedestrians.

2.3.3 Housing

The Austrian Tenants' Association[30] is a non-profit association that advises citizens on housing issues and also represents them in court in rental law disputes. Furthermore, it pursues interest politics in the field of housing. All members, who also finance the association, receive advice and service. There are regional offices in all nine federal states.

2.3.4 Nutrition

In the field of nutrition, the association 'die Tafeln'[31] is particularly noteworthy. The Wiener Tafel[32] was founded 20 years ago by four students as the first Austrian initiative for food rescue and distribution and was modeled after the Hamburger Tafel. There are currently nine local organizations in Austria that collect and distribute food regionally.

---

[24] See https://www.global2000.at/ueber-global-2000, accessed on 17.01.2020.

[25] See https://www.vcoe.at/ueber-vcoe/ueber-vcoe, accessed on 21.01.2020.

[26] See https://www.oeamtc.at, accessed on 21.01.2020.

[27] See https://www.arboe.at, accessed on 21.01.2020.

[28] See https://www.radlobby.at, accessed on 20.01.2020.

[29] See https://www.walk-space.at, accessed on 20.01.2020.

[30] See https://mietervereinigung.at, accessed on 18.12.2019.

[31] See https://dietafeln.at, accessed on 13.12.2019.

[32] See https://www.wienertafel.at, accessed on 17.02.2020.

2.3.5 Digitalization

The association NYOB ('None of your business') was founded by data and consumer protectors and advocates for the observance of data protection as well as the expansion of digital personal rights and freedoms. It is financed by donations and memberships.[33]

2.3.6 Economy and Social Issues

Südwind[34] is a NGO founded in Austria in 1979, whose main concern is development policy and which advocates for more global justice. The NGO is particularly committed to fair working conditions in the global South, i.e., for jobs that mainly concern the production of consumer goods for the European market, such as textiles, electronics, toys, etc. Thus, consumer policy is implicitly a topic of this organization.

Other NGOs active in the field of economic or social policy include, for example, Attac[35] or the Poverty Conference.[36] Although consumption is implicitly a relevant topic for these NGOs, their activity in the field of consumer policy is usually very low, which is why these NGOs are not discussed in more detail.

3 'Consumer Policy from Below': Cooperative Self-Organizations

'Consumer policy from below' can be seen as a counter-model to a state-controlled macro-politically prescribed approach. The activism comes from the middle of civil society. These are therefore social movements, also referred to as grassroots movements, which are structured here as cooperative consumer self-organizations. In contrast to the representative form (see Sect. 2.3), these are characterized by the fact that the individuals are not only formally members, but can actively contribute to the definition, organization and implementation of the goals and tasks of the initiative.

[33] See https://noyb.eu/konzept, accessed on 30.01.2020.

[34] See https://www.suedwind.at, accessed on 14.01.2020.

[35] See https://www.attac.at, accessed on 30.01.2020.

[36] See http://www.armutskonferenz.at, accessed on 30.01.2020.

3.1 Overview of Austrian Initiatives[37]

When looking at the Austrian landscape, it is predominantly initiatives that test alternative consumption models and are located in the field of sustainability. Many of the following initiatives exist in similar form in other countries. The methodological approach was carried out through internet research in the various consumption areas. Since there are also many locally active movements without an internet presence, the following presentation does not claim to be complete. The aim is to provide an overview of the involvement of civil society based on exemplary initiatives and to locate these in the consumer policy landscape. Subsequently, an attempt will be made to analyze the commonalities of the initiatives and to outline the resulting potentials for consumer policy.

3.1.1 Consumer Goods

In Austria, there are—predominantly in larger cities—various free and exchange stores, as well as rental stores. In free and exchange stores, no longer used items can be dropped off and other things can be taken; in the free store even without the principle of exchange. In rental stores, on the other hand, as the name suggests, items of use such as drills or tents are lent for a certain period of time. The primary focus is on conserving resources by reusing used items.[38] However, some stores also represent further societal and political goals such as promoting

[37] The following will also introduce various initiatives that are generally subsumed under 'sharing' such as in the area of home exchange, clothing exchange, etc. Precise classification, to what extent these are initiatives in the sense of consumer self-organizations or merely a form of individualized 'prosum', is sometimes difficult. Digital (brokerage) platforms are often also involved, which further complicate an ideal-typical separation. Here, a distinction must again be made as to whether one considers the platform itself or the individuals acting within the platform as actors. If one focuses on the former, for example, Fragnebenan.at is a local initiative that offers the opportunity to request individual services such as assistance in assembling a lamp or similar. On the other hand, platforms like the carpooling platform Blablacar are profit-oriented companies that generate income through the brokerage fee. However, the participants are actors who offer or use alternative forms of consumption; although they exercise this individually, their interests are collectively represented by the platform and may generate a sense of identity. In the sense of a 'politics with the shopping cart', sharing initiatives are therefore to be understood as consumer politics from below, which is why I have decided to include these forms in this article.

[38] Cf. https://www.leila.wien, accessed on 18.12.2019.

communal usage and social justice[39] or are seen as an expression of anti-capitalist action and as promoting solidarity.[40] These are civil society organized initiatives, which often exist alongside second-hand stores run by municipalities or charitable organizations.

Open bookcases are usually located in public spaces; here, no longer needed books can be offered to other people for further use. The Wikipedia page 'List of public bookcases'[41] lists (without claiming to be complete) over 100 such cabinets throughout Austria (as of January 2020). These cabinets are usually adapted, no longer needed public telephone booths and are organized and operated by both the municipal side and private individuals.

Clothing swap parties are initiated and carried out by individual people or small groups, but also by charity organizations. According to research, there is no private initiative that operates this regularly. Most of the time, these are one-time events of various individual initiators. These parties are run for ecological reasons, to give clothing a second use, but also for the fun factor and for personal supply. As a rule, a small contribution towards expenses is paid. Each participant brings their own old clothes for exchange. From the existing pool, you can take as many clothes back as you have given.

3.1.2 Services

In addition to goods, services are also exchanged in so-called talent exchange circles. These are usually activities that are common in neighborhood assistance, such as help with shopping or babysitting. The aim is to extend neighborhood assistance in the region. The accounting is often done in time units rather than in monetary units. The underlying socio-political claim is to consider time as equally available and valuable for all people, thereby balancing the market-typical price differences between intellectual and manual labor as well as between women's and men's work, and to evaluate work in a more socially just manner.[42]

'Fragnebenan' is a platform whose goal is digitally organized neighborhood assistance.[43] Since direct neighbors often do not really know each other in larger

[39] Cf. http://www.transition-tirol.net/gruppen-initiativen/leihladen-innsbruck, accessed on 19.11.2019.

[40] Cf. https://www.kostnixladen.at, accessed on 19.11.2019.

[41] Cf. https://de.wikipedia.org/wiki/Liste_öffentlicher_Bücherschränke_in_Österreich, accessed on 19.11.2019.

[42] Cf. https://www.tauschkreis-kaernten.at, accessed on 22.11.2019.

[43] Cf. https://fragnebenan.com, accessed on 22.11.2019.

cities, the platform is intended to help network people who need or can offer support. The initiative was founded by private individuals and initially limited to the Vienna area. Meanwhile, the organization has been transformed into a GmbH (limited liability company) and aims to expand to other German-speaking cities.

Repair cafes have also become increasingly popular in Austria in recent years, an idea from the Netherlands. Under the guidance of volunteer repair experts, consumers can bring their broken household appliances and repair them (or have them repaired). There are numerous repair cafes in most federal states, which are offered more or less regularly.[44] A networking of these repair initiatives has been taking place since 2017 with the support of RepaNet.[45] Sewing cafes work in a similar way; here, old clothes are mended or subjected to upcycling, or new clothes are sewn. In addition to the repair or production of a product, social aspects such as communication and mutual support also play an important role.

3.1.3 Nutrition

Community gardens are a form of 'urban gardening', where in addition to self-sufficiency with fruits, vegetables, herbs, etc., the social component is also important. Some initiatives address specific target groups such as children, older people, or migrants to promote social integration. Community gardens are also political, social, pedagogical, and ecological action spaces. In Austria, there are more than 200 such gardens.[46] Community gardens are founded and maintained by committed citizens, but also by municipalities or associations.

'Foodcoops' are self-managed cooperatives for self-supply of food. The members select the producers according to certain criteria agreed upon collectively and organize the purchase of food and sale to their own members. Through contact with the producers, greater transparency about working and production conditions can be created than in the retail food trade. The socio-political goal is to create an 'alternative to the currently prevailing food system' and to achieve food sovereignty. Currently, there are about 100 food cooperatives in Austria.[47]

---

[44] An incomplete overview can be found here https://www.repanet.at/projekte-2/reparatur-cafes_initiativen/, accessed on 22.11.2019.

[45] Repanet is a voluntary representation of interests of the social economy-oriented re-use companies as well as the repair networks and repair initiatives, https://www.repanet.at, accessed on 21.1.2020.

[46] Information from the Gartenpolylog association, by email on 21.01.2020.

[47] See https://foodcoops.at, accessed on 23.01.2020.

'Foodsharing' is an initiative that fights against food waste.[48] It was founded in 2012 in Germany and has expanded to Austria, Switzerland, and other European countries in recent years. Volunteer workers, known as 'Foodsavers', rescue food by collecting no longer needed but still edible food from cooperating businesses and then use it for their own supply or distribute it to other people. The Foodsharing initiative sees itself as a complement to food banks. Unlike these, however, need is not assessed in food sharing; anyone can pick up food. According to their own statistics, about 2600 'rescue missions' are carried out daily, 65,000 food savers volunteer, and 6000 businesses regularly cooperate with the initiative.[49] The organization and coordination is carried out via the platform foodsharing.network. From the Austrian side, the initiative is sponsored by the Federal Ministry for Sustainability and Tourism as well as the Viennese food banks.

In addition to these initiatives, which primarily serve their own supply, there are also groups where political goals are in the foreground. Food councils emerged in the USA in the early 1980s and have been experiencing a boom in German-speaking countries for several years. So far, there are two food councils in Austria, namely in Vienna[50] and Innsbruck,[51] and in Upper Austria, the agricultural council is calling for a foundation.[52] The food councils aim to contribute "to an ecologically sustainable and socially just food system" (FIAN Austria 2019, p. 7). The goal is to bring together the various actors in the food sector, who often act in isolation from each other, to relocalize food production and to draw attention to the needs of civil society. In Vienna and Innsbruck, the initiatives are organized by civil society and consist of committed individuals from research, the food industry, gastronomy, NGOs, and private individuals. On a global level, the Nyéléni initiative is committed to democratizing the agricultural and food system.[53]

---

[48] See https://foodsharing.at, accessed on 29.01.2020.

[49] The data refers to all participating countries, see https://foodsharing.at/karte, accessed on 22.11.2019.

[50] Cf. https://ernaehrungsrat-wien.at, accessed on 23.01.2020.

[51] Cf. http://ernaehrungsrat-innsbruck.at, accessed on 23.01.2020.

[52] Cf. https://www.max-hiegelsberger.at/oberoesterreich-ernaehrungsraete, accessed on 23.01.2020.

[53] Cf. http://www.ernährungssouveränität.at, accessed on 23.01.2020.

3.1.4 Finance

As a consequence of the financial crisis, committed private individuals founded a cooperative in 2014 with the idea of establishing a 'Bank for the Common Good'[54] as a bank of trust, which was to serve as a counter-model to the 'bad banks'. The original intention was to establish a full-service bank that could offer all the services of a universal bank such as lending, deposit business, services, and investments. However, the money was not to be speculated with, but invested in the common good-oriented real economy. The Austrian Financial Market Authority, however, rejected the application for a full banking license. Since mid-2019, there has been a common good account for cooperative members, made possible through cooperation with a regional bank. The common good account is linked to a so-called environmental guarantee, which ensures that the bank invests the deposited funds exclusively in ecological and social projects.[55]

3.1.5 Energy

In the energy sector, the principle is self-supply apart from commercial market offers. These are mainly associations or cooperatives at the local level, which join together for communal energy production and use. There is no structured overview of how many such initiatives there are in Austria. The 'Clean Energy Package' of the European Union could give a boost to communal energy production, as it aims to increasingly promote and support citizen energy communities in the future.

3.1.6 Mobility

In the field of mobility, there are privately or municipally organized car-sharing initiatives[56] as an alternative to commercial providers, but also platforms for private car sharing. Platforms can in turn be private initiatives,[57] but also commercial providers.[58] They offer not only the mediation but also the logistical handling (such as insurance). The car providers and users only have to take care of the

[54] Cf. https://www.gemeinwohl.coop, accessed on 23.01.2020.

[55] Cf. https://www.gemeinwohlkonto.at, accessed on 23.01.2020.

[56] An overview can be found here https://www.umweltberatung.at/carsharing-mitfahrboersen, accessed on 22.01.2020.

[57] For example in the form of a cooperative like a car-sharing platform for Vorarlberg: https://www.carusocarsharing.com, accessed on 22.01.2020.

[58] Cf. https://at.getaround.com, accessed on 22.01.2020.

rental, which reduces the self-work of the participants. The consumers offer their private cars for rent. Non-commercial car sharing is also offered by municipalities or associations founded by citizens. However, there is usually a separate fleet available for this purpose.[59] Especially municipalities in rural areas promote alternative mobility offers as a supplement to public transport.

Carpools are usually offered via (commercialized) platforms.[60] The trade union has founded an alternative carpooling exchange for the federal state of Styria.[61]

Private bicycle sharing is not widespread in Austria. In Vienna, a private initiative offers cargo bikes for rent.[62] In the larger state capitals as well as in the federal state of Lower Austria and in some smaller cities, there are bicycle rental systems; however, these are often initiated and promoted by the public sector (state or municipality).

The initiative 'Geht-doch'[63] advocates for the needs of pedestrians in Vienna and for consumer-free spaces in public areas.

3.1.7 Living

In recent years, communal living forms have gained importance. Building groups are initiatives where interested individuals collectively construct living space, usually in the form of multi-story residential buildings. The aim is to be able to actively participate in the planning and implementation of personal wishes for the design of the living space.[64] Not only individual living, but also the coexistence of the house community plays a central role, which is why emphasis is placed on the establishment of community rooms such as kitchens, workshops, saunas, etc. Many building groups also deal with socio-political aspects such as the creation of affordable housing and alternative offers to commercial real estate carriers. The 'Sargfabrik' in Vienna is considered 'Austria's largest self-managed residential and cultural project'.[65] In 1996, the residential building was built by a group

---

[59] Cf. https://www.mobilesmarchtrenk.at, http://www.carsharing-seekirchen.com, accessed on 22.01.2020.

[60] Such as https://greendrive.at or https://www.blablacar.de, accessed on 22.01.2020.

[61] Cf. https://www.mitfahrboerse.st, accessed on 22.01.2020.

[62] Cf. https://www.lastenradkollektiv.at, accessed on 22.01.2020.

[63] Cf. https://geht-doch.wien, accessed on 22.01.2020.

[64] This is hardly possible, especially with multi-story residential buildings.

[65] According to self-presentation see https://www.sargfabrik.at, accessed on 16.01.2020.

of committed families after more than ten years of planning. An association is the landowner, builder, operator of the residential complex, and landlord for the 112 residential units. Commitment of the people living in this project is a prerequisite, e.g., in the care of the garden or library. There is a bathhouse and regular cultural events that are open to the public.

In the living area, sharing is understood as the free provision of a sleeping place,[66] on the one hand, and short-term rental for a fee, on the other hand.[67] In both cases, (commercialized) platforms act as intermediaries between consumers who provide accommodation and those who are looking for it. In their initial phase, the social aspect and getting to know other cultures were in the foreground. However, short-term rental has also become a lucrative side income for providers, which is why the financial incentive should not be ignored here.

3.1.8 Environment and Socio-Ecological Transformation

The initiative 'System change, not climate change'[68] works at the political level. Its goal is to initiate a socio-ecological transformation and thus to enforce other forms of economy and coexistence in order to combat climate change. The focus is on combating political projects that would have fatal ecological consequences, such as the planned construction of the third runway at Vienna-Schwechat airport in Austria.

The global movement 'Fridays for future' also has a community in Austria.[69] At the beginning of 2020, there were 29 local groups committed to a sustainable living environment and fighting for radical environmental policy based on the 1.5°C target for more climate justice.

3.2 Commonalities, Challenges, and Potentials

The following attempts to elaborate on the similarities and differences of the presented initiatives. Kuhlmann (1990) identifies three factors that serve as motivation to participate in cooperative consumer self-organizations: first, material advantages; second, social integration into the group; and third, societal benefit.

---

[66] See https://www.couchsurfing.com, accessed on 16.01.2020.

[67] See https://www.airbnb.at, accessed on 16.01.2020.

[68] See https://systemchange-not-climatechange.at, accessed on 23.01.2020.

[69] See https://fridaysforfuture.at, accessed on 29.01.2020.

These factors are found in the grassroots movements presented and will be summarized in the next chapter. Furthermore, the structural challenges faced by the initiatives will be identified, as well as the potential they offer for consumer policy.

3.2.1 Similarities and Differences

Sustainable forms of consumption and lifestyles are recognizable as a common denominator in almost all initiatives and reflect a societal trend. These can be complementary offers to municipal or charitable institutions, e.g., in the area of second-hand and exchange shops, or alternatives to profit-oriented companies like car sharing. Initiatives also cover market economy supply gaps and supplement them, e.g., building groups. In some initiatives, self-supply away from market economy offers is in the foreground, which often offers financial advantages, e.g., in the area of mobility and energy. Desires for greater transparency regarding production conditions in ecological and social terms also play a major role. The movements thus express their dissatisfaction with market economy offers and at the same time show alternatives. Ecological and/or social sustainability are sometimes desired side effects. Ideological reasons or social and ecological needs can also be the main motivation for founding such initiatives (Seyfang and Smith 2007, p. 591).

The 'European Environmental Agency' attests grassroots movements a high potential to force socio-ecological transformation, as they take on societal pioneering roles, which can trigger socio-political reforms (European Environmental Agency 2019, p. 52). Specifically, the 'Transition Towns' movements, community energy production associations ('Community Energy'), as well as 'Urban Farming' and organic and 'Less-Meat' initiatives are mentioned. Private carpooling, car and bike sharing initiatives play an important role in the mobility sector (ibid.).

The regional action radius of civil society groups varies. Some groups operate very locally, as the involved persons have to coordinate, organize, and supply themselves on site. However, this does not exclude that they can network (digitally) with other local groups and thus can have a larger regional reach (in the case of 'Fridays for Future' even globally). Digitalization helps here to spread ideas and also to find common coordination forms and political positions.

Many of the presented initiatives have (locally) a relatively small number of members. This makes them very flexible on the one hand, but on the other hand, the persistence of the initiative is often precarious. Voluntariness is paramount in the associations, which is why access is generally low-threshold; but also an exit can quickly occur (Kuhlmann 1990). The danger with high fluctuation is that the grassroots movement suffers overall or disappears entirely if a very committed member drops out (Seyfang and Smith 2007). The movements are mostly organized in associations or cooperatives, but can also function as loose groupings. Apart from content-related focal points, there is a not to be underestimated logistical and organizational effort to be managed, which must be coordinated. Several questions arise, such as in what form the initiative is organized, e.g., whether an association/cooperative should be founded; what infrastructure is needed, e.g., a (business) premises or similar; how the movement is financed; what prerequisites membership includes; how the initiative becomes visible to the outside world, and much more. This requires a lot of initiative and time resources from the individual participants. In most cases, this is done on a voluntary basis. Sometimes members of an initiative work professionally in a similar field, such as the Food Council or the Bank for the Common Good, who bring their expertise privately.

In general, financing is of course a topic that also depends on a certain degree of success (especially in terms of consistency) of the initiatives. A certain amount of basic capital is needed for infrastructure such as premises, communication, etc., which is covered, for example, by membership fees. A basic financial security helps to maintain the basic operation. The required sums are quite different for the initiatives presented. While a lending shop only needs a room, higher amounts are needed for implementation at the common good bank or car sharing with its own fleet. These amounts are raised from membership fees or donations from the population as well as support from the public sector, in many cases at the municipal level.

Municipalities are important players in many cases, supporting civic engagement at the local level. However, many initiatives also work without support and finance themselves. This is not based on specific criteria and can vary quite a bit from case to case. For example, a repair café in one place can be built entirely on its own initiative, while in another place it can be organized, financed and carried out by the municipality. Self-financing or external financing by municipalities both have risks. Initiatives that finance themselves through membership fees or donations are politically independent and only responsible to themselves and can shape their goals and activities more freely. This independence also makes it possible to be an experimental field for alternative and new forms of consumption and living; they have the freedom to take very radical positions that do not yet seem politically feasible. However, they are dependent on the number of members as well as their willingness and morality to pay. In the case of external financing, there are dependencies in terms of possible counter-demands, favors and general (political) goodwill.

Community-based, non-profit oriented ideas are being commercialized and thus commodified. This trend has increased significantly in recent years, especially with the rise of the 'Sharing Economy'. The social practice of communal use or lending, but also the passing on of goods such as cars or tools, has long existed in the private sector, but mainly took place between known individuals (Behrendt et al. 2018, p. 5 ff.). With digitalization, sharing among strangers became easier. At the same time, the financial aspect of sharing has gained importance with increasing anonymization. Especially in large cities, the sharing economy has negative effects on the housing market. In 2017, there were about 8600 Airbnb offers in Vienna. 40% of the providers have more than one apartment on offer, in total 70% of the providers offer a whole living unit and not just a sleeping place or a room, which is why Seidl et al. (2017) assume that a commercial calculation is behind the majority of the offers. The short-term rental apartments are thus withdrawn from the housing market, which further increases the already high housing prices in the conurbations. The ideas of communal sharing and cultural exchange also play hardly any role anymore. One danger is that the original solidarity idea of sharing is pushed into the background by the appropriation of commercial providers and increased profit opportunities. In relation to sharing, it is necessary to question whether these are social movements that want to implement transformation processes, or rather other forms of individual prosumption (Blättel-Mink and Hellmann 2010) or/and forms of political consumption in the sense of "individualized collective action" (Lamla 2013, p. 45).

The increasing digitalization through Web 2.0 also offers opportunities. It enables networking on a larger scale and thus promotes consumer political engagement. Communication exchange is facilitated; a larger circle of interested parties can be addressed; entry barriers for new members are reduced and public attention is sometimes easier to reach. Platform-based offers enable better matching by reaching a larger circle of interested parties (e.g. for lending or passing on goods). Further digital developments simplify certain processes; e.g. digital locks in car sharing do not require personal presence at the vehicle handover. From a consumer policy perspective, trends can be more easily identified through digitalization, allowing political measures to be (further) developed.

On the other hand, possible rebound effects must also be taken into account. Car sharing can have negative ecological effects, for example, if car sharing is increasingly used instead of public transport. Also, the initial expectations that a large number of people would no longer own a private car have not been fulfilled; the number of new registrations in Berlin and Hamburg has remained the same (AT Kearney 2019, p. 6). Negative ecological effects can also occur in other areas; through the practice of sharing, consumers can save money. In the negative case, this can merely lead to shifts in consumption or even increased consumption (Behrendt et al. 2018, p. 71 ff.).

Digitization facilitates political consumption, which is often criticized as 'checkbook membership' or 'click activism' because they are very non-binding forms of political participation (Baringhorst et al. 2007). Political consumption also includes calls for boycotts and buycotts, which, however, encompass a very individualized form. These are distinct from initiatives that are based on networks and thus fulfill social functions such as inclusion or knowledge transfer and establish a link between citizens and the state from a political perspective (Stolle et al. 2004, p. 159). Even if initiatives have an integrative character, there is a risk of social exclusion on the other hand. It can be assumed that the population is not represented proportionately. As Seyfang and Smith (2007, p. 599) note: "Grassroots initiatives exhibit their own micro-politics and can be exclusive to some and inclusive to others." Since the mentioned initiatives focus on the area of sustainable consumption, it can be assumed that people from the 'post-material milieu' are primarily addressed. This group mainly includes people with a higher level of education, middle-aged, and with a tendency towards higher income (Brunner 2014, p. 6 f.). Which social groups actually participate in initiatives requires further empirical investigation.[70]

In view of the major challenges of climate change in the near future, large transformation processes in our Western consumption and lifestyles are necessary. Based on the points described, the question arises from a socio-political perspective about the effects and steering effects for the entire society. Politics can draw inspiration from grassroots movements for other forms of consumption and lifestyles and develop measures accordingly. If it can be assumed that these are movements that address a very small part of society and are probably still far from having a broad societal impact, a further major challenge is how the potential of this civic engagement can be politically utilized and made majority-capable.

Methodological support and scientific accompaniment can be provided by so-called 'real-world laboratories' or 'living labs', even if their actual effects have

[70] In this context, a historical comparison would also be interesting. The beginnings of consumerist movements came more from the trade union movement (Lamla 2013). In Austria, there were consumer cooperatives from the mid-nineteenth century, which emerged from the workers' movement and led to the founding of the retail chain 'Konsum' in the 1970s, but had to file for bankruptcy in the mid-1990s, see Höfferer et al. (2016).

not yet been evaluated (Wagner and Grunwald 2019). In 'real-world laboratories', societal and ecological problems are addressed, solutions are developed and tested. The inclusion of societal actors such as individual citizens or civil society initiatives is sought (Schäpke et al. 2018). 'Real-world laboratories' are more than citizen participation processes; a crucial element is the scientific accompaniment of the experimental fields, in order to gain insights regarding the potentials for socio-ecological transformation (Wagner and Grunwald 2019). This can in turn bring enriching insights for consumer research (Tröger 2017). In Germany, 'real-world laboratories' have been increasingly widespread in recent years and are often initiated and funded by the public sector or research.[71] The 'Real-world Laboratories of Sustainability' network lists more than 40 projects within Germany on their website; the subject areas include, among others, mobility, energy, climate protection, housing.[72] The pioneer is Baden-Württemberg.[73] Since 2015, the Ministry of Science has funded a total of 14 projects with 18 million EUR. In Austria, there are five 'mobility labs', funded by the Austrian Federal Ministry for Transport, Innovation and Technology (BMVIT), which analyze regional challenges in four cities and aim to contribute to the transformation of the mobility system.[74] Compared to Germany, the development of 'real-world laboratories' in Austria is still very modest and expandable; of course, it also requires public funds to support corresponding projects.

3.3 Further Development, Professionalization

As already mentioned in Sect. 3.2.1, consistency is certainly a major challenge for initiatives. A critical mass of people is necessary to ensure that the initiative continues to exist even when certain individuals leave. Infrastructure and a financial foundation are also important for the continued success of an initiative.

The degree of impact initiatives aim to achieve depends entirely on their goals and orientation. For many, local reach and self-sufficiency are desirable goals.

[71] However, Wagner and Grunwald (2019) note a certain arbitrariness in the use of the term and call for a clearer delineation.

[72] See https://www.reallabor-netzwerk.de, accessed on 16.01.2020.

[73] See https://www.baden-wuerttemberg.de/de/service/presse/pressemitteilung/pid/forschung-fuer-nachhaltigkeit-erfolgsmodell-reallabor-made-in-bw-1, accessed on 16.01.2020.

[74] See https://mobilitaetderzukunft.at/de/artikel/mobilitaetslabore, accessed on 16.01.2020.

Looking at representative consumer self- and other organizations (see Chap. 2), history shows that many of these important actors in today's consumer policy landscape have emerged from small initiatives, such as GLOBAL2000; the Chamber of Labour also developed out of the labour movement.

Processes of stabilization are likely to lead to the employment of full-time staff who are paid for their activities. A certain potential for volunteer staff may/must sometimes remain. In the case of many smaller local associations with similar ideals and objectives, an umbrella organization or similar can develop, representing the common interests of the individual groups. Increased visibility also makes it easier to attract financial supporters or more members to maintain the initiative. These development steps usually require a certain professionalization of public appearance and communication work. The locally operating 'Foodcoops' in Austria, for example, have founded an interest group with which they network with each other, develop common positions and support 'Foodcoops' in their founding phase and ongoing operation. With a certain size and visibility, initiatives can indeed achieve broader socio-political effects. With these steps, the transition from cooperative to representative self-organizations would be completed (see Sect. 2.3). With these steps towards professionalization, the structures change; certain advantages of cooperative self-organizations are also lost. The direction in which initiatives develop and the goals they pursue are somewhat at their own discretion, but of course also depend on political and social conditions.

4 Conclusion

One aim of this article was to locate grassroots movements in the Austrian consumer policy landscape, which is why a rough outline of the main actors in Austria was given at the beginning, apart from state actors such as ministries or arbitration bodies. The Chamber of Labour (AK) and the Association for Consumer Information (VKI) are the main polyvalent consumer organizations (CEO) that offer citizens services in the form of advice and information, conduct association, model and class actions, and advocate for an improved legal situation for consumers. Mono-thematic consumer protection organizations are primarily present in Austria in the fields of finance, internet, environment, and energy, serve as advisory bodies, and are funded by the public sector. In addition, there are representative consumer self-organizations (CSO), which are predominantly financed by membership fees and are active mainly in the fields of environment, mobility, housing, nutrition, and economy.

A special focus of this article, however, was on 'consumer policy from below', which is why civil society consumption initiatives in Austria were first introduced, from which ideal-typical similarities and differences of grassroots movements can be derived. Subsequently, socio-political challenges and potentials were worked out. Nationwide, there are civil society initiatives or cooperative consumer self-organizations in various consumption fields, such as nutrition, finance, energy, mobility, housing, and consumer goods as well as services, which offer supplements, but also alternatives to the existing market economy offer. For the majority of the grassroots movements presented, self-supply is in the foreground. In many cases, ecological and social sustainability is a significant element of their self-image. Small initiatives have various advantages compared to large organizations, such as self-determination and flexibility in action as well as opportunities to experiment due to political independence, but also disadvantages such as lack of funding and high fluctuation, which can sometimes endanger the continuation of the initiative. Digitalization enables and simplifies the coordination of actors among each other, increases the level of awareness, and helps to gain new members.

In particular, consumer organizations focus their support services primarily on consumer problems in the market and try to balance the imbalance between companies and consumers through information and interest politics (Nessel 2016). People who are looking for alternatives to the market economy have to become active themselves. Based on a significant number of various initiatives, it can be assumed that there is a general dissatisfaction with the market economy consumption offer and a desire for more socially just and ecologically viable supply systems. In various areas such as nutrition, housing, energy, and mobility, attempts are made to take over the task of intermediaries, apart from market economy companies such as food retailers, developers, energy providers, or commercial sharing platforms, in order to gain more control and transparency over the offer.

Grassroots movements—here equated with 'consumer policy from below'—are important actors in the consumer policy landscape, through which alternative forms of consumption can be demonstrated and societal transformation processes can be stimulated, which are more necessary and topical than ever today. However, this is associated with a lot of self-work and requires high societal commitment from individuals. It should not be forgotten that these are predominantly niche phenomena; these initiatives are often far removed from the everyday consumption of the majority of the population and can also be exclusive. Digitalization, on the other hand, offers a chance for interesting approaches to spread quickly, thereby gaining societal presence and influencing consumer policy.

It is the task of politics to set suitable framework conditions here to enable measures to have a broad impact. Currently, it is primarily the municipalities that promote initiatives; however, further measures would be necessary for a societal effectiveness. Therefore, further empirical research is needed regarding social inclusion and exclusion processes and the actual environmental effectiveness. For an evaluation and analysis of how this could be implemented, 'real laboratories' could be used.

References

Arbeiterkammergesetz. 1992. https://www.ris.bka.gv.at/GeltendeFassung.wxe?Abfrage=Bundesnormen&Gesetzesnummer=10008787. Accessed 30 Jan 2020.

AT Kearney. 2019. *The demystification of car sharing: An in-depth analysis of customer perspective, underlying economics, and secondary effects*. https://www.de.kearney.com/automotive/article?/a/the-demystification-of-car-sharing.

Baringhorst, Sigrid, Veronika Kneip, Annegret März, and Johanna Niesyto, eds. 2007. *Politik mit dem Einkaufswagen. Unternehmen und Konsumenten als Bürger in der globalen Mediengesellschaft. Medienumbrüche*. Bielefeld: transcript.

Behrendt, Siegfried, Christine Henseling, and Gerd Scholl, eds. 2018. *Digitale Kultur des Teilens: Mit Sharing nachhaltiger Wirtschaften*. Wiesbaden: Gabler.

Blättel-Mink, Birgit, and Kai-Uwe Hellmann. eds. 2010. *Prosumer revisited. Zur Aktualität einer Debatte*. Konsumsoziologie und Massenkultur Wiesbaden: VS.

Brunner, Karl-Michael. 2014. *Nachhaltiger Konsum und soziale Ungleichheit. Working papers Verbraucherpolitik, Verbraucherforschung*. Wien: AK Wien. http://resolver.obvsg.at/urn:nbn:at:at-akw:g-593244. Accessed 30 Jan. 2020.

Bundeskammer für Arbeiter und Angestellte. 2019. *Tätigkeitsbericht Bundesarbeitskammer 2018*. https://www.arbeiterkammer.at/taetigkeitsbericht. Accessed 31 Oct 2019.

European Environmental Agency. 2019. *Sustainability transitions: Policy and practice. EEA Report 9*. https://www.eea.europa.eu/publications/sustainability-transitions-policy-and-practice. Accessed 7 Nov 2019.

FIAN Österreich. 2019. *Ernährungsräte. Auf dem Weg zu einer demokratischen Lebensmittelpolitik*. Wien: Ernährungsrat Wien.

Höfferer, Peter, Florian Jagschitz, and Siegfried Rom. 2016. *160 Jahre Konsumgenossenschaften in Österreich*. Wien: Konsumverband.

Klug, Martin. 2017. *Die Repräsentation von Verbraucherinteressen. Organisation, Aggregation, Legitimation*. Policy-Analyse 12. Baden-Baden: Nomos.

Kollmann, Karl. 1986. *Konsumentenschutzpolitik in Österreich. Theorie und Praxis der Gewerkschaften*, Vol. 19. Wien: Verlag des Österreichischen Gewerkschaftsbundes.

Kuhlmann, Eberhard. 1990. *Verbraucherpolitik. Grundzüge ihrer Theorie und Praxis. Vahlens Handbücher der Wirtschafts- und Sozialwissenschaften*. München: Vahlen.

L&R Sozialforschung. 2005. *Grundsätzliche Organisationsform des Konsumentenschutzes in Österreich: mit dem Ziel der bestmöglichen operativen Aufgabenverteilung unter Einbeziehung aller gesellschaftlich relevanten Gruppen. Studie im Auftrag des Bundesministeriums für soziale Sicherheit, Generationen und Konsumentenschutz.* Wien.

Lamla, Jörn. 2013. *Verbraucherdemokratie: Politische Soziologie der Konsumgesellschaft.* Berlin: Suhrkamp.

Nessel, Sebastian. 2016. *Verbraucherorganisationen und Märkte: Eine wirtschaftssoziologische Untersuchung.* Wiesbaden: Springer VS.

Schäpke, Niko, Franziska Stelzer, Guido Caniglia, Matthias Bergmann, Matthias Wanner, Mandy Singer-Brodowski, Derk Loorbach, Per Olsson, Carolin Baedeker, and Daniel J. Lang. 2018. Jointly experimenting for transformation? Shaping Real-World Laboratories by comparing them. *GAIA – Ecological Perspectives for Science and Society* 27:85–96. https://doi.org/10.14512/gaia.27.s1.16.

Seidl, Roman J., Leonhard Plank, Justin Kadi, Roman Seidl, and Leonhard Plan. 2017. *Airbnb Wien: Eine Analyse – Interaktiver Forschungsbericht.* https://wherebnb.in/wien/. Accessed 17 July 2019.

Seyfang, Gill, and Adrian Smith. 2007. Grassroots innovations for sustainable development: Towards a new research and policy agenda. *Environmental Politics* 16:584–603. https://doi.org/10.1080/09644010701419121.

Stolle, Dietlind, Marc Hooghe, and Michele Micheletti. 2004. Zwischen Markt und Zivilgesellschaft: Politischer Konsum als bürgerliches Engagement. In *Zivilgesellschaft – National und transnational*, eds. D. Rucht, W. van den Daele, and J. Kocka, 151–172. WZB-Jahrbuch Berlin: Edition Sigma.

Tröger, Nina. 2017. Welche Potenziale bietet Transdisziplinarität für die Verbraucherforschung und die Verbraucherpolitik? In *Abschied vom eindimensionalen Verbraucher*, eds. C. Fridrich, R. Hübner, K. Kollmann, M.-B. Piorkowsky, and N. Tröger, 47–74. Kritische Verbraucherforschung Wiesbaden: Springer VS.

Verein für Konsumenteninformation. 2019. *Tätigkeitsbericht 2018.* https://vki.at/sites/vki.at/files/attachments/vki-tatigkeitsbericht_2018.pdf. Accessed 31 Oct. 2019.

Wagner, Felix, and Armin Grunwald. 2019. Reallabore zwischen Beliebtheit und Beliebigkeit: Eine Bestandsaufnahme des transformativen Formats. *GAIA – Ecological Perspectives for Science and Society* 28:260–264. https://doi.org/10.14512/gaia.28.3.5.

Nina Birkner-Tröger, Sociologist and consultant at the Vienna Chamber of Labour, Department for Consumer Policy. Main research interests: Social inequality, sustainability and social development processes. Co-initiator of the network "Konsum neu denken" (www.konsumforschung.at).

Self-organisation of Consumers as a Sociological Utopia of Consumption

Heiko Steffens

Abstract

A self-organization of consumer interests "from below", that is, through participatory engagement of consumer citizens, would best fulfill democratic standards such as legitimation and self-financing through membership fees. This article explores the real and utopian dimensions of this ideal-typical form of participation. A historical example is the founding of the Working Group of Consumer Associations AgV (Arbeitsgemeinschaft der Verbraucherverbände) in 1953, where opportunities and risks of representing their interests through the market power of consumers or through large associations such as trade unions, housewives' associations, or through their own special-purpose association were also discussed. The dependence of subsidized consumer organizations on the government is illustrated in the context of the AgV structural reform from 1995 to 2001 and culminates in the question of whether public welfare-oriented politics can act as selfless allies of organized consumer interests.

Keywords

Working Group of Consumer Associations AgV · External organization · Budget law · Self-organization · Consumer policy · Consumer associations

H. Steffens (✉)
ALOENK, Berlin, Germany
e-mail: steffens.heiko@tu-berlin.de

K.-U. Hellmann et al. (eds.), *Consumer Policy from Below*,
https://doi.org/10.1007/978-3-658-44478-5_12

1 Introduction

Would the establishment of consumer organizations 'from the bottom up', i.e., through the personal initiative of active consumers, be a panacea for all the legitimatory, political, organizational, and financial problems that accompany the process of institutionalization, including in terms of operational and work capability? Indeed, this question about the civil society status of consumer interest representatives is one of the oldest, most complex, and consequential issues in consumer policy. Even without theoretical flights of fancy and ideological somersaults, it is almost a priori that a consumer organization with a few million natural persons as registered members would have a secure base legitimacy for its consumer policy actions and demands. It could also generate the necessary financial resources through the membership fees of its individual members. Suppose a survey were to ask who should actually finance consumer organizations a) the consumers themselves, because their benefits would be great, the costs small; b) the state, because it does not want to risk its influence on consumers; or c) the economy, because it could prevent business-damaging consumer protection, a majority of respondents would probably favor self-financing by consumers. The control question of whether they themselves are members of the consumer center in their federal state, they would probably deny just as likely and perhaps also counterfactually claim that there are no individual members in consumer organizations. Respondents who notice the contradiction between the two answers would correct themselves and place the financing of consumer organizations in the public hand, which obtains the means from the pots of value-added and consumption taxes. This survey scenario is by no means trivial. To explain the outlined fickleness of consumers, behavioral consumer research establishes a connection between the interest-conforming services of consumer organizations and the theory of public goods. No one can be excluded from the enjoyment of public goods, and a contributor does not acquire exclusive property rights to the collective good. But if one can enjoy the benefits of a public good, such as preventive consumer protection, enlightening consumer information, labeling regulations, and other services of organized consumer representation, without having to participate in the costs of their creation, then there is a systematic incentive for free riding in the individual cost-benefit calculation, i.e., for the free use of the also monetary benefits that have been fought for by organizations (Hansen and Schrader 1997, p. 450).

After this introductory résumé of consumer research approaches, the view drifts back to the 1950s founding years of consumer organizations.

2 Self-help as the Historical root of Consumer Representation

The founding history of the Working Group of Consumer Associations (Arbeitsgemeinschaft der Verbraucherverbände, later AgV) is most succinctly revealed from the original wording of its anniversary publication on the occasion of its 40th anniversary in 1993:

> "After the currency reform, considerations began for the first time in the Federal Republic of Germany on how to combine the consumer organizations—in particular the traditional associations of consumer cooperatives and housewives' associations—which had hitherto worked largely in isolation from each other, into a powerful consumer representation. It is primarily the merit of the social scientist Professor Gerhard Weisser to have brought the necessity of consumer self-help into the consciousness of politics and the public. Together [with others—H.St.] Professor Weisser—then State Secretary in North Rhine-Westphalia—founded the 'Permanent Committee for Self-Help' in Cologne in 1949. This committee, which included representatives of non-profit institutes, associations, and organizations, set itself the goal from the outset of strengthening the 'solidary self-help will of the tendentially weak economic citizens'. These population groups included, for example, displaced persons, refugees, or unemployed people. A 'Subcommittee on Consumer Advice' was given the task of looking for ways to achieve effective consumer representation" (Arbeitsgemeinschaft der Verbraucherverbände 1993, p. 8).

In the communications of the Permanent Committee for Self-Help, Weisser, with argumentative foresight, demanded the creation.

> "of an organized representation of consumers, which must intervene where the individual consumer cannot sufficiently assert consumer interest through his demand. Although large organizations such as trade unions, consumer and housing cooperatives, or women's associations are repeatedly forced by life to deal with consumer problems. However, it cannot be denied that this cannot remain an unsystematic activity, starting here and there. After all, these are tasks that must be solved in an orderly manner. Weiser explicitly named three such tasks:
>
> 1. Representation of consumers to the government and state.
> 2. Representation of consumers to other economic partners.
> 3. Informing the public about the importance of the consumer in the economy and society, as well as appropriate behavior in the market" (Weisser, cited after Rick 2018, p. 192, footnote 613).

Based on these conceptual guidelines, the Working Group of Consumer Associations (AgV) was founded in Cologne in 1953, to which the majority of the associations represented in the Consumer Advice Subcommittee belonged as member associations. Only with the establishment of consumer centers at the state level, which took place from 1957 to 1962 and in many cases was based on home economics advice centers, and through the accession of large associations such as the German Tenants' Association, did the membership base reach a politically relevant strength in the early 1970s. In the anniversary publication on the 30th anniversary of the AgV, the political significance of the 'indirect membership' is emphasized. Because through the associations belonging to the AgV as an umbrella organization, such as the German Housewives' Association or the German Tenants' Association, "more than eight million consumers are connected with the AgV" (Arbeitsgemeinschaft der Verbraucherverbände 1983, p. 28).

When the AgV was founded as an association of associations (legal entities), this association solution was in principle a renunciation of an organization with mass membership of individual consumers.

The founding fathers and mothers apparently thoroughly discussed the reasons for consideration and impact assessments of their decision. According to the AgV's representations, the argumentation of its President O. Blume, who distinguished the ability to organize in the area of income generation from the ability to organize in the area of income use, ultimately prevailed:

> "While in the area of income generation the interest of self-employed and dependent working producers was sufficiently pronounced to be able to work successfully on the basis of individual membership [e.g. in the case of trade unions—H.St.], this was not the case with regard to income use. Here, the motivation of consumers was not sufficient to form a powerful organization that could have worked successfully as a counterweight to the numerous economic associations" (Blume, cited after Steffens 2015, p. 491).

From the government's point of view, the AgV's foundation according to this model was a stroke of luck despite all concerns in this or that direction. Because what was missing were a) a mobilizable and powerful membership base; b) financial and thus also political independence; c) the institutional prerequisites for conflict strategies and negotiating power vis-à-vis the economic associations and politics (Martiny and Klein 1977, p. 160; Scharpf 2002, p. 8).

Despite this genetic defect, the potential emergence of citizen initiatives in the form of consumer associations remained a perennial concern of politics. For example, a 'meta-survey on the development of institutions serving the consumer', commissioned by the Federal Ministry of Economics in 1975, already predicted a 'trend towards member associations', and further:

> "If numerous member associations emerge, they will exert pressure for the streamlining of consumer institutions; the AgV will take on the role of being the service center at the federal level for the associations as well. The influence of the federal and state governments will decrease, not least because of the expected self-financing of the associations; nevertheless, it must already be started now to establish member associations with state aid and to promote them over the first years, so that there is not an unconnected and thus uncontrollable private consumer movement" (Metaplan 1975, p. 6).

This statement sheds a telling light on the concern of the federal and state governments that the emergence of numerous self-financed member associations and the representation of their interests in the AgV as an umbrella organization could diminish the influence of the federal and state governments. What appears to be a contradiction in view of the dogma of consumer self-organization, namely the establishment of member associations with state aid, i.e., with financial grants as an incentive, turns out to be a means of securing state influence upon closer inspection. The conclusion from this analysis would be that the state wants to prevent the emergence of self-financed consumer organizations with mass membership by promoting the establishment of consumer organizations through state financial aid.

3 Active Consumers in Consumer Centers and Consumer Associations

In the history of the AgV, the year 1971 stands for a far-reaching organizational expansion and a well-intentioned, but ultimately misleading name change. In order to achieve 'a concentrated approach of all consumer organizations in public', the Working Group of Consumer Associations (AGV), the Consumer Centers of the States, the Working Group Home Economics, and the Federal Committee for Economic Education (BAVA) joined together in October 1971. The new name resembled the old one except in one important point. The new federal association called itself "Working Group of Consumers (AGV)" (Federal Government 1972, p. 35), although in its structure it remained what it was, an association of associations or, colloquially speaking: The AgV was not what it claimed to be by name. Neither in the first report of the federal government on consumer policy from November 1971 nor in the interim report of 1972 are there any reasons given for the new name. Only three years later in the "Concept for Consumer Information and Advice" presented by the Interministerial Committee for Consumer Affairs (BMWI 1975, p. 59) is the paradigm of the 'active consumer' not discussed at the high level of an association of associations, but below, i.e., at the level of the "establishment of consumer associations on the basis of individual membership" (ibid., p. 59).

> "The formation of such consumer associations would correspond to the concept of an active consumer who takes it upon himself to assert his interests and rights in the market. The federal government would welcome a stronger commitment of consumers also in this sense" (ibid., p. 60).

Without a doubt, this grassroots organizational and political model is worthy of all honor and would also be a classic basis for legitimacy. However, if it fails, for whatever reason, to fill the name part 'the consumer' with life and to win numerous individual consumers for membership through the opening "downwards", then the seal of approval becomes a false label. And so it happened soon. In his book 'Consumer Interest and Consumer Policy' from 1975, Gerhard Scherhorn (then a member of the Consumer Advisory Board) ties in with G. Weisser's concept of self-help and coins the pair of terms self-organization and external organization as a distinguishing norm. These terms were defined as follows: 1) Self-organization as 'organization of consumers in associations with individual membership' and 2) External organization as a form of organization in which not the consumers themselves as natural persons, but only associations as legal entities are admitted as members (Scherhorn 1975, p. 136). A working group of consumers, on the other hand, only pretends to have the basic legitimacy of a representation of interests supported by numerous consumers as members and, in Scherhorn's terminology, corresponds to the prototype of an external organization. It cannot be ruled out that the socio-political implications of the two terms 'self-organization' and 'external organization' were inspired by the value system of the terms 'self-determination', 'external determination' and 'co-determination', which were part of the argumentative basis of trade union counter-power politics at the same time as Scherhorn's classification in the course of political and scientific discussions about the opportunities and risks of self-determination, external determination and co-determination in the context of the legislation on employee co-determination of 1976.

Even after the re-conversion of the name 'Working Group of Consumers' into 'Working Group of Consumer Associations' in 1986, the characterization of the AgV as an external organization was not corrected and is also diagnosed by recent contemporary research as a serious genetic defect. This uncritical use of terms is very clear in Kevin Rick, who laments that the

> "structure of the AgV as a so-called external organization of consumer interests, i.e. as an organization that did not admit individual consumers as members, but only consumer-oriented associations, has not yet been reflected or systematically (by research) included in the analysis of its history—despite the far-reaching consequences of this form of organization for political legitimacy and practical work" (Rick 2018, pp. 30, 31, 238, 406 ff.).

But if the founding of the AgV in 1953 by consumer cooperatives, women's associations and other member associations was the founding of a federal association, then the question of the quality of the non-value-neutral term 'external organization' arises anew. Is a federal association that only registers legal entities, but no natural persons as individual members, therefore automatically an external organization? Then, for example, the German Trade Union Confederation DGB, which only counts individual trade unions among its members, would be an external organization that derives its legitimacy from an indirect membership of employees in the individual trade unions. According to this reading, the DGB would not be a self-organization of employees.

By the way, since the reorganization of the AgV in 1971, the eleven consumer centers (VZ) of the states that were admitted as member associations allowed individual membership of natural persons and had anchored this clause as well as the membership of associations in their statutes. On their own initiative, they repeatedly tried in field trials to win consumers for membership in the VZ. The success of such campaigns was low. As a result, the scientific advocates of self-organization put all their hope on self-founded and local consumer associations, in the founding of which they also personally participated.

For example, one of the pioneers of the critical theory of consumer policy, Bernd Biervert, conducted an empirical study commissioned by the Ministry of Economics in North Rhine-Westphalia in 1979 on 'Consumer associations as a form of self-organization of consumers' (Biervert et al. 1979). Despite the authors' passion for self-organized consumer associations and their axiom that

> "currently there is a considerable potential for self-organization of consumers […] it could not be sufficiently clarified in the context of this study, what successes can be achieved in terms of the state of self-organization of consumers" (ibid., p. 240 ff.).

In plain language, this means that even in consumer associations, there are significant difficulties in self-organization, which the authors explicitly name:

> "There is a significant gap between the willingness to self-organize in the sense of active participation in self-organized consumer associations and the possibilities of realizing the willingness to organize that can be found there. The reason for this can be seen in […] partly restrictive formal and content-related organizational conditions in the existing self-organized consumer associations" (ibid., p. 240).

The success of consumer associations also fell far short of expectations. As a counterexample, critics of the thesis of consumers' lack of willingness to self-organize often highlight the founding and success story of the Consumer Initiative in 1985. At a hearing in the Bundestag in 1998, the then chairman of the Consumer Initiative made a pointed statement:

> "The membership of the Consumer Initiative e. V. is made up predominantly of ecologically motivated individuals who see their membership fee as a political solidarity contribution. Our attempts to recruit new members with classic consumer topics have been fruitless" (Verbraucherinitiative 1998, p. 187).

The question of whether the findings cited from research projects, hearings or other sources are random or universally valid, relics of the past or burdens for the future, is a matter of debate. So far, such insights from empirical research provide a comparatively high level of evidence for findings of institutional economics. A fitting example: In 'The Rise and Decline of Nations', Mancur Olson (1991, p. 44) stated:

> "In no major country are large groups that do not have access to selective incentives generally organized—the masses of consumers are not in consumer organizations, the millions of taxpayers are not in taxpayer organizations, the considerable number of people with relatively low income are not in organizations for the poor […]. These groups are so scattered that it is not possible for any non-governmental organization to force them […]. There also seems to be no source of positive selective incentives that could give individuals in these categories an incentive to cooperate with the many others with whom they share common interests".

From this, one can conclude that at the current state of knowledge, neither empirical nor theoretical sciences give much chance to the realization of consumer self-organization. However, this does not mean that the normative fascination of self-organization is banished from the practical-political context to the beyond of practice-remote utopia. Quite the contrary. In the practical-political context, a paradoxical win-win situation arises instead.

4 Public Welfare-Oriented Politics as a Selfless Ally of Consumer Policy?

The 'public welfare-oriented politics' (Scharpf) or the state itself subsidize or finance the 'externally organized' consumer organizations through institutional and/or project-related funding, thereby compensating for the precarious situation of consumer organizations resulting from the inadequate organization of consumers. As a result, the existence, operational capability, and negotiating power of consumer organizations, secured at a relatively solid level, are subject to public budget law and can be guided to comply with rules and politically correct behavior using its means. A fundamental resistance against this would be futile, as the subsidy provider would then again bring the fundamentally superior self-organization with self-financing as an alternative into play. In such a situation, negotiation democracy ultimately leads to a vicious circle that turns the grassroots democratic norm of self-organization into a tool of power for public welfare-oriented politics. Conversely, consumer organizations depend on public welfare-oriented politics to compensate for their powerlessness in self-organization and self-financing.

The structural reform of the AgV and its integration into the Consumer Centre Federal Association vzbv (1996–2001) serves as an example to document that these considerations are not simply logical mind games. On February 19, 1997, the Federal Ministry of Economics presented the so-called 'ifo report', which was supposed to explore stronger self-financing of consumer organizations and identified "the lack of a larger member organization" (ifo 1996, p. 252) as the main obstacle on this path. Although the result of the structural reform in early 2001 was the merger of previously legally and economically independent institutions (AgV, Consumer Institute Foundation and Consumer Protection Association), the main goal of improving the framework conditions for significant self-financing could not be achieved (Steffens 2018, p. 14). This also maintained the high dependency on public subsidies, the close ties to public budget law, and the associated patronization.

Despite its utopian status, however, the self-organization of consumers remains a normative basic principle for good reasons, which will not disappear from the civil society and political demand catalog of a democratic consumer policy.

References

Arbeitsgemeinschaft der Verbraucherverbände. 1983. *30 Jahre AgV*. Bonn: AgV.

Arbeitsgemeinschaft der Verbraucherverbände. 1993. *40 Jahre AgV*. Bonn: AgV.

Biervert, Bernd, et al. 1979. *Verbrauchervereine als Form der Selbstorganisation von Verbrauchern in der Bundesrepublik Deutschland*. ed. NRW Ministerium für Wirtschaft. Düsseldorf: NRW Ministerium für Wirtschaft.

Bundesregierung. 1972. *Bericht der Bundesregierung: Es geht um den Verbraucher*. Bonn: Bundesregierung.

Bundesministerium für Wirtschaft. 1975. *2. Bericht der Bundesregierung zur Verbraucherpolitik + Konzeption für die Verbraucherinformation und -beratung*. Bonn: BMW.

Hansen, Ursula, und Ulf Schrader. 1997. A modern model of consumption for a sustainable society. *Journal of Consumer Policy* 20:443–468.

Ifo Institut für Wirtschaftsforschung. 1996. *Finanzierung der Verbraucherorganisationen in der Bundesrepublik Deutschland*. München: Ifo.

Martiny, Anke, und Otfried Klein. 1977. *Marktmacht und Manipulation*. Frankfurt a. M.: Europäische Verlagsanstalt.

Metaplan. 1975. *Metaenquête über die Entwicklung der den Verbrauchern dienenden Institutionen*. Quickborn: Metaplan.

Olson, Mancur. 1991. *Aufstieg und Niedergang von Nationen*. Mohr (Siebeck): Tübingen.

Rick, Kevin. 2018. *Verbraucherpolitik in der Bundesrepublik Deutschland (1945–1975)*. Baden-Baden: Nomos.

Scharpf, Fritz. 2002. Lobbyismus für Verbraucherinteressen in der Verhandlungsdemokratie. In *Verbraucherschutz im globalen Markt*. ed. Vzbv. Berlin: vzbv.

Scherhorn, Gerhard. 1975. *Verbraucherinteresse und Verbraucherpolitik*. Göttingen: Schwartz.

Steffens, Heiko. 2015. Verbraucherpolitik als Stärkung der Selbsthilfe. In *Lebenslagen. Beiträge zur Gesellschaftspolitik*, eds. H. Romahn and D. Rehfeld, 489–507. Marburg: Metropolis.

Steffens, Heiko. 2018. *Von der AgV zum vzbv. Strukturreform*. Unveröffentlichtes Manuskript, Berlin. https://www.aloenk.tu-berlin.de/fileadmin/fg165/Publikationen/Strukturreform-Ziele-des-ifo-Gutachtens-13-03-18-fin_Korr_vP-Imprimatur-1.pdf

Verbraucherinitiative. 1998. *Stellungnahme bei einer Anhörung des Wirtschaftsausschusses des Deutschen Bundestages am 9.02.1998*. Protokolle des Wirtschaftsausschusses, Bonn: Deutscher Bundestag.

Heiko Steffens, TU professor from 1981 to 2003, subject area economics/labour studies, individual member of the Verbraucherzentrale Berlin since 1976, president of the Arbeitsgemeinschaft der Verbraucherverbände AgV from 1995 to 2001, member of the Economic and Social Committee of the EU from 2002 to 2006, founder of the TOWER PERSON AWARD FOR CONSUMER EDUCATORS 2000–2018, honorary doctor of the University of Economics in Bratislava 2006. Numerous publications.

The Critical and Mature Consumer

Georg Abel

Abstract

Consumers have power, they decide on products, companies, shopping routes, and their personal lifestyle. The individual purchasing decision for or against a product is a direct opportunity to influence. Consumers say in surveys what their expectations are of manufacturers and trade. However, they are not manufacturers themselves or have the technical expertise on the various supply chains. They delegate these tasks to the "professionals" of the companies. However, they want to know who did what when with what success. And only then do they (possibly) consider these products for their personal purchase. They therefore indirectly influence in this way—almost as "clients". More influence from consumers is also exerted by non-governmental organizations through media criticism or through various cooperations with companies. Relatively new is the prosumer approach to product design.

Keywords

Information overload label · Prosumer · Non-governmental organizations · Corporate cooperations · CONSUMER INITIATIVE · Consumer power · Consumer values

G. Abel (✉)
VERBRAUCHER INITIATIVE e. V., Berlin, Germany
e-mail: georg.abel@verbraucher.org

K.-U. Hellmann et al. (eds.), *Consumer Policy from Below*,
https://doi.org/10.1007/978-3-658-44478-5_13

Without genetic engineering, without child labor, and without animal suffering—the demands of consumers as formulated in representative surveys are clear. The real difference between the demands of consumers and their actual (demand) behavior is a challenge. For politics, businesses, and civil society.

Consumers have power. In the face of stagnating and even declining markets—keyword demographic change—this power is likely to grow. Experienced shoppers decide which products are in vogue or not. Consumers also decide which companies are successful or not. Customers choose their individual lifestyle and of course also the shopping method that suits them: Brick-and-mortar retail or internet is just one question. Online shopping, i.e., conveniently shopping from home in an unlimited range of products around the clock, will continue to grow in the coming years. Shopping events like 'Black Friday' or 'Cyber Monday' increasingly invite bargain hunting, an estimated €3.1 billion were generated in Germany alone on 'Black Friday'. Older consumers, changed household sizes, and changed eating habits—the demand for out-of-home consumption is increasing—are further trends. Sensationalist media reports, the opportunity for direct exchange on social networks, and a general loss of trust are further challenges. The multioptional, vagabonding, and price-fixated consumer is a reality—when looking at the entirety of consumers. However, individual groups exhibit a different, very conscious demand behavior. They set strong trends in the short term and thus influence the product range, the retail landscape, and the expectations of the broad masses of tomorrow.

1 Offering What the Customer Wants

Even the food retail industry, which is one of the few sectors not yet affected by the online boom, is facing significant changes: The concentration process in the industry continues; increasingly more food sales are currently being achieved through drugstores. New distribution channels such as direct marketing, organic supermarkets, and vegan markets have emerged. The trade acts as a mediator between manufacturers and customers—in terms of quality and price.

However, the traditional full-range suppliers have made significant ground against the seemingly unbeatable discounters, which have been growing for years, with their differentiated range of goods in terms of quality and price, and their service offerings. Supermarkets like the REWE market Richrath in the center of Cologne show where the journey is heading: For example, with products from the region, whose suppliers are introduced by name and location. A large wine department with regular wine tastings, a wide range of different food offerings from Italian to Asian, and a coherent product presentation on two levels make shopping there and in many model markets of other providers an experience and are an alternative to online shopping.

The discounters will have to follow suit. A narrowly defined, flat assortment with fast-moving items garnished with non-food promotional goods was yesterday. A minimalist effort for product presentation and store furnishings is no longer contemporary. Accordingly, this market segment will continue to change: Larger areas with more products taking into account dietary trends, the listing of branded products, more elaborate presentation are the already visible harbingers of major changes. Whether this quality strategy by ALDI and Co. will succeed, however, remains to be seen; price-sensitive customers could switch to other providers.

The food retail industry is responding to these developments with a changed awareness of quality. Because for some years now, consumers have been willing to spend (somewhat) more money on food. However, they expect more than just an appealing presentation.

For many years, the slogan 'Greed is cool' was on everyone's lips, but today other things are more important. This is evidenced, among other things, by the current Nestlé nutrition study 'So is(s)t Germany 2019': Good food and drink are an expression of one's own quality of life, nutrition has become a personal statement. The quality of food replaces price as the most important criterion. Higher expenditures for organic, fair and regional are real market changes. They demonstrate the changes in personal value ranking and thus in individual expenditure management by consumers. But anyone who wants to get more money from the customer must be able to credibly convey where the corresponding added value lies.

Surveys indicate that consumers in an often arbitrary society increasingly rely on values. Trends such as 'regional', 'without child labor' and 'animal welfare' are examples of these strong values. 'Sustainability' is the possible substantive bracket for this!

2 Consumer in Transition

Despite all representative surveys, many of the trends do not reflect in actual demand behavior or, despite high percentage growth rates, ultimately lead a niche existence.

Consumers will continue to be contradictory in their behavior in the future, making them difficult to predict. Some examples: Knowing about the fine dust problem, fireworks are temporarily disposed of in the air for €133 million, which corresponds to over 15% of the fine dust emissions from road traffic in a year. Knowing about the climate problem, second and third vacations are very popular. Knowing about illegal child labor, cheap clothes are hauled home by the bagful.

However, changes can also be observed: Cities block areas for the archaic black powder firecrackers, retailers delist corresponding products. Massive investments in more environmentally friendly means of transport, in a tighter rail network ('Germany schedule'), new mobility offers such as the Berlin ride-sharing service Berlkönig or different (car-) sharing offers also in suburbs or in rural regions are keywords here alongside the prohibition rhetoric of some politicians. Textile retailers are committed to improved working conditions and participate in the Textile Alliance or voluntarily use the 'Green Button', the state seal for sustainable textiles.

But ultimately it depends on the consumer. He must at least demand these offers from companies or become more of an actor in the future than before. The first of these challenging options is the easier one, namely solvable through communication and motivation.

3 Information Overload

Consumers are individual, multi-optional, and contradictory in their behavior. Anyone who wants to score points with consumers must provide diverse information, for example about the company, business conduct in the supply chain, and products. Given tight time budgets and in a media society overloaded with stimuli, however, there is little time for comprehensive information processes. Here, consumers have the choice between different information offers: Test reports from institutions such as Stiftung Warentest or Öko-Test belong to this category, as do a multitude of different car magazines. Monthly magazines like Finanztest with around 200,000 copies sold or the weekly free newsletter from finanztip.de, according to its own statements with more than 600,000 subscribers Germany's largest non-profit advisor, offer advice on money matters.

Daily newspapers provide tips on often weekly consumer pages, as do consumer magazines on radio and television, taking into account test results as well as tips from non-governmental organizations or government institutions. Government web portals such as the Consumer Information System/VIS, an offer from the Bavarian state government with the participation of several departments, provide information on topics such as nutrition, food, consumer rights, finances, and data protection. A multitude of often non-profit organizations such as consumer, environmental, senior, or animal protection organizations also offer consumer information. Web portals like utopia.de, karmakonsum.de, smarticular.net or globalmagazin.com prepare topics for a sustainability-affine clientele and use the different social media channels for this purpose.

Another source of information about product quality are labels. Without them, nothing works in our world of goods anymore. Far more than 1,000 different signs stick on products, distinguish services or internet offers. Originally intended as quick advice for purchase decisions, labels have rather lost this function for many consumers due to their sheer number.

4 Labels—The Quick (Perceived) Advice

Organic, regional, fair, vegan—consumers' interests are becoming more diverse. Therefore, the 'quick' advice from credible senders is in demand. An increasing information offer are labels. As a guide for buyers, a guidance system in retail, an added value for products, or a guidance system for procurement, they fulfill different functions. The multitude of signs and the lack of consumer knowledge about the backgrounds of the individual labels are, however, two of the hurdles that limit their effect. Thanks to long-lasting, intensive communication work, the organic seal, the Fairtrade logo, or the Blue Angel have a high, at least perceived, level of awareness. However, even with these signs, awareness does not automatically mean that this is reflected in actual purchasing behavior.

Since the year 2000, the information service label-online.de has been providing more transparency for labels in Germany. The portal is now the most comprehensive service for quality marks in Europe. In it, the CONSUMER INITIATIVE ('Verbraucher Initiative') evaluates over 800 symbols in 16 different categories according to a cross-industry matrix. A free app allows for a label check on the go. With accompanying communication (label theme booklets, press services, ready-to-broadcast radio contributions, video, etc.), the topic of labels is placed in different media in a target group-specific manner.

A representative consumer study by Kantar EMNID on behalf of the non-profit federal association dealt in 2017, among other things, with consumers' handling of labels, expectations and requirements for product seals, and the corresponding information sources. When it comes to labels, consumers are divided. While pictograms on products are generally seen positively in terms of additional information and their function as orientation aids, their innumerable number causes confusion. It is therefore not surprising that only 16% of respondents rate their knowledge of the meaning of labels as 'very good or rather good'.

In contrast, 44% of those interviewed state that it is 'very important or important' to them to know what the respective product seal means.

Most consumers see labels as useful additional information about certain properties or the quality of products: 69% of respondents express themselves accordingly, 62% generally see them as helpful in making a purchase decision. Consumers have clear expectations of product labels: credibility, comprehensibility, and independent testing and awarding are at the forefront. However, consumers consider labels differently depending on the industry. Product labels are particularly important for electrical and household appliances as well as in the food sector.

Depending on the product group, those who at least pay strong attention to product seals also formulate the quality criteria: In contrast to other product groups, health compatibility plays a particularly important role in food—similar to cosmetics and drugstore items. It is significantly ahead of environmentally and socially compatible production as well as safety (see Figs. 1 and 2).

Fig. 1 Relevance of seals: Product groups. *Source* DIE VERBRAUCHER INITIATIVE e. V.

Fig. 2 Desired quality criteria for product seals. *Source* DIE VERBRAUCHER INITIATIVE e. V.

Consumers inquire about information on labels. The most important information channels are the internet and packaging. The credibility of the information sources is also evaluated differently. Information offers on product seals from environmental and consumer organizations and government agencies are particularly well received. In contrast, manufacturers of products are met with skepticism.

The multitude of similar symbols is not helpful from a consumer perspective and rather contributes to consumer confusion. Thus, the discussion about the different approaches to animal welfare is rather counterproductive. Here, a variety of approaches have been responded to a consumer desire articulated in surveys, from industry approaches (Initiative Tierwohl) to labels (Neuland, Tierschutzbund, Vier Pfoten, etc.) to the repeatedly placed idea of a state symbol. However, for the target group, the nuances of the individual approaches are difficult to recognize, as a standard comparison by the CONSUMER INITIATIVE showed in 2018. From the perspective of a consumer organization, more cooperation would be sensible.

The uniform four-stage husbandry form labeling of the Initiative Tierwohl (haltungsform.de) is a helpful approach for consumers to recognize more animal welfare.

The basic consideration of labels—whether by listing corresponding products, upgrading own brands through co-labeling, or by developing corresponding orientation systems at the point of sale—are a helpful tool in customer communication. It makes sense to pay more attention to existing symbols in order to use their familiarity and thus also increase the effect of these labels on consumers. By the way, there must be no standstill in the quality of the symbols: they must continuously develop in content, even more intensive cooperation of individual label systems or even a merger, as recently with UTZ and Rainforest Alliance, makes sense from a consumer's point of view.

On Label-online, labels are evaluated according to a uniform matrix. For example, it is examined what claims labels make, how independent their award is, what controls are provided and how transparent this process is for consumers. The matrix was developed on the basis of an extensive stakeholder process, in which representatives of companies, associations, science and various federal ministries were involved. An advisory board occasionally accompanied the development of the website as well as the selection and evaluation of the labels; this evaluation matrix is also used in Austria, among others.

Each individual criterion is evaluated in the matrix with 1 or 0 points. The final evaluation ranges from 'not recommended' (under 5 points) to 'highly recommended' (12 points). Labels that are committed to sustainability and include ecological and social aspects in their certification process are marked with a . This is additional information that does not flow into the evaluation of the labels.

5 NGOs as Representatives of Civil Society

In addition to the consumer as a demanding actor, companies themselves make decisions about the further development or new development of products. With the increased offering of private labels, particularly in the food and drugstore product sectors, retailers become manufacturers and decide on the product quality of these offers. Thus, trade has two levers: on the one hand, it can decide on the listing of branded products, on the other hand, it creates its own brands.

Both manufacturers and trading companies use not only data from market research for product development. Increasingly, they take into account different dialogue formats to involve other actors. For example, Nestlé has been exchanging ideas with a volunteer, 18-member 'consumer advisory board' for several years. The committee sees itself as an advisor and impulse giver. Nestlé itself emphasizes that this 'critical dialogue' provides the company with valuable feedback on the quality and sustainability of its products.

Increasingly important for companies in recent years has been the exchange with different actor groups, for example at (annual) stakeholder forums. Thus, the REWE Group created a 'dialogue forum' in 2009 as an exchange format for more sustainability in trade and society. The goal was to enable an 'open, constructively critical dialogue' with actors from politics, trade, economy, science, and society.

Non-governmental organizations willing to talk are part of this exchange process. This applies broadly to this stakeholder format. In individual cases, however, the cooperation between NGOs and companies goes beyond this. For example, since 2009 there has been a 'partnership' between EDEKA and the World Wide Fund For Nature (WWF), among other things with the aim of reducing the company's ecological footprint. Consumers benefit from this cooperation; around 400 more sustainable private label products are marked with the WWF panda.

The REWE Group is also concerned with the further development of its own brands. In a 'strategic partnership' with the Nature and Biodiversity Conservation Union (NABU), these are to be further developed sustainably. In addition to this bilateral cooperation, the company has been offering a 'navigation system for more sustainable products' to customers since 2009 with the PRO PLANET label. An independent, five-member 'sustainability advisory board' is actively involved in the award process. The committee includes PROVIEH, SÜDWIND, and the CONSUMER INITIATIVE.

Other companies also rely on exchanges with non-governmental organizations. For several years, a three-member advisory board, which includes the Global Nature Fund (GNF) and the CONSUMER INITIATIVE, has been supporting REAL in the distribution of permaculture products and assisting with the corresponding range expansion.

In addition to non-governmental organizations that do not rule out cooperation, organizations like Foodwatch pursue a different 'business model'. The association, financed by supporting memberships and donations, deals with 'consumer-unfriendly practices in the food industry and the weaknesses in legislation' and wants to put politics and companies under pressure.

6 Other Approaches to Cooperation

Not only in the field of agriculture and nutrition have new initiatives emerged in recent decades that have more closely interlinked consumers and producers. These include local FOOD-Coop initiatives, at the center of which is joint direct purchasing. The interlinking of producers and consumers is generally important. For example, the regional initiative 'som/skat' enables decisions on selected textile products; in workshops, it is decided whether a design is produced and the corresponding demand exists. The nationwide tea campaign has been offering direct trade of selected tea varieties in advantageous bulk packaging since 1985. Another example is the EVG LANDWEGE founded in 1988 in the Lübeck region. In the producer-consumer community, individual groups of actors from consumers, farmers, and employees decide together. The idea of 'Solidarity Agriculture/SOLAWI' focuses on the cooperation of farmers with their buyers.

The consumer community e. V. pursues a path for consumers to have more influence on nutrition with their initiative 'You are the boss here!'. The aim of the non-profit association is the transparent co-design of sustainable products by consumers and the fair and just remuneration of agricultural producers. The first product is expected to be a milk to be introduced in spring 2020 under the consumer brand 'You are the boss here!'. With a product questionnaire comprising eight questions, which has been available on the website since December 2019, consumers can decide for themselves which product features are important to them in the milk, how it should be produced, and at what price they would be willing to buy it. The aim is to design a valuable, fair, and sustainable product that is offered as fresh and UHT milk in full-fat and low-fat versions.

"Milk offers the opportunity to address many of the important issues of our initiative such as environmental protection and biodiversity, animal welfare, remuneration for farmers together," explains Nicolas Barthelmé, founder of the initiative. The current milk price does not allow many dairy farmers in Germany to produce at cost. An alliance between consumers and farmers is intended to change this. The questions of the first product questionnaire were developed together by consumers, farmers, and a dairy: Are the cows allowed to graze? What is fed to the animals and where do the feedstuffs come from? How fair should farmers be paid? What quality should the milk have: conventional or organic? How sustainable should the packaging be? Which future measures—conversion to pasture farming, to organic farming or to mother-bound calf rearing—should be prioritized for co-financing?

On the website www.youarethebosshere.com every consumer can decide for free on the relevant product features and at the same time see how the price of the milk changes accordingly. “Once we have reached about 5000 completed questionnaires, we summarize the results in a specification book,” explains Nicolas Barthelmé. In order for the ‘consumer milk’ to also find its way onto supermarket shelves, farmers, dairies, and retailers are won as partners. The model for ‘You are the boss here!’ is the French initiative ‘C’est qui le patron?!’, which also started with milk in 2016 and now sells over 50 million liters annually. This benefits 330 French dairy farmers who now produce exclusively for the initiative and receive a fair and just remuneration between €0.39 and €0.41 per liter. The term ‘prosumer’, which was coined in 1980, is now used more broadly and also includes the (re)distribution and repair of products.

7 Approaches of the CONSUMER INITIATIVE

The Federal Association of Critical Consumers has long relied on a mix of different strategic approaches to implement its consumer policy objectives. The nonprofit association, founded in a Bonn living room in June 1985, emerged from the environmental movement. According to the invitation to the founding assembly at the time, the aim was to ‘establish an independent nationwide consumer initiative that strives to coordinate the many individual activities and represent the interests of critical consumers’. Campaigns on cans and disposable bottles (‘Disposable is no way’) or signature campaigns for an EC-wide ban on radioactive irradiation of food characterized the first years of the association financed by membership fees and donations.

In October 1991, a 16-page ‘manifesto’ of the association titled ‘The Responsibility of Consumers’ was published. In it, the association sees itself as part of an ‘eco-social’ consumer movement. Among other things, it called for ‘a fundamental rethink of consumption and buying habits’, an ecological consumer and economic policy, promotion of fair trade as well as women- and family-friendly companies. ‘The CONSUMER INITIATIVE wants to contribute with its work to people taking responsibility in their everyday life’, it says about the future tasks of the association.

The Federal Association therefore limited itself to a few subject areas such as environment, nutrition and health, and initially relied on the factor of communication through theme campaigns. In the following years, the then print-based own media were expanded and occasionally books were published. It was recognized early on that one must act in theme cooperations. Accordingly, the association was one of the co-founders of the Neuland brand meat program in 1988 together with the German Animal Welfare Association and the BUND, or a founding member of Transfair in 1992.

Over the decades, however, the strategic approach has changed: A target group-specific approach to individual consumer policy issues was not possible in the past. The concept of regional consumer events for older consumers developed by the Federal Association in 2009 has since enabled direct targeting of this growing target group in several federal states. An average of 70 participants were directly reached at the approximately 150 half-day regional events on the topics of internet, health, rip-offs and energy. Thousands more consumers were addressed with the corresponding topic brochures that were displayed in town halls, adult education centers, etc. Several million consumers were reached through the accompanying media work on these topics. In addition to the content theme setting, strengthening volunteer work on site is an approach pursued by the association.

Also, studies and market research on topics such as animal welfare, Corporate Social Responsibility (CSR), sustainability, fair trade or labels were not conceivable and financeable in earlier years. Communication in the digital age has changed. The small Federal Association now has various websites, a quarterly widely distributed consumer magazine and a monthly brochure series currently covering 150 individual topics. Target group-specific nationwide information campaigns, the regular offer of ready-to-broadcast radio contributions and the placement of articles in weekly newspapers were not feasible in the past due to lack of financial resources.

Even today, the CONSUMER INITIATIVE operates in alliances and is a co-sponsor, among others, of the Green Electricity Label, belongs to boards such as the Platform for Nutrition and Exercise/peb, supports new movements like 'You are the boss here', participates in signature campaigns on change.org on the subject of merino wool and uses membership in committees such as the Board of Trustees of QS Quality and Safety GmbH for political exchange and influence.

The participation of the CONSUMER INITIATIVE in the advisory boards of various companies is a strategic challenge. The federal association has formulated various minimum criteria for this internally. Necessary among other things is a clear goal and task definition, the long-term and broad anchoring of this approach in the company itself, as well as an independent body supported by actors with various content approaches. Since its foundation in 2009, the federal association has been a member of the Sustainability Advisory Board (formerly PRO PLANET Advisory Board) of the REWE Group (REWE, Penny, toom) and leads the multi-member advisory boards on the topic of permaculture at REAL and the multi-thematic Nestlé advisory board.

However, the multifaceted work of a non-profit non-governmental organization is particularly dependent on the resources available. The original approach of full financing through membership fees and donations from individual consumers has not proven successful. Today, the CONSUMER INITIATIVE therefore relies on a mix of income from traditional revenues, sales proceeds from the brochure series, project funds, and the surpluses of the association's own GmbH, which are booked as own income and which, among other things, carry out orders for state ministries.

8 Example Animal Welfare

Another component of the consumer policy work of the CONSUMER INITIATIVE is the exchange with different stakeholders from civil society, politics, and business. In 2018, a comprehensive standard comparison of important animal welfare approaches was carried out, as well as a comprehensive survey of various institutions in ten actor groups from trade to farmers to animal protection. The corresponding study was discussed in a stakeholder workshop with selected actors and presented directly to important national actors such as the state animal welfare officers or parliamentarians.

For example, consumers want the animals to be well. According to the study 'Conscious Enjoyment—Sustainable Profits' from 2013, about 26% of them consciously buy sustainably, socially, and ecologically. In this group, enjoyment and social responsibility have already moved closely together. This group is informed, pays attention to labels, shops consciously, sets trends, determines public discussion, and initiates changes. Consumers of this group can and must be communicated additional commitment in various ways.

Consumers wish—or at least they claim—that the farm animals are well in life, while growing up, and in death. They should, for example, be healthy, be able to develop according to their species, and receive healthy and species-appropriate feed. However, consumers cannot check these 'felt expectations' themselves. Because they do not keep the animals, they do not collect the eggs, they do not cut the fillet from the pig. They delegate these steps to the professionals: farmers, slaughter and cutting operations, processors, and last but not least, trade. Consumers expect them to solve the existing problems and communicate this in a comprehensible way. They themselves can only decide what to buy from it. For this, they expect information: They want to recognize and believe the services of the professionals. They want to know whether, what, and how something was done with what success. The fact that the answers sometimes do not match the idealized ideas of laypeople is the special challenge (also for communication).

However, orientation towards 'animal welfare' is not so easy for industry professionals either. Because consequently, the animal is at the center. This is new, so far it has always been the human being with needs such as safety, sufficient quantity, or cheap prices. The art will be to develop measurable and implementable criteria for 'animal welfare' and to build a bridge between the deceptive idyll of 'felt animal welfare' and the agricultural and scientific reality.

The duty of responsible animal owners already commands that livestock be kept in a manner that is appropriate to their species, healthy, sustainable, and dignified. For this self-evident fact to finally become the standard, the industry and trade must rethink and no longer place the responsibility for product quality and prices on the consumer. The consumer neither determines how production is carried out, nor does he set the prices. He merely chooses from the offer that manufacturers and trade make to him. Therefore, for livestock farming to actually become animal-friendly, it largely depends on trade. Because efforts to improve animal welfare must not stop with conscious, enlightened, committed customers. The goal must be to reach the mass market. As a mediator between the production side and its customers, trade is the most important ambassador for standards, concepts, and qualities. While it is the task of the meat industry to develop a minimum standard for animal welfare and to implement it reliably, trade must find an honest, animal-friendly pricing policy. Anyone who seriously commits to animal welfare will also no longer use meat and sausage as a bait offer. This dumping contradicts the idea of animal welfare and destroys the price feeling and the trust of consumers in the quality of the goods. Consequently, trade will in the future only list such meat products that reliably meet at least the basic requirements for animal-friendly products. Only in this way can it be ensured that 'cheap' does not come at the expense of the animals.

Consumers want animal-friendly livestock farming. This is a mandate for agriculture, the meat industry, trade, and politics. Agriculture and trade are already in motion. They show with various animal welfare programs, labels, and husbandry labeling that they have understood the signals and that changes are possible. It would be consistent and committed if the federal government were to pick up these approaches and roll them out across all stables. But this is not happening.

The policy of the Federal Minister of Agriculture on animal protection/animal welfare in livestock farming has for years not been doing justice to either animal protection or committed farmers or the demands of consumers. Consumers are not waiting for the x-th voluntary sign, but for far-sighted course settings for animal-friendly and economically viable livestock farming. For this, the CONSUMER INITIATIVE demands:

- *Implement laws:* Violations of existing animal protection laws must be consistently recorded and eliminated in all stables.
- *Keep an eye on animal health:* A nationwide mandatory 'system for recording animal-related characteristics' on living and dead animals allows for the identification of deficiencies. The results must be returned to the farmers and, if necessary, linked to the obligation to make improvements.
- *Fair financing:* More animal-friendly livestock farming must be paid for. The Federal Minister must develop a viable financing system for animal-friendly livestock farming that does not solely depend on the individual decisions of laypeople at the end of the value chain, but also includes large consumers, processors, and the catering industry.
- *Learn from pioneers:* Agriculture and trade are moving. This is welcome. The Federal Minister must use the existing experiences, requirements, and control systems to bring more animal welfare into the mass of stables.
- *Support commitment:* The federal government must promote investments by farmers that contribute to animal welfare. This includes not only structural changes but also measures that serve animal health (including species-specific behavior) or herd management.
- *Be a role model and use purchasing power:* In the federal government's catering establishments, animal products should only be offered from reliably animal-friendly husbandry. The federal government can lead by example here.

9 Outlook

In their work, the CONSUMER INITIATIVE, as a critical consumer organization, pursues the guiding principle of the enlightened, responsible, and informed consumer. It is not easy to maintain an overview and behave responsibly as a committed consumer in the jungle of products and services. What is needed is good, preferably individual advice, which is not really easy in a media-saturated society. Not only in the age of fake news, consumers rightly ask themselves who and what they can believe, what interests are behind information, or how current such information is. This is where the provider-independent work of the CONSUMER INITIATIVE comes in: with credible information and the demonstration of feasible options for action.

The CONSUMER INITIATIVE therefore sees itself as a political federal association and pursues the guiding principle of a livable and more sustainable society. However, promoting a more sustainable lifestyle is a cross-sector task and cannot be achieved by individual actors alone.

The federal association therefore relies not only on strategic, thematic, and cross-actor alliances in the area of animal welfare. To advance topics in terms of content and to spread them widely in a media society, this approach is without alternative. A focus on the consumer is too short-sighted, other stakeholders are also in demand. A mix of governmental and voluntary measures is necessary.

More sustainable consumption is not sufficient as the only perspective. We need to move away from the 'growth fixation' in the long term. The vision 'How can we live in the future' must be widely discussed and agreed upon in society. All stakeholders, not just consumers, are logically required for this. This vision is missing.

This debate is about 'less', not just more sustainable consumption. The growth of organic, regional & fair is niche and not mass market. Approaches such as producer cooperatives, FOOD coops, urban gardening, and solidarity agriculture are also important approaches. However, they only replace consumption with another form of consumption.

Habits, rituals, lack of time, setting up in social media groups, sensory overload: We need a different 'discussion and debate culture' and not reflexive reactions etc. A broad societal alliance is needed as a basis. Since all citizens are consumers, consumption topics are of great importance for this debate. The nature of the debate, the results, and their experience in one's own environment have considerable explosive power in civil society/politics. 'Renunciation' must be sold, i.e., recharged differently. For this overall societal 'development process' we need:

- thematic alliances
- time, which we actually don't have
- different thinking and acting (not only in election periods or in 140 characters on Twitter etc.)
- honesty (it will also hurt!)
- all actors
- bundles of measures (political guidelines, individual actions of companies/consumers)
- global view/approach.

Animal welfare, plastic bags, and sustainability are just three examples of the changing quality demands of consumers. As with CSR, manufacturers and retailers are gradually making progress in these areas. The goals are large and far from being achieved, and communication is often difficult. In addition, consumers neither have the time, the attention, nor the will to immediately respond positively to every industry initiative with their shopping basket and change their long-standing habits. Therefore, real changes require a long breath. It will help to fulfill the three wishes that unite consumers regardless of their personal shopping behavior, their quality demands, and their individual value canon:

1. Take responsibility. Producers, manufacturers, and retailers determine under what conditions and how products are made. They must solve the problems.
2. Provide options for action. Consumers do not want to search, preferably not leave their usual shopping places, and not become specialists. Products of special, sustainable quality must therefore be offered everywhere, clearly recognizable and understandably labeled. Their usage qualities (taste, durability, etc.) must be as convincing as the price.
3. Communicate convincingly. Not everyone needs all the information. However, labels must be clear, and the messages from the industry must be consistent. Transparency in the supply chain may not be used by everyone—but it is expected. This kind of corporate openness is more directed at the small group of particularly interested consumers, non-governmental organizations, and politics.

Georg Abel has been working as the Federal Executive Director of VERBRAUCHER INITIATIVE e. V. since 1994 and focuses on the topics of consumer communication and sustainability.

BUND Berlin e. V.'s Commitment to Strengthening the Initiative Scene

Daniel Affelt

Abstract

The Bund für Umwelt und Naturschutz Deutschland (BUND) Berlin e. V. supports civic engagement and initiatives in the city in various ways. Concrete examples of these activities, such as sewing cafes, repair cafes, and clothing swap parties, are presented in the text. In addition, BUND Berlin e. V. qualifies volunteers and interested parties through workshops to become energy-saving and waste advisors. As part of the 'Berlin's Path to Zero Waste' project, it offers opportunities for networking within the Berlin initiative scene. As a practical partner, BUND participated in the transdisciplinary Citizen-Science research project REPARA/CUL/TURE, which dealt with questions of appropriation and dissemination of repair and DIY practices.

Keywords

Berlin initiative scene · Volunteers · Repair café · Resource protection · Networking

Consumer policy traditionally focuses on the relationship between consumers and producers or providers. In recent years, many consumers have been trending towards becoming more independent from providers and the consumer society.

D. Affelt (✉)
Bund für Umwelt und Naturschutz Deutschland (BUND) Berlin e. V., Berlin, Germany
e-mail: affelt@bund-berlin.de

K.-U. Hellmann et al. (eds.), *Consumer Policy from Below*,
https://doi.org/10.1007/978-3-658-44478-5_14

The reasons for this are diverse and can be found in the economic, social, and ecological sectors. Small, decentralized projects and structures are being built by civil society, aiming to increase the independence of consumers from the consumer and consumption society. This is achieved through grassroots initiatives, social commitment, and mutual voluntary support of consumers with little or no institutional framework. The BUND Berlin e. V. supports such civic engagement in the city in various ways. Some examples will be briefly presented here, especially with regard to the changed role of 'consumers'.

1 Repairing, Borrowing, Exchanging

In the field of repair, borrowing, and exchanging, for example, a diverse initiative scene has developed in recent years, often built and supported by great voluntary commitment. The goal of all these initiatives is to create alternatives to established consumption habits that are participatory in design and cause less environmental impact and also less cost for users. Consumers consciously create spaces oriented towards their consumption or non-consumption needs, which would not be conceivable within commercial and profit-oriented structures. Many initiatives and structures are poorly networked and coordinated by a small number of very active volunteers. This always carries the risk that committed individuals are personally overwhelmed or that the initiative is threatened by the departure of key people. Individual groups often lack knowledge and organization to apply for certain funding for projects or to even consider such possibilities. In addition, funding instruments are usually not sustainably designed, so that even very successful projects often do not receive further funding in the sense of a continuation. Another disadvantage is that each group builds similar structures anew, often without benefiting from the 'know-how' and 'lessons learned' of other initiatives.

The BUND Berlin has made it its mission to strengthen the Berlin initiative scene through networking. As part of the project 'Berlin's Path to Zero Waste', funded by the Foundation for Nature Conservation, networking meetings for initiatives in the fields of repair, 'upcycling', textiles, and food are regularly offered, for example. The BUND also acts as a mediator, taking up the specific needs of the actors and bringing them to politics and administration. The long-term goal is to create conditions and funding instruments that contribute to the securing, continuation, and better networking of the diverse initiative scene and thus bring about a change in consumer behavior towards less waste production and conservation of resources from the bottom up. The aim is not to homogenize the initiatives or to prescribe goals and structures, but to support the diverse and creative initiatives and the committed individuals who have built and carry them.

Consumer policy from below can also mean gaining a degree of independence from producers by not immediately resorting to new products when something no longer works, but instead trying to repair the existing, but no longer (fully) functional product. The fall in prices of consumer goods, coupled with high personnel costs and the design of many products that are deliberately not constructed to allow easy repair, means that the common procedure, for example with a broken printer or hairdryer, is to dispose of them and get a new product. Repair Cafés aim to provide an alternative here. Since 2015, BUND Berlin e. V. has been running a Repair Café in the Schöneberg district of Berlin. More than 20 volunteers are now involved in the areas of repair, guest care, and buffet. The Repair Cafés are deliberately designed so that the social aspect and mutual exchange are important components. Especially since there can be waiting times during the repair, which can be bridged with a piece of cake and exchange with other visitors. On average, 30 repairs are undertaken at these monthly events held by BUND. The consumers are always involved in the sense of self-help and are also somewhat qualified and empowered to possibly dare to take a first inspecting look inside the housing themselves the next time there is a problem at home. Often, new committed and active people have been won from the circle of users of the Repair Cafés. For further deepening and qualification for repairs that require soldering, soldering courses for beginners are also regularly offered. The BUND's Repair Café activities have already prevented a lot of waste, especially electronic waste, and have shown and enabled consumers an alternative to buying new.

The range of volunteers extends from the 14-year-old student who was introduced to repairing by his father, to the retired physicist who feels valued with his knowledge in the Repair Café. Technicians and engineers are also active in the BUND Repair Cafés. However, male repairers are still clearly in the majority here as in most Berlin Repair Cafés. To specifically inspire female and diverse volunteers for engagement in Repair Cafés, BUND advised and supported the women's center Schokofabrik in the Berlin district of Kreuzberg in the founding of a Repair Café by women* for women*. The protected framework is intended to facilitate entry and ultimately help to make the volunteer structures in other Repair Cafés more diverse.

The motivations of the visitors to the Repair Café are different. Often it is also a conscious decision not to buy a new product, but to preserve the old one if possible. Since commercial repair providers or specialist retailers often consider repairs of older or cheaper devices to be uneconomical and rather advise customers to buy new, Repair Cafés do not see themselves as competition, but as a socially demanded supplement. Repair Cafés aim to strengthen the idea of repair in society, from which commercial repair providers and spare parts dealers also benefit. Depending on the know-how of the active participants and also the spatial possibilities, there are limits to what can be worked on in the Repair Café. Large household appliances and complicated bicycle repairs cannot be carried out in the BUND Repair Cafés.

2 Repair Café, Sewing Café, Workshops, and Clothing Swap Parties

With a comprehensive climate and resource protection project involving a Repair Café, Sewing Café, workshops, and clothing swap parties, BUND is actively involved in the Steglitz district of Berlin, providing a reliable framework for many volunteers. At the sewing cafés, clothing items are repaired and mended, and guidance and assistance are provided to repurpose old clothing and create something new from it. Users come to the sewing café to get professional support for their projects, because they do not have their own sewing machine at home, or simply to pass on their knowledge to others.

Clothing swap parties and sewing cafés are part of a counter-movement to large clothing chains, where you can buy clothes at very low prices, which are then worn only a few times and then discarded. Clothing swap parties strengthen consumers' awareness that in addition to buying goods, there is also the long-forgotten option of bartering. Consumers are actively choosing to use their options to refuse consumption and satisfy their needs in other ways, rather than acting as pure consumers.

In addition to economic aspects, ecological factors are an important motivator for participating in clothing swap parties. Due to increased reporting on the consumption of raw materials in the clothing industry, many consumers are asking whether there are other options than always buying factory-new clothes, and thus come to the clothing swap parties. For consumers, it is also a positive experience to see that their discarded clothing has found new users.

3 BUND Project Berlin Energy and Waste Check

In the BUND Project Berlin Energy and Waste Check, volunteers are trained as energy saving and waste advisors, who can then pass on their knowledge at information stands and in household advice to interested parties. The aim here is for consumers to be better informed about how they can save waste or, if it has already been generated, how it can be recycled in the most resource-efficient way. With a better understanding of energy-saving options, consumers are enabled to better assess the energy consumption of consumer goods when making their next purchase and to include this in their decision. The free advice service, on an equal footing from consumers for consumers, enables households from different milieus to have easy access.

To bring consumers together with local initiatives in the areas of repair, exchange and sharing, giving, donating and buying used goods, the ReMap Berlin (www.remap-berlin.de) was developed as part of the Berlin Energy and Waste Check advisory project. Using a search function, users can quickly and easily find suitable offers. The step towards environmentally friendly action and becoming active oneself is often only a few minutes' walk away.

4 Research Project REPARA/CUL/TURE

To shed light on the motivation and personal backgrounds of activists in the field of repair and DIY, BUND, together with TU Berlin, the Association of Open Workshops, and the Isinova Institute, participated in the citizen science research project REPARA/CUL/TURE. Among others, activists from Repair Cafés and Open Workshops in Berlin, Hamburg, and Munich were involved in the research process. The method 'Cultural Probes', originally from design research, was tested and adapted for social science application.

In addition to researching the culture of repair and DIY and its creators, the project also aims to promote places of repair and DIY. In several workshops, concrete challenges and questions from initiatives in the respective institutions in Greifswald, Berlin, and Dresden were addressed and a vision for the future was created. The results of the research project have led to an activating interactive traveling exhibition that is also intended to motivate visitors to become active themselves. In this context, BUND Berlin, as a practical partner, played an important role as a mediator between co-researching consumers and the participating scientists.

Daniel Affelt has been a member of the waste and resource policy working group at BUND Berlin e. V. since 2013 and has also worked there full-time as a project coordinator for local climate and resource protection projects since 2015. His work focuses on repair cafés and repair initiatives, waste avoidance and reuse, environmental education and volunteer coordination.

Understanding Commitment to Sustainable Consumption. Insights from the Work of the Consumer Association of NRW with Local Initiatives

Jonas Grauel

Abstract

In recent years, many groups have emerged that collectively advocate for the appreciation of food and limited resources, such as Repair Cafés or food sharing groups. The article presents findings from the work of the Consumer Association of NRW with local initiatives. First, the typical forms of commitment and expected contributions to sustainable development are reflected upon. The article then addresses the support needs of the groups and presents previously tested offers for this target group. The conclusion shows: potentials exist, among other things, in making the already existing commitment known to a wider public and establishing a more professional member management. In order to make the practices of the initiatives accessible to an even wider audience, further developments and new business models appear necessary.

Keywords

Engagement · Initiatives · Sustainable consumption · Resource conservation · Social innovation

---

J. Grauel (✉)
Bereich Ernährung und Umwelt, Verbraucherzentrale NRW, Düsseldorf, Germany
e-mail: jonas.grauel@verbraucherzentrale.nrw

K.-U. Hellmann et al. (eds.), *Consumer Policy from Below*,
https://doi.org/10.1007/978-3-658-44478-5_15

1 Introduction

In recent years, a multitude of groups has emerged in Germany and many other countries that collectively organize or practice climate-friendly and sustainable forms of consumption and advocate for the appreciation of food and limited resources. Examples include community gardens, open repair workshops, free cargo bike rentals, community-supported agriculture, food sharing groups, gift initiatives such as free stores and give boxes, barter rings, and zero waste initiatives.[1] In recent years, the commitment in these groups has increasingly come into the focus of politics and societal institutions, which are working to make consumption in Germany sustainable (Rückert-John et al. 2015). A promising strategy is seen in observing the pioneers of sustainable consumption and their experiments in order to learn from them and promote them further (Federal Environment Agency 2014, p. 6).

In the guiding principle of the Consumer Association of NRW, sustainability is named as one of four basic values and the goal is formulated to support and motivate consumers in the implementation of sustainable and responsible lifestyles. Since 2016, the Consumer Association of NRW has been carrying out measures to support and network the commitment in initiatives, initially within the framework of the MehrWert NRW project funded by the EU and the state of NRW, and from October 2018 within the framework of the MehrWertKonsum project funded by the same donors. Various offers for committed groups were tested and further developed. In addition, the 'Initiative Consultation' from the MehrWert NRW project was extensively evaluated (CO Concept & USV Agrar 2018). This article links insights from practical work with the initiatives with the professional debate and provides answers to the following questions: What does the work of the initiatives look like? What contributions do those involved in the initiatives make to strengthen sustainable consumption? What challenges are the initiatives facing? How can commitment to sustainability be effectively supported and promoted?

The rest of the article is structured as follows: In Chap. 2 the initiatives for sustainable consumption are first classified and presented against the background of consumer research. In addition, the specific characteristics of the commitment

[1] For simplicity, these different groups will be collectively referred to as *initiatives* or *committed groups* throughout the rest of this article—the addition of 'for sustainable consumption' is always implied.

in the initiatives are worked out and the contributions of the initiatives for more sustainable consumption are presented. Chapter 3 presents the findings of the Consumer Association of NRW on the challenges and support needs of the initiatives. This is followed by Chap. 4 dealing with the approaches and tools of consumer work around commitment to sustainable consumption that have been tested so far. Finally, a conclusion is drawn in Chap. 5.

2 Foodsharing, RepairCafé & Co.: Initiatives for Sustainable Consumption

Firstly, the question arises as to how the aforementioned initiatives can be classified sociologically and against the background of consumer work: What kind of group with what organizational forms can we observe here? Are we dealing with a new form of consumer organizations?

Historically, the role of the consumer only emerges with the development of a rich assortment of goods and the supplier-demand dualism associated with these goods markets (Brewer 1997, p. 52; Klug 2017, p. 14). Classical consumer protection is based on this dualism, aiming for a balance of power and seeking to reduce structurally conditioned imbalances between suppliers and "non-commercial end consumers" (Klug and Gartner 2017, p. 267), who are understood as private individuals. This image of the consumer as a private individual also fits with the understanding of neoclassical economic theory with its guiding principle of the 'Homo oeconomicus'. In this, consumers are thought of as atomistically acting individuals or households who appear on the market as demanders and want to maximize their utility with respect to a given preference order (Hedtke 2001, p. 19).

However, consumer research of the last two decades has dealt with the various 'dissolutions of consumption' (Lamla and Kenning 2017) and pointed out that the procurement of products and services can occur not only through purchase on the market, that consumers can act not only as individuals but also in community, and that the consumer role cannot be completely separated from the whole person with their other roles: The debate on 'prosuming' refers to various mixtures between production and consumption, including 'commoning' as a communal and non-market-based form of procurement, production, and use of resources (Blättel-Mink 2017, p. 26). Collaborative forms of consumption include, for example, swapping, borrowing, or gifting (Klug and Gartner 2017). While communal forms of consumption are historically nothing really new, they were increasingly pushed back with the emergence of the modern consumer society and strong tendencies towards individualization (Loske 2016, p. 44). Against the background of recent decades, community-based forms of consumption now appear as 'Social Innovations for Sustainable Consumption' (Jaeger-Erben et al. 2017).

Also helpful for classification is the term 'consumer citizen', with which Lamla (2013, p. 182 ff.) has pointed to the intertwining of the roles of the consumer and the political citizen. Global environmental problems, global warming, and the exploitation of natural resources are important occasions for both politically motivated consumption and the politicization of consumption (ibid., p. 13). Although the core activity of the initiatives is not in the organization of political protest or the articulation of explicit political demands (Grauel et al. 2018, p. 83), but rather in the attempt to "counteract the negatively experienced consequences of societal modernization through self-initiative on a small scale and locally" (ibid., p. 85). However, the activities of the initiatives are indeed also (societal-) politically motivated (Boddenberg et al. 2017, p. 135; Urban Gardening Manifest 2014). Therefore, it is obvious to understand the initiatives as the pragmatic action-oriented arm of the environmental movement (Grauel et al. 2018, p. 84).

Against this background, the initiatives for sustainable consumption can now be described in more detail: These are originally self-initiated and self-organized groups of individuals who commit themselves to sustainable consumption through volunteer work.[2] The exact focus of the commitment can take various forms: Some of the groups take the form of self-help groups that devote themselves to communal forms of consumption (e.g., production for personal use in community gardens and community-supported agricultures, or exchange of products and services in exchange rings). Some groups organize platforms that enable third parties to consume collaboratively (e.g., cargo bike rentals, give-away boxes, or free stores). In other groups, the focus is more on consumer education and political advocacy for sustainable consumption (e.g., Slow Food Youth, Zero Waste initiatives). Finally, the commitment can also aim to eliminate negative consequences of the consumer society—such as the garbage collection actions of the Clean-Up groups.

Table 1 provides an overview of the different types of initiatives supported by the Consumer Association of NRW, their consumer relevance and their references to climate protection and resource conservation, as well as the number of groups committed locally in NRW (as of September 2019).

---

[2] Due to their independence from providers, the Consumer Association of NRW does not support groups that pursue commercial purposes, such as unpackaged stores.

Table 1 Overview of the initiatives supported by the Consumer Association of NRW. *Source* own representation

Type of initiative	Consumer relevance	Reference to climate protection and resource conservation
Rental of free cargo bikes	Enabling the communal use of cargo bikes	Saving of car kilometers for smaller transports
Community gardens	Communal cultivation of fruits, vegetables, and herbs for personal consumption (in small quantities); often also activities for consumer education	Demand-oriented and pesticide-free cultivation and consumption of seasonal and regional (organic) foods, short transport routes. Improvement of air quality and space for biodiversity in the city
Community-supported agriculture (CSA)	Communal cultivation of fruits, vegetables, and herbs for personal consumption (in quantities sufficient to meet needs)	Demand-oriented and pesticide-free cultivation and consumption of seasonal and regional (organic) foods, short transport routes
Foodsharing	Communal procurement and distribution of rescued food	Reduction of food waste, advocacy for the appreciation of food
Slow Food Youth	Community actions, political commitment to an ecologically and socially sustainable food economy	Reduction of food waste, commitment to the appreciation of food
Shopping Cooperatives	Joint purchase of food directly from the farmer or producer at more favorable conditions.	CO_2 savings through shortened supply chains
Repair Cafés	Repair of defective items under the guidance of experienced repairers, free of charge or for a small donation	Resource saving through longer and more intensive use of products, possibly avoiding new purchases
Swap Rings	Free exchange of products and services	Resource saving through longer and more intensive use of products, possibly avoiding new purchases
Lending Shops	(Lending) of products for a small donation	Resource saving through longer and more intensive use of products, possibly avoiding new purchases
Free Shops	Enable the free acquisition of used items	Resource saving through longer and more intensive use of products, possibly avoiding new purchases

(continued)

Table 1 (continued)

Type of initiative	Consumer relevance	Reference to climate protection and resource conservation
GiveBoxes/Book-shelves	Free acquisition or passing on of used items and books	Resource saving through longer and more intensive use of products, possibly avoiding new purchases
Zero Waste	Actions, educational work and political commitment to avoid (plastic) waste	Awareness building to avoid (plastic) waste
Clean-Up	Trash collection actions	Prevention of environmental consequences due to contamination by microplastics in waters and soils
Refill	Enabling the free supply of tap water at refill stations	Prevention of plastic waste that would have been generated by the purchase of e.g. PET bottles

2.1 What is the Nature of the Commitment in the Initiatives?

Various forms of commitment are often mistakenly lumped together as voluntary work. However, the term voluntary work does not do justice to the informal, low-threshold, individual and voluntary character of the commitment in the initiatives. In the following, these characteristics will be elaborated on against the backdrop of the change in forms of commitment. In general, commitment can be understood as an "umbrella term for people taking action for their own and/or others' concerns" (Evers et al. 2015, p. 3).

The classic voluntary work has its roots in the 19th century, when municipal self-government and charitable organizations emerged and clubs flourished (Roß 2017, p. 1). Voluntary work is characterized by its closeness to the state and a high degree of obligation, is associated with social prestige, is embedded in clear hierarchies, and is often carried out over long periods of time by the same person (Evers et al. 2015, p. 3). Voluntary positions are often integrated into existing, hierarchically organized and influential civil society clubs and associations—and it is usually clearly defined what tasks are to be performed within the framework of a voluntary position. The integration of classic voluntary work into established organizations also brings a number of advantages for those involved: for example, volunteers in clubs and associations usually enjoy insurance protection and are reimbursed for travel and material costs. Often there is also professional support from full-time contact persons and supervision in certain fields of work.

With the self-help movement of the 1970s, new forms of commitment emerged that are more closely associated with self-initiative, voluntariness, and self-determination and are referred to here as grassroots commitment (Roß 2017, p. 1). These forms of commitment are typically found in newly emerging or young organizations characterized by flat hierarchies and a high degree of participatory decision-making (Grabs et al. 2016, p. 100). The commitment in the initiatives for sustainable consumption is more akin to grassroots commitment than to classic voluntary work. Although there are indeed voluntary positions in the initiatives, such as the board or treasurer of a club. However, German association law is seen quite ambivalently in the initiatives: on the one hand, it offers opportunities such as the ability to collect donations as a non-profit club, on the other hand, the question arises whether club structures – which are sometimes perceived as rigid – are still contemporary. Therefore, some initiatives make conscious efforts to 'de-hierarchize' their structures and instead design them as democratically as possible (CO Concept & USV Agrar 2018, p. 15). Also, in grassroots commitment, roles and responsibilities are usually less clearly defined: each member should be able to contribute in the way they wish with their individual skills.

The access to commitment has also changed: as the term suggests, the exercise of voluntary work is a special honor, which per se cannot be bestowed on everyone and which requires certain qualifications and comes with obligations. In contrast, community gardens and repair workshops are often labeled as 'open': anyone interested can spontaneously drop by and participate. In community-supported agricultures, there is a certain threshold, through the payment of a membership fee and the obligation to receive a share of the harvest, usually for one year. However, some community-supported agricultures specifically use mechanisms to enable access for people with low income. Each member decides on the amount of the membership fee, a solidarity overpayment by people with higher income is intended to enable participation for people with lower income. An exception among the initiatives for sustainable consumption is Foodsharing. While everyone is welcome here too, Foodsharing has a classic hierarchical organization with a federal board at the top and roles with defined duties and powers ('Foodsharer', 'Foodsaver', 'Ambassador'), which is reminiscent of a classic voluntary structure.

Two further aspects of voluntary engagement are to be highlighted in conclusion: On the one hand, the low-threshold access is also associated with the idea of inclusivity of all people regardless of gender, age, level of education, and origin (Urban Gardening Manifest 2014). On the other hand, the low-threshold access and the high degree of voluntariness favor the trend towards "temporarily limited, project-like [...] forms of engagement" up to "short-term engagement"

(Roß 2017, p. 2 f.), which is not only observable in the area of the initiatives discussed here for sustainable consumption. Grassroots engagement thus offers a high degree of freedom for those involved. However, a disadvantage from the perspective of the volunteers is that accompanying services such as travel expense reimbursement or professional support—which are often offered in traditional volunteering—do not exist here. For the initiatives, the low degree of commitment also results in the possibility of withdrawal at any time and thus often results in a high fluctuation of members. A challenge for the initiatives is therefore continuous member management (see Section 3.1). The background to this development are societal processes of individualization of life courses and forms as well as increasing demands for flexibility in work and private everyday life. These developments have led to many people desiring a higher degree of flexibility and self-determination also within the framework of their engagement (Roß 2017).

2.2 Contributions of the Initiatives to a Sustainable and Climate-Friendly Society

After the sustainability references of the initiatives have already been highlighted (see Table 1), this section will reflect on the already realized and potentially realizable contributions of the initiatives for a 'Great Transformation' to a sustainable and climate-friendly society (WBGU 2011). In order to classify the contributions of the initiatives, the following will draw on theories of social innovation, as they can be used to describe how new societal practices develop, spread, and eventually become a widely accepted self-evidence (Gillwald 2000; Howaldt and Schwarz 2010).

It can be considered certain that initiatives create spaces in which sustainable consumption practices are made possible. For example, a study on the potentials of Repair Cafés concludes: "Spaces are created in which more sustainable alternatives to the non-sustainable 'mainstream' (i.e., discarding or disposing of broken devices) are fundamentally possible." (Jaeger-Erben et al. 2019, p. 59) For social innovations, protected spaces fulfill an important function: New practices can initially be further developed in niches and optimized until they function convincingly enough to make them accessible to a wider audience. The activities of the initiatives typically are based on such an innovative reconfiguration of social practices.

Beyond the creation of protected spaces, the next step is the dissemination of the developed practices. Committed individuals can potentially take on the role of pioneers, showing other consumers ways in which sustainable consumption styles can be practically lived. Peuker and Rückert-John (2017) assume a high potential of community-based forms of consumption based on results from a representative population survey. For example, 56% of respondents say they can imagine repairing things together with others in an open workshop—three percent say they are already doing this. 50% can imagine cultivating a garden together with others, nine percent are already doing this (ibid., p. 13). Typical ways of diffusing new practices are firstly the multiplication of projects within the niche, secondly the growth in size of existing projects, and thirdly the translation of niche ideas into the context of the mainstream (Seyfang and Haxeltine 2012, p. 384). Based on personal observations, it seems plausible that the first method of dissemination—the establishment of additional local projects—predominates among the initiatives. A noticeable dynamic can be observed here: For example, the number of repair initiatives known to the Consumer Association in NRW has more than doubled from around 110 in 2016 to around 230 in 2019; the number of community gardens has increased from around 100 to around 170 over the same period.[3] The second mentioned method of dissemination through the strong growth of individual projects—as is known from social media, e.g. Facebook—is not observed in the initiatives, as the individual groups rather aim for a 'right size' instead of continuous growth (see Section 3.1). Therefore, it is particularly interesting for the further establishment of the novel practices whether a translation of niche ideas into the mainstream can succeed. The need for such a translation is plausible, as consumption forms based heavily on community and self-initiative pose significantly higher transformation requirements for consumers than individual consumption forms, which can rely on existing market offers (Rückert-John et al. 2015, p. 85). A larger leap in the adaptation and acceptance of the new practices is therefore most likely to be expected when new variants are developed that tailor the niche ideas to the needs of a broader mass of consumers and make them more easily accessible. In the course of such adaptation processes and changes—which are typical for social innovations (Gillwald 2000, p. 33)—parts of the original character of the practices, such as sense of community, may also be lost. This raises the question of whether the initiatives are interested in such a diffusion into the mainstream at all, whether this can be achieved within their formats, or

[3] It should be noted that the change in the aforementioned numbers between 2016 and 2019 is not solely due to actual new establishments, but possibly also to a changed search methodology in online research. Nevertheless, the assumption remains plausible that there is indeed a noticeable dynamic of establishment. Further research would be useful to describe this dynamic qualitatively and quantitatively and to investigate its causes.

whether this needs to be driven forward in a different form and possibly by other actors. It can be assumed, for example, that the principle of repair will diffuse into the mainstream more quickly the more other (business) models for repairs beyond Repair Cafés are established. However, impulses for this may possibly be given from the initiative networks: For example, the German "Netzwerk Reparatur-Inititiativen" (Network of Repair Initiatives) has joined forces with other associations and companies to promote the strengthening of the repair idea and local economic development.[4] The decisive breakthrough for social innovations is seen precisely in the fact that new practices become socially widely accepted routine or a matter of course (Howaldt and Schwarz 2010, p. 90). This step is still pending for practices such as 'saving food' or 'gardening together', but a further spread of local groups is likely.

Regardless of their prevalence, the activities of the initiatives themselves can be attributed to positive contributions to climate and resource protection. Landholm et al. (2019) quantified greenhouse gas savings for 38 community initiatives in the areas of food & nutrition, energy, transport, and waste prevention from six European countries. For this, the activities of the initiatives (e.g., cultivation of regional organic vegetables in a community-based agriculture) were compared with a baseline scenario (e.g., purchase of the same amount of vegetables in stores or supermarkets assuming the country-specific market share of organic quality). The difference between de facto activities and the baseline scenario results in the greenhouse gas savings. Furthermore, it was calculated how many people can cover their total needs (e.g., for energy or food) from the activities of the initiative and how many percent of the personal CO_2 footprint would be reduced as a result. The results show that the initiatives in the energy sector perform best both in terms of absolute savings and in reducing the personal CO_2 footprint. For example, six electricity-producing initiatives were able to save around 454 t CO_2 per year. 210 people benefited from the electricity, which corresponds to a reduction of the average personal footprint by 24% (Landholm et al. 2019, p. 933). Four initiatives that save food also achieved a high total saving of 145 t CO_2 per year. However, since these savings were spread over more than 2,000 people, the reduction of the personal CO_2 footprint per person involved was less than 2% (ibid.). As part of the MehrWert NRW project, a workshop was

[4] At first glance, it seems strange to describe repair as a 'social innovation', as repair techniques have been applied as a matter of course for thousands of years and have only been increasingly displaced by a throwaway culture in recent decades. However, innovations can also consist of reviving old solutions—this is then referred to as 're-novation'.

also held in which the greenhouse gas savings for eight initiatives were calculated together with experts from the Öko-Institut and the ifeu. Here too, a food sharing initiative showed the greatest potential.

For example, according to our calculations, Foodsharing Düsseldorf saved approximately 160,000 kg of food in 2017, thus avoiding 93.8 t CO_2 (Öko-Institut and ifeu 2018). The CO_2 saving through the cultivation of regional vegetables in community-supported agricultures is strongly dependent on how many car kilometers are needed for transport to the end consumer. One involved initiative achieved a saving of 3.9 t CO_2 in one year. However, inefficiently organized or too long transport routes can completely nullify possible savings in community-supported agricultures. Thus, another initiative resulted in a barely positive CO_2 balance. Savings can also be quantified for cargo bikes, community gardens, and repair initiatives, but these are small and amount to less than 1 ton per per initiative and year.

Overall, the activities of food sharing initiatives can be attributed moderate greenhouse gas avoidance potentials. For all other types of initiatives from Table 1, the potentials are to be classified as low. However, it should be noted that indirect emission reductions, which are triggered, for example, by the role model character of the committed individuals or by educational activities, cannot be quantified. In addition, CO_2 savings are just one of many indicators to measure the societal and ecological benefits of the initiatives. For example, community gardens have various positive effects: They improve air quality in the city, serve as bee pastures, strengthen communities in the neighborhood, and offer city dwellers opportunities for relaxation. Therefore, the contributions of the initiatives should rather be viewed broadly, e.g., in the sense of the global Sustainable Development Goals (United Nations 2015), and not one-sidedly based on the amount of CO_2 savings.

3 Challenges and Support Needs in Locally Engaged Groups

After the contributions of the initiatives for change towards a sustainable society and thus their worthiness of support were presented in the previous chapter, the focus should now be on the challenges of the groups. Both the survey of committed individuals as part of the evaluation and the direct experiences in working with the committed individuals have repeatedly shown that there is a relatively high level of problem-solving and self-help skills in the initiatives. An important basis for this is certainly that a large part of the committed individuals in the initiatives have higher educational degrees (Sekulova 2016, p. 32 f.; Müller et al. 2015, p. 40). For example, a survey of committed individuals in open-access workshops found that three quarters have an academic degree (Lange et al. 2016, p. 28). Self-initiative and motivation are usually high, at least among the core of particularly committed members. Specialized skills in the area of the respective activities of the initiatives (e.g., woodworking, vegetable cultivation, repair, IT skills, etc.) are usually present at least among some of the members, who can then instruct less experienced members. Some initiatives, like the community-supported agricultures, even create paid positions for professionals. Overall, a pronounced 'do it yourself/do it together' culture can be observed. Both steady tasks and short-term challenges are "first tried to be dealt with independently by the surveyed initiatives" (CO Concept & USV Agrar 2018, p. 38). In addition, the initiatives rely on self-help networks such as the 'Network Repair Initiatives', the 'Network community-supported agricultures', 'Urban Oases' or the 'Transition Initiatives'. The Foodsharing association has a more formalized structure with a nationwide umbrella organization. The networks and umbrella organizations prepare expert knowledge and communication materials and offer nationwide meetings for exchange and networking. The Network of Community-supported agricultures also advises individual local groups. In addition, it is common for newly founded groups to seek contact with already longer existing groups in their vicinity to exchange ideas and benefit from their experiences.

Nevertheless, there is certainly a need for further support from various institutions and organizations. Limits to self-help capacities exist in that the networks and associations usually cannot financially support local groups. On the other hand, the capacities of the networks for 'help for self-help' are also limited by their personnel possibilities. Thus, there are further needs for networking and support at the local and regional level.

Own surveys on the challenges and the associated support needs of the initiatives were carried out in various ways. In the fall of 2016, an online survey was first conducted among 358 initiatives. 69 initiatives responded, resulting in a response rate of about 20%. Since the various needs were not systematically known at this time, open questions were asked and the answers were then coded and categorized. As part of the project-accompanying evaluation, interviews were conducted with 12 initiative representatives (CO Concept & USV Agrar 2018, p. 30 f.). And in the fall of 2018, a resume workshop was held at the end of the first project with nine participating initiatives, where the areas of need were discussed in detail.

Furthermore, continuous discussions were held with representatives of the initiatives at various events, which also repeatedly addressed needs. Due to the diverse channels and different methods of needs assessment, quantification is not possible. However, the qualitative findings can be considered well saturated, as similar answers kept appearing across the various survey methods. Based on the collected knowledge, a total of six central fields can be described in which significant challenges for the initiatives lie and where "help for self-help" or direct support is desired:

1. Attracting and motivating members
2. Acquiring financial and material resources
3. Increasing public awareness
4. Networking with other initiatives and potential supporters
5. Securing legal framework conditions
6. Improving internal communication and organization

These challenges will be examined in more detail in the following.

3.1 Attracting and Motivating Members

In most initiatives, there is a core group of highly committed members who significantly drive the development of projects, and a further circle of members who participate irregularly or with a small amount of time in activities (CO Concept & USV Agrar 2018, p. 14 f.). The sometimes small core group often wishes for relief and more members who take responsibility for tasks and engage reliably. In a 2016 online survey, 38 out of 69 surveyed initiatives stated that they wish for 'more members in the core team'—given the open-ended question, this is a remarkably high number. Also frequently mentioned were a 'fair division of tasks' as a significant challenge, as well as complaints about the 'lack of commitment of some members'. Also, in the context of the evaluation of the MehrWert NRW project, eight out of twelve surveyed initiative representatives named the 'finding of responsible participants' as a central challenge (CO Concept & USV Agrar 2018, p. 24). A reliable, steady commitment in the core group is often more important to the initiatives than growth of the wider circle, as many members in the wider circle can sometimes mean additional coordination effort for the core group. Therefore, it is not only about attracting new members for the initiatives, but also about winning existing members from the wider circle for more intensive cooperation. Many initiatives do not strive for growth through ever more members, but for the 'right size' that allows participation of all members (Kropp 2016, p. 3).

A possible explanation for the difficulty in finding enough members for responsible tasks is the understanding in the initiatives that all committed individuals should contribute voluntarily and according to their abilities. Interested parties are given low-threshold access, but there is also no strong binding force. This understanding contrasts with the commitment in volunteering, where a high degree of obligation is rewarded with high societal recognition (see Sect. 2.2). Therefore, interested parties can easily join an initiative, but can also easily leave again (Grauel et al. 2018, p. 85 ff.). For this reason, it is important for the initiatives to motivate members and possibly develop new solutions for member management, beyond attracting new interested parties.

3.2 Acquiring Money and Material Resources

Depending on the type of initiative, different methods are used to obtain relevant resources. The 'bottom-up' structure of the groups is reflected in the acquisition process, as they prefer to use as low-threshold and unbureaucratic methods as possible, such as asking around in their circle of acquaintances or making calls for donations in their support network via social media. However, depending on the type of initiative, there are different focuses in the acquisition of resources.

A critical resource for community gardens is the ability to use an often urban (fallow) area free of charge. The support of the municipality, which can allocate appropriate areas and is often also responsible for other important concerns such as water connections or sanitary facilities, is of great importance here. In addition, materials such as wood, soil or garden tools are often acquired through in-kind donations in support networks. Another important source of funding for community gardens are low-threshold municipal funding pots, which provide small amounts of money without complicated application procedures. For example, the city of Düsseldorf awards up to 250 € as part of its environmental project funding.

In contrast to the gardens, cargo bike rentals focus on resource acquisition. Due to the high purchase costs for the cargo bikes as well as ongoing costs such as insurance, maintenance and care, the cargo bike initiatives depend on the acquisition of funding and do not shy away from more complex application procedures. Important for them are suitable funding programs, with which cargo bikes can be largely or fully financed, such as the program 'Kurze Wege für den Klimaschutz' (Short Paths for Climate Protection), which was launched by the Federal Ministry of the Environment as part of the National Climate Protection Initiative. However, own funds often also have to be raised, for which the initiatives collect donations.

Repair Cafés, on the other hand, finance themselves, among other things, through donations from people who bring devices for repair. In community-supported agricultures, monthly membership contributions for harvest shares usually make up the largest part of the financing. Foodsharing groups often only need small financial resources. Pick-ups of food from supermarkets or bakers are usually possible with the private bicycles of the members, the online platform is provided by the umbrella organization. However, prize money and funding are gladly used, for example, to purchase refrigerators for distribution stations or cargo bikes for the transport of food.

3.3 Increasing Public Awareness

Public awareness is a key success factor for many initiatives. Because awareness is a prerequisite for their services, such as repairs or cargo bike rentals, to be used and appreciated, as well as to recruit new members. In addition, resonance experiences are important for maintaining the motivation of the committed individuals. Other groups, such as community-supported agricultures, operate as a closed group during a harvest year. But as soon as it comes to planning the following year, they depend on finding enough interested parties who want to draw a harvest share. Beyond potential users, most initiatives also want to be "recognized by as broad and large a public as possible. Concrete actors mentioned include: citizens, politics, administration, media, other initiatives, companies, students, children or neighborhood residents" (CO Concept & USV-Agrar 2018, p. 27). Through the attention of administration, politics or companies, the initiatives hope for support, sponsorship or patrons.

For their public relations work, initiatives use their own homepage, social media, but also information stands or press interviews. The survey of twelve initiatives as part of the evaluation of the MehrWert NRW project concludes that while the initiatives do intensive public relations work, they perceive their visibility in the public as rather low (CO Concept & USV-Agrar 2018, p. 28). The TESS project ('Towards European Social Sustainability') has extensively studied 63 initiatives in six European countries and concludes that the initiatives report that on average 91% of their users live in the immediate neighborhood (Sekulova 2016, p. 32). Even though it is not directly asked about awareness, the result can at least be read as an indication that the initiatives are primarily known in their immediate environment. Overall, these results suggest that the public awareness of the initiatives could certainly still be expanded and is often limited to the immediate environment and possibly also to certain milieus.

3.4 Networking with Other Initiatives and Potential Supporters

Networking with similar initiatives and like-minded people is considered extremely important by those involved. A study from the TESS project examined the network contacts of 63 initiatives in six European countries in detail. It concludes that 85% of the initiatives studied consider external networks with similar initiatives to be 'very important' or even 'extremely important' for their own work (Celata and Jungmee 2016, p. 150 f.). The largest share of network contacts, at 35%, is with other initiatives. Also important network partners with many contacts are intermediary network organizations such as the initiatives networks (14% of contacts) and municipal administrations with 10% of contacts (ibid., p. 166 f.). Other groups of actors such as non-governmental organizations, education centers, authorities and administrations at regional and national level, and social movements each account for about 5–7% of the counted contacts (ibid.). About half of all contacts are thus with the scene of initiatives and their networks, which once again underlines the 'do-it-yourself/do-it-together' mentality mentioned above. The interviews conducted as part of the evaluation from the MehrWert NRW project show that an exchange with initiatives from other cities at events is experienced as beneficial, but a constant exchange in everyday life is primarily sought with initiatives in the immediate vicinity or in the same city (CO Concept & USV Agrar 2018, p. 58), as this provides specific points of contact for planning joint actions or appearances, using spaces together.

On the other hand, the results of the TESS study also show that the initiatives network with a wide variety of actors beyond like-minded people. Because municipal administrations, foundations, associations, and other organizations often act as supporters who can provide information, knowledge, legal advice, or financial resources. As already mentioned in Sect. 3.2, depending on the type of initiative, various sponsors may be relevant.[5] In particular, this section will once again focus on municipal administrations as central actors on site. In the context of the online survey 2016, seven initiatives stated that they would like to cooperate with the municipality, eight others complained about a lack of support from the municipality. Since the initiatives are usually locally anchored, the municipalities are important contacts for them, with different concerns to the municipality

[5] An overview of various organizations that support initiatives can be found at www.mehrwert.nrw/werkzeuge/links (accessed on 10.09.2019).

or interfaces to the municipality showing up depending on the type of initiative. Foodsharing groups and community gardens are particularly dependent on cooperation with municipal administrations: For foodsharing groups, good contacts with health departments and food authorities are important in order to be able to assess risks, take preventive measures in the area of food hygiene, and clarify the legality of the so-called 'fair distributors' at an early stage (CSCP 2019, p. 13 f.). For community gardens, approvals for the (interim) use of unused areas and infrastructure such as water connections are a central concern to municipalities (see also Section 3.2). Similar questions can also arise in Community-based agricultures. Here, however, arable land is sometimes also contributed by participating farmers, and compared to urban gardens, there are more opportunities to lease land from private individuals. Repair initiatives or cargo bike rentals are less dependent on municipal support. For these initiatives, suitable spaces are important, which can be provided in municipal facilities such as community centers or council rooms, but for which there are also private alternatives.

3.5 Securing Legal Framework Conditions

Another important area of need for the initiatives is support in legal matters. Fundamental for volunteers is initially the clarification about the choice of the suitable legal form of the group, which is always connected with liability and insurance issues. Thus, groups that do not explicitly determine a legal form for themselves are treated as a civil law partnership (GbR) in Germany, and each member is liable with their private assets. Basic information about liability and insurance issues in volunteering has already been prepared by various organizations and is easy to find online. In addition, in discussions with initiatives, the need for more in-depth advice on specific legal issues has been repeatedly mentioned. For example, the question arose as to how shares in a Community supported agriculture are to be assessed for tax purposes. Another group planned the foundation of an economic association and wished for individual advice. While there are lawyers who offer, for example, association consultations, these services are usually not free of charge and are difficult for most initiatives to finance. In the future, low-threshold funding offers could be set up here.

Finally, the initiatives are partly affected by existing legal uncertainties that go beyond the situation of individual groups and can only be solved at a collective level. Affected are, for example, food sharing groups, because they

> "meet the requirements for a 'food business' and are therefore also subject to the obligations anchored in hygiene law. If they do not comply, they can expect all forms of legal consequences; from the prohibition of operation to fines and penalties" (CSCP 2019, p. 13).

Although food sharers can prevent such consequences through risk analyses and good agreements with the local health department, a basic establishment of legal certainty would be desirable here. The Italian 'Good Samaritan Law' can serve as a model here (Scientific Services German Bundestag 2019, p. 12 ff.). Repair Cafés are also affected by legal uncertainties in liability issues. The groups usually have the users sign a general disclaimer. However, this leaves gaps and is potentially legally vulnerable (Werkstadt Stuttgart e. V. n. d., p. 2). Initiatives to establish legal certainty would have to be introduced into the legislative process through lobbying groups. In the area of repair, this could, for example, be done through the 'Round Table Repair', in which associations, companies and also the Repair Initiatives Network jointly advocate for better conditions for repair.

3.6 Improving Internal Communication and Organization

Last but not least, internal communication and organization is a challenge for the initiatives. In the 2016 online survey, 14 out of 69 initiatives mentioned improving internal communication as an important point in an open question. In the interviews conducted as part of the project evaluation, corresponding concerns were also mentioned, e.g. 'enabling self-reflection for the initiative' and 'help with organizational questions (e.g. workshops for group formation processes)'.

4 Approaches of Consumer Work to Engagement for Sustainable Consumption

Based on the needs analysis presented above, the Consumer Association of NRW tested a number of formats to strengthen and support engagement for sustainable consumption. Some offers were developed further and carried out to this day due to demand, good feedback from the target group and/or good fit with the strategy and organizational development of the Consumer Association of NRW. Other offers were continued by cooperation partners after testing, individual offers were discontinued due to lack of demand or too high costs in relation to the benefit. In total, a number of formats were tested that focus on networking (see Section 4.1), competence building (Section 4.2) and public announcement (Section 4.3) of the initiatives, Section 4.4 also presents further approaches.

4.1 Approaches to Networking Initiatives

Regional Co-Working Spaces The all-day events provide committed individuals from various initiatives and cities with a space for networking, exchange, and creative work. The co-working spaces have been tested in various versions and continuously developed. In 2017, a focus was placed on the topic of 'recruiting members'. As part of the events, the participating initiatives developed a measure suitable for their situation using a creative method. In a follow-up survey, it was found that eight out of 21 surveyed initiatives had actually implemented the developed measure, five of which stated that they had successfully recruited new members. An advantage of this format was the clear focus on impact; a disadvantage was the thematic restriction to only one area of need, which led to lower participant numbers. For this reason, an open barcamp format was tested in 2019, where the committed individuals can bring in their own topics. The open creative work was supplemented by expert input in the important areas of need. For example, a speaker from the Foundation for Environment & Development NRW presented on financing opportunities, or an expert from the Consumer Association of NRW answered questions about insurance in volunteering. This format was in high demand and the combination of the opportunity to address one's own topics with expert input was well received by the target group.

Sustainability Roundtable From 2016 to 2018, sustainability roundtables were tested in Düsseldorf and Dortmund for local networking. On a monthly or bimonthly basis, committed individuals from initiatives met at various 'places of sustainability' with additional guests such as municipal representatives. The roundtables were handed over to local partners and continued by them.

Local Networking Meetings As part of the 'GlücksTaten' (Practicescts of Happiness) campaign (see Sect. 4.3), networking meetings were organized in various cities in NRW, where both representatives of the initiatives and potential supporters from the city, such as from the municipal administration, were invited.

4.2 Approaches to Skill Building

Workshops To contribute to skill building in the initiatives, one to two-hour workshops were developed, in which a brief expert input is given on a selected area of need such as 'recruiting and motivating members', 'financing', and 'public relations'. Afterwards, the group develops their own approaches to action using creative methods.

Online Toolbox The 'toolbox' is accessible via the website www.mehrwert.nrw/tools and serves to build the skills of the initiatives in various areas of need (see chapter "Empowered Consumers—A Practice-Theoretical Revision"). Relevant action knowledge is prepared in the three categories 'Getting Started' (guides to founding an initiative), 'Everyday Aids' (tips on financing, member recruitment, public relations) and 'Legal' (tips on liability, insurance and legal form). In addition, a collection of useful links to other supporting actors is provided.

4.3 Approaches to Public Announcement of Initiatives

Statewide Actions The Consumer Association of NRW has 61 consumer advisory centres throughout NRW, 19 of which have a special environmental consultation. The advisory centres can help to make the initiatives visible locally. In 2017, as part of the 'NRW repairs' campaign, a cooperation with Repair Cafés was tested for the first time: Here, ten advisory centres of the Consumer Association of NRW conducted repair workshops together with Repair Cafés. In addition, 16 Repair Cafés took advantage of the offer to schedule an appointment during the campaign period, which was advertised under the campaign umbrella 'NRW repairs'. The goal of making initiatives known was further pursued in 2019 under the campaign title 'GlücksTaten' (Practices of Happiness). The name 'GlücksTaten' refers to small acts for more sustainability and climate protection, such as repairing objects or cooking with leftovers to avoid waste. It is intended to show that these acts can bring joy and fun, especially when done together with others.[6]

[6] A theoretical foundation is provided by Kate Soper's concept of 'alternative hedonism': Soper (2007) assumes that materialistic consumption hedonism is increasingly disenchanted by knowledge and experience of the negative consequences. Alternative hedonism, on the other hand, proposes a different conception of the *beautiful, eventful life,* by emphasizing the pleasure and often very simple sensual pleasures associated with sustainable lifestyles.

The advisory centres provide information on the topic during the campaign period and carry out actions in public spaces. The approach is to first talk to people about what they are already doing for the appreciation of food or limited resources, and then to show them possibilities for further steps, also together with others—e.g. in the family, with neighbours, in clubs, but also to become active in the initiatives. Where possible, local initiatives such as food sharing groups or community supported agriculture are integrated into the actions to show directly on site what 'Acts of Happiness' can look like.

Online Offers for Committed Individuals With www.mehrwert.nrw a platform has been created around the commitment to sustainable consumption, which addresses both already committed individuals and interested consumers. Three core offers on the website are a map showing local initiatives in the whole state, a subsite with practical advice for volunteers and a subsite for upcoming events. The 'Participation Map' represents over 600 initiatives in NRW and their locations (e.g. food sharing distributors, cargo bike locations). The appointment tips inform about events of the initiatives and topics related to sustainable commitment. The toolbox provides concrete answers to all important fields of action of the initiatives (see Sect. 4.2). Committed individuals and interested parties thus receive bundled information on where, when and how they can participate or get involved. These three offers are accompanied by portraits of selected initiatives and information on opportunities for individual consumers to personally commit to climate-friendly consumption. The offers are publicized via social media channels on Facebook, Instagram and Twitter as well as at information stands at various public events.

Starter Workshops In order to introduce interested consumers to the opportunities for commitment, a separate format was developed, which is carried out at events of third parties (e.g. sustainability fairs, city festivals) and encourages consumers to become active in their own everyday life or in community with others.

4.4 Further Approaches

Consultation Hour for Initiatives In Münster, the format of a weekly consultation hour at the local advisory center was tested in 2017. Münster is a city with a lively initiative scene. However, the demand proved to be too low to establish the format permanently.

District Projects From 2017 to 2018, specific projects were accompanied on-site in Bonn, Cologne, Bochum, and Herne to gather insights about the founding of new initiatives in districts and to test their transferability to other contexts. To this end, cooperations with the district management and various local organizations were initiated and impulses for new initiatives were given: In Bonn-Tannenbusch, a Repair Café was newly founded; in Cologne-Chorweiler, a cargo bike rental was launched; in Herne-Wanne, a swap cabinet was created; in Bochum-Hamme, citizens were informed about the possibilities for self-initiated and organized local food supply. The local projects were successful and were handed over to the cooperation partners; in Cologne, Bonn, and Herne, the projects could be permanently established. However, the external support of local projects proved to be relatively complex. The coordination and support of such projects should ideally be located in the district itself.

5 Conclusion

The aim of this article was to better understand the commitment to initiatives for sustainable consumption and to gain insights into how this commitment can be further meaningfully supported and strengthened. To this end, insights from the Comsumer Association of NRW from three years of work with Repair Cafés, community gardens, Foodsharing groups and other initiatives were linked to the expert debate.

Firstly, it was shown that the commitment in the initiatives is low-threshold and characterized by a high degree of voluntariness and self-determination. The grassroots commitment in the initiatives differs in many respects from voluntary commitment in established clubs and associations. On the one hand, the openness and flexibility is a strength of the initiatives, as the diversity of different people with their individual competencies is utilized. On the other hand, the grassroots commitment lacks the favorable conditions of traditional volunteering, such as professional support. Therefore, it seems promising to examine to what extent elements of the volunteer support established in clubs and associations can be transferred to the specific conditions of grassroots initiatives.

Secondly, the spread dynamics of the initiatives were described with reference to the debate on social innovations: In recent years, more and more groups have been founded, but a translation into mainstream society is not foreseeable and certainly not the goal of the initiatives in part. For the further spread of new groups and the adoption of innovative practices by broader sections of the population, it seems important on the one hand that the initiatives and their practices become better known. On the other hand, based on theories of social innovation, it is plausible that a push of sustainable practices into the mainstream seems more conceivable the less they rely on individual initiative and coordination with others in a group.

Thirdly, six fields were identified in which the initiatives face challenges and can be meaningfully supported by third parties. In connection with the two insights presented above, two points should be highlighted again here.

On the one hand, in view of the ongoing search for responsible persons, it seems sensible to support the initiatives in the area of member management. The Consumer Association of NRW has so far prepared knowledge on how to recruit members and has conducted creative workshops. In addition, knowledge and measures for designing a holistic member management could be developed or existing approaches from volunteer management could be adapted for the specific grassroots context of the initiatives.

On the other hand, it should be considered how the novel practices of the initiatives, which are very welcome in terms of sustainable consumption, can be further disseminated. The first step in this direction is certainly to create more public awareness for the initiatives and their activities, in order to open up new consumer groups for the low-threshold offers of the initiatives and to mobilize new commitment. Furthermore, it would be worth considering how sustainable consumption practices such as repairing can be reintegrated into the mainstream economy beyond the Repair Cafés. In this context, it might also be necessary to promote different framework conditions and new business models that can introduce consumers to practices such as repairing, saving food, etc.

Finally, the question arises as to whether and to what extent the work with the initiatives will possibly provide new impulses for consumer work, in which debates about the organization of consumer interests and the support of consumer organizations are also conducted. Depending on the point of view, it would be worth discussing whether the initiatives for sustainable consumption examined and supported here can be described as consumer groups or organizations. It is clear that the activities of these groups comprise a complex mixture of prosumption, self-help, (political) commitment and leisure activities. These activities go beyond the classic consumer action on provider markets in the narrower sense, but in a broader sense they affect in many ways consumer-related aspects of the procurement, use and disposal of goods. Consumer work is thus faced with the question of how to deal with forms of consumption that are firstly not organized in a market-oriented way and thus take place outside the provider-consumer dualism, and in which secondly the consumer role merges with the citizen role.

References

Blättel-Mink, Birgit. 2017. Varieties of Prosuming – konzeptionelle Überlegungen und empirische Befunde zur veränderten Rolle von Konsument_innen. In *Entgrenzungen des Konsums. Dokumentation der Jahreskonferenz des Netzwerks Verbraucherforschung*, eds. J. Lamla and P. Kenning, 17–31. Wiesbaden: Springer Gabler.

Boddenberg, Moritz, Max Heinrich Frauenlob, Lenard Gunkel, Sarah Schmitz, Franziska Vassen, and Birgit Blättel-Mink. 2017. Solidarische Landwirtschaft als innovative Praxis – Potenziale für einen sozial-ökologischen Wandel. In *Soziale Innovationen für nachhaltigen Konsum. Wissenschaftliche Perspektiven, Strategien der Förderung und gelebte Praxis*, eds. M. Jaeger-Erben, J. Rückert-John, and M. Schäfer, 125–148. Wiesbaden: Springer VS.

Brewer, John. 1997. Was können wir aus der Geschichte der frühen Neuzeit für die moderne Konsumgeschichte lernen? In *Europäische Konsumgeschichte Zur Gesellschafts- und Kulturgeschichte des Konsums (18. bis 20. Jahrhundert)*, eds. H. Siegrist, H. Kaelble, and J. Kocka, 51–75. Frankfurt a. M.: Campus.

Celata, Filippo, and Cary Yungmee. 2016. WP 4: Case studies integration and policy recommendations. D4.1: Case Study integration report. TESS Project (Grant Agreement n° 603705). http://www.tess-transition.eu/wp-content/uploads/2016/11/TESS_D4.1_Case-study-integration-report.pdf.

CO Concept & USV-Agrar. 2018. *Qualitative Studie zur Evaluation der Initiativenberatung im Projekt MehrWert NRW auf Basis von Befragungen von Engagierten in lokalen Verbraucherinitiativen. Projektendbericht.* Unveröffentlichtes Manuskript im Auftrag der Verbraucherzentrale NRW. Das Manuskript kann angefordert werden unter mehrwert@verbraucherzentrale.nrw.

Collaborating Centre on Sustainable Consumption and Production (CSCP), ed. 2019. *ProMoNa – Prosumptionsmodelle und ihre Nachhaltigkeitspotentiale am Beispiel von Ernährung und Bekleidung. Handlungsempfehlungen für die Verbraucherpolitik zur Förderung eines nachhaltigen Prosumierens.* https://www.scp-centre.org/wp-content/uploads/2019/03/ProMoNa_report_Handlungsempfehlungen.pdf. Accessed 10 Sept 2019.

Evers, Aadalbert, Thomas Klie, and Paul-Stefan Roß. 2015. Die Vielfalt des Engagements Eine Herausforderung an Gesellschaft und Politik. *Aus Politik und Zeitgeschichte* 65(14–15):3–9.

Gillwald, Katrin. 2000. *Konzepte sozialer Innovation.* Wissenschaftszentrum Berlin für Sozialforschung (WZB), Discussion Paper S. 00–519. http://hdl.handle.net/10419/50299. Accessed 29 Aug 2019.

Grabs, Janina, Nina Langen, Gesa Maschkowski, and Niko Schäpke. 2016. Understanding role models for change: A multilevel analysis of success factors of grassroots initiatives for sustainable consumption. *Journal of Cleaner Production* 134:98–111 (Special Volume: Transitions to Sustainable Consumption and Production in Cities).

Grauel, Jonas, Johannes Gorges, Myriam Stenger, and Arno Becker. 2018. Lokale Verbraucherinitiativen für einen nachhaltigeren Konsum als ‚soziale Innovation' – Reflexionen aus soziologischer und evaluatorischer Perspektive. In *Soziale Innovationen lokal gestalten. Band 1 der Reihe Sozialwissenschaften und Berufspraxis*, eds. BDS, H.-W. Franz, and C. Kaletka, 81–99. Wiesbaden: Springer VS.

Hedtke, Reinhold. 2001. *Konsum und Ökonomik. Grundlagen, Kritik und Perspektiven.* Konstanz: UVK-Verlagsgesellschaft.

Howaldt, Jürgen, and Michael Schwarz. 2010. Soziale Innovation – Konzepte, Forschungsfelder und -perspektiven. In *Soziale Innovation. Auf dem Weg zu einem postindustriellen Innovationsparadigma*, eds. J. Howaldt and H. Jacobsen, 87–109. Wiesbaden: VS Verlag.

Jaeger-Erben, Melanie, Jana Rückert-John, and Martina Schäfer. 2017. *Soziale Innovationen für nachhaltigen Konsum. Wissenschaftliche Perspektiven, Strategien der Förderung und gelebte Praxis*. Wiesbaden: Springer VS.

Jaeger-Erben, Melanie, Magdalena Meissner, Sabine Hielscher, and Marco Vonnahme. 2019. Herausforderung soziale Teilhabe: Repair-Cafés als Orte inklusiver nachhaltiger Entwicklung? *Soziologie und Nachhaltigkeit* 5:44–65.

Klug, Martin. 2017. *Die Repräsentation von Verbraucherinteressen. Organisation, Aggregation, Legitimation*. Baden-Baden: Nomos.

Klug, Martin, and Sarah Gartner. 2017. Soziale Innovationen als Herausforderung für die Verbraucherarbeit. In *Soziale Innovationen für nachhaltigen Konsum. Wissenschaftliche Perspektiven, Strategien der Förderung und gelebte Praxis*, eds. M. Jaeger-Erben, J. Rückert-John, and M. Schäfer, 263–285. Wiesbaden: Springer VS.

Kropp, Jürgen. 2016. *TESS research for low-carbon initiatives policy brief: Success factors of community-based sustainability initiatives*. http://www.bcnuej.org/wp-content/uploads/2016/11/Tess_Policy-Brief_Success.pdf. Accessed 9 Sept 2019.

Lamla, Jörn. 2013. *Verbraucherdemokratie. Politische Soziologie der Konsumgesellschaft*. Berlin: Suhrkamp.

Lamla, Jörn, and Peter Kenning. 2017. *Entgrenzungen des Konsums. Dokumentation der Jahreskonferenz des Netzwerks Verbraucherforschung*. Wiesbaden: Springer Gabler.

Landholm, David M., Anne Holsten, Federico Martellozzo, Dominik E. Reusser, and Jürgen P. Kropp. 2019. Climate change mitigation potential of community-based initiatives in Europa. *Regional Environmental Change* 19:927–938.

Lange, Bastian, Valentin Domann, and Valerie Häfele. 2016. *Wertschöpfung in offenen Werkstätten. Eine empirische Erhebung kollaborativer Praktiken in Deutschland.* Berlin: Schriftenreihe des IÖW 213/16. https://www.ioew.de/fileadmin/user_upload/BILDER_und_Downloaddateien/Publikationen/Schriftenreihen/IOEW_SR-213_Wertschoepfung_in_offenen_Werkstaetten.pdf. Accessed 18 Sept 2019.

Loske, Reinhard. 2016. Neue Formen kooperativen Wirtschaftens als Beitrag zur nachhaltigen Entwicklung. Überlegungen zur Wiedereinbettung der Ökonomie in Gesellschaft und Natur. In *Prosuming und Sharing – Neuer sozialer Konsum. Aspekte kollaborativer Formen von Konsumtion und Produktion*, eds. C. Bala and W. Schuldzinski, 31–63. Düsseldorf: Verbraucherzentrale NRW.

Müller, Christa, and Karin Werner. 2015. Neuer Urbanismus. Die New School grüner politischer Utopie. *INDES. Zeitschrift für Politik und Gesellschaft* 4:31–43.

Öko-Institut & ifeu. 2018. *Kurzbericht. Evaluation des Projekts MehrWert NRW mit Fokus auf der Darstellung mittelbarer Beiträge zu THG-Minderungen.* Unveröffentlichtes Manuskript im Auftrag der Verbraucherzentrale NRW. Das Manuskript kann angefordert werden unter mehrwert@verbraucherzentrale.nrw.

Peuker, Birgit and Jana Rückert-John. 2017. Potenziale und Herausforderungen von Gemeinschaftlichkeit und Gemeinwohl für den sozial-ökologischen Wandel. Ergebnisse einer repräsentativen Bevölkerungsumfrage. *ISInova Beiträge zur Sozialinnovation* Nr. 19. https://www.isinova.org/images/BzS19.pdf. Accessed 16 Sept 2019.

Roß, Paul-Stefan. 2017. *Alles im Wandel – Beim Engagement alles beim alten?!* https://www.ehrenamt-verbindet.de/wpD4/wp-content/uploads/2017/04/Engagment-4-0_KISS.pdf.

Rückert-John, Jana, René John, and Melanie Jaeger-Erben. 2015. Neue Formen des Konsums aus Sicht der Politik. *Forschungsjournal Soziale Bewegungen* 28:77–89.

Sekulova, Filka. 2016. WP 3: *Analysis of success factors*. D 3.3: Report on qualitative success factors. TESS Project (Grant Agreement n° 603705). http://www.tess-transition.eu/wp-content/uploads/2016/05/04.29.2016-Deliverable3.3_Final-rectified.pdf. Accessed 28 July 2017.

Seyfang, Gill, and Alex Haxeltine. 2012. Growing grassroots innovations: Exploring the role of community-based initiatives in governing sustainable energy transitions. *Environment Planning C: Government and Policy* 30:381–400.

Soper, Kate. 2007. Re-thinking the ‚Good Life': The citizenship dimension of consumer disaffection with consumerism. *Journal of Consumer Culture* 7:205–229.

Umweltbundesamt. 2014. *Soziale Innovationen im Aufwind. Ein Leitfaden zur Förderung sozialer Innovationen für nachhaltigen Konsum*. https://www.umweltbundesamt.de/sites/default/files/medien/376/publikationen/soziale_innovationen_im_aufwind_bf_1.pdf. Accessed 3 Sept 2019.

United Nations. 2015. *Transforming our world. The 2030 agenda for sustainable development*. https://sustainabledevelopment.un.org/content/documents/21252030%20Agenda%20for%20Sustainable%20Development%20web.pdf. Accessed 11 Oct 2019.

Urban Gardening Manifest. 2014. http://urbangardeningmanifest.de/. Accessed 1 Aug 2017.

Werkstadt Stuttgart e. V. o. J.. *Elektroreparaturen in ehrenamtlich betriebenen ReparaturCafés*. https://www.reparatur-initiativen.de/files/kcfinder/pages/13483/files/Interview%20150706_ensmann_elektroreparaturen%20final.pdf. Accessed 11 Sept 2019.

Wissenschaftlicher Beirat der Bundesregierung Globale Umweltveränderungen (WBGU). 2011. *Welt im Wandel*. Berlin: Gesellschaftsvertrag für eine Große Transformation.

Wissenschaftliche Dienste Deutscher Bundestag. 2019. *Regelungen gegen Lebensmittelverschwendung in ausgewählten Ländern*. https://www.bundestag.de/resource/blob/648932/7c64ad8483b3e289ce6896fc36198be0/WD-5-046-19-pdf-data.pdf. Accessed 11 Sept 2019.

Jonas Grauel, Dr. phil. (sociologist), completed his doctorate on food consumption and everyday morality at the University of Siegen in 2012. He then conducted research on climate change and the transformation to a more sustainable economy at the University of Hamburg. He has been working at the Consumer Association of NRW since 2016, since 2023 he is director of the MehrWertRevier project.

Rethinking Consumption—To Make Things Better

Stefan Schridde

Abstract

Below, I describe personal views on the topic of consumption, from which I justify my commitment to consumer policy. In this description, I am deliberately pointed and intensifying in the presentation at times, in order to provide an impulse for a debate on the renewal of guiding principles in consumption. By 'we' in the text, I mean the consumers.

Keywords

Citizenship · Planned obsolescence · Climate crisis · Consumption academy · Consumption balance · Consumption crisis · Circular society · Resource protection · Consumer policy

1 Consumption is More Than Commerce

We consume always and from birth. Consumption is something we humans do to make ourselves and those closest to us better off. Dialogue and consumption are what form our human communities. At the origin of Neolithic societies, consumption is self-sufficiency in a natural context. With the increasing division of labor and urbanization, we have delegated tasks in consumption to third parties,

S. Schridde (✉)
MURKS? NEIN DANKE! e. V., Berlin, Germany
e-mail: stefan@schridde.org

K.-U. Hellmann et al. (eds.), *Consumer Policy from Below*,
https://doi.org/10.1007/978-3-658-44478-5_16

developed the division of labor and its administration, and established money as a substitute for goods. Production, distribution, and barter trade were taken over by independent organizational forms. The financial markets have been independent since around 1750. Since and through industrialization in the 19th century, we have largely forgotten the competence for self-sufficiency and experienced an explosive expansion of externally determined forms of consumption. Use value became exchange value. The economic role of 'employee' was added to the second role as 'consumer' for the common people. Today, the citizen is supposed to become a 'user' in the circular economy. The exchange value becomes the utility value.

2 Consumption Becomes Commercialized Stress

Today, more and more people experience consumption as stress. Floods of goods plunge us into decision dilemmas. Information floods overwhelm our cognitive abilities. Decollectivization leads us into loneliness. Alienation and loss of attachment lead to an increase in social and personal crises. Uninhibited predatory competitions destroy our living space. Global political failure destroys future prospects.

Consumption without the justified concern that damage to ourselves or others may have already occurred before the acquisition of goods through their production and distribution is hardly possible anymore. The necessary effort to avoid the damage that occurred before purchase and that arises from use is becoming increasingly large, even to the point of hopelessness for the desired result. The expected effect that we and those closest to us will be better off through consumption in the future has become unreliable. Although the purchasing citizen should be at the forefront of the celebrated customer orientation, we still stand defenseless and helpless against a 'flood of everything' that overwhelms us and makes us feel more like victims than kings as purchasing citizens. Although the economy is only a subsystem of society, most people see themselves only as the smallest cog in an inhuman gear of global competition.

The erosion of society as a positive utopia is already experienced in the production of its goods. The insatiable pursuit of efficiency in industrialization has not only increased wealth, but also the increase of waste, environmental damage, social upheavals, and the current climate crisis. Since industrialization, there has been an ever-increasing gap between rich and poor. The acceleration of everything creates ever greater distances between global communities, which are only further enlarged by digitalization.

3 What It's About

We are in a consumption crisis. At least, that's what we are led to believe by politics, research, retail companies, and manufacturers. Because the problems caused by the way everyday items are globally produced and distributed worldwide are ultimately blamed on the consumer. We buy the end products and are therefore supposed to take the greatest responsibility for the circumstances and characteristics under which they have found their way onto the shelf. We are mistakenly treated as if we had ordered these things this way. However, it is always business decisions that determine the shapes in competition and the quality of the goods produced. This also applies to the underlying assumptions and economic models.

As enlightened and responsible consumers, we are supposed to make the decision 'at the shelf' as to whose products stay in the race. The problems caused by inadequately regulated competition in ruinous orientation are supposed to be solved at the point of purchase by the 'end customer' as the 'last place before the landfill' in the global value chain. It is not global competition that is supposed to generate the best solution for everyone, but the swing voter in the assortment.

Instead of letting the purchasing citizen participate and contribute as a. an employee or b. future user already in the idea finding and product development, he is supposed to separate the wheat from the chaff at the end of the value chain. For example, 10,000 different washing machine model variants as front loader models make it into the European assortment, although probably about 500 model variants for about five different household forms would be completely sufficient from a consumer's point of view. It is this ruinous and predatory competition behind the shelf that has triggered the major crises of sustainability in this world.

4 We Buy Other People's Problems

In the worldwide competition for the greatest power, the maximum return, the largest market shares, the greatest economic efficiency, the fastest business deals and accelerated turnovers, the most pressing challenges to enable prosperity for all have fallen behind. Some ruthlessly strive for the highest 'Return-on-investment' (ROI), while leaving the 'Return-of-damage' (ROD) to society. We are dealing with destructive predatory competitions that accept the survival of generations and the death of billions.

The consequences of this development are all too familiar. The global climate crisis and the global extinction of species are now questioning our future on this planet. The scenarios of research suggest a planet where only one billion people and a few species will survive. The survival of all is even being questioned.

The increasing global resource shortages are causing significant geo-political upheavals. Species extinction and slash-and-burn agriculture endanger countless life forms and ecosystems. Wars, poverty, and hunger rob many peoples of any perspective. The lack of modernization of democracies creates new power spaces for autocratic systems. Anyone who wants to push the citizen back into the passively responsible consumer role deprives him of any further right as a democratic sovereign. We need active consumption, with which we can effectively and emancipatedly enforce our interests for a carefree life democratically.

5 A Campaign is Born

In April 2011, I saw in a documentary how children on a huge garbage dump in Accra, Ghana, tried to recover the metallic resources from the illegally dumped electronic waste there by melting it in countless open fires, in order to resell them.[1] According to the documentary, the main cause of these immense electronic waste dumps from Europe was the so-called 'planned obsolescence'. In this deliberate shortening of the potentially possible service life of consumer goods under otherwise equal conditions by business decisions for the purpose of sales and profit maximization, no rationally justified action can be recognized. In my estimation, it is one of the main causes of the crises described above. Therefore, I am concerned with ensuring a rapid end to planned obsolescence.

In February 2012, I launched the website www.murks-nein-danke.de. This platform provided information about the background and harmful effects of planned obsolescence. At the same time, I invited citizens to submit their own experiences with planned obsolescence. These are still being published today[2] after internal review. Since then, driven by the broad media presence of 'MURKS? NEIN DANKE!', a rapidly growing civic movement against planned obsolescence has emerged, which more and more organizations, companies, parties, NGOs, and associations are joining.

[1] Documentary 'Buying for the landfill' by Cosima Dannoritzer.

[2] See www.murksbarometer.org.

In March 2013, the study 'Planned Obsolescence' commissioned by the parliamentary group of Alliance90/The Greens was published[3] , which elevated the public debate in the political sphere to a higher level and was downloaded more than 30,000 times from my site. In April 2013, the association 'MURKS? NEIN DANKE!' was founded. This organization, recognized as a non-profit, advocates for sustainable product qualities, i.e., for circular durability, optimal usability, easy repairability, free spare parts supply, regional service providers, better warranties, sustainable resource efficiency, and ethical circular economy. More than 40,000 people support the work of the organization both online and offline.

'MURKS? NEIN DANKE!' has sparked a broad debate in the media and at the societal and political level about planned obsolescence, thus putting the issue on the political agenda in a very short time.[4] Initial hostilities against the campaign as an alleged conspiracy theory quickly subsided. The pursuit of durability was recognized as a strong lever for coping with global crises. Corporations, companies, and associations also confirm planned obsolescence as a problem that urgently needs to be addressed due to its harmful effects.

The rapid and broad effectiveness of the cross-media campaign work of 'MURKS? NEIN DANKE!' is due to the high relevance of durability in the daily (ex)perience of the affected consumers. We all experience the erosion of our living conditions and things in various forms in daily life. The acceleration of everything, the growth-driving urge for ever more efficiency, and the ruinous competition in the global hamster wheel have created a world in which the individual feels isolated, lonely, and trapped in consumer and work stress.

As consumers, we experience this directly in our dealings with things. Things are perceived as products of a throwaway economy. The role assigned to us in this ruinous economic model as 'responsible consumers' reduces us to the 'last parking space before the landfill' of a global supply chain that still disregards the requirements of climate and resource protection and social justice. Ultimately, we only rent things for a short period of use. The purchase price is a rent in this understanding. Even in advertising, providers only announce a three to five-year usage period for many everyday goods.

---

[3] See https://www.schridde.org/download/Studie-Obsoleszenz-aktualisiert.pdf.

[4] The 'Green New Deal' of the EU Commission also demands effective measures against planned obsolescence.

6 What is Planned Obsolescence?

Our consumer society has a history. In this history, the acceleration of the turnover frequency of capital has led to a constant reduction in usage periods. This is how planned obsolescence came about, i.e., the deliberate reduction of and influence on the usage periods of goods in favor of increasing returns.

7 Definition 'Planned Obsolescence'

'Planned obsolescence' is the umbrella term for operational strategies and methods of manufacturers and trade that lead to a shortening of the expected lifespan by the consumer, thus accelerating the repurchase. The first description of this relationship goes back to Paul M. Gregory (1947, p. 24), who still called planned obsolescence 'purposeful obsolescence':

> "Purposeful obsolescence exists a) whenever manufacturers produce goods with a shorter physical life than the industry is capable of producing under existing technological and cost conditions; or b) whenever manufacturers or sellers induce the public to replace goods which still retain substantial physical usefulness".

Originally, Bernard London (1932) referred to 'planned obsolescence' with positive goals such as job security and economic stability. Politics should legally prescribe the lifespan and demand the repurchase. Jack Sloan of General Motors introduced the annual models for model diversity and corporate organization. The ruinous consequences of industrialization for society and the environment were already discussed in the late 19th century, but their subsequent effects were not taken seriously enough.

Today, we are finally dealing with issues such as climate change, resource transition, and post-growth on a broader level. The termination of planned obsolescence is recognized as a crucial lever for addressing global problems.

The term 'obsolescence'[5] generally denotes the inherent property of wear and tear and aging in all things. All business processes are always subject to planning

[5] Obsolescence—lat. Obsolescere = to age, to become obsolete, to lose value and reputation, to wear out.

and decision-making processes. Therefore, 'planned obsolescence' is to be distinguished from natural obsolescence and refers to operational processes in the areas of product development, manufacturing, and sales that lead to a shortening of the product lifespan (compared to the technically and cost-possible product lifespan). It is also to be distinguished from consumer behavior that leads to shortened product use (human-ethological obsolescence), as far as these are not brought about by methods of planned obsolescence (psychological obsolescence).

With comprehensibly presented and justified scenarios, the Green Party's study on planned obsolescence in 2013 clearly showed that the financial damage of planned obsolescence, depending on the assumptions made, is between 67 and 137 billion EUR per year for Germany alone.[6] Due to the demonstrably immense damage caused by planned obsolescence, rapid and effective action is required. This is what 'MURKS? NO THANKS!' e. V., a civic NGO, is committed to.

The forms and measures to reduce and end planned obsolescence are diverse. Options for action are available at all levels of society, e.g., individuals, civil society initiatives, NGOs, trade unions, companies, authorities, ministries, parties, and parliament. In total, there are more than a hundred known measures. The potential societal impacts that would result from a complete reduction of planned obsolescence reveal considerable economic and ecological potentials and provide a high incentive.

8 The Citizenry is Changing

Consumer policy from below is emancipating itself. The sovereign realizes that he is at the top. The baby boomers are unfolding old youth ideas. The LOHAS generation is seeking their work-life balance in a modern consumption beyond commerce. The youth are taking to the streets to enforce their legitimate demands. Science too is beginning to emancipate and politicize itself in the course of climate debates, to provide the argumentative basis for societal demands. In urban consumption, people realize their life ideals. Consumption is being rethought and decoupled from economic concepts. Non-monetary and self-sufficient forms join monetary consumption as equal alternatives.

[6] Cf. https://www.schridde.org/download/Studie-Obsoleszenz-aktualisiert.pdf.

9 There is Another Way

'MURKS? NO THANKS!' stands as a non-profit organization for a new consumer model, which is intended to counteract the ruinous market models and their planned obsolescence with a new durable market model.

Consumption should be carefree, emancipated, and effective. Consumption goes with money and also without money, self-sufficient or reductive. Such consumption takes place on different (exchange) markets and mostly in urban areas. We assume that the economy as a whole, as a subsystem of society, is only a supplier and society should tell the supplier what to deliver and under what conditions. This corresponds to the business conditions and regulations already common among business customers, so it does not question a free market. This would rather exclude normative societal influence. The democratically constituted society orders differently than companies or individuals. The democratically constituted society names its requirements to the supplier not only individually through the individual consumer, but also collectively through the democratically legitimized organs (e.g. SGD, eco-design guidelines, laws, regulations) and commissioned institutions (e.g. standards and specifications by ISO, CEN, CENELC, DIN, DKE, VDE).

Municipal public services are based on monetary and non-monetary markets. Municipalities should primarily support the infrastructure of non-monetary markets with the money (e.g. business taxes, levies) that they have taken from the monetary markets. Often, the mere provision of unused infrastructure can be a strong lever for non-monetary generated prosperity effects. If, for example, the school auditoriums could be used every three months for a clothing swap party free of charge or at cost by non-profit organizations, this would already significantly alleviate a bottleneck for the expansion of this social innovation. Neighborhood repair culture should be given the same municipal support as sports.

In this way, carefree emancipated consumption can be made possible and corresponding social innovations can be strengthened and enforced. Carefree means that we as purchasing citizens should finally be able to rely on the fact that only those products are present in the retail offer, the purchase of which does not cause or even contribute to damage to ourselves, our next and future relatives, in our living space and the environment. Emancipated means that the gradient of well-informed suppliers and purchasing citizens is brought back into a balanced power balance. It should apply that goals decided by society as a democratically organized community, such as the UN sustainability goals (SDGs), are directly incorporated into product development and consistently taken into account. The public provision of infrastructure for public services may also be extended to new market segments in this balance. Non-profit organizations, cooperatives, and municipal enterprises are particularly suitable legal forms at the municipal level to organize an emancipated participation and participation of citizens in regional monetary and non-monetary markets.

Manufacturers like to prove themselves as innovators and suppliers of ever better offers. The optimum achievable for the customer and society can best be achieved if the future user is involved in the development of ideas. All products and services must be developed participatively as solutions for general prosperity.

Why should the purchasing citizen research again and each for himself which product on the shelf is junk or the best solution? Trade must become a procurement logistician for carefree consumption. Trade must clean up its shelves and delist cheap products that pass on the already caused and still expected damage to the customer.

10 Responsible Consumption Makes an Impact

Sustainable consumption gets involved. We should use all opportunities to influence production processes on an equal footing. This starts right on the shelf. The place of trade is a public place where the requirements for the assortment need to be re-discussed. Producers are also responding and offer, for example, in Living-Labs and real laboratories various opportunities to participate directly in product development as a customer. Such methods are not a one-way street and can also be initiated by society.

11 Employees and Employers Act Together

Consumers have previously earned their money. At the workplace, we can also become active to achieve something for carefree consumption. However, protective interests on the part of the employees need to be strengthened. An engineer who represents sustainable consumer interests at work (e.g., as an engineer in product development for exhaust aftertreatment systems) should not feel threatened in his job as a result. Whistleblower protection also needs to be strengthened so that management decisions harmful to society can be exposed.

12 The Consumption Academy Strengthens Consumer Policy Through Active Consumption and Citizenship

'MURKS? NO THANKS!' wants to strengthen these developments in urban consumption through education, further training, and empowerment. With the Consumption Academy, we want to turn the city into a campus for new consumption and establish a new platform for this. Consumption should be carefree and emancipated for all citizens. Today's consumer world is still characterized by commerce, floods of goods and information, and planned obsolescence. But consumers are seeking and developing new ways. The Consumption Academy provides the skills for this, connects regional expertise in the citizenry, and shows new ways. The participatory educational formats meet people in everyday consumption, show new effective ways for everyday solutions and more sustainability, and lead through a total of five development levels from co-consumption (collective consumption) to prosuming (entrepreneurial consumption).

The Consumption Academy wants to develop trade, libraries, fruit meadows, and many other places in Berlin into learning places for new consumption. Because recognizing and avoiding junk is best learned on site on the shelf, and solutions already exist in many places in the city.

But consumption is also possible without money. The Consumption Academy teaches consumption skills for monetary, non-monetary, self-sufficient, and reductive consumption. Swapping, borrowing, gifting, and shared consumption are the newly discovered forms of consumption for carefree and effective consumption. Social innovations, civic initiatives, and new business concepts emerge from the middle of society. The Consumption Academy provides the know-how for this and also trains consumption trainers.

The Consumption Academy is being created and invites you to participate. The bUm (www.bum.berlin) is the central place. From here we start the construction in Berlin. Initial information events, workshops, and basic seminars such as 'Discover Your Consumption Balance' will invite you to discover the offers of the Consumption Academy.

References

Gregory, Paul M. 1947. A theory of purposeful obsolescence. *Southern Economic Journal* 14:24–45.

London, Bernard. 1932. *Ending the depression through planned obsolescence*. Madison: University of Wisconsin. Quelle. https://upload.wikimedia.org/wikipedia/commons/2/27/London_%281932%29_Ending_the_depression_through_planned_obsolescence.pdf.

Stefan Schridde, Dipl. Betriebswirt (FH), since 1986 in specialist and management positions, since April 2011 initiator of the campaign MURKS? Nein Danke! against planned obsolescence. As founder of MURKS? NEIN DANKE! e. V., Stefan Schridde has been making a significant contribution to the debate on the damaging consequences of planned obsolescence and its termination throughout Europe since 2012. To this end, he is in direct exchange with political parties, parliamentary groups, members of parliament, ministries, authorities, companies, universities, institutes, research facilities, trade unions, professional associations, NGOs and other friendly networks.

The 'Humboldt Consumer Law Clinic' as an Example of Civil Society Strengthening of Consumer Rights

Reinhard Singer, Kristina Schimpf and Kathrin Steinbach

Abstract

'Law Clinics', which are based on the voluntary commitment of students in legal advice, have significantly improved access to justice for consumers. On the one hand, they fulfill a didactic function by allowing students to deal with real cases, to prepare legal information in an understandable way, and to get to know current developments in legal professions, especially through the digitization of legal advice. On the other hand, 'Law Clinics' fulfill a social function: They strengthen the enforcement of consumer law by overcoming the so-called rational disinterest, by providing free out-of-court legal advice and low-threshold information offers. Against this background, the article explains the concept of the 'Humboldt Consumer Law Clinic' of the Humboldt-Universität zu Berlin and addresses current challenges in consumer legal advice.

Keywords

Blog · Access to information · Legal education · Law Clinic · Legal Tech · Access to justice

R. Singer (✉) · K. Schimpf · K. Steinbach
Humboldt Universität zu Berlin, Berlin, Germany
e-mail: reinhard.singer@hu-berlin.de

K. Schimpf
e-mail: kristina.schimpf@rewi.hu-berlin.de

K. Steinbach
e-mail: kathrin.steinbach@rewi.hu-berlin.de

K.-U. Hellmann et al. (eds.), *Consumer Policy from Below*,
https://doi.org/10.1007/978-3-658-44478-5_17

1 Introduction

'Law Clinics' have democratized access to justice through free out-of-court legal advice in consumer law and are rooted in voluntary commitment. They make an important contribution to consumer policy, which is anchored in civil society. With their pro bono work, 'Law Clinics' address a need for advice that is usually not covered by traditional legal advice concerning small claims. The 'Humboldt Consumer Law Clinic' (HCLC) is a student legal advice service in consumer and residential tenancy law at the Faculty of Law of Humboldt-Universität zu Berlin, founded in 2012, and is the first consumer law 'Law Clinic' in Germany.

The HCLC offers students the opportunity to gain first practical experience in legal advice during their studies by advising those seeking legal advice and working on 'real' cases. At the same time, consumers seeking legal advice are given the opportunity to receive free legal advice on consumer and tenancy law issues from the students, as well as assistance in enforcing their rights out-of-court.

Gaps in the enforcement of rights are among the current challenges of consumer law. The 'emissions scandal' has led to new movements in the field of collective redress with the introduction of the Model Declaratory Action. Innovations in the area of alternative dispute resolution are also progressing with the amendment of the Act on Alternative Dispute Resolution in Consumer Matters. However, events such as the insolvency of airlines or package tour operators also show that many consumers are unaware of their rights and that there is a need for improved consumer information.

In the area of tenancy law, it is primarily the so-called rent brake and the so-called Berlin rent cap that determine the current discussion on tenancy law and show that regulatory approaches are intended to stop ever-increasing rents in tense housing markets. This diversity of consumer and residental tenancy law also shows the need for expanded access to advice and information services, to which the HCLC contributes.

The following will first address the legal permissibility of free legal advice by students. The main part of the contribution deals with both the didactic and the social function of 'Law Clinics'. These two functions are highlighted using the three sub-projects of the HCLC: legal advice, the consumer blog, and the 'Legal Tech' project.

2 The Development and Permissibility of Free Legal Advice by Students

The idea of the 'Law Clinic' comes from the Anglo-American legal sphere (Dastis and Udich 2013, p. 721; Schmidt 2017, § 6 RDG para. 9; Singer 2016, p. 93 f.). In the USA, the basic idea was to limit the theory-ladenness of legal studies through an expanded practical orientation in teaching, the 'Clinical Legal Education'.

Until 2008, legal advice was reserved for lawyers (Singer 2016, p. 94; Vogler 2013, p. 135). In addition, legally qualified persons were long prohibited from providing pro bono legal advice. It was not until a decision in 2004 that the Federal Constitutional Court (Bundesverfassungsgericht) made it clear that such a prohibition which is punishable by fine violates the fundamental right to general freedom of action under Art. 2 para. 1 GG (BVerfG NJW 2004, 2662).

3 The Permissibility of Student Legal Advice

With the enactment of the Act on Out-of-Court Legal Services (RDG) in 2008, which replaced the Legal Advice Act (RBG) from 1935, a legal basis was created with § 6 para. 2 RDG that enabled the establishment of many 'Law Clinics' (Hannemann and Dietlein 2017, p. 449; Schmidt 2017, § 6 RDG para. 69, 72). The standard thus represents a "milestone" for 'Law Clinics' (Paal 2016, p. 1). Since 2008, various 'Law Clinics' have been established in Germany (Dastis and Udich 2013, p. 721; Kilian and Wenzel 2017, p. 963).

According to § 1 para. 1, the RDG regulates the authorisation to provide out-of-court legal services the Federal Republic of Germany. Legal services, according to § 2 RDG, are activities in a concrete affair of others that require an assessment of the individual case. The central point of § 2 RDG is the required "special assessment in individual cases" (BT-Drs. 16/3655, p. 46). This does not apply if only a simple schematic application of the law is required. Thus, for example, general legal advice and mere information provision, such as in the form of legal blogs, fall outside the scope of the law.

According to § 3 RDG, legal services are subject to a permit requirement, i.e., legal services require a legal basis (Römermann 2008, § 3 RDG para. 1). Such authorisation follows in the case of free advice from § 6 RDG. The RDG serves both the "protection of those seeking legal advice" and the "strengthening of civic engagement" (BT-Drs. 16/3655, p. 1). The previously existing complete prohibition of free legal advice is not justified for consumer protection interests (BT-Drs.

16/3655, p. 39). § 6 RDG aims to enable civic engagement (BT-Drs. 16/3655, p. 58). According to § 6 RDG, out-of-court, free legal services can be provided by anyone. However, for legal services that occur outside of family, neighbourly or similarly close personal relationships, the involvement of a legally qualified person is required for the protection of those seeking legal advice (BT-Drs. 16/3655, p. 1 f.). Legally qualified persons are individuals who are qualified to hold judicial office, i.e., fully qualified lawyers according to § 5 para. 1 of the German Judicary Act (DRiG) or university professors according to § 7 para. 1 DRiG (Hannemann and Dietlein 2017, p. 451). According to § 6 para. 2 RDG, the legal service must also be provided free of charge, i.e., it must not be associated with a fee-based activity (Römermann 2008, § 6 para. 6). Legal services against payment are generally only permitted to lawyers (Hannemann and Dietlein 2017, p. 456).

According to § 6 para. 2 RDG, it must be ensured that the free legal service is either "provided by a person qualified to hold judicial office or under the instruction of such a person". The instruction requires according to § 6 para. 2 RDG "an induction and training which is oriented to the scope and content of the legal services to be provided, as well as involvement in the provision of the legal service, as far as this is necessary in the individual case". The requirements regarding the instruction should not be "too demanding" (BT-Drs. 16/3655, p. 40). It is necessary to instruct the legal advisors, and a legally qualified person must be available if the expertise of the non-legal advisors is not sufficient (BT-Drs. 16/3655, p. 58). At the same time, it must be ensured that the advising persons are informed about legal changes, for example through appropriate events or newsletters.

4 Conformity of the HCLC with the RDG

The students of the HCLC participate in educational courses before they start their legal advice. These courses specifically prepare the students for giving legal advice and the subject of advice. The students of the 'Consumer Law Clinic' also receive guidelines for handling mandates and contact with clients and the opposing side, and are also trained in an introductory workshop on student legal advice. They must also sign a declaration on data protection and confidentiality regarding the personal data they have become aware of through giving legal advice to clients. The close contact and constant consultation with the legally qualified supervisors ensure the instruction required by § 6 para. 2 RDG.

5 Didactic Function of 'Law Clinics'

Although the legislator only created a legal basis for free out-of-court legal services about ten years ago, there are now 'Law Clinics' at almost all law faculties in Germany (Kilian and Wenzel 2017, p. 963). In addition to the social objectives (see point 18), 'Law Clinics' fulfill an important didactic function in legal education and university teaching (Riehm and Heiß 2016, p. 23). This was also highlighted by the Wissenschaftsrat in 2012 in an expert opinion, emphasizing that 'Law Clinics' promote the practical relevance of legal studies (Wissenschaftsrat 2012, p. 57 f.).

6 Confrontation of Students with Real Cases

Almost 80% of graduates become lawyers after completing their law studies (Jahn 2008, p. 6). However, the legal studies are designed in such a way that many students usually only handle real cases after the First Legal State Examination, i.e. after about five years of study, during their legal clerkship.

7 Education Concept of 'Law Clinics'

'Law Clinics' start here and enable students to gain important practical experience in the first semesters of their studies, thus facilitating the transition from theory to practice. Student legal advice therefore has an essential didactic function by preparing students for their future professional life. Within the framework of legal advice, students deal intensively with legal issues. In this process, knowledge transfer is strengthened by the practical relevance of substantive law and the students' awareness of problems is sharpened by advising those seeking legal advice.

Legal advice also strengthens communicative, linguistic, organizational, and strategic skills of students and therefore makes an important contribution to practical professional training. It imparts important 'soft skills' such as rhetorical skills and negotiation techniques, which are essential for later professional life. In addition, early client contact leads to students not only working on the legal situation theoretically, but also conducting conversations with those seeking legal advice, in which they determine the individual facts of the case and provide case-specific information about their rights.

Working in a 'Law Clinic' also creates a learning and networking effect, as students exchange ideas with the qualified lawyers who supervise them about possible career perspectives and learn directly from them (Schubert 2014, p. 248). However, 'Law Clinics' are not part of the mandatory program to be completed during studies, but rather represent optional, extracurricular teaching offers (Kilian and Wenzel 2017, p. 965).

8 Structure of the HCLC

An important goal of the HCLC is the training of students in the field of consumer law through a combination of theoretical events and practical solutions to real cases, as well as through insights into the practice of different actors in the field of consumer law. The HCLC's teaching offer is coordinated within the curriculum of the Faculty of Law. Students can have their participation in the HCLC credited as a key qualification (professional additional qualification).

The structure of the HCLC includes a one-year training cycle. In the winter semester, students deepen their knowledge in substantive consumer and tenancy law through basic courses and workshops and are prepared for the legal advisory activity, which takes place in the summer semester, through various practice-related workshops.

9 Theory Semester

The theoretical training of students in the winter semester consists of two pillars: lectures on consumer law and practice-oriented workshops. As part of a lecture on consumer law, students are taught knowledge about, for example, the right of withdrawal, sale of consumer goods, and the law of general terms and conditions, thus providing them with important substantive legal knowledge for legal advisory work.

In parallel, a lecture series on consumer law takes place. As part of this lecture series, practitioners give talks on various particularly practice-relevant consumer law topics from their professional everyday life and illuminate substantive legal questions from a practical perspective. Speakers from law firms and consumer organizations report on topics such as air passenger rights, cross-border consumer protection, and consumer protection in banking law. At the same time, the lecture series deals with presentations on collective redress and the Model Declaratory Action, as well as planned legal changes at the European level in the area of law enforcement.

The out-of-court settlement of consumer disputes and current consumer policy developments are also discussed. In this context, an insight into the protection mechanisms and working methods of various institutions such as the Verbraucherzentrale or the Mieterverein is also provided. The lecture series provides students with an understanding of the diversity of the consumer law enforcement landscape by demonstrating different forms of asserting rights. The lecture series serves, on the one hand, to give participants of the 'Law Clinic' as comprehensive an overview as possible of current developments in consumer protection legislation. On the other hand, it also offers the opportunity to exchange ideas and network with practitioners.

Events such as a rhetoric seminar and various workshops on legal advice specifically prepare students for advising those seeking legal advice and impart important 'soft skills' that are not only crucial for work within the HCLC, but also for later professional practice. The practice-oriented workshops focus not only on drafting legal briefs, but also on client conversations and negotiations with the opposing party. In this context, students are to learn, among other things, essential skills for comprehensive fact-finding and at the same time for dealing with different opposing parties and for negotiation.

At the same time, a lecture in tenancy law takes place, which serves to impart in-depth knowledge of residential tenancy law to students. Tenancy law is characterized by a multitude of specific case law and is only part of the mandatory legal studies in its basic features. A further training event thus specifically prepares students for the advice of the HCLC in tenancy law.

The two pillars in the form of events on consumer law and practice-oriented workshops pave the way for practical work in the summer semester.

10 Practical Semester

During the practical phase, students work in teams of two to three advisors under the instruction of qualified lawyers on their own assigned cases. To this end, the students first record the facts of the case from the clients and request additional documents from the clients if necessary, or arrange a meeting. They are in close consultation with the fully qualified lawyers supervising them. Based on the facts of the case, the students make a legal assessment of the case. Depending on the client's request, either only consultation takes place or the students draft a letter addressed to the opposing party. After the letters have been checked by the supervising qualified lawyers, they are forwarded to the clients. With their consent, the letters are sent to the opposing party. In addition, regular meetings of the 'Law

Clinic' staff with the students take place, which serve to answer further questions about case management and to exchange information in the plenary about the cases currently being dealt with. Case work forms the core of the practical work in the summer semester.

The HCLC's consulting semester is also supplemented by various practice days, which are intended to give students a comprehensive insight into various areas of consumer law. The students thus have the opportunity to spend a day at the Verbraucherzentrale Berlin e. V. and the Schlichtungsstelle für den öffentlichen Personenverkehr e. V., long-standing cooperation partners of the HCLC, to gain an insight into the institutions and their practical work to effectively enforce consumer rights. At the same time, the students attend a court hearing to experience consumer law from a procedural perspective. The HCLC students should also gain an insight into consumer law from a legal policy perspective, which is why the Federal Ministry of Justice and Consumer Protection (BMJV) is also visited.

11 Information Processing for Non-Lawyers

Linguistic competencies are crucial in law studies and for the later legal professional life, as language is considered the most important, sometimes even the only tool of lawyers (Jahn 2008, p. 6, 9). The language of lawyers is often referred to as 'legal German' and classified as technical language. However, the later professional life of legal advisors is characterized by the fact that they have contact with lawyers on the one hand, but also with the client himself, who is usually not a lawyer. This implies that not only different social, but also linguistic approaches are necessary to explain legal problems.

12 The Didactic Concept of the HCLC Consumer Blog

Legal blogs, in which students write posts on various legal issues, convey and improve these skills to transfer between the levels of linguistic understanding. They pursue different approaches depending on the target audience. Blogs, whose posts are intended for the professional public, are to be distinguished from blogs that are specifically addressed to those seeking legal advice. The latter serve to inform those seeking legal advice about legal issues or legal policy developments. Laws are difficult for many lay persons in legal matters to understand, but they still form the basis for the legal coexistence between the different parties.

Consumer blogs present the legal situation in typical consumer cases in an easily understandable, accessible language, so that consumers can inform themselves about their rights. Therefore, students acquire the important practical ability of explaining complex legal problems in an understandable way during their training. Rephrasing in their own words and condensing complicated facts also leads to a deeper understanding of the legal matter among the students. 'Law Clinics' also serve to strengthen techniques of scientific work such as research and argumentation skills and to promote the critical thinking of students (Science Council 2012, p. 58). Not only does legal advice aim at these goals by having students identify legal problems in case processing, research them and at the same time strengthen their oral and written argumentation skills through conducting client interviews and written communication with the opposing side. Writing blog posts as part of the 'Clinic' activity also serves these goals, as the students intensively and critically engage with a topic for their blog posts and prepare it scientifically and argumentatively.

13 The Process of the Blog Project

The HCLC began its work on a consumer law blog in the winter semester of 2018/2019 and wants to become more involved in the field of consumer information and expand the scope of activities for participating students. For the 2018/2019 cycle, the HCLC launched two new projects based on this concern. In addition to the 'core' of the HCLC, the traditional legal advice, students can now participate in the 'Legal Blog' and 'Legal Tech' projects.

As part of the 'Legal Blog' project, students write blog posts for consumers on various consumer law topics. In the 'Legal Tech' project, students conceptualize and develop 'Legal Tech' applications for consumers. Both new sub-projects of the HCLC were awarded the Teaching Prize for Innovative Teaching 2019 by the Faculty of Law at Humboldt-Universität zu Berlin.

The blog was born out of the desire to make the HCLC's legal advisory services available to a wider public, independent of individual cases. The knowledge that students acquire through participation should thus be made publicly accessible beyond the advised mandates, in order to support more consumers in enforcing their rights. The advice is naturally very dependent on individual cases. In addition, consumers sometimes lack easily accessible, independent information on consumer law issues relevant to everyday life.

To remedy this, the establishment of the information platform began in the winter semester of 2018/2019, on which basic consumer law questions, current leading cases in the field of consumer law, and landmark decisions are reported. The blog can be accessed on the HCLC website (hclc-berlin.de).

In this way, the HCLC also wants to contribute to a consolidation of the insights gained in the context of training work. Frequent and practical problem areas are, for example, termination for cause of contracts for the performance of a continuing obligation (e.g., gym or mobile phone contracts) or air passengers rights. In preparation for the blog activity, the students attend a seminar that introduces them to the basics of writing blog posts and running a blog. Furthermore, various seminars in the form of writing workshops take place throughout the year, where the students and staff of the HCLC evaluate the drafts of the blog posts in a mutual exchange. In this context, there is also a discussion about current consumer law topics and important basic consumer law questions to determine the topics of the individual blog posts. The posts thus also reflect legal policy developments in consumer law, so that the blog participates in the legal policy discourse.

14 Preparing for the Digitization of the Legal Profession: Technological Development

The majority of law students will practice law after their legal clerkship (Jahn 2008, p. 6). In addition to training students' communicative and strategic skills through independent handling of real cases, digitization and partial automation of legal work presents a future challenge for students. This development is driven by 'Big Data' (Mayer-Schönberger and Cukier 2013, p. 8 ff.), growing computing and storage capacities, and the increasing networking of data sources. In the legal field, this is often discussed under the term 'Legal Tech': a uniformly used definition of what Legal Tech encompasses does not yet exist. It seems sensible to first differentiate whether it is about the digitization or automation of law firm organization or the original legal activity; Hartung (2018, p. 8) thus distinguishes 'Office-Tech' from 'Legal Tech' in the narrower sense. The former only supports the traditional work of the legal profession, without significant influence on the business model, while the latter "directly affects the provision of legal services" (ibid.). 'Legal Tech' in the narrower sense includes, for example, automated document creation or software-based processing and enforcement of claims (ibid., p. 8 f.). This is particularly known in the context of rights, but there are now further applications in tenancy law, labor law or sales law. It is therefore a "utilization of information technology for law" (Kuhlmann 2018, p. 88).

Increasingly common is also the evaluation of case law via so-called 'Predictive Analytics' tools, which primarily determine the chances of success of lawsuits using statistical methods (Chen 2019, p. 17 ff.). Here, the relationship between lawyers and judges approaches the Holmesian ideal (1897, p. 461) of law as experience-based prediction. This trend is particularly prevalent in the USA, but has already led to the French legislator creating a norm that prohibits, among other things, making predictions about their 'professional practice' from data of judiciary members (Art. 33 of the Loi n° 2019-222 du 23 mars 2019 de programmation 2018–2022 et de réforme pour la justice).

In light of the outlined advancing digitization and automation of the legal profession, the question arises in the university environment how students can best be prepared for this professional world.

15 Challenges for the Legal Profession due to Digitalization and Automation

Firstly, it is important to realize which qualifications and skills of a lawyer are gaining and losing importance: Simple but extensive research tasks, such as the comparison of certain contract clauses, are increasingly being automated (Susskind and Susskind 2015, p. 68 f.). Ideally, this would also allow newcomers to the profession to quickly focus on the complex aspects of a mandate. Some areas of law, such as tax, insurance, or social law, are particularly suitable for automated processes due to their inherent quantitative references (from a governmental perspective Martini and Nink 2017). The same applies to areas of law where data is collected automatically and extensively, for example in traffic accident law due to vehicle sensor technology.

With the advancing digitalization and automation of the legal profession, interdisciplinary work comes into focus. Lawyers will increasingly work with programmers when it comes to developing efficient solutions for legal problems. This requires at least a basic understanding of the technological contexts and functionalities on the part of the lawyers. Therefore, basic knowledge in decision tree methods, statistics, and machine learning is useful (a comprehensible introduction to machine learning is offered by Alpaydin 2016). Law firms have responded to this in recent years by offering so-called hackathons, events where law students and programmers try to develop a software solution for legal or firm-specific problems in a limited time. Ideally, law students even acquire programming skills themselves, which enable them to design tailored offers or to assess the usefulness of software for their work as a lawyer.

This knowledge ultimately serves not only to keep pace with the change in the lawyer's professional image, but also promotes a sense for the limits of automation. A lawyer who has at least basic knowledge in the aforementioned fields will be able to assess more quickly which legal aspects are suitable for automated processing or which skills will be in demand in the future job market.

16 Training Concept of the HCLC's 'Legal Tech' Project: Basic Procedure

The motivation to initiate the 'Legal Tech' project of the HCLC arose from observing this technological development and the associated opportunities and challenges for the legal profession. The project pursues two goals: On the one hand, it aims to prepare students for legal work in an increasingly digital and automated working world, with the practically oriented further education program primarily targeting interface activities (didactic function). On the other hand, 'Legal Tech' should be used to develop solutions that sustainably provide legal assistance to a large number of consumers (social function, see point 27).

Regarding the didactic concept, it should first be noted that currently only a few state law faculties in Germany integrate 'Legal Tech' in its practical dimension into teaching, and then usually only within the framework of occasional events or as an additional qualification. Breidenbach (2018, p. 206 f.) therefore emphatically calls for the integration of 'Legal Tech' approaches into legal education in view of technological development. As a consequence of this university 'gap', it is currently up to student initiatives to deal with the topic. The HCLC is one of the first 'Law Clinics' nationwide that wants to specifically link 'Legal Tech' with consumer protection. The concept envisages that the students receive a theoretical and practical introduction in the form of lectures and workshops in the winter semester and try to solve a consumer law problem with 'Legal Tech' in the summer semester, for example in the form of classifications or automatically generated template letters. In parallel, the students participate in the compulsory consumer law events in the summer semester—together with the students who focus on traditional legal advice. The didactic concept is therefore based on a combination of theory and practice as well as knowledge transfer in consumer law. Students should learn to handle 'Legal Tech' software in a project-related manner and get a feel for the challenge of translating legal facts and norms into 'code' and also considering user-friendliness for the consumer.

The first 'Legal Tech' project of the HCLC started in the winter semester 2018/2019 with ten students. The theoretical framework consisted of lectures and workshops on the topics 'Legal decision logics and their digital translation', 'Agile project work', 'Software introduction for the areas of document automation and decision trees' as well as the lecture 'IT for lawyers', in which cross-sectional knowledge of information technology is conveyed. Regarding the methodological approach, the focus was therefore on decision trees. This deductive approach has the advantage that 'Legal Tech' concepts of the students do not depend on elaborate data collections or access to external data sets, which are necessary for machine learning, for example. A central question at the beginning of the project was therefore which software can be made available to the students in the practical phase to model decision trees without programming knowledge. Initially, cooperations with commercial providers or the use of prototypes from other university projects were considered. Ultimately, two participants of the 2018/2019 class developed an open-source program ('OpenDecision') that can be used to create and connect decision trees (Rothmann and Schädlich 2019, p. 22). The goal of the two students is to make this software available to future participants, but also to external institutions such as consumer associations.

17 Experiences from the Practical Phase

The concrete consumer law project phase started in the summer semester: The students formed groups that worked on different sub-projects. One group developed the aforementioned program 'OpenDecision' to provide the Legal Tech project with open source software. This guarantees the project long-term independence from commercial licenses, external data storage, etc. Another group designed a decision tree to optimize the internal case management of the HCLC. So far, those seeking legal advice usually contact the HCLC by email. Depending on the case presentation, the examination of whether the case can even be accepted by the 'Law Clinic' takes some time. The primary concern is whether the facts of the case can be assigned to consumer law, whether possible claims are already statue-barred or are about to become statute-barred or are about to expire, and whether the limit of the amount in dispute is being adhered to (see point 22 for details). The latter, however, can require a legally complex examination—for example in tenancy law—and is therefore not easily standardized. Contact details, claim requests, details of contracts etc. can, however, be efficiently classified via decision trees.

The third group finally aimed to develop assistance in substantive consumer law. It proved very difficult to identify suitable legal questions that can be solved with 'Legal Tech' in a relatively short period of time. On the one hand, an inventory had to be taken of which public consumer law 'Legal Tech' applications already exist. For example, consumer associations offer a so-called debt collection check (https://www.verbraucherzentrale.de/inkasso-check). On the other hand, legal questions that depend on indefinite legal concepts and are therefore not binary schematizable are not suitable for translation into a decision tree. In this respect, the basic problem of deductive legal informatics has remained since the 1950s (see Gräwe 2011, pp. 44, 222). The idea was finally to automatically generate termination letters for mobile phone or gym contracts, as these contracts are often concluded and usually have long terms—although the BMJV is currently planning a further restriction of term agreements for certain consumer contracts under § 309 No. 9 BGB (draft bill of the BMJV 2020: Law for Fair Consumer Contracts). The advantage over the sample letters from the consumer advice centers would be that the automated content could be more individualized and the letter, unlike numerous internet templates, comes from a public institutional source. However, this sub-project has not yet been completed.

Various options are conceivable for future cohorts of the 'Legal Tech' project. With regard to the practical phase, it would be possible to continue working on largely independent sub-projects or to decide on a total project in advance in which all students are involved. The latter option has the advantage that the actual project implementation can be started more quickly, as this year's experience shows that it is very time-consuming to commit to several suitable sub-projects. It is also planned to cooperate more intensively with other 'Legal Tech' initiatives and research institutions in order to use knowledge exchange and synergy effects.

18 Social Function of 'Law Clinics'

'Law Clinics' have a social function, particularly through the offer of free legal advice (Schubert 2014, p. 250), and serve to promote the charitable commitment of students. By improving access to information and recognizing the opportunities created by digitization in legal advice, ways are created to improve and expand access to justice.

19 Access to Justice by Overcoming Rational Disinterest

Having rights does not always mean getting rights: From this perspective, the HCLC's legal advice service is provided. Consumers are protected by a multitude of laws; however, there are often gaps in the enforcement of consumer rights. For a long time, the focus in consumer law was on the constant strengthening of consumer rights by the legislator, by adopting further consumer protection regulations. However, the focus is increasingly on the enforcement of these rights. This is particularly evident in the expansion of collective redress through the Model Declaratory Action. The substantive consumer law with its protective provisions does not always represent the reality of perceived consumer protection, as many consumers often do not assert or enforce their existing rights, regardless of them.

20 Rational Disinterest

There are various reasons for the enforcement deficit in consumer law. An important reason for this is the so-called rational disinterest (also called rational apathy) of consumers (BT-Drs. 19/2507, p. 1; Fries 2016, p. 57 f.). Rational disinterest occurs in cases where the damage suffered is particularly small compared to the time and cost of enforcing rights (Berlin 2020, para. 16). This is often the case in consumer law, as the damages suffered are usually financially minor. This leads to many consumers being deterred from enforcing their rights. According to a study, the dispute value at which citizens in Germany go to court for financial damage suffered averages 1950 EUR.[1]

Due to the existing fee schedule according to the Act on the Renumeration of Lawyers (RVG), consumers often do not seek legal advice from lawyers in small claims, let alone do they pursue going to court. Also, obstacles of a social or psychological nature, e.g. the fear of visiting a law firm or confronting the landlord, lead to many consumers refraining from enforcing their rights.

Although legal aid and litigation cost assistance, as well as legal protection insurance, are important tools for consumers to access justice regardless of their financial situation (Dastis and Udich 2013, p. 721; Weber 2013, p. 326). Nevertheless, the use of these tools presents obstacles for some consumers. Consumers are sometimes unaware of the possibility of legal aid and litigation cost assistance or are deterred from using them due to language or psychological reasons (Singer 2016, p. 113).

Another contribution to reducing rational disinterest is consumer conciliation (BT-Drs. 18/6904, p. 66). The main legal basis for consumer conciliation is found

[1] See Roland Rechtsschutz-Versicherungs- AG. Ed. Roland Legal Report 2014, p. 8.

in the Act on Alternative Dispute Resolution in Consumer Matters. In addition to specific dispute resolution bodies for individual areas of consumer disputes, such as the Schlichtungsstelle für den öffentlichen Personenverkehr e. V. or the Schlichtungsstelle beim Deutschen Sparkassen- und Giroverband e. V.[2] There is also an online dispute resolution tool for disputes over contracts concluded on the Internet between consumers and companies, based on the European Union's Regulation on online dispute resolution for consumer disputes (OJ EU L 165/1 of 18.06.2013). The German contact point is the Europäische Verbraucherzentrum Deutschland in Kehl. The use of consumer dispute resolution is free of charge and, due to easily accessible complaint forms, represents a quick, efficient way for many consumers to access justice. However, companies are not generally obliged to participate in consumer dispute resolution (Berlin 2020, para. 116). Furthermore, there is a lack of personal advice or the opportunity to make oral statements in the context of consumer dispute resolution, as the procedure is generally conducted in writing (on this Fries 2016, p. 215 f.).

21 Legal Advice Through 'Law Clinics'

Student legal advice services offer a social, low-threshold opportunity for those seeking legal advice to obtain it without any cost risk, thus improving access to justice. 'Law Clinics' provide social assistance by offering legal advice in areas and cases where rights would otherwise not be enforced or where enforcement is weakened. They thus contribute to reducing the rational disinterest of consumers. Consumers approach 'Law Clinics' with their everyday disputes, which they would often refrain from enforcing due to cost and time factors. The existence of the previously described legal advice services does not mean that there is no need for student legal advice services for improved access to justice; rather, the different strands of legal enforcement complement each other and compensate for individual deficits. The variety of legal advice services for consumers, who would not seek legal advice without these services, therefore leads to a global strengthening of access to justice for these consumers.

[2] Allgemeine Verbraucherschlichtungsstelle, Further consumer dispute resolution bodies can be found at https://www.verbraucher-schlichter.de/was-ist-schlichtung/weitere-schlichtungsstellen [As of: May 18, 2020].

Access to justice is improved not only by the out-of-court representation by 'Law Clinics', but also by the individual advice given to those seeking legal advice. These different approaches also follow the different concerns of those seeking legal advice. Some consumers only seek advice, as, for example, in residential tenancy law, conflicts with the landlord are often avoided and a final assessment of this is facilitated by advice. Others, however, have not been able to enforce their rights on their own, as, for example, there is no response from the other party to their asserted claim, and they seek representation in their legal matters.

Civic engagement is only a limited part of legal studies. 'Law Clinics', among others, provide a remedy for this. For students who are still in legal training, working within a 'Law Clinic' is usually an extracurricular, voluntary commitment (Wenzel and Killian 2017, p. 965), so that students pursue social goals with their participation in a 'Law Clinic', which benefit consumers through the advice offered.

22 The Legal Advice of the HCLC

The case inquiries from those seeking legal advice reach the HCLC mostly by email. The HCLC team checks these for their 'Clinic' suitability. Only cases that fall within the field of consumer or residential tenancy law, are submitted by consumers or tenants, and do not exceed the amount in dispute of 1000 EUR can be accepted for advice. In addition, no relevant deadlines, such as the imminent expiry of the limitation period, may apply. The range of cases at the HCLC ranges from delayed flights and desired compensation payments to unjustified telephone bills and subscription traps. The limit of the amount in dispute is due to the insurance conditions of the professional liability insurance, which regulates the liability for the advice of the HCLC. The limit of the amount in dispute is quickly reached in rental disputes due to the dispute value calculations, for example in the case of unjustified rent increases, the refusal to grant a subletting permit or disputes around the so-called rent brake, so that many rental disputes could not be accepted. From October 2019, the dispute value limit in tenancy law was therefore raised to 5000 EUR. The students advise those seeking legal advice in teams under the instruction of the qualified lawyers who supervise them.

23 Access to Justice Through Information

Only those who are informed about their rights can enforce them and make use of them. Therefore, consumers' ignorance of their rights is a reason for the deficit in enforcing rights in consumer law. This ignorance has different reasons. It is due to a lack of access to information, but also to the way it is conveyed.

24 Relevance of Information in Consumer Law

Information are an important tool in consumer law, as consumers often have an information deficit compared to businesses. This is also due to the information model prevalent in European consumer law (Heiderhoff 2016, para. 260). Information, in particular, have the function of enabling consumers to make independent decisions (Schürnbrand and Janal 2018, p. 3). Information also serve to protect consumers themselves (Sedlmeier 2012, p. 124).

However, an 'excess' of information can have the opposite effect (Heiderhoff 2016, para. 249; Enste et al. 2016, p. 12). Many consumers, due to the mass of information, can no longer distinguish between important and unimportant information and therefore feel ignorant about their rights and the legal situation despite the many information available to them. This phenomenon shows that it is important to convey a balanced amount of information.

Information also control the market behavior of consumers and increase market transparency (Hagen and Wey 2009, pp. 5, 11; Sedlmeier 2012, pp. 124 f.). They contribute to better decisions by consumers (Howells et al. 2018, p. 31). Essential is also the indication of cost-efficient information procurement. This is often not possible, as consumers lack easily accessible or understandable information.

25 Consumer Model

Consumers are diverse. Not all consumers desire individual advice, but some want to inform themselves independently about the legal situation (Bala and Schuldzinski 2018, p. 11). In this context, no comprehensive consumer concept should be assumed. Because just like in consumer associations (ibid., p. 10), the questions and consumers seeking legal assistance in 'Law Clinics' are also very diverse.

Especially the responsible consumer of the consumer triad of vulnerable, trusting, and responsible consumers sometimes wants to inform themselves and uses existing information sources (Enste et al. 2016, p. 23). Even if the problem of 'information overload' is recognized, it cannot be denied that information are important to support the consumer in their decisions.

26 The Social Significance of the Consumer Blog

The HCLC meets the social claim of consumer protection to inform consumers about their rights by providing easily accessible and understandable information on common consumer questions within the framework of their blog. The choice of certain consumer questions is particularly due to their relevance and frequency in individual legal advice, but also results from the topicality of certain consumer law or tenancy law topics.

Within the framework of the blog, legal changes are also informed about, and consumers can thus inform themselves about their rights before a conflict arises. This is a crucial point for the effective enforcement of consumer rights by reducing existing information deficits. The HCLC aims to contribute to this. It is important to bundle the information offers, as many offers already exist, but they are not easily findable and specialized. The legal advice offer and the blog complement each other in many ways, by pointing out contact addresses on the blog, the consumers seeking legal assistance are also referred to the legal advice of the HCLC or to further legal advice offers. In addition, consumers who do not desire individual advice from the HCLC can take advantage of a direct information offer.

27 Access to Justice Through Digitalization

The provision of free legal advice within the framework of 'Law Clinics' has always served the function of enabling those seeking access to justice in the sense of enforcing their rights. However, what does access to justice mean in the context of digitalization? The 'Legal Tech' project of the HCLC aims, on the one hand, to democratize legal advice as a service and, on the other hand, to offer efficient help to the largest possible number of consumers through economies of scale.

28 Democratization of Legal Advice

Digitalization has initially led to low-threshold access to information for consumers in the form of blogs, template letters, or references to advice centers. However, improved access to information does not always lead to the consumer enforcing their rights. In the depicted overcoming of rational disinterest, the cost factor as well as the time factor play a crucial role. This is where Legal Tech can come in: It allows the consumer to transmit the facts of the case in a standardized manner or to receive an assessment of their legal situation in simple cases, regardless of location (Hartung 2017, p. 20). In addition, it removes the fear of threshold, which prevents some people seeking justice from consulting a lawyer, regardless of financial considerations.

29 Permissibility Under the RDG

However, legal advice as a service is heavily regulated in Germany. While the classic out-of-court legal advice within the framework of a 'Law Clinic' is now relatively unproblematic due to § 6 para. 2 RDG, the free offer of 'Legal Tech' applications raises new questions: When do such constitute a legal service and what does the instruction of a person qualified to hold judicial office according to § 6 para. 2 RDG specifically mean in this context? If one does not already deny the 'activity' in the sense of § 2 para. 1 RDG for a software, at least for pure digital information offers or sample letters that do not take into account the individual situation of the person seeking legal advice, there should already be no legal service in the sense of § 2 para. 1 RDG (Remmertz 2017, p. 56). Within the framework of the permission fact of § 6 para. 2 RDG, for example, it could be based on the fact that the person qualified to hold judicial office supervises the development process of the software or controls the end product (Fordan and Renz 2019, p. 76 f.).

The desired democratization of legal services as access to justice through digital offers is to be distinguished from the liberalization of the legal market: In the current debate on the liberalization of the legal market through 'Legal Tech', free legal advice plays a subordinate role, as the lines of conflict usually run between the legal profession and the 'Legal Tech' companies (Singer 2019, p. 213). Thus, the FDP parliamentary group presented a draft law for the modernization of the RDG (BT-Drs. 19/9527) and the final report of the federal working group on

'Legal Tech' was also presented at the 90th Conference of Ministers of Justice.[3] The judgment of the Federal Court of Justice (Bundesgerichtshof) of November 27, 2019 on the scope of the collection license of Legal Tech companies was widely noted. The Federal Court of Justice broadly interpreted the term collection service in § 10 para. 1 sentence 1 no. 1 RDG and saw the assertion of claims and declaratory requests in connection with the so-called rent brake by the company 'Lexfox' as covered by it. The partial advocacy of an opening of the legal market is done here from the perspective of legal service providers and is likely to be economically motivated, as they depend on success fees as profit-oriented companies. A possibly improved access to justice on the part of consumers is rather a side effect.

30 Open Source Technological Infrastructure

For the HCLC's 'Legal Tech' project, this means that a true democratization of the legal market can only be achieved through a non-profit and sustainable technological infrastructure. This includes open source software, connecting to developments of other 'Law Clinics', or collaborating with consumer centers. The project thus joins other initiatives that aim to improve access to government services through digitization and artificial intelligence.[4] Any potential amendment to the RDG should take this into account by also creating legal certainty for free legal advice through 'Legal Tech'.

31 Utilization of Scale Effects

The provision of free legal advice is always a question of available capacities, especially for 'Law Clinics' that rely on the voluntary work of students and supervisors. The requests from consumers seeking legal advice far exceed the process-

---

[3] Available at https://schleswig-holstein.de/DE/Schwerpunkte/JUMIKO2019/Downloads/190605_beschluesse/TOPI_11_Abschlussbericht.pdf?__blob=publicationFile&v=1 [As of: May 18, 2020].

[4] For example, the Federal Ministry for Family, Seniors, Women and Youth (Bundesministerium für Familie, Frauen, Senioren und Jugend) launched the Innovation Office 'Digital Life' in the summer of 2019, see https://www.bmfsfj.de/bmfsfj/aktuelles/alle-meldungen/gesellschaft-soll-staerker-von-digitalisierung-profitieren/136620 [As of: May 18, 2020].

ing capabilities of the HCLC each year, despite a growing number of students and supervisors volunteering.

The Consumer Law Blog and the 'Legal Tech' project were therefore also created with the desire to make information permanently easily accessible and to help those seeking legal advice efficiently. The aim is thus to 'produce' more legal advice with unchanged resources. In the context of 'Legal Tech', this is facilitated by the previously described internal case management, i.e., a standardized and partially automated review of whether the case can be accepted by the 'Law Clinic' at all.

On the other hand, in the future, a partially automated substantive processing of consumer law cases could lead to more cases being successfully completed, and thus ultimately the HCLC could better meet the high demand from those seeking legal advice. However, the HCLC neither intends nor has the technological and personnel resources to compete with legal advice, especially since it can only advise out-of-court. 'Legal Tech' can, however, be a way to use existing capacities efficiently.

32 Conclusion

'Law Clinics' make an important contribution to practical legal education. At the same time, this creates the positive effect of offering those seeking legal advice free access to the law in cases where they would often refrain from asserting their rights because the costs are disproportionate to the value in dispute. By offering free legal advice, they fulfill an important social task by ensuring low-threshold access to the law for those seeking legal advice who cannot afford legal advice.

The work of the HCLC leads to a strengthening of consumers' knowledge of their rights and their enforcement. Societal discussions about current topics in the field of consumer and tenancy law show that consumer law is a highly topical area of law. This is also reflected in the HCLC's consumer blog. By increasingly making the findings of the students available to the public, the blog project also contributes to a deepening of the HCLC's activities in the field of consumer policy. At the same time, the 'Law Clinic' takes advantage of the opportunities of digitization to increase the HCLC's consulting capacities, expand information offers, and prepare students for the changing legal profession. Thus, the HCLC is an actor driven by voluntary commitment and ensures consumer policy 'from below'.

References

Alpaydin, Ethem. 2016. *Machine learning – The new AI*. Cambridge: MIT Press.

Bala, Christian, and Wolfgang Schuldzinski. 2018. Einleitung: One size does not fit all! In *Jenseits des Otto Normalverbrauchers. Verbraucherpolitik in Zeiten des ‚unmanageable consumer'. Beiträge zur Verbraucherforschung*, Vol. 8, eds. C. Bala and W. Schuldzinski, 8–16. Düsseldorf: Verbraucherzentrale.

Berlin, Christof. 2020. § 24a Schlichtung und sonstige alternative Streitbeilegung. In *Verbraucherrecht Beratungshandbuch*, 3rd edition, eds. M. Tamm, K. Tonner, and T. Brönneke, Rn. 1–157. Baden-Baden: Nomos.

Breidenbach, Stephan. 2018. Juristenausbildung und Legal Tech. In *Rechtshandbuch Legal Tech*, eds. S. Breidenbach and F. Glatz, 205–210. München: Beck.

Chen, Daniel L. 2019. Judicial analytics and the great transformation of American Law. *Artificial Intelligence and Law* 27:15–42.

Dastis, Juan C., and Julian Udich. 2013. Gutes pro bono leisten: Wie gründet man eine Law Clinic? *Anwaltsblatt* 63:721–731.

Dietlein, Georg, and Jan-Gero A. Hannemann. 2017. Studentische Rechtsberatung in Deutschland. *Juristische Ausbildung* 39:449–460.

Enste, Dominik H., Mara Ewers, Christina Heldman, and Regina Schneider. 2016. *Verbraucherschutz und Verhaltensökonomik*. IW-Analysen Nr. 106. Köln: Institut der deutschen Wirtschaft.

Fordan, Dennis Ch., and Clara Renz. 2019. Stärkung des Verbraucherschutzes durch studentische Rechtsberatung 2.0. *Legal Revolution* 70–77.

Fries, Martin. 2016. *Verbraucherrechtsdurchsetzung*. Tübingen: Mohr Siebeck.

Gräwe, Svenja L. 2011. *Die Entstehung der Rechtsinformatik – Wissenschaftsgeschichtliche und -theoretische Analyse einer Querschnittsdisziplin*. Hamburg: Dr. Kovač.

Hagen, Kornelia, and Christian Wey. 2009. Verbraucherpolitik zwischen Markt und Staat. *Vierteljahreshefte zur Wirtschaftsforschung* 78:5–29.

Hartung, Markus. 2017. Legal Tech und Berufsrecht. *Neue Juristische Wochenschrift-Sonderheft: Innovationen & Legal Tech* 20–21.

Hartung, Markus. 2018. Gedanken zu Legal Tech und Digitalisierung. In *Legal Tech – Die Digitalisierung des Rechtsmarkts*, eds. M. Hartung, M. Bues, and G. Halbleib, 5–18. München: Beck.

Heiderhoff, Bettina. 2016. *Europäisches Privatrecht*, 4th edition. Heidelberg: C. F. Müller.

Holmes, Jr., Oliver Wendell. 1897. The path of the law. *Harvard Law Review* 10:457–478.

Howells, Geraint, Christian Twigg-Flesner, and Thomas Wilhelmsson. 2018. *Rethinking EU Consumer Law*. London: Routledge.

Jahn, Joachim. 2008. Klares Deutsch für Juristen. *Juristische Schulung-Magazin* 3:6–9.

Killian, Matthias, and Lisa Wenzel. 2017. Law Clinics in Deutschland: Zahlen, Typologien und Strukturen. *Anwaltsblatt* 67:963–965.

Kuhlmann, Nico. 2018. Legal Tech – Zugang zum Recht im Zeitalter der Digitalisierung. In *Digitalisierung im Spannungsfeld von Politik, Wirtschaft, Wissenschaft und Recht*, eds. C. Bär, T. Grädler, and R. Mayr, 87–101. Berlin: Springer Gabler.

Martini, Mario, and David Nink. 2017. Wenn Maschinen entscheiden... – Vollautomatisierte Verwaltungsverfahren und der Persönlichkeitsschutz. *Neue Zeitschrift für Verwaltungsrecht Extra* 36:1–14.

Mayer-Schönberger, Viktor, and Kenneth Cukier. 2013. *Big data – A revolution that will transform how we live, work, and think*. London: Murray.
Paal, Boris P. 2016. Geleitwort – Studentische Rechtsberatung: Ein Beitrag – nicht nur – zur juristischen Ausbildung an Universitäten. *German Journal of Legal Education* 3:1–3.
Remmertz, Frank R. 2017. Legal Tech – Rechtliche Beurteilung nach dem RDG. *BRAK-Mitteilungen* 48:55–61.
Riehm, Thomas, and Thomas A. Heiß. 2016. Alternative Streitbeilegung in der studentischen Rechtsberatung. *German Journal of Legal Education* 3:21–35.
Römermann, Volker. 2008. Kommentierungen des §§ 3, 6 RDG. In *Rechtsdienstleistungsgesetz*, eds. V. Römermann and B. Grunewald. Köln: Otto Schmidt.
Rothmann, Aaron, and Finn Schädlich. 2019. Open Decision – Ein quelloffenes System zur Entscheidungsautomatisierung. *Rethinking Law* 2:22–26.
Schmidt, Karl-Michael. 2017. Kommentierung des § 6 RDG. In *Rechtsdienstleistungsgesetz Handkommentar*, 2nd edition, ed. M. Krenzler. Baden-Baden: Nomos.
Schubert, Andreas. 2014. Legal Clinics – Juristische Ausbildung mit Praxisbezug am Beispiel der Freiburg Legal Clinics und Pro Bono Studentische Rechtsberatung Freiburg. *Ordnung der Wissenschaft* 4:247–252.
Schürnbrand, Jan, and Ruth Janal. 2018. *Examensrepetitorium Verbraucherschutzrecht*, 3rd edition. Heidelberg: C. F. Müller.
Sedlmeier, Kathleen. 2012. *Rechtsgeschäftliche Selbstbestimmung im Verbrauchervertrag*. Tübingen: Mohr Siebeck.
Singer, Reinhard. 2016. Studentische Rechtsberatung. Legal Clinical Education an der Humboldt-Universität. In *Anwaltsorientierung im Studium: Aktuelle Herausforderungen und neue Perspektiven. Bielefelder Schriftenreihe für Anwalts- und Notarrecht*, Vol. 29. eds. S. Barton, S. Hähnchen, and F. Jost, 93–123. Hamburg: Dr. Kovač.
Singer, Reinhard. 2019. Durchsetzung von Verbraucherrechten durch Inkassounternehmen – Chancen und Grenzen. *BRAK-Mitteilungen* 50:211–219.
Susskind, Richard, and Daniel Susskind. 2015. *The future of the professions – How technology will transform the work of human experts*. Oxford: Oxford University Press.
Vogler, Ralf J. 2013. Legal Clinic – Innovatives Studienmodell oder unerlaubte Rechtsberatung? *Zeitschrift für das Juristische Studium* 135–140.
Weber, Franziska. 2013. Gegenwärtige Verbraucherrechtsfälle und Bedarf an staatlicher Rechtsdurchsetzung. *Verbraucher und Recht* 9:323–332.
Wissenschaftsrat, ed. 2012. *Perspektiven der Rechtswissenschaft in Deutschland. Situation Analysen, Empfehlungen 2012*, WR-Drs. 2558–12.

Reinhard Singer is Professor of Civil Law, Labour Law, Lawyers' Law, Family Law and Sociology of Law at Humboldt-Unversität zu Berlin and heads the 'Humboldt Consumer Law Clinic'.

Kristina Schimpf is a research associate at the 'Humboldt Consumer Law Clinic' at the Faculty of Law of the Humboldt-Universität zu Berlin.

Kathrin Steinbach is a research associate at the 'Humboldt Consumer Law Clinic' at the Faculty of Law of the Humboldt-Universität zu Berlin.

An Afterword

The main title of the event in the summer of 2019, 'Consumer Politics from Below', as well as this anthology of the same name in the aftermath, preserves a small difference in meaning, even though the research field of 'Political Consumerism' was almost synonymously set with it in the introduction. Because the 'below' inevitably refers to an 'above' and reflects an imbalance, a tension, possibly even a permanent conflict line (Baule 2012).

The term 'Consumer Politics from Below' implies a counter-model to state consumer policy, namely a civil society dimension that aims to make itself politically noticeable and effective. Otherwise, it would hardly be justifiable to speak of 'Consumer *politics*'. This impetus, which claims political relevance, and not just for the periphery of the political system, but with a view to the political center, in order to initiate fundamental changes in the decision-making and legal situation, is understood here as a *conditio sine qua non* to speak of 'Consumer Politics from Below' at all.

The effectiveness of such consumer politics from below 'naturally' does not solely lie in the responsibility of the protagonists of such politics, but depends, among other things, on the system-internal resonances that are stimulated by it, i.e., how the political system (personnel) reacts to it. Niklas Luhmann (1986) has run through this problem of intention-adequate system resonance functionally comparative shortly after Chernobyl.

In retrospect, a brief look will now be taken at a few aspects that are associated with the efforts for a problem-adequate consumer policy from below.

K.-U. Hellmann et al. (eds.), *Consumer Policy from Below*,
https://doi.org/10.1007/978-3-658-44478-5

1 Paradoxes

Paradoxes are embarrassing. They reveal a certain inability to appear without contradiction. In the case of political consumption, one might question why the 'attitude-behavior-gap' seems so insurmountable. Never before have the problematic side effects of modern consumption received more attention. The mass media report on it incessantly; even the social sciences are now extensively addressing the corresponding phenomena; and in the private sector, one can hardly escape the guilty conscience. Nevertheless (taking into account the beginning of 2020 as time of consideration), it gives the impression that almost nothing changes, nowhere a radical reversal, a fundamental sociotechnical 'disruption' is emerging, neither at the macro nor at the micro level.

Even worse, political consumption might repeat what has happened with regard to political populism: The more one rises above it or speaks out against it, explicitly rejects and sharply condemns it, the stronger it becomes, quasi dialectically conditioned, but without the prospect of a synthesis, because the mutual irreconcilability makes any cross-camp understanding impossible (Reckwitz 2019; Koppetsch 2019; Manow 2019). Transferred to political consumption, the vehement advocacy, even demand for radical upheavals, be it in the field of nutrition, energy production or mobility, to name just a few examples, may achieve exactly the opposite, namely defense, persistence, entrenchment, largely immobility. Populist consumption has a future, so to say.

In this context, it remains to be clarified how purpose and means are actually distributed in the case of political consumption. Jörn Lamla and Sighard Neckel made this ambiguity clear about seventeen years ago by contrasting 'Politischer Konsum—konsumierte Politik' (Lamla and Neckel 2006). Is the politicization of consumption a means or an end? Do we politicize consumption to influence the political agenda? Or to give our own consumption a different appearance through politicization? Perhaps to enhance oneself, to practice 'Lifestyle Politics' (Shah et al. 2007), because it is incredibly hip? And to what extent does the politicization of consumption reproduce politics in the original sense? Or does this not rather lead to now also consuming politics as we already consume education, culture, love, medicine, sports? So just another stage of colonization through consumption (Hirschman 2001; Leatherman and Goodman 2005; Hellmann 2019, pp. 295–316; Landry 2019). The situation remains diffuse.

2 Perspectives

The image of man in neoclassically oriented economics, i.e., the 'homo oeconomicus' with its assumption of a self-interested, utility-maximizing economic subject (consumer) within the framework of methodological individualism, has had a wide-ranging influence on consumer science research and the consumer role model debate. At the same time, it is constantly under criticism. In this respect, behavioral economics has particularly stood out (Oehler and Reisch 2008).[1]

However, it often remains unclear what the starting point of the 'homo oeconomicus' refers to, whether to anthropological foundations, normative guidelines, specific empirical results, or model-theoretical considerations. This applies even to terms such as 'utility' and 'rationality', which are interpreted differently and framed scientifically. Revisions, extensions, and creative-conceptual reinterpretations of mutually enriching orthodox and heterodox economic approaches, as well as interdisciplinary theory constellations, are the result.

All of this leads to entirely new requirements for consumer research, which has to deal with a growing range of theoretical approaches and a significantly increasing inter- and multidisciplinarity. It is also noticeable that there is a new complexity, especially with regard to an adequate consumer role model, which now has to meet expanded differentiation requirements. It is therefore not surprising if finally a 'farewell to the one-dimensional consumer' (Fridrich et al. 2017) is taken and a 'multiperspective consumer research' (Nessel et al. 2018) is demanded. But what does this mean in practical-political terms?

To put it very simply, German consumer policy from above has been characterized for decades by two guiding principles: the *model of the active-responsible consumer* and the *model of the passive-evasive consumer*.[2] Mature consumers

---

[1]Furthermore, experimental economics, economic psychology, information economics, new institutional economics, neuroeconomics, and other approaches.

[2]If one sticks to the topic of guiding principles, one can distinguish between a legal and a political-economic understanding of consumers since the beginning of the Federal Republic. The legal development, which is based on significantly greater continuity, started from the fleeting, indifferent consumer who relies on legislation, with a transformation into the guiding principle of the average informed, attentive, and understanding consumer taking place under the influence of the EU and the ECJ. In the political-economic sector, tensions were inherent between variously contoured, yet diffuse guiding principles. The uninformed, passive consumer was supposed to receive information support for his purchasing decisions on the one hand, and on the other hand, due to his low self-responsibility, he was supposed to be supported and protected from harm by paternalistic protection mechanisms from

need significantly less protection, strictly orthodoxly considered almost none, because they are capable of autonomously ensuring their own lifestyle within the framework of societal conditions, and can negotiate sovereignly with manufacturers and dealers. In contrast, the symptoms in fleeting-trusting consumers suggest an acute need for action, because they are structurally inferior to their market partners, have too little information, and their material and action-related resources are limited.

Since the BSE crisis in 2000, such simplifying evaluations have increasingly complicated (Janning 2011). By now, there are not only the two guiding principles of the passive-fleeting (including the trusting and the vulnerable) and the active-mature consumer, which together cover their own bipolar dimension, but also another role model, namely the *guiding principle of the responsible consumer* (Reisch et al. 2003; Schrader 2007; Micklitz et al. 2010). This has also introduced another evaluation dimension into the field, as it is now not only about the difference *in need of protection/not in need of protection,* but also about the difference *responsible/irresponsible* or more specifically *sustainable/not sustainable consumption,* which is orthogonal to the former.

That this dimension has been added should not be surprising in view of the currently heated sustainability debate. But does this already represent multiperspectivity? Just think of the ten consumer types as they appear in Yiannis Gabriel and Tim Lang (2015). According to them, there is the 'Activist', the 'Chooser', the 'Citizen', the 'Communicator', the 'Explorer', the 'Hedonist', the 'Identity-seeker', the 'Rebel', the 'Victim' and the 'Worker'. The 'Victim' consumer corresponds to the fleeting-vulnerable-trusting consumer guiding principle, while the 'Citizen' consumer corresponds to the responsible one. But what speaks against making consumer policy in the future also for the 'Activist', the 'Chooser', the 'Communicator', the 'Explorer', the 'Hedonist', the 'Identity-seeker', the 'Rebel' or the 'Worker'? Are these less important needs?

Sustainability reasons may rightly deserve more attention, even if it is currently primarily (still) about clientele and symbolic politics. But do the other types therefore deserve no attention at all? And indeed, there are already further consumer guiding principles in circulation, such as the 'active consumer'

---

above. Furthermore, another guiding principle can be identified, which ranges from Ludwig Erhard's demand for the 'conscious consumer' to the informed consumer to the guiding principle of the reflective, mature consumer, including corresponding forms of action and corresponding (self-) organizations.

(Czerwonka et al. 1976), the 'critical consumer',[3] the 'new consumer',[4] the 'multidimensional consumer' (Heiner 1989), the 'stubborn consumer' (Hainer 2006), the 'moral consumer' (Seeber 2006), the 'informed consumer' (Schwan 2009), the 'overwhelmed consumer' (Grunwald 2013; Strünck 2015), the 'transparent consumer' (Bala and Müller 2014a), the 'vulnerable consumer' (Bala and Müller 2014b) the 'digitally seduced, clueless consumer' (Schleusener and Stevens 2015), the 'ignorant consumer' (Klug 2015), the 'self-determined consumer' (IHK 2016), the 'generous consumer' (Kübler 2017), the '(self) experiencing consumer' (Hellmann 2018), the 'naive consumer' and the 'active consumer' (Müller 2019; Ullrich 2019) as well as the 'hypocritical consumer' (Hoffmann 2019). Which one do you prefer, which one do you neglect? What could further syntheses look like? What should a common consumer-related foundation be like, which underlies the various approaches and perspectives? Which traditional strands can be meaningfully linked to, both normatively and empirically, in reference to changed political, social, economic and cultural developments? How can, for example, an emancipatory practice be established in terms of personnel, civil society and politics, with a view to a renaissance of the concept of maturity—understood normatively, prescriptively, state- and process-oriented?

Without continuing this debate here, it should have become apparent that a plea for more multiperspectivity opens up broad discursive spaces and options for action, especially for consumer research, future guiding principle discussions and consumer policy from above as well as from below.

3 Problematisations

Problematisations: What may sound so harmless has, in the case of Michel Foucault, triggered considerable consequences, not least for the interpretation of his complete works (Foucault 1986, p. 19). This refers to societal discourses that testify to a certain problem, tension, unrest that cannot simply be regulated, repressed, suppressed in society (Klöppel 2010). Something is, so to speak, rumbling, not running smoothly, resisting and communicating through problematising

[3]See https://www.addf-kassel.de/fileadmin/user_upload/Dossiers/Meibom/Meibom_Der_kritische_Verbraucher_AddF_NL-K-16_A-34.pdf.

[4]In 1987, the (German) Marketing Journal launched a whole series of articles under the title 'Der neue Konsument', cf. Hellmann (2003, pp. 114–121).

positions and processes. Phenomenologically, this is almost a social symptomatology at work here.

What we encounter in what is called ‘consumer policy from below’ here can probably also be understood as such a problematisation. Be it the search for (a) contemporary consumer model(s), be it the demand for a radical change in our way of life, indeed the structure of society as such: These points have been discussed for decades, and more than ever it seems to be about the very essence, about the future of humanity as such, without a reasonable, globally functioning solution being discernible.

What should be particularly emphasized in this context, however, is the emphasis on the willingness to independently launch and drive much more problematizations in the field of consumer policy, to deliberately irritate and cause unrest (Baule et al. 2019). Despite all activism, for example, the consumer model debate proves to be extremely sluggish, incoherent, and little innovative. Contradictory positions are repeatedly juxtaposed without much movement, much like in a positional war that costs some victims without the prospect of victory for one side or the other, a pure battle of material.

It would be highly desirable to problematize this immobility much more strongly, ultimately to eliminate and overcome it, if necessary through significantly more unconventional argumentation maneuvers, subversive strategies, breaking taboos. And by this, it is not meant, to stay in the picture, to switch from a positional war back to a war of movement, but to fundamentally leave this scenario and to embark on completely new design and mediation paths.

References

Bala, Christian, and Klaus Müller, eds. 2014a. *Der gläserne Verbraucher. Wird Datenschutz zum Verbraucherschutz?* Düsseldorf: Consumer Center NRW.

Bala, Christian, and Klaus Müller, eds. 2014b. *Der verletzliche Verbraucher. Die sozialpolitische Dimension der Verbraucherpolitik.* Düsseldorf: Consumer Center NRW.

Baule, Bernward. 2012. §72 Kommerzkultur, Verbrauchermacht, moralischer Konsum—zur Verbraucherpolitik im Föderalismus. In *Handbuch Föderalismus. Föderalismus als demokratische Rechtsordnung und Rechtskultur in Deutschland, Europa und der Welt, Bd. III Entfaltungsbereiche des Föderalismus*, ed. I. Härtel, 515–613. Berlin: Springer.

Baule, Bernward, Dirk Hohnsträter, Stefan Krankenhagen, and Jörn Lamla, eds. 2019. *Transformationen des Konsums. Vom industriellen Massenkonsum zum individualisierten Digitalkonsum.* Baden-Baden: Nomos.

Czerwonka, Christine, Günter Schöppe, and Stefan Weckbach. 1976. *Der aktive Konsument. Kommunikation und Kooperation. Untersuchung über Möglichkeiten funktional angemessener, frühzeitiger Einflussnahme der Konsumenten auf das Güterangebot.* Göttingen: Schwartz.

Foucault, Michel. 1986. *Der Gebrauch der Lüste. Sexualität und Wahrheit 2.* Frankfurt a. M.: Suhrkamp.

Fridrich, Christian, Renate Hübner, Karl Kollmann, Michael-Burkhard Piorkowsky, and Nina Tröger, eds. 2017. *Abschied vom eindimensionalen Verbraucher.*. Wiesbaden: Springer VS.

Gabriel, Yannis, and Tim Lang. 2015. *The Unmanageable Consumer.* Los Angeles: Sage.

Grunwald, Armin. 2013. Überforderte Verbraucher—Warum ökologischer Konsum die Umwelt nicht rettet. In *Umweltverträglicher Konsum durch rechtliche Steuerung. Dokumentation des Symposiums in der Landesvertretung Sachsen-Anhalt in Berlin*, ed. Environmental Agency, 6–18. Berlin: UBA.

Hainer, Herbert. 2006. *Der störrische Konsument. Marketing und Wertewandel. Materielle, soziologische und fiskalische Ursachen, gesellschaftliche und betriebswirtschaftliche Trends und Lösungen.* Vortrag anlässlich der Mitgliederversammlung 2006 der Wirtschaftswissenschaftlichen Gesellschaft an der Humboldt-Universität zu Berlin e. V. Berlin, May 2, 2006.

K.-U. Hellmann et al. (eds.), *Consumer Policy from Below*,
https://doi.org/10.1007/978-3-658-44478-5

Heiner, Heinz. 1989. Der multidimensionale Konsument 'beackert' zwölf Konsumfelder. *Markenartikel* 51:332–334.

Hellmann, Kai-Uwe. 2003. *Soziologie der Marke*. Frankfurt a. M.: Suhrkamp.

Hellmann, Kai-Uwe. 2018. Verbraucherleitbilder, Konsumerlebnisse und die mentale Dimension des modernen Konsums. Zum Menschenbild der akademischen Verbraucherforschung. In *Jenseits des Otto Normalverbrauchers. Verbraucherpolitik in Zeiten des 'unmanageable consumer'*, ed. C. Bala, 19–51. Düsseldorf: NRW.

Hellmann, Kai-Uwe. 2019. Der Konsum der Gesellschaft. 2., erweiterte Auflage. Wiesbaden: Springer VS.

Hirschman, E. C. 2001. Ethnicity, racism, and the colonization of consumption. *American Marketing Association. Conference Proceedings, Suppl. 2001, AMA Educators' Proceedings* 12:236-244.

Hoffmann, Stefan. 2019. *Der hypokritische Konsument—Einsichten der Verbraucherforschung. Vortrag auf der Jahreskonferenz 2019 des Netzwerks Verbraucherforschung*. Berlin: BMJV.

Industrie- und Handelskammer (IHK) für München und Oberbayern. 2016. Kernelemente einer modernen Verbraucherpolitik: Der selbstbestimmte Verbraucher in der digitalen Welt. *Positionspapier*. https://www.ihk-muenchen.de/ihk/Positionspapier-Verbraucher.pdf.

Janning, Frank. 2011. *Die Spätgeburt eines Politikfeldes. Die Institutionalisierung der Verbraucherschutzpolitik in Deutschland und im internationalen Vergleich*. Baden-Baden: Nomos.

Klöppel, Ulrike. 2010. Foucaults Konzept der Problematisierungsweise und die Analyse diskursiver Transformationen. In *Diskursiver Wandel*, ed. A. Landwehr, 255–263. Wiesbaden: VS Verlag.

Klug, Martin. 2015. Der ignorante Verbraucher als Leitbild der Verbraucherpolitik. In *Abschied vom Otto Normalverbraucher. Moderne Verbraucherforschung, Leitbilder, Information, Demokratie*, eds. C. Bala and K. Müller, 79–92. Essen: Klartext.

Koppetsch, Cornelia. 2019. *Die Gesellschaft des Zorns. Rechtspopulismus m globalen Zeitalter*. Bielefeld: transcript.

Kübler, Dorothea. 2017. Der freigebige Verbraucher. In der Ära der Digitalisierung schwindet die Privatsphäre—wie auch der Datenschutz. *WZB Mitteilungen* 155: 26–29.

Lamla, Jörn, and Sighard Neckel, eds. 2006. *Politisierter Konsum—konsumierte Politik*. Wiesbaden: VS Verlag.

Landry, Deborah. 2019. 'Stop calling it graffiti': The visual rhetoric of contamination, consumption and colonization. *Current Sociology* 67(5):686-704.

Leatherman, Thomas L., and Alan Goodman. 2005. Coca-colonization of diets in the Yucatan. *Social Science & Medicine* 61:833-846.

Luhmann, Niklas. 1986. *Ökologische Kommunikation. Kann die moderne Gesellschaft sich auf ökologische Gefährdungen einstellen?* Opladen: Westdeutscher.

Manow, Philip. 2019. Politischer Populismus als Ausdruck von Identitätspolitik? Über einen ökonomischen Ursachenkomplex. *Aus Politik und Zeitgeschichte* 69: 9-11. https://www.bpb.de/apuz/286510/politischer-populismus-als-ausdruck-von-identitaetspolitik-ueber-einen-oekonomischen-ursachenkomplex.

Micklitz, Hans-W, Andreas Oehler, Michael-Burkhard Pierkowsky, Lucia A. Reisch, and Christoph Strünck. 2010. *Der vertrauende, der verletzliche oder der verantwortungsvolle Verbraucher? Plädoyer für eine differenzierte Strategie in der Verbraucherpolitik. Stellungnahme des Wissenschaftlichen Beirats Verbraucher- und Ernährungspolitik beim BMELV.* Bonn: BMELV.

Müller, Robert Caspar. 2019. *Konsumentenbilder als produktive Fiktionen. Eine theoretische und ethnographische Untersuchung. Mit einem Geleitwort von Prof. Dr. Jürgen Schulz.* Wiesbaden: Springer Gabler.

Nessel, Sebastian, Nina Tröger, Christian Fridrich, and Renate Hübner, eds. 2018. *Multiperspektivische Verbraucherforschung. Ansätze und Perspektiven.* Wiesbaden: Springer VS.

Oehler, Andreas and Lucia A. Reich. 2008. *Behaviorial Economics—eine neue Grundlage für Verbraucherpolitik? Eine Studie im Auftrag des Verbraucherzentrale Bundesverbandes.* Berlin: VZBV. https://www.vzbv.de/sites/default/files/downloads/studie_behavioral_economics_12_2008.pdf.

Reckwitz, Andreas. 2019. *Das Ende der Illusionen. Politik, Ökonomie und Kultur in der Spätmoderne.* Berlin: Suhrkamp.

Reisch, Lucia A., et al. 2003. *Strategische Grundsätze und Leitbilder einer neuen Verbraucherpolitik. Diskussionspapier des Wissenschaftlichen Beirats für Verbraucher- und Ernährungspolitik beim BMELV.* Bonn: BMELV.

Schleusener, Michael, Saraah Stevens, et al. 2015. *Der digital verführte, ahnungslose Verbraucher. Working Papers des KVF NRW, No. 1.* Düsseldorf: Consumer Research Network of the Consumer Advice Centre NRW.

Schrader, Ulf. 2007. The Moral Responsibility of Consumers as Citizens. *International Journal of Innovation and Sustainable Development* 2:79–96.

Schwan, Patrick. 2009. *Der informierte Verbraucher? Das verbraucherpolitische Leitbild auf dem Prüfstand. Eine Untersuchung am Beispiel des Lebensmittelsektors.* Wiesbaden: VS Verlag.

Seeber, Günther. 2006. Was haben Lebensmittelskandale mit Wirtschafts- und Unternehmensethik zu tun? Das Beispiel Gammelfleisch. *Forum Ware* 34:81–84.

Shah, Dhavan V., Douglas M. McLeod, Eunkyung Kim, Sun Young Lee, Melissa R. Gotlieb, S. Shirley Ho, and Hilde Breivik. 2007. Political Consumerism: How Communication and Consumption Orientations Drive 'Lifestyle Politics'. *The Annals of the American Academy of Political and Social Science* 611:217–235.

Strünck, Christoph. 2015. Der mündige Verbraucher: Ein populäres Leitbild auf dem Prüfstand. In *Abschied vom Otto Normalverbraucher. Moderne Verbraucherforschung, Leitbilder, Information, Demokratie*, eds. C. Bala and K. Müller, 19–28. Essen: Klartext.

Ullrich, Wolfgang. 2019. Konsum als Arbeit. *Pop. Zeitschrift für Kultur und Kritik.* http://www.pop-zeitschrift.de/2019/04/01/konsum-als-arbeitvon-wolfgang-ullrich01-4-2019/.

MIX
Papier aus verantwortungsvollen Quellen
Paper from responsible sources
FSC® C105338

FSC
www.fsc.org

If you have any concerns about our products,
you can contact us on
ProductSafety@springernature.com

In case Publisher is established outside the EU,
the EU authorized representative is:
Springer Nature Customer Service Center GmbH
Europaplatz 3, 69115 Heidelberg, Germany

Printed by Libri Plureos GmbH
in Hamburg, Germany